Principles
of Instructional
Design

Principles of Instructional Design

Second Edition

Robert M. Gagné   Leslie J. Briggs
Florida State University

Holt, Rinehart and Winston
New York   Chicago   San Francisco   Dallas
Montreal   Toronto   London   Sydney

Library of Congress Cataloging in Publication Data

Gagné, Robert Mills, 1916-
  Principles of instructional design.

  Includes bibliographies.
  1.Learning, Psychology of.   2. Lesson planning.
I. Briggs, Leslie J., joint author. II. Title.
LB1051.G196   1979   371.3   78-27628

ISBN: 0-03-040806-7

Preface

We are glad to have had the opportunity of preparing a revised edition of this book. We perceive a continuing need, as expressed in the first edition, for "knowledge of how instruction may be systematically designed, on the part of teachers, curriculum developers, instructional leaders and managers, and those in related educational professions." The revision makes possible the inclusion of some up-to-date material and references, the correction and elaboration of particular points, and the addition of such topics as media and group instruction, as suggested by instructors who have used the previous edition. The purpose of the volume remains that of describing an intellectually consistent basis for practical procedures of instructional design.

It is our expectation that this revised edition will fill a need in teacher education courses, at both undergraduate and graduate levels. With its current scope and emphasis, the book may find a place in courses which deal with instruction as system design, including those which approach the selection of media within the tradition of educational technology as technique. Instructors of courses in teaching methods, instructional planning, curriculum theory, and classroom techniques should find the book useful. In graduate-level education, the text may be of use in these same areas, as well as in courses on learning and educational psychology.

The field of instructional design is dealt with as an instance of system design, in which identifiable stages are systematically related to both prior and succeeding stages, and decisions reflect the "outputs" of prior stages while conforming to system goals. Within this framework, methods are derived which can be used to design lessons, topics, modules, and courses of instruction in a variety of subject-matter areas. These methods have their origin in principles of performance analysis and human learning research, including learning theory.

In this edition, the attempt has been made to bring about an improved integration of the book as a whole by way of the theme of system design. Procedures of instructional design are related to the goals of various models of teaching. Several features are intended to contribute to the integration of chapters and a balance of content: (1) a page of transitional explanation is included for each of the four sections of the book; (2) added coverage is given to the topics of media characteristics and media selection; and (3) a chapter on modes of group instruction is added to match the discussion of individualized instruction. While a good deal of the substance of the first edition has been retained, revisions have been made throughout to reflect recent research findings and other developments in instructional design technology.

In Part One, an introductory chapter presents a rationale for instructional design as derived from human learning principles and carried out in accordance with system design concepts. Chapter 2 outlines fourteen stages of instructional system design, beginning with needs and goal analysis and proceeding through the stage of installation and diffusion of programs.

Beginning Part Two, chapter 3 defines and illustrates the major classes of learning outcomes for programs of instruction, including intellectual skills, cognitive strategies, information, attitudes, and motor skills. Chapters 4 and 5 describe the conditions of learning applicable to the acquisition of these capabilities, and accordingly to the design of instruction having these objectives.

Part Three is devoted to an account of the procedures of design. These begin with the classification of the types of objectives intended by the design, as one of the primary outcomes of task analysis described in chapter 6. The definition of specific objectives is taken up in chapter 7, followed by an account of procedures for determining sequences of instruction in chapter 8. Chapter 9 describes the derivation of a basis for events of instruction as they apply to each single learning episode, and the following chapter, 10, relates these events to the selection of appropriate instructional media. In chapter 11, the design of the individual lesson is related to varieties of learning outcomes and to appropriate instructional events. Procedures for assessing outcomes of learning by the use of criterion-based and norm-based measures are taken up in chapter 12.

Delivery systems for instruction is the general topic of Part Four. Chapter 13 discusses the application of instructional design products and principles to group instruction, while chapter 14 takes a similar approach with individualized instruction. The final chapter, 15, deals with procedures for evaluation of instructional programs, within the larger framework of educational systems.

Tallahassee, Florida   R. M. G.
October 1978   L. J. B.

Contents

Principles
of Instructional
Design

INTRODUCTION TO INSTRUCTIONAL SYSTEMS

While the major portion of this book is devoted to the principles of instructional design, and to procedures derived from these principles, this initial section is intended as an orientation to the general concept of instructional design.

The two chapters which make up this section are intended to do several things for their readers:

1. Indicate how the design of instruction may be related to human learning, a major theme of the entire book.
2. Introduce readers to a number of concepts related to instructional design, some of them perhaps new, so that they will begin to become familiar.
3. Give a general outline of the topics to be covered in the chapters of the book, and the order of presentation.
4. Define what is meant by *instructional system* design; in other words, the application of a "systems" approach to this enterprise.
5. Provide an indication of the ways in which systematic instructional design is carried out, and by whom.

6. Describe fourteen stages of instructional system design, beginning with the analysis of needs and continuing through a final stage of installation.

We look upon these introductory chapters as being of considerable importance for those who will be reading and learning from the book. We hope that the framework provided by this section, oriented on the one hand to the human learner who is a student, and on the other to a systematic set of technical procedures, will help to establish a point of view which can be maintained as the rest of the book is processed by the reader.

chapter 1

Introduction

Instruction is a human undertaking whose purpose is to help people learn. While learning may happen without any instruction, the effects of instruction on learning are often beneficial and usually easy to observe. When instruction is designed to accomplish a particular goal of learning, it may or may not be successful. The general purpose of this book is to describe what characteristics instruction must have in order to be successful, in the sense of aiding learning.

Instruction is a set of events which affect learners in such a way that learning is facilitated. Normally, we think of these events as being external to the learner —events embodied in the display of printed pages or the talk of a teacher. However, we also must recognize that the events which make up instruction may be partly internal, when they comprise learner activity called "self-instruction."

Why do we speak of "instruction," rather than "teaching"? It is because we wish to describe *all* of the events which may have a direct effect on the learning of a human being, not just those set in motion by an individual who is a teacher. Instruction may include events that are generated by a page of print, by a picture, by a television program, or by a combination of physical objects, among other things. Of course, a teacher may play an essential role in the arrangement of any of these events. Or, as already mentioned, the learners may be able to manage instructional events themselves. Teaching, then, may be considered as only one form of instruction, albeit a signally important one.

Considered in this comprehensive sense, instruction must be planned if it is to be effective. In detail, of course, a teacher may not have much time to plan instruction on a moment-to-moment basis. Each new event of the classroom requires one or more decisions on the part of a teacher. However, instruction is usually planned, which means that it is designed in some systematic way. Despite varying moment-to-moment decisions, a teacher follows the plan of a lesson design. The lesson is part of the larger design involved in the presentation of a topic (a course segment), and this topic in turn makes up part of a still more comprehensive design of the course or curriculum.

The purpose of designed instruction is to activate and support the learning of the individual student. This aim is characteristic of instruction wherever it occurs, whether between a tutor and a single student, in a school classroom, an adult-interest group, or in an on-the-job setting. Instruction for the support of learning must be something which is planned rather than haphazard. The learning it aids should bring all individuals closer to the goals of optimal use of their talents, enjoyment of life, and adjustment to the physical and social environment. Naturally, this does not mean that the planning of instruction will have the effect of making different individuals more alike. On the contrary, diversity among individuals will be enhanced. The purpose of planned instruction is to help each person develop as fully as possible, in his or her own individual directions.

Basic assumptions about instructional design

How is instruction to be designed? How can one approach such a task, and how begin it? There must surely be alternative ways. In this book we describe one way which we believe to be both feasible and worthwhile. This way of planning and designing instruction has certain characteristics that need to be mentioned at the outset.

First, we adopt the assumption that instructional design must be aimed at *aiding the learning of the individual.* We are not concerned here with "mass" changes in opinion or capabilities, nor with education in the sense of "diffusion" of information or attitudes within and among societies. Instead, the instruction we describe is oriented to the individual. Of course, we recognize that learners are often assembled into groups; but learning nevertheless occurs within each member of a group.

Second, instructional design has phases that are both *immediate and long-range.* Design in the immediate sense is what the teacher does in preparing a lesson plan some hours before the instruction is given. The longer-range aspects of instructional design are more complex and varied. The concern will more likely be with a set of lessons organized into "topics," a set of topics constituting a course or course sequence, or perhaps with an entire instructional system. Such design is sometimes undertaken by individual teachers as well as groups or teams of teachers, by committees of school people, by groups and organizations of curriculum planners, by textbook writers, and by groups of scholars representing academic disciplines.

The immediate and long-range phases of instructional planning are best performed as separate tasks, and not mixed together. The job of the teacher in carrying out instruction is highly demanding in terms of time, effort, and intellectual challenge. The teacher has a great deal to do in planning instruction on an immediate, day-to-day or hour-to-hour basis. Such a task can be greatly facilitated when the products of careful long-range instructional design are made available in the form of textbooks, teachers' guides, audio-visual aids, and other materials. Trying to accomplish both immediate and long-range instructional design, while at the same time teaching twenty or thirty students, is simply too big a job for one person, and can readily lead to the neglect of essential teaching functions. This is not to suggest, however, that teachers cannot or should not undertake long-range instructional design, either on their own or as part of a larger team. Teachers have essential contributions to make to long-range instructional design, and such contributions are best made during non-teaching periods.

A third assumption to be made in this work is that *systematically designed instruction can greatly affect individual human development.* Some educational writings (e.g., Friedenberg, 1965; Barth, 1972) indicate that education would perhaps be best if it were designed simply to provide a nurturing environment in which young people were allowed to grow up in their own ways, without the imposition of any plan to direct their learning. We consider this an incorrect line of thinking. Unplanned and undirected learning, we believe, is very likely to lead to the development of many individuals who are in one way or another incompetent to derive personal satisfaction from living in our society of today and tomorrow. A fundamental reason for instructional design is to insure that no one is "educationally disadvantaged," and that all students have equal opportunities to use their individual talents to the fullest degree.

The fourth idea to be given prominence is that instructional design should be *conducted by means of a systems approach.* This is discussed more fully in Chapter 2. Briefly, the systems approach to instructional design involves the carrying out of a number of steps beginning with an analysis of needs and goals, and ending with an evaluated system of instruction which demonstrably succeeds in meeting accepted goals. Decisions in each of the individual steps are based upon empirical evidence, to the extent that such evidence allows. Each step leads to decisions which become "inputs" to the next step, so that the whole process is as solidly based as is possible within the limits of human reason. Furthermore, each step is checked against evidence that is "fed back" from subsequent steps to provide an indication of the validity of the system.

A fifth and final point to be expanded in the next section, and also throughout the book, is that *designed instruction must be based on knowledge of how human beings learn.* In considering how an individual's abilities are to be developed, it is not enough to state what they should be; one must examine closely the question of how they can be acquired. Materials for instruction need to reflect not simply what their author knows, but also how the student is intended to learn such knowledge. Accordingly, instructional design must take fully into account *learning conditions* that need to be established in order for the desired effects to occur.

SOME LEARNING PRINCIPLES

At this point, it seems appropriate to expand upon the idea of basing instructional design on knowledge of the conditions of human learning. What sort of knowledge of learning is needed in order to design instruction?

The process of learning has been investigated by the methods of science (mainly by psychologists) for many years. As scientists, learning investigators are basically interested in explaining how learning takes place. In pursuing this interest, they usually construct *theories* about structures and events (generally conceived as occurring in the central nervous system) that could operate to bring about the remarkable behavior that can be directly observed as "an act of learning." From these theories, they deduce certain consequences which they can test out by a set of controlled observations.

In the course of this entire scientific process of theory-building and experimentation, much knowledge is accumulated. The effects of particular events on learning may be, and usually are, checked again and again under a great variety of conditions. In this way a body of "facts" about learning and a body of "principles" which hold true under a broad variety of conditions are collected. As an example, a rather well-known principle of learning is the following: When a fact such as the name of a person is learned, and is immediately followed by the learning of other persons' names, the first-learned name is likely to be forgotten. It is interesting to note that even such a well-known principle has to be stated with careful denoting of conditions. To attempt to simplify by stating something like, "whatever is learned is forgotten over time" would be quite incorrect.

Some of the facts and principles of human learning which have been accumulated in this manner are highly relevant to the design of instruction, while others are less so. For example, it has been found that lists of nonsense syllables with unfamiliar letter combinations, like ZEQ and XYR are more difficult to learn than those with familiar letter combinations, such as BOJ or REK. While such a finding has some importance to theory-making, it is of little direct relevance to the design of instruction, because the latter is hardly ever concerned with this kind of nonsensical learning task. A contrasting example is provided by the discovery that a list of words like MAN AND BOY WENT FAR AWAY is easier to learn and remember than the sequence FAR BOY AWAY MAN AND WENT (Miller and Selfridge, 1950). In this case, the principle *has* some relevance, because instruction sometimes does concern itself with the learning of words, classes of words, and word sequences. There are many examples of this sort in the scientific literature on human learning (Hulse, Deese, and Egeth, 1975).

Similar comments may be made about learning theories themselves—some of their ideas are highly relevant to instruction, while some are not. For example, a theory of learning might propose that a single event of learning produces a particular change in the chemical composition of the activated nerve cells. This may be an exciting theory, but by itself it cannot be expected to be relevant to the task of designing instruction. A different theory might hold that the presentation of an "alerting" signal just prior to presentation of the stimulus for learning, activates some particular neural circuits in such a way as to facilitate learning. Were such a theoretical idea to be verified, it would probably be considered of importance for the design of instruction. Those aspects of learning theory which are important for instruction are those which relate to *controllable events and conditions.* If we are concerned with designing instruction so that learning will occur efficiently, we must look for those elements of learning theory that pertain to the events that an instructor can do something about.

Some time-tested learning principles

What are some of the principles derived from learning theory and learning research, which may be expected to be relevant to instructional design? First, we shall mention some principles that have been with us for many years. Basically, they are still valid principles. But they may need some new interpretations in the light of modern theory.

Contiguity   This principle states that the stimulus situation to which one wants the learner to respond must be presented *contiguously in time* with the desired response. One has to think hard to provide an example of a violation of the principle of contiguity. Suppose, for example, one wants a young child to learn to print an E. An unskilled teacher might be tempted to do it as follows: First, give the verbal instruction, "Show me how you print an E." Following this, show the child a printed E on a page, in order to illustrate what it looks like and leave the page on the child's table. The child then draws an E. Now, has the child learned to print an E? Referring to the principle of contiguity, one would have to say, probably not yet. What has been made contiguous in this situation is:

Stimulus situation: a printed E
Child's response: printing E

whereas what is intended as an objective of the lesson is:

Stimulus situation: "Show me how you print an E."
Child's response: printing E

Somehow, in order for the principle of contiguity to exert its expected effect the first set of events must be replaced by the second, by a staged removal of the intervening stimulus (the printed E). In the first case, the verbal instructions were *remote from* the expected response, rather than contiguous with it.

Repetition   This principle states that the stimulus situation and its response need to be repeated, or practiced, in order for learning to be improved and retention more certain. There are some situations where the need for repetition is very apparent. For example, if one is learning to pronounce a new French word like *variété,* repeated trials certainly lead one closer and closer to an acceptable pronunciation. Modern learning theory, however, casts much doubt on the idea that repetition works by "strengthening learned connections." Furthermore, there are many situations in which repetition of newly learned ideas does not improve either learning or retention (cf. Ausubel, 1978; Gagné, 1977). It is perhaps best to think of repetition, not as a fundamental condition of learning, but merely as a practical procedure ("practice") which may be necessary in order to make sure that other conditions for learning are present.

Reinforcement Historically, this principle was stated in the following form (Thorndike, 1913): learning of a new act is strengthened when the occurrence of that act is followed by a satisfying state of affairs (that is, a "reward"). Such a view of reinforcement is still a lively theoretical issue, and there is a good deal of evidence for it. For instructional purposes, however, one is inclined to depend on another conception of reinforcement, which may be stated in this form: A new act (A) is most readily learned when it is immediately followed by an "old" act (B) which the individual performs readily, in such a way that doing B is made contingent on doing A (Premack, 1965). Suppose a young child is fond of looking at pictures of animals, and it is desired that he learn how to make drawings of animals. The new capability of animal drawing, according to this principle, will be most readily learned if one "attaches" it to looking at additional animal pictures. In other words, the opportunity to look at animal pictures is made *contingent* upon drawing one or more animals. In this form, the principle of reinforcement is a most powerful one.

Some newer learning principles

As the study of human learning has proceeded, it has gradually become apparent that theories must be increasingly sophisticated. Contiguity, repetition, and reinforcement are all good principles, and one of their outstanding characteristics is that they refer to controllable instructional events. The designer of instruction, as well as the teacher, can readily devise situations which include these principles. Nevertheless, when all these things are done, an efficient learning situation is not guaranteed. Something seems to be missing.

The missing conditions are to be sought *within* the individual, rather than in the external environment. They are states of mind that the learner brings to the learning task; in other words, they are *previously learned capabilities* of the individual learner. These capabilities appear to be a highly important set of factors in insuring effective learning.

Internal processes in learning

An act of learning requires the presence of some varieties of internal states that have been previously learned. For example, a student who is learning about the mechanical advantage of levers, expressed in the equation $Fd = F'd'$, must have readily accessible the information that F is a symbol for force, which may be expressed in pounds; that d stands for distance from the fulcrum, stated in feet; and similar *information* of this sort. Second, he must have some *intellectual skills,* such as that of substituting specific values of variables in proper places, solving simple equations, and others. And third, his learning will be facilitated to the extent that he has the kind of "self-management" *strategies* that govern his own behavior in attending, in storing and retrieving information, and in organizing problem solution. Each of these kinds of internal states depends, to a greater or lesser extent, upon *prior learning.*

Other kinds of internal events important for learning are *motivation* and an *attitude of confidence* in learning (sometimes included in the idea of "self-concept"). These internal states are essential for successful learning. It should be noted that we do not deal with them directly in our discussion of learning processes. They are, instead, assumed to be present as preconditions for the instruction to be designed. Initial stages of instruction, preceding those we shall describe, are often concerned with the establishment and channeling of motivation.

Factual information must be brought to bear upon an act of learning. Actually, this can occur in three different ways. First, and most obviously, it may simply be communicated to the learner in a form that remains accessible. For example, printed "directions" may remain available for reference throughout an act of learning. Second, it may have been just previously learned. For instance, students who are presented with a problem in mechanical advantage may have been told on a previous page that "*d* is a symbol for distance, and is usually expressed in feet." They may then keep this in their working memories, while learning to solve problems in mechanical advantage. Third, factual information may need to be retrieved from their memories, because it has been learned and stored months or years ago. In this case, the students must search their memories for the information.

Intellectual skills needed for learning must be recalled, in order for learning to occur. The learner has to have ways of doing things, particularly with language and other symbols, in order to learn new things. There may be stimulation to recall these intellectual skills by means of some verbal "cues." For example, the student faced with the learning of a rule about mechanical advantage may be told, "You remember how to find the value of a variable in an equation," or something similar. It is important to note that an intellectual skill typically cannot be conveyed by "directions." It must have been previously learned, in order to be available for recall at the proper moment. Can it not be learned just immediately prior to the new learning, or perhaps almost simultaneously? Yes, it can. But this procedure may make the learning more difficult.

A learning event requires the activation of strategies for learning and remembering. The individual may bring into play *strategies* of attending to complex stimulation; of selecting and coding parts of it; of solving problems; and of retrieving what has previously been learned. Much learning, except that of the youngest children, is aided by these capabilities of "self-management" of the learning process. In contrast to intellectual skills, strategies are highly general in their applicability to a variety of situations. Self-management strategies may show improvement over a period of many years. For any particular learning event, the strategies brought into play may be simply the best the learner has available at the moment. They may be expected to improve with continued practice. In most cases of instruction, learning is supported by stimulation provided by the teacher. As the learners gain experience in learning, they come to depend increasingly upon internalized strategies. In other words, they become more and more "self-learners."

A learning event involves several internal processes, each of which may be influenced by the external factors of instruction. Modern theories treat learning as a matter of *information-processing,* having several successive stages (Reynolds & Flagg, 1977). Thus, stimulation from the learner's environment is originally subject to brief internal registration. Subsequently, this information is transformed for storage in a temporary fashion in "short-term memory." Still another transformation, called *semantic encoding,* occurs when the information enters "long-term memory." Performances which are based upon recall of this stored information depend upon a process of *retrieval* of information from the learner's long-term memory. Thus, a single learning event, even though it may take only a few seconds to complete, includes these various internal processes, each of which may be differentially affected by the set of external events called "instruction." A more complete description of the implications of information-processing theory for the design of instructional events will be given in Chapter 9.

Figure 1–1 depicts the two categories of factors involved in a learning event. Older learning theories gave greatest weight to *external* factors, and the model of what was required internally consisted almost entirely of "connections to be strengthened." The newer model places greater emphasis on the importance of factors which originate from the *internal* source of the individual's memory. The influences of these factors occur through memories of what has previously been learned. Thus the design of instruction must take into account not only the immediate external situation stimulating the learner, but also those capabilities which learners bring with them. Instructional planning must also provide for the prior learning of these latter capabilities, and timely recall or reactivation of them.

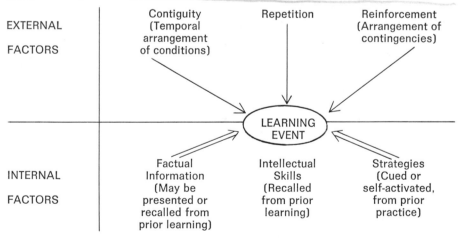

FIGURE 1–1   External and Internal Factors Affecting the Learning Event

Learning emphases in instruction

There are several varieties of learned capabilities that instruction aims to establish. For purposes of illustration, we have already mentioned three—*infor-*

mation, intellectual skills, cognitive strategies—and we may complete the list with *motor skills* and *attitudes*. Any of these may represent a category of what is to be learned. Any or all of them may need to be recalled as a previously learned capability at the time of new learning. Which of these should be the primary aim of instruction? Is it possible to assign priorities to them on theoretical or practical grounds?

Concentrating instruction on any one type of capability alone, or any two in combination, is insufficient. Factual information, in and of itself, would represent a highly inadequate instructional goal. Learning intellectual skills leads to practical competence. Yet these, too, are insufficient for new learning, because such learning makes use of information as well. Furthermore, the learning of intellectual skills does not by itself equip the learners with the strategies of learning and remembering which they need to become independent self-learners. Turning to cognitive strategies themselves, it is apparent that these cannot be learned or progressively improved without the involvement of information and skills—they must, in other words, have "something to work on." Attitudes, too, require a substrate of information and intellectual skills to support them. Finally, motor skills constitute a somewhat specialized area of school learning, not representative of the whole. In sum, *multiple aims* for instruction must be recognized. The human learner needs to attain several varieties of learned capabilities.

Information   Since learning principles have frequently been derived from studies of information learning, one might draw the implication that priority in instruction should be given to the learning of information. Effective learning and problem solving require the accessibility of information. However, information for problem solving *can* be made available to a student as part of the communication which states the problem. Alternatively, it can be looked up in convenient reference sources; it doesn't really have to be stored in all cases. Certain information can be recalled and retrieved at the time of a learning event; other information can be communicated as part of the problem description; still other things can be looked up and stored in memory for the duration of the learning event. Because all of these alternatives are feasible, the design of instruction around factual information seems a highly inadequate course of action.

Cognitive Strategies   Some educational theorists appear to award priority consideration to cognitive strategies as an instructional aim. These are emphasized, for example, in the writings of Bruner (1960, 1971). In some respects, this emphasis is reasonable and desirable. It is based upon the idea that an ultimate goal of instruction is to insure that the student becomes an efficient self-learner. The learning of strategies, however, cannot be critically affected by instruction on a minute-to-minute basis. Such capabilities are improved in quality and effectiveness over relatively long periods of time—months and years. For example, over a period of years a person who continues to read will become a more efficient reader, a more insightful reader, a reader with greater virtuosity. Entire sequences of instruction may be planned so that learners will improve their cognitive strategies of attending, of coding verbal information, of storing and retrieving what they have learned, of attacking and solving problems. Plans for attainment of such strategies appear to require arrangements for a variety of practice situations, extending over a period of many months.

Intellectual Skills as Building Blocks for Instruction   For purposes of planning instruction in scope ranging from entire systems to individual lessons, intellectual skills have a number of desirable characteristics as components of a design framework (Gagné, 1970). An intellectual skill cannot be learned by being simply looked up, or provided to the learner by a verbal communication. It must be learned, recalled, and put into use at the proper time. As an example, consider the intellectual skill of spelling words containing a "long *a*" sound. When the learner possesses this skill, he is able to perform such spelling rapidly and without the necessity of looking up a set of rules. His performance shows that he is able to recall such rules and put them immediately into effect. At the same time, learning the necessary rules for spelling words with "long *a*" is not something that takes a period of many months to accomplish (as seems to be true of cognitive strategies). Essentially flawless performance calling upon such an intellectual skill can be expected to be established in a short space of time.

There are other advantages to intellectual skills as a major framework for instruction and instructional design. Such skills come to be highly interrelated to each other, and to build elaborate internal intellectual structures of a cumulative sort (Gagné, 1977). The learning of one skill aids the learning of other "higher-order" skills. Suppose an individual has learned the skill of substituting specific numerical values for letters in a symbolic expression like the following:

$$\sigma^2 = E(X-m)^2.$$

Such a skill will aid the learning of many kinds of advanced skills, not simply in mathematics, but in many areas of science and social studies. Intellectual skills are rich in transfer effects, which bring about the building of increasingly complex structures of intellectual competence.

Another advantage of intellectual skills as a primary component in instruction is the relative ease with which they can be reliably observed. When a learner has attained an intellectual skill, as, for example, "representing quantitative increases graphically," it is not difficult to see what must be done to show that the skill has indeed been learned. One would provide the person with numerical values of any increasing variable, and ask him to construct a graph to show the changes in that variable. An intellectual skill can always be defined in operational terms; that is, it can always be related to a class of human performances—to something the successful learner *is able to do.*

The choice of intellectual skills as a primary point of reference in the design of instruction, then, is based mainly upon practical considerations. In contrast to factual information, skills cannot be simply looked up or made available by "telling," but must be learned. In contrast to cognitive strategies, intellectual skills are typically learned over relatively short time periods, and do not have to be refined and sharpened by months or years of practice. Intellectual skills build upon each other in a cumulative fashion to form increasing elaborate intellectual structures. Through the mechanism of transfer of learning, they make possible an ever-broadening intellectual competence in each individual. And finally, such skills can be readily observed, so that it is easy to tell that they have been learned.

THE RATIONALE FOR INSTRUCTIONAL DESIGN

The design of instruction must be undertaken with suitable attention to the conditions under which learning occurs—conditions which are both external and internal to the learner. These conditions are in turn dependent upon *what* is being learned.

In order to design instruction systematically a rationale for what is to be learned must first be established. This requires going back to the initial sources that have given rise to the idea of employing instruction to meet a recognized need. A *system* of instruction may then be constructed step by step, beginning with a base of information that reflects identified goals.

The planning of instruction in a highly systematic manner, with attention to the consistency and compatibility of technical knowledge at each point of decision, is usually termed the "systems approach." This kind of design uses various forms of information, data, and theoretical principles as input at each planning stage. Further, the prospective outcomes of each stage are checked against whatever goals may have been adopted by those who manage the "system" as a whole. It is within this systems framework that we seek to apply what is known about the conditions of human learning to instructional design.

The derivation of an instructional system

The rational steps in the derivation of an instructional system, to be described more completely in the next chapter, may be outlined briefly as follows:

1. The *needs* for instruction are investigated as a first step. These are then carefully considered by a responsible group to arrive at agreements on the *goals* of instruction. The *resources* available to meet these goals must also be carefully weighed, along with those circumstances that impose *constraints* on instructional planning.

2. Goals of instruction may be translated into a framework for a *curriculum,* and for the individual courses contained in it. The goals of individual courses may be conceived as *target objectives,* and grouped to reflect a rational organization.

3. *Objectives* of courses are achieved through learning. In this book the lasting effects of learning are defined as the acquisition of various *capabilities* by the learner. As outcomes of instruction and learning, human capabilities are usually specified in terms of the classes of *human performance* which they make possible. We need to consider what kinds of capabilities may be learned. We shall describe

the varieties of human performance made possible to the learner by each kind of learned capability—intellectual skills, cognitive strategies, information, attitudes, and motor skills.

4. The identification of these categories of human capabilities is a useful step. Without them, we should only be able to deal with learning principles on a very general basis. With them, it becomes possible to infer what *kinds of internal effects* learning is having. As a further step, it is possible to describe what *conditions,* internal and external, will be needed to bring about learning with greatest efficiency.

5. The inference of conditions for learning makes possible the planning of *sequences of instruction.* This is so because the information and skills which need to be recalled for any given learning event must themselves have been previously learned. As a simple example from language study, learning the intellectual skill of using a pronoun in the objective case when the object of a preposition, requires the recall of other "subordinate" skills of identifying prepositions, pronouns, the cases of pronouns, and the concept "object of." Thus by tracing backwards from the outcome of learning for a particular topic, one can identify the sequence of intermediate (or "prerequisite") objectives that must be met to make possible the desired learning. In this way, instructional sequences may be specified that are applicable to topics, to courses, or even to entire curricula. The sequences thus derived are like *terrain maps* of intellectual development to be visited when students progress from one level of capability to another.

6. Continued planning for instruction proceeds to the design of units that are smaller in scope and thus more detailed in character. At some point, the consideration of target objectives must also lead to increased attention to a larger array of detailed objectives, called *performance objectives.* They are objectives in that they identify the expected or planned outcomes of the events of learning. They represent instances of human performance which can be reliably observed and thus assessed as outcomes of learning.

7. Once a course has been designed in terms of target objectives, and an appropriate sequence determined, detailed planning of instruction for the *individual lesson* can proceed. Here again the first reference for such planning is the performance objective which represents the outcome of the lesson. Attention centers on the arrangement of *external conditions* which will be most effective in bringing about the desired learning. What are the events that must be arranged by the teacher, or by the instructional designer, which will insure learning on the part of the student? These events, together with their arrangement and sequencing, comprise *instruction.* The determination of the conditions for instruction also involves the choice of appropriate media and combinations of media that may be employed to promote learning.

8. The additional element that is required for completion of instructional design is a set of procedures for *assessment* of what students have learned. In conception, this component follows naturally from the definitions of instructional objectives. The latter statements describe domains from which "items" are se-

lected. These in turn may be teacher observations, or assembled as tests. Assessment procedures are designed to provide *criterion-referenced* measurement of learning outcomes (Popham, 1971). They are intended as direct measures of what students have learned as a result of instruction on specified objectives. We call this *objective-referenced* instruction and assessment.

9. The design of lessons and courses with their accompanying techniques of assessing learning outcomes makes possible the planning of entire *systems.* Instructional systems aim to achieve comprehensive goals in schools and school systems. Means must be found to fit the various components together by way of a management system, sometimes called an "instructional delivery system." Naturally, teachers play key roles in the operation of such a system. A particular class of instructional systems is concerned with *individualized instruction,* involving a set of procedures to insure optimal development of the individual student.

Finally, attention must be paid to *evaluation* of whatever instructional entity has been designed. Procedures for evaluation are first applied to the design effort itself. Evidence is sought for needed revisions aimed at the improvement and refinement of the instruction ("formative evaluation"). At a later stage, "summative evaluation" is undertaken to seek evidence of the learning effectiveness of what has been designed.

WHAT THE BOOK IS ABOUT

Designing instruction is described in fifteen chapters of this book, arranged into four parts, as follows:

Part 1—introduction to instruction systems

Chapter 1, the Introduction, outlines our general approach to instruction, and gives a brief account of some principles of human learning which will be incorporated into the following description of instructional design.

Chapter 2 introduces the reader to instructional systems and the systems approach to the design of instruction. The stages of instructional system design are described, to be developed further in subsequent chapters.

Part 2—basic processes in learning and instruction

Chapter 3 introduces the reader to the five major categories of instructional outcomes—the human capabilities that are learned with the aid of instruction. The varieties of human performance which these capabilities make possible are described and distinguished.

Chapter 4 enters into an intensive description of the characteristics and conditions of learning for two of these categories of learning outcomes—intellectual skills and cognitive strategies.

Chapter 5 extends this description of learned capabilities to the three additional categories, with definitions and examples of information, attitudes, and motor skills.

Part 3—designing instruction

Chapter 6 begins with a consideration of the purposes and goals of instruction; and describes a system of task analysis which aims for the classification of these objectives of instruction. The uses of such a classificatory system in instructional planning are described.

Chapter 7 deals with the derivation and description of specific instructional objectives (performance objectives). These are related on the one hand to the categories of objectives previously defined, and on the other to the particular learned capabilities that are the focus of interest for instruction.

Chapter 8 describes procedures for constructing sequences of lessons in making up larger units of instruction, such as "topics," "modules," and courses.

Chapter 9 deals with sequences of instructional events within single lessons, and shows how these may be related to the stages of information-processing involved in learning.

Chapter 10 discusses the important matter of media selection, and provides a systematic procedure for conducting such a step as a part of instructional design.

Chapter 11 gives an account of the design of individual lessons, including the placement of parts of lessons in sequence, the arrangement of effective conditions of learning, and the use of media for instructional delivery.

Chapter 12 deals with methods of assessing student performances as outcomes of instruction, describing appropriate uses of criterion-referenced and norm-referenced tests.

Part 4—delivery systems for instruction

Chapter 13 opens this part of the book by discussing the special features of design needed when instruction is to be delivered to groups of various sizes.

Chapter 14 presents a complementary account of how systematic procedures may be designed to accomplish individualized instruction.

Chapter 15 describes the basic logic of evaluation of designed products and procedures, from lessons to systems.

SUMMARY

Instruction is planned for the purpose of supporting the processes of learning. In this book, we describe methods involved in the design of instruction aimed at the human learner. We assume that planned instruction has both short-range and long-range purposes in its effects on human development.

Instructional design must take into account some principles of human learning, specifically, the conditions under which learning occurs. Theories of learning have identified a number of conditions for learning, some of which are controllable by the procedures of instruction. Older theories emphasize particularly the external conditions for learning, embodied in the principles of contiguity, repetition, and reinforcement. Modern theories add to these some internal conditions, those that arise within the learner. Internal processes control several stages in the transformation of learning matter for long-term storage. In addition, contributions to new learning are made by the recall of previously learned material from the learner's memory.

An act of learning is greatly affected by these internally generated processes and states. In particular, new learning is influenced by the recall of previously learned information, intellectual skills, and cognitive strategies. These and other human capabilities, established by learning, will be described in the chapters to follow. These varieties of learned capabilities, and the conditions for their learning, constitute the basis for instructional planning. Derived from these principles is the rationale for a set of practical procedures for the design of instruction.

Students who use this book will find it possible to follow up the ideas derived from research on human learning with further exploration and study of the references at the end of each chapter. Those who are interested in becoming skillful in designing instruction will need to undertake practice exercises that exemplify the procedures described. Because of the anticipated variety of particular courses and educational settings in which this book might be used, it has been our general expectation that such exercises would be supplied by a course instructor. Examples and exercises of particular relevance for such a purpose are provided in two previously published volumes by Briggs (1970, 1972).

References

Ausubel, D. P., Novak, J. D., and Hanesian, H. *Educational Psychology: A Cognitive View.* 2d ed. New York: Holt, Rinehart and Winston, 1978.

Barth, R. S. *Open Education and the American School.* New York: Agathon Press, 1972.

Briggs, L. J. *Handbook of Procedures for the Design of Instruction.* Pittsburgh, Pa.: American Institutes for Research, 1970.

Briggs, L. J. *Student's Guide to Handbook of Procedures for the Design of Instruction.* Pittsburgh, Pa.: American Institutes for Research, 1972.

Bruner, J. S. *The Process of Education.* Cambridge, Mass.: Harvard University Press, 1960.

Bruner, J. S. *The Relevance of Education.* New York: Norton, 1971.

Friedenberg, E. Z. *Coming of Age in America: Growth and Acquiescence.* New York: Random House, 1965.

Gagné, R. M. *The Conditions of Learning,* 3d Ed. New York: Holt, Rinehart, and Winston, 1977.

Hulse, S. H., Deese, J., and Egeth, H. *The Psychology of Learning.* New York: McGraw-Hill, 1975.

Miller, G. A., and Selfridge, J. A. Verbal context and the recall of meaningful material. *American Journal of Psychology,* 1950, *63,* 176–185.

Popham, W. J. (ed.). *Criterion-Referenced Measurement.* Englewood Cliffs, N.J.: Educational Technology Publications, 1971.

Premack, D. Reinforcement theory. In D. Levine (ed.), *Nebraska Symposium on Motivation.* Lincoln: University of Nebraska Press, 1965.

Reynolds, A. G., and Flagg, P. W. *Cognitive Psychology.* Cambridge, Mass.: Winthrop, 1977.

Thorndike, E. L. *The Psychology of Learning: Educational Psychology,* Vol. 2. New York: Teachers College, 1913.

chapter 2

Designing Instructional Systems

There are many ways to approach the task of designing instruction. It is possible, for example, to attend primarily to the content of a textbook, and assume that the printed communications provided by the book are all that need to be designed. In contrast, one might devote principal attention to the procedures to be employed by teachers for achieving different sorts of educational *goals* or *outcomes*. From the latter point of view, some of the approaches best known to teachers and curriculum planners have been summarized by Joyce and Weil (1972) as "models of teaching." Each of these models incorporates a major type of educational outcome sought or valued, along with the teaching procedures considered most effective in realizing this outcome. Some of the major types of outcomes sought by such models may be described as "personal development," "social interaction," "basic skills," "scientific method." Phrases such as these are not the same as those employed in this book (Chapter 3) to describe the outcomes of instruction. However, they carry similar implications—namely, that different types of outcomes may be best fostered by different sets of teaching and learning conditions.

A major distinction needs to be made between a model of teaching and an instructional system. It appears that the purpose of a model of teaching is to provide a conceptual link between a desired outcome and an appropriate teaching method or set of methods. The purpose of an *instructional system,* however, is to provide the necessary means for achieving *all* the types of outcomes called for in the curriculum or course being considered. In this book designing an instructional system is shown as the construction of an over-arching framework for accomplishing whatever variety of learned outcomes the course (or curriculum) intends. The design of such an instructional system is drawn from the accumulated wisdom contained in teaching models, learning theory, and other relevant disciplines and experiences.

A "systems model" of instruction accepts whatever goals or outcomes may have been adopted by those who establish or manage the education (such as a school board, a corporate office, or a government agency). The type of goals will influence the entire implementation strategy designed to achieve those goals. Even the form of the instructional delivery system and the plans for later diffusion of the system will be affected. While special instructional systems have been designed to make maximum use of individualized instruction, or television, or a particular teaching style, the systems approach to instructional design, we believe, should be as unbiased as possible with respect to these more particular aims. While chapters in this book deal with such specific matters as media selection and individualized instruction, the stages in instructional system design are dealt with in general terms in this chapter. Although the reader will not always find a "stage," as described here, to correspond to each chapter title in the following sections of the book, these chapters will nevertheless be tied to the stages described.

DEFINITION OF INSTRUCTIONAL SYSTEM

A system is usually considered to be a human enterprise of a complex nature which serves a purpose valued by society. One could use the term "U.S. educational system" to include the operations of all the schools and other institutions having educational purposes in the nation as a whole. More frequently, "educational system" refers to all the schools in a city or district which operate under a single superintendent and school board. Within such a local school system, the term "instructional system" is often used to distinguish those operations dealing with the instruction of students from those that pertain to transportation, financial management, and other aspects of administration.

The scope of a system has no fixed boundaries. In a narrow sense, a single course or instructional method may be considered an instructional system. At the other end of the scale, the entire society of the United States may be called a social system, containing within it a business system, a government system, a school system, and several others. It is evident, then, that the use of the word *system* is relative and may mean any organized way of accomplishing certain goals, whether these pertain to a whole society, a portion of a society, or even to a single teacher. As the title of this chapter implies, we intend to deal with the design of instruction as an activity more or less independent of personnel administration, budgeting, and other aspects of school management.

Instruction is the means employed by teachers, designers of materials, curriculum specialists, and others whose purpose it is to develop an organized plan to promote learning. The system of instruction which is designed may be intended for use in public or private schools, in industry, or in public-service training installations. No particular emphasis is placed here on the distinction between education and training, since systems of both types are designed to promote learning which leads to outcomes of the various categories described in later chapters.

The systems approach and educational technology

In recent years, systematic efforts to design instruction have come to be identified as examples of the "systems approach." This mode of planning has become familiar to managers of business concerns, industrial and military operations, and school systems. While not enough time has elapsed for emergence of a widely accepted standardized meaning of this phrase, generally it may be said that the contents of the present volume are compatible with a systems approach to instructional design. This is particularly evident in its emphasis upon learning outcomes as the goals of an instructional system, and in its attempts to bring systematic knowledge of the learning process to bear on the design of instruction.

Instructional system designing utilizes a kind of knowledge called *educational technology.* This term has sometimes been associated with computers and other media hardware used for instruction. However, there is a growing tendency to relate educational technology to the *process of planning* by which an instructional system is developed, implemented, controlled, and evaluated. The procedures to be described in this chapter for planning instructional systems are consistent with this latter meaning of educational technology (cf. Davies & Hartley, 1972).

In providing a historical framework for educational technology, Davies (1971) points out that it is an outgrowth of a number of converging influences upon present concepts and practices in instructional design. According to Lumsdaine (1964), these earlier influences include the following developments: (a) *interest in individual differences* in learning, as seen in educational and military research and development programs, in self-instructional devices such as those of Pressey (1950) and Briggs (1960) and the branching programs of Crowder (1959), and in computer applications to instruction; (b) *behavioral science and learning theory,* as seen in Skinner's emphasis upon contingencies of reinforcement and in his teaching machines (1968), and in other learning theories; and (c) *physical science technology,* as represented in motion-picture, television, and video-tape instruction; and in audio-visual devices to supplement printed media. All of these streams of development, along with the conceptions of learning outcomes categories and their associated instructional events described in this volume, can be harmoniously utilized in the design of instructional systems which give primary attention to the individual learner's activities and to the testing of their outcomes.

INSTRUCTIONAL SYSTEM DEVELOPMENT

The process of instructional system design and development is presented as a series of stages in Table 2–1, as described in the next section. Often these procedures and their relationships to each other are shown in flow charts or diagrams. In employing a list, we also emphasize that in practice there is much "recycling" —going back over previous work, modifying it in view of insights gained later. There are also "forward projections" which are later revised. This cyclical or iterative nature of the process is real, but its details cannot be shown accurately in advance, either by feed-forward and feedback loops in diagrams or by arrows connecting numbered stages in a list. These second attempts to improve work at various stages, while costly in time and effort, actually do improve and strengthen the system, as do the later changes which are occasioned by formative evaluations and field tryouts. Even experienced designers have learned to expect imperfections in their first efforts. It is this very recycling, based on empirical testing of the system, that leads to its later effectiveness. Designers can set a design objective, which describes the kind of acceptable evidence of a successful system operation, and work until that point of quality has been reached. Even when depletion of resources ends the effort to bring added improvements, the data can show how close the effort came to the design target, and how much improvement from initial results the gains represented.

From this book as a whole, it will be apparent that much systematic thinking and planning go into the design effort, making use of all theory and research evidence available, and that this planning can be supplemented by the iterative, self-correcting process of empirical tryout and revision. The entire procedure, while lacking the elegant precision and predictive power of the natural sciences, is closer to a science of education than are other approaches to the design of instruction which do not include measurement of their effects. The ability to determine whether the system has met its design objectives—whether student performance shows that needs were met—provides the basis for accountability in results.

Who designs instructional systems?

Designing a system of instruction is an enterprise that is likely to involve a variety of specialized people and agencies. The size of such an effort will of course depend upon whether the design is for a single lesson or module, for a new curriculum to be installed in an existing school system, or for a totally new system of education.

Most current instruction has not been designed as an instructional system, following the steps of Table 2–1. Instead, different agencies, acting almost entirely independently from each other, have provided some of the resources used in conventional instruction. Universities have trained teachers; publishers have provided textbooks; and local communities have constructed the school buildings and employed the people to operate the schools. Teachers perhaps deserve more credit than they customarily receive for trying to adapt components of instruction which do not fit well together because there has not been sufficient coordination to make them compatible. It is not easy to use available instructional materials to accomplish objectives for which the materials were not designed, or to try to effect individualization of instruction with materials not suited for such systems.

It seems evident that a joint effort of schools, industry, universities, and other agencies, organized as a consortium and applying a systems approach, represents the ideal model of instructional systems design in the future. Other sorts of efforts to bring about improvements in instruction also have merit and will doubtless be tried. For example, closer joint-sharing of teacher-training responsibilities between schools and universities seems a likely development. However, production of instructional materials also needs to be integrated with other aspects of the total educational endeavor, in order that optimal systems development can be undertaken.

When attempts are made to design entire school curricula by a systems approach but with piecemeal methods, problems are usually encountered. Separate curricula for different school subjects, designed by independent groups, appeal from the point of view of a single discipline, but are less appealing in meeting system goals. Efforts by a single teacher or department within a school to install a new partial curriculum may flounder because it is out of step with the rest of the school. Even the school building itself may not be appropriately designed to accommodate a new system of instruction.

In an ideal situation, a group of people, possibly representing a number of organizations, would be given the responsibility for designing an entire school system. For example, in the Model Cities Program (City of Tampa, Florida, undated), a portion of a city might literally be torn down and rebuilt to suit the needs of the community. Plans for school buildings would be made only as an integral part of the design of the entire section of the city. No assumption would even be made about the nature of school buildings until the educational and other needs of the people in the community were analyzed. Then all buildings would be designed to accommodate the learning activities chosen by the people and suiting their needs.

Designing systems of instruction in this complete sense seems likely to be the most promising course of action to follow if highly satisfactory results are to be achieved. Most communities, however, would undoubtedly prefer to seek gradual improvement of their schools and their curricula rather than literally building entirely new systems of instruction. This may mean that the changes undertaken are not as satisfactory in the long run. Nevertheless, it is possible to design and install new systems of instruction within existing conventions. Such programs are more likely to be intended for a single classroom, school, or subject area, than for entire schools or curricula. Even relatively small efforts may meet some new needs, or more satisfactorily meet long-recognized needs.

For example, the school system of the city of Duluth, Minnesota, by its own efforts, first introduced individualized instruction into all curriculum areas of three elementary schools (Esbensen, 1968). Thereafter the methods were adopted by other schools. The American Telephone and Telegraph Company replaced numerous locally developed courses in first aid (accomplished by the member Bell Companies) with a new, uniform, contractor-developed first-aid course (Markle, 1967). Training time was reduced with concomitant large gains in trainee performance. The new course, developed by a systems approach, was found to be more economical than the former courses. This course, now made available by the American Red Cross, has since been used to train over two million persons (see Markle, 1977), and plans have been made to update its content. The first example (Duluth) involved all the instruction in entire schools; the second example

(AT&T) involved 7.5 clock hours of instruction. Thus, the systems approach can involve any amount of instruction one wishes to undertake in a single, coordinated planning and development effort.

Other large curriculum design efforts have tended to center on the individual subject areas such as science and mathematics, but three programs for individualized instruction in several subject areas began within university or private research settings, and then expanded with adoption by hundreds (in some cases thousands) of schools. The three systems, known respectively as Project PLAN (Program for Learning in Accordance with Needs), IPI (Individually Prescribed Instruction) and IGE (Individually Guided Instruction) are described in a book edited by Weisgerber (1971).

STAGES OF DESIGN

The various stages of design of instructional systems, as viewed in this book, are listed in Table 2–1. While there are many other ways in which the entire process could be outlined, the stages shown in that table will now be discussed in turn.

TABLE 2–1 Stages in Designing Instructional Systems

System Level

  1. Analysis of Needs, Goals, and Priorities
  2. Analysis of Resources, Constraints, and Alternate Delivery Systems
  3. Determination of Scope and Sequence of Curriculum and Courses; Delivery System Design

Course Level

  4. Determining Course Structure and Sequence
  5. Analysis of Course Objectives

Lesson Level

  6. Definition of Performance Objectives
  7. Preparing Lesson Plans (or Modules)
  8. Developing, Selecting Materials, Media
  9. Assessing Student Performance (Performance Measures)

System Level

10. Teacher Preparation
11. Formative Evaluation
12. Field Testing, Revision
13. Summative Evaluation
14. Installation and Diffusion

Stage 1: analysis of needs, goals and priorities

Recent writings treating the topic of needs analysis have defined a need as a discrepancy or gap between the way things "are" and the way things "ought to be" (Burton and Merrill, 1977; Kaufman, 1976). In elementary and secondary schools, these writers suggest, the "ought to be" should be established by public consensus, expressed in terms of what school children should be learning and how well. Any gap between that consensus and the present achievement of the pupils would be taken as a need. Needs then should be arranged in priority order, so that the most pressing needs may receive priority attention.

Training needs in industry are often derived from a job analysis, or from a comparison of the present performance of personnel with the performance desired of them (Branson, 1977). Needs in higher education, writers suggest, are often set by precedent rather than by serious analysis (Branson, 1977; Wager, 1977).

All these writers, however, warn of the danger of too quickly concluding that any performance gap observed may best be solved by education or training. Often a change elsewhere in society itself or in how one of its institutions operates would close an apparent gap. So, most of these writers caution, "don't worry about how to solve a problem until you are sure there is one." Their corollary is, "if the trouble doesn't really lie in education or training, don't try to solve the problem there." These warnings seem especially useful at a time when various kinds of test scores of students *are* falling but when many other problems of great concern seem almost beyond solution by the entire society.

Returning to matters of definition, we have cited one current meaning of "need." Other definitions would place a need as just a step broader than a goal. So there is not complete agreement. Suffice it to say that the prevailing view appears to be that the general public, including the learner, should help determine what the instructional goals of the schools should be. Perhaps for convenience and economy the general public should participate in defining goals at logical intervals in the schooling system, such as at the close of elementary education, then middle school, then high school. It would appear wasteful and frustrating to involve a cross section of the population in deciding goals for each year of schooling, for example.

The instructional designer can help citizens articulate their intent in ways that can be recorded and put to a consensus test. Burton and Merrill (1977) documented step-by-step procedures for helping citizen groups reach and express a consensus, so that the more detailed specification of year-by-year performance objectives (then expressed at the yearly or "course" level) could be completed.

When such groups of citizens, parents, educators, and pupils are convened, a systematic sorting and winnowing of ideas occurs and a true consensus does result. During this process, if the group wishes, information on current resources and constraints which would facilitate or retard the achievement of desired goals may be provided. While detailed decisions on means, methods, and materials might not be accomplished in such groups, the group might identify constraint-removal actions to be initiated, such as changes in a local or state law, budget, or an administrative procedure. The total actions of such a group would probably help with the first two, and perhaps the third, stage of design listed in Table 2–1. Certainly significant progress on any of those stages facilitates getting to the fourth stage, and so on.

This discussion of the role of citizens-groups does, however, pertain most directly to Stage 1, (Analysis of needs, goals, and priorities for system development). We have placed the first three stages under system design and development in Table 2–1 because generally the initial broad planning is complete when the curriculum scope and sequence has been spelled out, often in chart form, so that others can fill in the year-by-year details. Practice has varied at this point, however. In some cases, the same team goes right on into the activities labelled under "Course Level" in Table 2–1. Continuity in planning and support are most needed but some continuity in team design membership facilitates later stages of work.

It is apparent that in the past, needs have been identified by many means other than the citizen consensus groups recommended by current needs-analysis writers. Often school officials have consulted authorities in the academic disciplines, sometimes represented by professional societies, presuming that school-board approval represents the only form of citizen consensus needed. Or, groups of teachers in the school have joined together and agreed upon new directions for the instruction. Professional associations have sometimes assumed the task of needs analysis, as was done, for example, by the AAAS Commission on Science Education (1967) in undertaking the development of a new science curriculum called *Science—A Process Approach* which recognized the need to teach children the intellectual skills of science. Also, government agencies and private foundations have sponsored curricula based on recommendations contained in proposals from scientists in universities.

As the tempo of change in society increases, it may be increasingly important to review needs frequently, not only to keep abreast of changes in society but also to attend to increased feelings of alienation by many in an increasingly pluralistic society. The needs of individuals should be considered as well as society's general concerns.

No matter how the needs and goals are first identified, a next step is to arrange them either into a curriculum scope and sequence statement if an entire curriculum is being planned, or to state them as course objectives if a single course is being planned. In either case, there is a continued refinement in the way the goals are stated in order to achieve two purposes: (a) to state them in increasing detail, in layers arranged from general to specific and (b) to express them ultimately in performance (behavioral; measurable) terms. These two points, and the reasons for them, will be examined again in a later section of this chapter.

Stage 2: analysis of resources, constraints, and alternate delivery systems

When needs and goals have been identified, instructional planners need to pause and ask questions like these: How would children (or students, or trainees) learn to do the things our goals describe? From whom would they learn? Where would they find the resources, or materials, or help they need? What would it take to teach the goals as first conceived? Are there any reasons why it couldn't be done that way? Do we have to compromise somewhere? What would it cost? Do we have that much? Can present personnel of our schools do this? What alternatives exist? Once such questions are pursued, some alternate "delivery systems" suggest themselves.   *emerge from answering questions*

A delivery system may be defined as everything it takes to make a particular instructional system operate as it was intended to operate, where it was intended to operate. Thus a system can be designed to fit a particular physical plant, or to require a new one. The basic decision about instructional delivery can directly affect the kind of personnel, media, materials and learning activities that can be carried on to reach the goals. Must some of the goals be sacrificed, or a new building constructed, or the budget increased, or a more efficient system be designed? All such questions, deliberations, and alternative plans are pondered in the search for a way to meet the needs, given available resources and constraints. Can any of the resources and constraints be changed? That may be a key question at several stages of planning, including this one.

Should the new set of needs and goals, as first defined, appear out of the reach of any delivery system that the planning group can conceive within existing resources and constraints, no further detailed planning is possible until either (a) some goals are changed, (b) some resources and constraints are changed or (c) another delivery system can be conceived. This may lead to the use of "piecemeal" planning with generally unsatisfactory results. It may be wiser to face the original issue squarely, working a while longer for a satisfactory solution. Failure to do this at this early stage may result in various kinds of waste: (a) equipment and materials sitting unused due to lack of supporting personnel, (b) laboratories not used because supplies were not budgeted for, (c) learning activities disrupted due to faulty planning of time schedules, (d) goals not reached because essential prerequisite learning experiences were not provided.

Once the planners have seen a way to plan a delivery system suitable for a set of goals (possibly somewhat modified) within resources and constraints as identified, the team may be enlarged for more detailed work. Perhaps by this point few goals really have had to be abandoned; a few may have changed in priority, and the level of expected performance of students reduced somewhat for others, but the critical, high-priority ones survived unchanged. Perhaps only the range of planned materials has been reduced, or some media substitutions have been made to save money or space. Perhaps larger classrooms than wished for must be utilized, but by changing the ratio of team teaching and individualized study material, the space is used more efficiently. Some pet ideas might have gone by the wayside, but on the whole, the decision to do a needs analysis is thought to be worth the effort.

At this point, many of the citizen team members may drop out of the work, leaving the more detailed planning to the professionals.

Stage 3: determination of scope and sequence of curriculum and courses; delivery system design

At this stage there is a need to restate the original needs and goals as performance objectives which are sufficiently specific and detailed to show progress on goals, year-by-year in the curriculum. In usual terminology, this stage corresponds to the end of curriculum development and the beginning of year-by-year plans for each course, or subject area, or competency area. However, in some cases, the same team of persons who developed the curriculum also continues to operate through course design, development, and implementation.

There are two reasons for working from goals to increasingly specific objectives, in as many layers as needed for each course design. (From this point on in this chapter, we use "course" to refer either to a single training effort in public service or industrial settings, or to a single year of study in a subject area in elementary school, or to a semester or quarter in secondary or postsecondary schools.) The first reason is to communicate at different levels to different persons. The general public may want to hear only the broad goals; administrators may want only the curriculum scope and sequence level; teachers and members of the course design team, including material writers and media producers, need the very detailed objectives, as of course, do the learners.

The second reason for increased detail is for supervision of all phases in development of the delivery system. The design team leader must coordinate the work of writers, media producers, and trainers of teachers, if the delivery system is to operate smoothly.

The reason for eventually stating all objectives in terms of learner performance (rather than in terms of what the materials present or what the teacher does) is to be able to measure that performance to determine when the objective has been reached. It is because of the importance of objectives to both learning and to the assessment of learning that we devote an entire chapter of this book to the defining of performance objectives (Chapter 7).

During Stage 3 the design team also begins to clarify the details of the delivery system to be developed. The forms of materials, space, and instruction have already had to be known well enough to estimate cost feasibility in Stage 2, but now that objectives are known year-by-year for the curriculum, rough quantity estimates can be made for amounts of print and nonprint materials to be purchased or developed, equipment to be used in various media forms, and so on. Space utilization plans for study areas of various sorts, as well as for classrooms and laboratories, begin to form. Decisions are made for ratios of group-paced versus pupil-paced study materials; spaces for various sized group activities are planned; and needed teacher guides are noted. Plans often begin at this stage for monitoring and recording pupil progress, for defining various teacher roles, and for devising assessment and guidance procedures. However, these plans are left loose enough to permit later adjustments after the analysis of each objective has been made and a teaching strategy has been designed for each objective, or for clusters of them.

The principal document which may emerge from this stage is often called a "curriculum scope and sequence," which outlines the major goals to be reached for each year in the curriculum.

Stage 4: determining course structure and sequence

At the close of Stage 3, the major skills to be learned during each year of an entire curriculum have been outlined, in the form of course goals for each year. These may be stated separately for each subject or skill area, or they may be arranged only by "grade level." In either case, the next major step is to consider the sequencing of major clusters of course objectives for each year in the curriculum; these clusters may be called "units of instruction," each perhaps requiring several weeks of study.

In the opening portion of Chapter 6, it is further shown that there is eventually a need to distinguish between *target objectives* which are to be reached only by the end of the course or year of study, and *enabling objectives* which are smaller in scope and are required in order to attain a target objective. It is the target objectives which are of concern in this Stage 4 of system design. If the course goals contained in the curriculum scope and sequence plan resulting from Stage 3 are not sufficiently explicit to serve the purposes of course target objectives, then the goals may require further analysis before the course structure and sequence can be accomplished.

The course target objectives are now to be grouped in some fashion to form a gross structure of the course. For a training course of short duration, or for some school subjects, it may not be necessary to group them into the familiar course "units." It may be sufficient simply to determine the order in which the objectives should be learned. Such a course may have one or two target objectives under which a dozen or more enabling objectives are simply listed.

More typically, perhaps for school learning, the original set of target objectives are grouped into units, each unit representing a skill area, an information area, or both. Sequence of instruction is then considered, first for the unit sequence, then for the objectives within each unit. In some areas such as mathematics, both levels of sequence may be crucial for effective instruction. It may matter greatly which unit comes first in the sequence, and which objective comes first under each unit. In other courses consisting mostly of information learning, some sequences may be easier or more interesting than others, but learning could go on in *any* sequence. In the first example, intellectual skills where sequence is crucial are being built; in the second case it may be a matter of arriving at any "logical" sequence.

In listing unit objectives, designers may at first choose only to use phrases rather than performance statements. For example, in a course entitled "Asian Culture" one might find units simply labelled "Japan", "China", and so forth. Then the performance objectives under each unit would specify what it is about each country that learners should state, classify, or generate a statement about. Another course with the same title might be organized differently. The units might be entitled "Legal System," "Education System," for example, with specific performance objectives calling for information or skill demonstration pertaining to Japan and China. To many, the acceptance of phrases in place of performance objectives at the unit level may be questionable. It may detract from the "traceability" of each specific objective back to a goal, but goals often exist first in non-performance terms, too. We simply suggest the use of performance statements at each level at which assessment of pupil performance is desired. If assessments are not to be made at the unit level, or at what might be called a "topic" level under units, then any phrasing which enables designers to get to the performance level where assessments are to be made seems acceptable to us. It must be recalled, of course, that assessments may be required to diagnose the need for remediation, for monitoring pupil progress, and for reporting to parents. So performance terms are recommended for all levels at which these assessments are to be made.

The final point of this stage of work then, is an overall sequence plan for the major units of the course. The next three stages, it will be seen, are needed to complete the sequence plan for more detailed elements of the course.

Stage 5: analysis of course objectives

Earlier in this chapter, the cyclical or iterative nature of the instructional design process was emphasized. This working and reworking of plans is especially likely to occur in Stages 4 through 6, as outlined in Table 2–1. Ideally one wishes to work from more general goals and objectives down to increasingly specific objectives. But in the process of doing so, one often sees other ways to organize the instruction. Furthermore, as stated at the opening of Chapter 6, one is often uncertain whether to state objectives first, and then analyze them, or vice versa. With these points in mind, a designer will be alert to exceptions to the planning sequence used for descriptive purposes here:

Stage 4: Determining Course Structure and Sequence
Stage 5: Analysis of Course Objectives
Stage 6: Definition of Performance Objectives

The work for Stage 5, then, consists of further analysis of course objectives (principally *target* objectives). Gagné (1977b) has shown that there is profit in undertaking three kinds of analysis of objectives at this point: (a) information-processing analysis, to reveal the sequence of mental operations in performance of the objective, (b) task classification, to categorize type of learning outcome in order to identify the conditions of learning, and (c) learning task analysis, to reveal the enabling objectives for which teaching sequence decisions need to be made. Chapter 6 expands on these three aspects of this stage of design, so only brief comment on each is needed here.

Information-processing analysis is valuable for revealing the mental operations that make possible the observed performances of learners which indicate that they have mastered a target objective or an enabling objective. Thus both the decisions and the actions of learners are noted in order to be sure that the enabling objectives are identified for further analysis and ultimate inclusion in sequences of lessons to be planned. An important estimate to be made for each decision and action revealed by an information processing analysis is whether the intended learners enter with these capabilities or whether they must be taught as a part of the instruction for the objective.

Task classification of both target and enabling objectives can assist in several aspects of instructional design. Classifying the target objectives can help one check whether any intended purpose of a unit of instruction is being overlooked. Wager (1977) has presented examples of how target objectives may be classified and then grouped into course units so that the resulting "instructional map" can be reviewed to check whether necessary information, attitude, and intellectual skill objectives are included in the instructional plan for the course unit. Thus, classifying the larger (target) objectives aids in reviewing the course structure to be sure that the desired domains of learning outcomes are represented in those objectives. It is also possible that grouping the objectives for each desired domain of outcome will help to spot neglected areas of instruction within each course unit. Classification of the enabling objectives which result from a learning task analysis of a target objective, on the other hand, is likely to help identify the appropriate conditions of learning to be incorporated into the teaching strategy to be accomplished by preparing lesson plans for the enabling objectives.

Finally, once a learning task analysis has been completed for each target objective, one has a sound basis for planning both the *sequence* of teaching the enabling objectives for each target objective and the *conditions of learning* to be established by each lesson plan.

The procedures for accomplishing these three major aspects of analysis of course objectives are presented in Chapter 6. The results of these aspects of analysis now enable the designer to (a) review the course structure and sequence which resulted from Stage 4 and to (b) proceed with greater confidence to the definition of performance objectives (Stage 5), which in turn becomes the focal point both for designing lesson plans (Stage 7) and for assessing learner performance (Stage 9).

Stage 6: definition of performance objectives

Prior to Stage 6, the designer has given much thought to how the needs and goals first specified for each course in the curriculum scope and sequence statement (Stage 3) may be translated eventually into instructional plans at the level of the individual lesson. Perhaps by this stage the designer has formulated and reformulated the results of various analyses into an arrangement of "layers" of purposes, course objectives, unit objectives, target objectives, and finally enabling objectives. Probably both the number of layers and even the names given to the layers have changed as the structure of the curriculum and then of each course has been reviewed. As emphasized repeatedly here, the designer, while working on each stage, has revised his thinking of work "done" in prior stages, and has had new thoughts about the nature of later stages.

Clarifications made up to this point enable the designer to define the performance objectives which are to guide all the later work in developing lesson plans (or modules) and in devising measures of learner performance to be used in monitoring pupil progress and improving the instruction.

The question now arises, at what "level" are performance objectives to be defined? At the level of course purposes, course objectives, target objectives, unit objectives, or enabling objectives? Clearly it might be non-functional to make elaborate, precise statements describing all these levels of objectives.

Chapter 7 acknowledges the above question, and it also suggests that non-precise statements of intents and purposes of a course are not only acceptable at some points in planning, but are also economical prior steps to the ultimate statement of objectives in terms of learner performance after relevant instruction. Examples are given in Chapter 7 of how a gradual process of clarification takes place in working from statements of intent and purpose on to identification and definition of performance objectives. Chapter 7 also shows what is meant by the term performance objectives, and the process for arriving at such objectives is illustrated.

It remains here, then, to suggest that performance objectives should be *identified, defined,* and *written down* on paper when the designers have accomplished sufficient analyses (in prior stages) to be able to do so. Many experiences have demonstrated that it is self-defeating to attempt to define such objectives too early in the design process or before the designer understands the intended relationship between objectives on one hand, and instruction and evaluation of pupil progress on the other hand.

Assuming that all the analyses described for Stages 1 through 5 have been accomplished satisfactorily, it is suggested that a performance objective be written for each lesson to be planned and for each level or unit in the course at which pupil accomplishments are to be assessed (but not necessarily at each point where feedback is to be given to the learner). It is entirely possible that a single lesson would be planned for an entire information objective in a unit of instruction for which an "instructional map" has been drawn, while for an objective in the area of intellectual skill there might be a separate lesson for each enabling objective. If performance needs to be formally checked for each of these, then an objective would be written for each. Such objectives also serve as guides in lesson plan development, and they aid the learners in their study efforts.

Recalling that some objectives (target objectives) may be reached only at the close of an entire course, some performance objectives (and their associated tests) thus become "end-of-course" objectives. In turn, some course units may represent prerequisites to target objectives, and hence require sets of objectives and performance measures. Other units, in courses consisting heavily of information objectives, may "stand alone"—in this case performance may be assessed at either the unit level or in smaller parts. This decision could determine how many objectives are needed for the unit.

In the case of intellectual skill objectives, a decision may be made to write an objective for each essential prerequisite sub-skill (enabling objective), or a single diagnostic test over the entire task may be planned, and hence only a single objective written.

It is evident that no generalization can be made concerning how many "levels" of objectives might best depict the structure of an entire course; it is equally impossible to say how many objectives should be written for each course or how many performance measures over the objectives should be prepared. These decisions should result from the total analysis made for each course.

In the above discussion of deciding at which course levels to write objectives, concern was focused on the classroom learning environment. That is to say, the *functions of objectives* were shown to be: (a) to focus the lesson planning upon appropriate conditions of learning, (b) to guide the development of measures of learner performance, and (c) to assist the learners in their study efforts. Thus the intimate relationships among *objectives, teaching,* and *evaluation* are emphasized. Briggs (1970) has referred to these three aspects of instructional design as the "anchor points" in planning, and he has emphasized the need to make certain that the three are in agreement (or congruence) with each other.

Due to the close agreement desired among the above three components or "anchor points," it is clear that the designer will need to carefully review his work after Stages 6, 7, and 9. That is to say, both the lesson plans and the evaluations of learner performance must be targeted on the objectives.

It is also apparent that the objectives should guide the instruction and the evaluation, not the other way around. Therefore the objectives should be determined before the lesson plans or the evaluation instruments. Almost all descriptions of the instructional design process place the objectives before the other two components. Practices differ, however, as to the sequential placement of lesson plan development and performance measures. Briggs (1977) placed the design of assessment instruments before lesson planning on the grounds (a) that the novice is more likely to stray from the objectives in developing tests than in preparing lesson plans, and (b) that if a designer had just finished selecting (or developing) instructional material as a part of lesson planning, he or she might inadvertently focus on "course content" rather than learner performance when next constructing the tests. On the other hand, if one looks at the sequence in which the experienced designer is most likely to work, the lesson plans might precede the development of performance measures. For this reason, the sequence in Table 2–1 places lesson planning before the actual development of performance measures, with the recommendation that the designer keep referring to the objective when designing either a lesson plan or a performance measure. Thus some *planning* for performance measures should come earlier than actual development of them.

Stage 7: preparing lesson plans (or modules)
Our use of the term lesson plan is intended to be non-restrictive. We do not intend to imply that all lessons must be teacher-centered or teacher-led. We used parentheses around the term module to help make this point. By lesson plan or module we intend to point out that there needs to be some plan to assist learners in their study efforts for each performance objective. The lesson plan can include activities for both the teacher and the learner, and either a list of references to

printed and non-printed materials to be used or the actual materials themselves in complete form (as is often the case with modules).

With the above flexibility in mind, we might restate the matter as follows. When teacher-led, group-paced instruction is planned, it is typical that the lesson plan is mainly a guide for the use of the teacher, who implements the intent of the lesson plan without necessarily conveying its exact content to the learners. The teacher gives directions, refers learners to appropriate materials, leads or directs class activities, and supplements the materials by direct instruction. On the other hand, when a learner-centered, learner-paced lesson is planned, a *module* is typically presented to the learner. It usually contains a statement of an objective, a list of materials to be read (and often the module *contains* the materials), a guide for activities to be performed, a self-check test, and an instruction to present completed work for another check-test by the teacher. In this case, the directions or suggestions in the module are to the learner rather than to the teacher. Under conventional school systems, the teacher is usually the author of the lesson plan of course. Under a modular system, designers provide teachers with teacher's guides to assist them in performing their roles.

Treating all instruction according to the systems view presented in this book, the purpose of teachers, lesson plans, modules, and the learner's study effort, is to *accomplish the events of instruction.* Those events are listed and discussed in Chapter 9, but they include such widely recognized functions as *directing attention, informing the learner of the objective, presenting the stimulus material,* and *providing feedback.* It matters little which of these are performed by modules and materials, which by the teacher, and which by the learner, as long as they are successfully performed. It may be noted further that these events of instruction are applicable to all domains of learning outcomes, although *how* they are implemented involves somewhat different sets of *conditions of learning* (Chapters 4, and 5; Gagné, 1977a). Thus there are both common elements across all teaching efforts and unique features selected for each type of desired outcome.

What has been said of the purpose of instruction, including instructional materials, pertains also to the *media* of instruction. The purpose of all is to *put instructional events into play.* It is a matter of selecting the best agent for each event. Teachers are unbeatable for providing learning guidance and feedback; materials in many media provide effective stimulus situations.

The purpose of instruction is to promote learning, and many agents (teachers, learners, materials, media) can be employed to accomplish the events of instruction.

It may now be appreciated that the *choice of the delivery system* indicates a general preference for emphasizing certain agents to accomplish instructional events; within such a general preference (such as for individualized, learner-paced modules) specific agents or media can be assigned, event-by-event, objective-by-objective. That is what we mean by lesson planning. Any materials specified but not contained in the lesson plan are subject to selection or development, as described in the following stage.

In Chapter 11 a procedure is described for designing lesson plans. Basically the recommendation is that these steps need to be included:

1. Listing the instructional events to be brought into play to accomplish the objective of the lesson.
2. Determining the materials, media, or agents to be employed for making each event possible.
3. Designing or planning learning activities, including plans for how media and materials are to be used.
4. Previewing the selected media and materials to plan the roles or events which the teacher needs to accomplish for the lesson.

Technically speaking, the purpose of all the above is to incorporate the appropriate sets of conditions of learning into a plan for bringing about each instructional event, in order that the learners achieve the objective of the lesson. It is at this point in the total design process that the designer needs to be able to combine knowledge of learning and design theory with experience with learners and objectives like those intended for the course being designed. Needless to say, creativity in lesson design will enhance these other knowledge and experience factors. It is clear that the best lesson designs will demonstrate *knowledge about the learners,* the *tasks reflected in the objectives,* and the *teaching strategies* which will make the instructional events effective. At this stage in instructional design, the professional designer functions on a team with teachers, subject-matter experts, and perhaps others. Needless to say, during formative evaluation of the lesson's effectiveness the learner is a key member of the design team.

As shown above, the selection or development of instructional materials is really a phase of lesson planning. However since different problems are involved in selection than in development of materials, a separate phase of design is devoted here to the materials. As shown below, two different lesson design procedures are related to the matter of whether existing materials are selected or whether new materials are designed.

Stage 8: developing, selecting materials, media

The word materials here refers primarily to instructional materials, whether in the form of printed or other media for conveying instructional stimuli and content which help implement the instructional events.

There is a distinct difference between an earlier design convention and system design procedures. In the earlier custom, materials are first produced and distributed, and then teachers design instruction, in part by *selecting* the materials to be used. In contrast, instructional systems design makes the *specification of materials to be produced* an important part of the design effort. As said earlier, teachers do well to succeed at all when there are no really suitable materials available for part of the planned objectives. So they improvise and adapt as best they can. In other instances, of course, teachers find exactly the materials they want, and then lesson planning can progress rapidly without the need for time out to devise "make-do" substitutes for the needed materials.

Probably the more well-established the objectives and hence the more precisely determined the desired content of materials, the more likely it is that suitable materials will already be on the market. But even so, such materials are often indexed by content, rather than by objective (to say nothing of their failure to list the instructional events they serve). For this reason the search may need to include previewing the actual material, not merely using indexes. Thus, many difficulties can be encountered when materials are produced *before* the instruction is planned. The case of the most serious failure of this practice would be complete absence of materials from the market for *newly identified needs, goals, and objectives*. This failure is clearly preventable by application of the system design model.

Recall from our earlier discussion that initial decisions often have to be reconsidered later. Suppose now that a design team has completed all stages through Stage 6, and is working on lesson plans. The objectives and the instructional events for each lesson have been listed, and the team is planning how to implement each event of each lesson. An earlier choice of a delivery system reflected a preference for learner-paced, individualized materials, packaged to be as self-instructional as practicable (e.g., the materials would contain many of the planned instructional events). But the search for available materials may indicate either that there were none, or that they were too costly, or too difficult to implement, within the total system plan. At this point the designers would decide to develop some new materials where no suitable materials exist, or to modify the delivery system generally preferred in order to select some available materials and media which are less costly than others available and less costly to purchase than to develop.

A few general principles thus emerge. First, the more innovative the objectives, the more likely it is that a greater portion of the materials must be developed, since they are not available for purchase. Second, the more rigidly the original choices of delivery system and supporting media are adhered to, the greater will be the costs due to the decision to develop materials when similar materials in other media or formats could be purchased. Third, it is not unreasonable to save costs by making flexible selections of available materials and media, if the lesson plans provide in some way for provision of all the desired instructional events for each objective. Fourth, the roles of teachers are affected by choice of delivery systems, media, and materials, because the lesson plans will call upon teachers to provide whatever needed instructional events are not supplied by the materials and activities or are beyond the maturity or skill of the learners to supply.

Some new curricula and instructional systems have intentionally been planned from the outset either to develop all new materials or to make as much use as possible of existing materials. The reason in the first instance is probably to insure that a central concept, method, theme, or body of content is carefully preserved. Since such programs are often recognized as experimental ones, the added development costs would be justified to preserve purity of the original concept. In the case of a decision to make maximum use of existing materials, cost is likely to be the prime consideration so that funds could be expended for other items vital to the original concept. An example of this latter kind of decision was that of

Project PLAN (Flanagan, 1975). The design of that individualized system called for maximum use of available instructional materials so that funds would be accessible for designing implementation plans, for performance measures to monitor pupil progress, and for computer costs to save teachers' time in scoring tests and keeping records.

It is beyond the scope of this book to describe how design teams operate to accomplish the various stages of instructional system design including the development of materials, but a general account has been given by Carey and Briggs (1977), and a book edited by Weisgerber (1971) gives some of the details for specific systems that have been developed. Suffice it to say here that there must be a project management plan if the systems design plan is to be successfully and economically coordinated and implemented.

Stage 9: assessing student performance (performance measures)

Since Chapter 12 discusses the design of measures of learner performances, we need here only to summarize the purpose of this design stage. As stated earlier, diagnostic tests are needed in many skill areas to pinpoint instructional needs of individual pupils in order to concentrate on the skills they lack and avoid unnecessary instruction. Such measures often focus upon rather detailed part-skills, each representing only a portion of a single performance objective, such as the separate skills in subtracting one three-digit number from another. Other diagnostic tests reveal larger areas of needed study. Examples of the latter for elementary language instruction would be word attack skills and sentence construction.

Performance measures designed to check pupil progress might typically be administered for each performance objective in a course or unit of instruction. Still other measures designed to determine school placement or promotion, or to serve as a basis for periodic reports to parents or administrators, might cover larger blocks of instruction. For pupils who have been in attendance at a school for a period of time, the record of performance on progress checks could also serve these latter purposes.

All these levels of performance measures can also be useful in evaluating the instructional system itself, either lesson-by-lesson, or in its entirety. These evaluations, designed to provide data on the basis of which to improve the instruction as a whole, or some single component such as instructional materials, are called *formative evaluations.* They are usually conducted while the course is still being formed and re-formed until its final makeup is achieved. When no further changes are planned, and it is time to determine the success and worth of the course in its final form, *summative evaluations* are conducted. Types of performance measures suitable for these various purposes are discussed in Chapter 12.

Some planning of performance measures may well be undertaken *before* development of lesson plans and instructional materials because one wishes the tests to focus on the performance objectives (what the learner must be able to do) rather than upon what the learner reads or what the teacher does. Thus the performance measures are not intended to test merely the learners' memory for the content they have read in the instructional materials, or their memory of what the teacher said and did. Rather, the intention is to measure the effects of these study and teaching efforts in terms of the stated performance objectives. Early planning for development of the measures before the development of the instructional content helps preserve the aim just stated.

Stage 10: teacher preparation

The term as used here does not refer to the initial education and training of new teachers, but rather to the special training of in-service teachers needed to operate and evaluate a new instructional system. We therefore offer no review of philosophies or current practices for pre-service training of teachers, nor can we recommend a single approach for special training that would apply to all new systems.

A major point to be made here is that while teacher training has to be placed somewhere in this list of stages, its planning actually should begin much earlier. In fact, teachers are usually members of the design team from the outset; such teachers assist in all stages of design, and they become trainers of other teachers or demonstration teachers when other teachers are to be trained. Each new instructional system usually requires special skills beyond those already possessed by most in-service teachers, and consequently the special training is designed to focus on those skills. Special workshops become one mode for such training, but visits to schools in which the system is first operating as a pilot test is another important mode. The teachers in training may first receive a general orientation by the design team, after which they observe the pilot teachers at work, and often begin assisting the pilot teachers until they feel comfortable in taking complete charge of a class.

In visits to schools first adopting an individualized instruction system, the consensus of teachers was that after initial training they needed a year of experience in their own classrooms with the new systems to feel skilled to the extent that they preferred the new systems to their prior practices (Briggs and Aronson, 1975).

Stage 11: formative evaluation

Formative evaluations provide data on the basis of which to revise and improve the materials, the lesson plans, the performance tests, and indeed the operation of the entire instructional system. Providing that materials or lessons are introduced to tryout learners having the appropriate prerequisite learning, small segments of the total instruction can be tried out and revised before later segments are ready. In an incremental fashion, such tryouts not only pinpoint needs for changes in specific small segments of instruction but also lead to the discovery of other usable insights to avoid similar problems in later segments of the instruction. As entire units are ready, larger segments can be tried out.

The successive tryouts for a particular segment usually begin with trials involving a few individual learners in a one-to-one, face-to-face situation, in which interview data can be combined with the learners' voluntary comments and observations of obvious misunderstandings or difficulties they are encountering. Then, the next edition or version of the segment is tried out in a small group situation, and finally a segment or unit is given in its entirety in a regular classroom situation. The detailed procedures and methods of data analysis appropriate for each stage have been outlined in more detail by Dick (1977).

Stage 12: field testing, revision

Once all instructional units have undergone several tryouts and revisions, as briefly sketched above, the entire system is first installed in one or more pilot schools for its field testing. In these tryouts, a few more needed improvements may be pinpointed in the details of instruction, but more likely this tryout reveals problems in space utilization, supplies, storage and access to materials, scheduling difficulties, record-keeping problems, and the like.

There is no standard number of formative evaluations that small components or segments or the entire system undergo. The number depends on the budgets and time available, the degree of excellence set as the system design objective, and the total circumstances surrounding the project. In some cases, increasingly large numbers of schools use the new system or curriculum each year, and provide various forms of data or feedback for use in making final revisions or in reaching a decision that a summative evaluation should now be made. Nor is there a uniform practice of ever conducting a summative evaluation, although the need for this appears to be increasingly well-recognized. Participating schools or the design team often publish newsletters or supplementary material in order to continue information-exchange. But it is the entire series of evalutions and revisions which is a chief distinguishing characteristic of a systems approach to instructional design.

Stage 13: summative evaluation

Studies of the effectiveness of the system of instruction as a whole are called *summative evaluations,* the basic form of which is described more fully in Chapter 15. As the term implies, a summative evaluation is normally conducted after the system has passed through its formative stage—when it is no longer undergoing point-by-point revision. Such a stage may occur at the time of the first field test, or as much as five years later when large numbers of students have been taught by the new system. If there is expectation that the system will be widely used in schools throughout the country, summative evaluations need to be conducted under an equally varied range of schools and conditions.

Stage 14: installation and diffusion

This stage of instructional system development has been anticipated in some of the preceding discussion. After an acceptable degree of merit has been reflected by one or more summative evaluations, the new system (course, or curriculum) is ready for widespread adoption and regular use.

In the course of "operational installation," a number of practical matters receive final attention or adjustment. For example, materials may have to be stored differently in some schools than in others, owing to differences in building design and space situations. Planned time schedules for the new system may require adjustment to fit the overall scheduling pattern for a particular school. These are inevitable practical problems, but most need not interfere with the success of the system as a whole. Cooperative school administrators can usually be counted upon to arrange satisfactory local adjustments to the basic system.

A problem frequently arising in large-scale instructional system revisions is the matter of securing adoption of a new system by enough schools to make the costs of system development worthwhile and economical. It is beyond the scope of this book to describe methods for bringing about such adoptions. Techniques relevant to the dissemination and diffusion of educational theory, research findings, and products have been the subject of considerable research. A useful source pertaining to methods for securing acceptance of new systems and new practices is Havelock *et al.* (1969).

When the design team is to be solely responsible or jointly responsible with a publishing company or other organization for diffusion and adoption efforts, plans for this function, like those for teacher training, begin early in the design of the system. If diffusion is a design team responsibility, this adds one more set of factors considered when resources and constraints are being reviewed for making initial decisions about the nature of the delivery system. In practice, designers may wish to employ a delivery system which uses some components or media which it would be difficult to persuade schools to accept. The design team and the funding source would then face a decision to plan for a less preferred delivery system in order to diffuse the system more widely, or to accept more limited adoptions in the future. In some cases, but by no means all, such a choice might also require abandonment or modification of some goals, needs, or system design objectives.

SUMMARY

The term, instructional system design, has been defined, along with a general description of the overall design process which is presented as fourteen different stages of analysis and development.

The "systems approach" to instructional design was related to "educational technology"; both were presented as *processes* of planning instruction which make use of research and learning theory and employ empirical testing data as a means for the improvement of the designed instruction. A general account was given of how design teams function, along with the role of citizen participation in determining educational needs and goals.

The fourteen-stage organization of design described in this chapter represents only one of many possible ways of conceptualizing the total process. It would be possible to describe the same overall viewpoint in either a larger or a smaller number of stages. It was acknowledged that there are other viewpoints on how instruction may be designed. Some of these have been conceptualized as "models of teaching." However, instructional system design was presented as a broad, overarching framework for accomplishing whatever variety of learned outcomes that a curriculum or course of instruction intends.

All fourteen stages of work were briefly discussed. Although the stages are listed in Table 2–1 as discrete steps shown in a sequential, linear fashion, emphasis was placed on the iterative nature of the design process. That is to say, in practice there is much working backwards and forward in a non-linear fashion, because work done at any one stage gives new insights into other stages. There results, then, much "working back and forth" as the total design work progresses.

The first three design stages focus upon the determination of needs and goals sought as the outcomes from an entire school curriculum or course of instruction. These needs and goals are reviewed in terms of resources available and the possible delivery systems which could be employed for the intended instruction. This early work broadly views the entire scope of outcomes desired, usually for several years of schooling. The goals at this point are thus broadly stated, and often arranged in the form of a curriculum scope and sequence statement, showing the desired outcomes for each year or course. These three stages are labelled as work done at the "system (or curriculum) level."

The next two stages of work consist of considering separately each year of study or each course to be planned. The two principal products are the determination of the overall structure of each course in terms of major units of instruction and a listing of the objectives to be achieved by the end of the course. These analyses are thus described as "course level" analyses.

The next four stages of work are described as working at the "lesson level." This consists of: (a) definition of detailed performance objectives, (b) preparing lesson plans (or self-instructional modules), (c) developing or selecting course materials and media, and (d) preparing measures for assessing student performance.

The concluding five stages of work include: (a) plans for special preparation of teachers, (b) conducting formative evaluations of materials to improve the instruction, (c) conducting field tests as a basis for further adjusting the instructional system to the realities of the school environment, (d) conducting summative evaluations of the worth, practicality, and effectiveness of the total instruction, and (e) securing adoptions of the system and subsequent installations of it in schools other than those involved in field testing and evaluation of the system.

The remaining chapters of this book do not simply expand upon the fourteen stages of work described in this chapter. Rather, certain critical stages are chosen so that more a comprehensive treatment of them can be offered. Some chapters deal with only a part of a stage, as outlined in this chapter. Examples of this are the chapters on the events of instruction and media selection. Still other chapters focus on a specific result of design decisions, such as the chapters on individualized instruction and group instruction. Finally, other chapters on the variety of learning outcomes are fundamental to the application of lesson planning as presented in this book, because the classification of objectives is crucial for the utilization of appropriate conditions of learning in the instructional strategy for each objective. To emphasize the key role of sequences of instruction and instructional events, separate chapters are also devoted to these stages of design.

The purpose of lesson planning, as presented here, is to be sure that necessary instructional events take place. Key steps in lesson planning (or design of self-instructional modules) therefore include: (1) classifying the lesson objectives, (2) listing the needed instructional events, (3) choosing a medium of instruction for each event, and (4) incorporating appropriate conditions of learning into the prescription for how each event will be accomplished by the lesson. Some events may be accomplished by the learner, some by the teacher, and others by the materials and activities planned for the lesson.

The entire design approach outlined here is considered to be internally consistent and in agreement with research findings on how learning takes place, and the resulting designs are amenable to both formative and summative evaluations. Thus a design objective can be stated in testable form so that the success of the design can be evaluated.

References

AAAS Commission on Science Education. *Science—A Process Approach. Hierarchy Chart.* New York: Xerox, 1967.

Branson, R. K. Military and industrial training. In L. J. Briggs (ed.), *Instructional Design: Principles and Applications.* Englewood Cliffs, N.J.: Educational Technology Publications, 1977.

Briggs, L. J. Teaching machines. In G. Finch (ed.), *Educational and Training Media: A Symposium.* Washington, D.C.: National Academy and Sciences-National Research Council, 1960 (Publication 789), Pp. 150–195.

Briggs, L. J. *Handbook of Procedures for the Design of Instruction.* Pittsburgh, Pa.: American Institutes for Research, 1970 (Monograph No. 4).

Briggs, L. J. *Student's Guide to Handbook of Procedures for the Design of Instruction.* Pittsburgh, Pa.: American Institutes for Research, 1972.

Briggs, L. J. (ed.). *Instructional Design: Principles and Applications.* Englewood Cliffs, N.J.: Educational Technology Publications, 1977.

Briggs, L. J., and Aronson, D. *An Interpretive Study of Individualized Instruction in the Schools: Procedures, Problems, and Prospects.* (Final Report, National Institute of Education, Grant No. NIE-G-740065). Tallahassee, Fla.: Florida State University, 1975.

Burton, J. K., and Merrill, P. F. Needs assessment: Goals, needs, and priorities. In L. J. Briggs (ed.), *Instructional Design: Principles and Applications.* Englewood Cliffs, N.J.: Educational Technology Publications, 1977.

Carey, J., and Briggs, L. J. Teams as designers. In L. J. Briggs (ed.), *Instructional Design: Principles and Applications.* Englewood Cliffs, N.J.: Educational Technology Publications, 1977.

City of Tampa, Florida. *Tampa Model Cities Program, Interim Report, Part I* (undated).

Crowder, N. A. Automatic tutoring by means of instrinsic programming. In E. H. Galanter (ed.), *Automatic Teaching: The State of the Art.* New York: Wiley, 1959, pp. 109–116.

Davies, I. K. *The Management of Learning.* London: McGraw-Hill, 1971.

Davies, I. K., and Hartley, J. *Contributions to an Educational Technology.* London: Butterworth, 1972.

Dick, W. Formative evaluation. In L. J. Briggs (ed.), *Instructional Design: Principles and Applications.* Englewood Cliffs, N. J.: Educational Technology Publications, 1977.

Esbensen, T. *Working with Individualized Instruction.* Belmont, Calif.: Fearon, 1968.

Flanagan, J. C. In H. Talmage (ed.), *Systems of Individualized Education.* Berkeley: McCutchan Publishing Corp., 1975.

Gagné, R. M. *The Conditions of Learning,* 3d Ed. New York: Holt, Rinehart, and Winston, 1977(a).

Gagné, R. M. Analysis of objectives. In L. J. Briggs (ed.), *Instructional Design: Principles and Applications.* Englewood Cliffs, N.J.: Educational Technology Publications, 1977(b).

Havelock, R. G., et al. *Planning for Innovation through Dissemination and Utilization of Knowledge.* Ann Arbor: Institute for Social Research, University of Michigan, 1969.

Joyce, B., and Weil, M. *Models of Teaching.* Englewood Cliffs, N.J.: Prentice-Hall, 1972.

Kaufman, R. A. *Needs Assessment: What It Is and How to Do It.* San Diego, Ca.: University Consortium on Instructional Development and Technology, 1976.

Lumsdaine, A. A. Educational technology, programmed learning, and instructional science. In H. G. Richey (ed.), *Theories of Learning and Instruction.* Chicago, Ill.: University of Chicago Press, 1964.

Markle, D. G. Final Report: *The Development of the Bell System First Aid and Personal Safety Course.* Palo Alto, Calif.: American Institutes for Research, 1967.

Markle, D. G. First Aid training. In L. J. Briggs (ed.), *Instructional Design: Principles and Applications.* Englewood Cliffs, N.J.: Educational Technology Publications, 1977.

Pressey, S. L. Development and appraisal of devices providing immediate automatic scoring of objective tests and concomitant self-instruction. *Journal of Psychology,* 1950, *29,* 417–447.

Skinner, B. F. *The Technology of Teaching.* New York: Appleton, 1968.

Wager, W. Instructional technology and higher education. In L. J. Briggs (ed.), *Instructional Design: Principles and Applications.* Englewood Cliffs, N.J.: Educational Technology Publications, 1977.

Weisgerber, R. A. *Developmental Efforts in Individualized Instruction.* Itasca, Ill.: Peacock, 1971.

PART TWO

BASIC PROCESSES IN LEARNING AND INSTRUCTION

This part of the book presents the theoretical foundation for our system of instructional design. We conceive of human learning as a set of internal cognitive processes that transform the stimulation presented to the learner into several successive phases of information processing. The outcome of this processing is the establishment in the learners (that is, in their memories) of certain types of capabilities evidenced by the human performances they make possible.

Learning, supported by instruction, may result in the establishment of five kinds of capabilities in the human learner. Briefly stated, these are:

1. intellectual skills, that permit the learner to carry out symbol-based procedures;
2. cognitive strategies, that the learner brings to bear upon his own cognitive processing;
3. information, the facts and organized "knowledge of the world" stored in the learner's memory;

4. attitudes, internal states that influence the personal action choices a learner makes; and
5. motor skills, the movements of skeletal muscles that are organized to accomplish purposeful actions.

The chapters of this section describe these learned capabilities, and provide instances of them as human performances. The descriptions of these types of capabilities continue with an account of the conditions of learning that are appropriate for each. As later portions of the book will show, it is from these principles that the detailed design of instructional events is to be derived.

The Outcomes of Instruction

The best way to design instruction is to work backwards from its expected outcomes. Some ways of working backwards, and their implications for the content of instruction, are described in this chapter. These procedures begin with the identification of human capabilities to be established by instruction. The instructional outcomes, introduced and defined here in terms of five broad categories, run throughout the book as a framework on which the design of instruction is based.

INSTRUCTION AND EDUCATIONAL GOALS

The basic reason for designing instruction is to make possible the attainment of a set of educational goals. The society in which we live has certain functions to perform in serving the needs of its people. Many of these functions—in fact, most of them—require human activities which must be learned. Accordingly, one of the functions of a society is to insure that such learning takes place. Every society, in one way or another, makes provision for the education of people in order that the variety of functions necessary for its survival can be carried out. *Educational goals* are those human activities which contribute to the functioning of a society (including the functioning of an individual *in* the society), and which can be acquired through learning.

Naturally, in societies whose organization is simple—often called "primitive" societies—the goals of education and the means used to reach them are fairly easy to describe and understand. In a primitive society whose economy revolves around hunting animals, for example, the most prominent educational goals center upon the activities of hunting. The son of a hunter is educated in these activities by his father, or perhaps by other hunters of the village to which he belongs. Fundamentally, educational goals have the same kind of origin in a modern complex society. Obviously, though, as societies become more complex, so must educational goals.

Every so often in our own society, we hold conferences, appoint committees, or establish commissions to study educational goals. One of the most famous of these bodies formulated a set of goals called the "Cardinal Principles of Secondary Education" (1918). The key statement of this document was as follows (p. 9):

> Education in a democracy, both within and without the school, should develop in each individual the knowledge, interests, ideals, habits, and powers whereby he will find his place and use that place to shape both himself and society toward ever nobler ends.

The composition of the "knowledge, interests, ideals, habits, and powers" was considered by this commission to fall into the seven areas of (1) health, (2) command of basic skills, (3) worthy home-membership, (4) pursuing a vocation, (5) citizenship, (6) worthy use of leisure, and (7) ethical character.

It might be supposed that more specific objectives for education could be derived from broad statements such as these. This sort of analysis, however, becomes a stupendous task, so great that it has never really been attempted for our society. Instead, we depend upon a number of different simplifications to specify educational goals in detail. These simplifying approaches condense information in several stages, and thus lose some information along the way.

Thus it has come about that we tend to structure education in terms of "subject matters" that are actually gross simplifications of educational goals, rather than activities reflecting the actual functions of human beings in society. It is as though the activity of shooting a bear in a primitive society were to be transformed into a "subject" called "marksmanship." We represent an educational goal with the subject-matter name of "English" rather than with the many different human activities which are performed with language. One of the best-known recent efforts on a national scale has been the formulation of educational goals within various subject-matter fields by the National Assessment of Educational Progress Program (Womer, 1970).

Goals as educational outcomes

The reflection of societal needs in educational goals is typically expressed in statements describing categories of *human activity*. A goal is preferably stated, not as "health," but as "performing those activities which will maintain health." The goal, or goals, are most inadequately conveyed by the topic of "citizenship"; they are more adequately reflected in a statement such as "carries out the activities of a citizen in a democratic society."

What would be desirable for educational scholars to accomplish, but which has not yet been accomplished, is the derivation of an array of human *capabilities* which would make possible the kinds of activities expressed in educational goals. It is these capabilities which represent the proximate goals of instruction. In order to carry out the activities required for maintaining health, the individual must possess certain kinds of capabilities (knowledge, skills, attitudes). In most cases these are learned through deliberately planned instruction. Similarly, in order to perform the various activities appropriate to being a citizen, the individual must have learned a variety of capabilities through instruction.

Educational goals are statements of the outcomes of education. They refer particularly to those activities made possible by learning, which in turn is often brought about by deliberately planned instruction. The rationale is not different in our society from that of a primitive society. In the latter, for example, the educational goal of "hunting activity" is achieved by a customary regime of instruction in the various component human capabilities (locating prey, stalking, shooting, etc.) that make possible the total activity of "hunting." The difference, however, is an important one. In the more complex society, the *capabilities* required for one activity may be shared by a number of others. Thus, the human capability of "performing arithmetic operations" serves not a single educational goal (such as making a family budget), but several others as well, including changing money and making scientific measurements.

In order to design instruction, one must seek a means of identifying the *human capabilities* that lead to the outcomes called educational goals. If these goals were uncomplicated, as in a primitive society, defining these human capabilities might be equally simple. But such is not the case in a highly differentiated and specialized society. Instruction cannot be adequately planned separately for each educational goal necessary to a modern society. One must seek, instead, to identify the human capabilities that contribute to a number of different goals. A capability like "reading comprehension," for example, obviously serves several purposes. The present chapter is intended to serve as an introduction to the concept of human capabilities.

Courses and their objectives

The planning of instruction is often carried out for a single *course,* rather than for larger units of a total curriculum. There is no necessary fixed length of a course, or no fixed specification of "what is to be covered." A number of factors may influence the choice of duration or amount of content. Often the length of time available in a semester or year is the primary determining factor. In any case, a course is usually defined rather arbitrarily by the designation of some topics which are understood within the local environment of the school. A course may take on a general title like "American History," "Beginning French," "English 1," and so on.

The ambiguity in meaning of courses with such titles is evident. Is "American History" in grade 6 the same as or different from the course of the same title in grade 12? Is "English 1" concerned with composition, literature, or both? These are by no means idle questions, because they represent sources of difficulty for many students in many places, particularly when they are planning programs of study. It is not entirely uncommon, for example, for a student to choose a course like "First-year French," only to find that he should have elected "Beginning French."

Ambiguity in the meaning of courses with title or topic designations can readily be avoided when courses are described in terms of the *objectives* (Mager, 1975; Popham & Baker, 1970). Examples of objectives in many subject areas are described in a volume by Bloom, Hastings, & Madaus (1971). Thus, if "English 1" has the objective "the student will be able to compose a unified composition on any assigned single topic, in acceptable printed English, within an hour" it is perfectly clear to everyone what a portion of the course is all about. It will not help the student, in any direct fashion, to "identify imagery in modern poetry," nor to "analyze the conflicts in works of fiction." It will, however, if successful, teach him the basic craft of writing a composition. Similarly, if an objective of "Beginning French" is that the student will able to "conjugate irregular verbs," this is obviously fairly clear. It will not readily be confused with an objective that makes it possible for the student to "write French sentences from dictation."

As usually planned, courses often have several objectives, and not just one. A course in social studies may have the intention of providing the student with several capabilities: "describing the context of (specified) historical events," "evaluating the sources of written history," and "showing a positive liking for the study of history." A course in science may wish to establish in the student the ability to "formulate and test hypotheses," to "engage in scientific problem solving," and also to "value the activities of scientists." Each of these kinds of objectives within a single course may be considered equally worthwhile. They may also be differentially valued by different teachers. The main point to be noted about them at this juncture, however, is that they are different. The most important difference among them is that each requires a different plan for its achievement. Instruction must be differentially designed, in order to insure that each objective is attainable by students within the context of a course.

Are there a great many specific objectives for which individual instructional planning must be done, or can this task be reduced in some manner? The task of instructional planning can be vastly simplified by assigning objectives to *five major categories of human capabilities.* Such categories can be formed because each leads to a different class of human performance and requires a different set of instructional conditions for effective learning. Within each category, regardless of the subject matter of instruction, the same conditions apply. Of course, there may be subcategories within each of the five categories. In fact, there *are* subcategories which are useful for instructional planning, as later chapters of this book will show. But for the moment, in taking a fairly general look at instructional planning from the standpoint of courses, five categories provide the comprehensive view.

FIVE CATEGORIES OF LEARNING OUTCOMES

What are the categories of objectives, expected as learning outcomes resulting from instruction? A brief description of each is given in the following section. This is later followed by a fuller description of their usefulness as human capabilities. Conditions necessary for learning these capabilities are to be described in following chapters.

Intellectual Skills   Intellectual skills are the capabilities that make the human individual *competent* (Gagné, 1977). They enable him to respond to conceptualizations of his environment. They make up the most basic, and at the same time the most pervasive, structure of formal education. They range from elementary language skills like composing a sentence to the advanced technical skills of science, engineering, and other disciplines. Examples of intellectual skills of the latter sort would be finding the stresses in a bridge, or predicting the effects of a currency devaluation. Their learning begins in the early grades with the three R's, and progresses to whatever level is compatible with the individual's interests, or to the limits of his intellectual capacity.

Learning an intellectual skill means learning *how to do something* of an intellectual sort. In particular, such learning contrasts with learning *that something exists,* or has certain properties. This *verbal information learning* will be described in a moment. Learning how to identify a sonnet by its rhyme pattern is an intellectual skill; learning that a sonnet's rhyme pattern is "a repeated *a b b a* followed by a repeated *c d e*" is an instance of verbal information. A learner may, of course, learn both, and often does. But it is perfectly possible for him to learn how to do the first (identify a sonnet) without being able to do the second (describe a sonnet's rhyme pattern). Likewise, as teachers know well, it is possible for a student to learn the second without being able to do the first. For these reasons, it is important to maintain this distinction between knowing *how* and knowing *that,* even while recognizing that instruction often involves both as learning objectives.

Cognitive Strategies   These are special and very important kinds of skills. They are the capabilities that govern the individual's own learning, remembering, and thinking behavior. For example, they control his behavior when he is reading with the intent to learn; and the internal methods he uses to "get to the heart of a problem." The phrase "cognitive strategy" is usually attributed to Bruner (Bruner, Goodnow, & Austin, 1956); Rothkopf (1971) has named them "mathemagenic behaviors"; Skinner (1968) "self-management behaviors." One expects that such skills will improve over a relatively long period of time as the individual engages in more and more studying, learning, and thinking. It has long been a goal of education to develop capabilities of creative problem solving in students. If this is indeed a trait, or possibly a collection of traits which can be learned and generalized, it deserves to be included with many simpler learning skills under the heading of cognitive strategy.

Provided it has previously been learned, a cognitive strategy may be selected by a learner as a *mode* of solving a novel problem. Often, for example, newly encountered problems can be efficiently approached by working backwards in stages beginning with the goal to be achieved by a solution. This "working backwards" approach is an example of a cognitive strategy. Intellectual skills (such as basic arithmetic operations) frequently have to be recalled by the learner and brought to bear upon a problem. But while these skills are essential, they are not sufficient. A *mode* of seeking a solution must also be used by the learner, a *cognitive strategy* which he has learned in the past, and perhaps used many times in a variety of situations.

Verbal Information   All of us have learned a great deal of verbal information, or verbal knowledge. We have readily available in our memories many commonly used items of information such as the names of months, days of the week, letters, numerals, towns, cities, states, countries, and so on. We also have a great store of more highly organized information, such as many events of U.S. history, the forms of government, the major achievements of science and technology, and the components of the economy. The verbal information we learn in school is in part "for the course only," and in part the kind of knowledge we are expected to be able to recall readily as adults.

The learner usually acquires a great deal of information from formal instruction. Much is also learned in an incidental fashion. Such information is stored in the learner's memory, but it is not necessarily "memorized," in the sense that it can be repeated verbatim. Something like the *gist* of paragraph-long passages are stored in memory and recalled in that form when the occasion demands.

Motor Skills   Another kind of capability we expect human beings to learn is a motor skill (Singer, 1975; Fitts & Posner, 1967). The individual learns to skate, to ride a bicycle, to steer an automobile, to use a can opener, to jump rope. There are also motor skills to be learned as part of formal school instruction, like printing letters, drawing a straight line, aligning a pointer on a dial face. Despite the fact that school instruction is so largely concerned with intellectual functions, we do not expect a well-educated adult to be lacking in certain motor skills (like writing) which he may use every day.

Attitudes   Passing now to what is often called the "affective domain" (Krathwohl *et al.,* 1964), we can identify a class of learned capabilities called attitudes. All of us possess attitudes of many sorts towards different things, persons, and situations. The effect of an attitude is to amplify an individual's positive or negative reactions toward some person, or thing, or situation. The strength of a person's attitude toward some item may be indicated by the frequency with which he *chooses* that item in a variety of circumstances. Thus, an individual with a strong attitude toward helping other people will offer his help in many situations;

whereas a person with a weaker attitude of this sort will tend to restrict his offers of help to fewer situations. The schools are often expected to establish socially approved attitudes such as respect for other people, cooperativeness, personal responsibility, as well as positive attitudes toward knowledge and learning, and an attitude of self-esteem.

Capabilities and human performance

Each of the five categories of learning outcome is an acquired capability of the person who has learned, as the previous examples have illustrated. Once learned, these capabilities can be observed again and again in a variety of human performances. They are called *capabilities* because they make possible the prediction of many particular instances of performance on the part of the learner. If he has acquired the capability (motor skill) of figure-skating, we infer that he carries this capability around with him. He may exhibit it on any specific occasion when he is on ice and wearing skates. The same holds true for the other kinds of capabilities, intellectual skills, cognitive strategies, verbal information, and attitudes. Of course, some of these may be forgotten more easily than others. Learned capabilities, until they have been forgotten, are exhibited as specific human performances. They are not the same as these performances; instead, they may be said to *mediate* the performances that are observed.

These categories of learned capabilities are distinguished from each other because they make possible distinctive categories of human performance. As we shall see in the following chapters, they also require different arrangements of conditions in order for the learning of each to occur. At this point, though, it will be worthwhile to summarize the distinguishing features of each class of learned human capability, including the category of performance that each makes possible. This information is given in Table 3–1.

TABLE 3–1 Five Kinds of Learned Capabilities

Kind of Capability	Example	Function	Performance Category
Intellectual Skill	Using a metaphor to describe an object	Component of further learning and thinking	Showing how an intellectual operation is carried out in specific application
Cognitive Strategy	Induction of the concept "magnetic field"	Controls learner's behavior in learning and thinking	Solving a variety of practical problems by efficient means
Verbal Information	"Boiling point of water is 100° C"	(1) Provides directions for learning; (2) Aids transfer of learning	Stating or otherwise communicating information
Motor Skill	Printing letters	Mediates motor performance	Carrying out the motor activity in a variety of contexts
Attitude	Preference for listening to music as a leisure activity	Modifies individual's choices of action	Choosing a course of action toward a class of objects, persons, or events

The first column of Table 3-1 contains the five kinds of capability which may result from learning. The second column contains an example of each capability. Next, column three describes the inferences one may make about the function served by each kind of capability. Current understanding of these functions seems likely to be incomplete at the present time, and additional clarification may be expected from research sources. Finally, the table contains a column which describes the category of human performance made possible by each of the capabilities.

Intellectual Skill   A student of the English language learns at some point in his studies what a metaphor is. More specifically, if his instruction is adequate, he learns to *use* a metaphor. (In the next chapter, we identify this particular subcategory of intellectual skill as a *rule.*) In other words, it may be said that the student has learned to use a rule to show what a metaphor is; or that he has learned to apply a rule. This skill then has the function of becoming a component of further learning. That is to say, the skill of using a metaphor now may contribute to the learning of more complex intellectual skills, such as writing illustrative sentences, describing scenes and events, composing essays.

If one wishes to know whether the student has learned this intellectual skill, one must observe a category of *performance.* Usually this is done by asking the student to "show what a metaphor is" in one or more specific instances. In other words, observations might be made to determine whether the student performed adequately when asked to use a metaphor to describe (1) a cat's movements, (2) a cloudy day, and perhaps (3) the moon's surface. As the fourth column of the table indicates, he is showing how this intellectual skill may be applied in specific instances.

Cognitive Strategy   Internally organized strategies that govern the learner's behavior come in several varieties. At present, it is not possible to identify them singly with any degree of confidence, much less name them. Nevertheless, their effects in determining human performance appear quite evident. The example given in the table is the process of *inference,* or *induction.* Suppose that a student has become acquainted with magnetic attraction in a bar magnet—noting that a force is exerted by each pole of the magnet on certain kinds of metal objects. Now the student is given some iron filings to sprinkle on a piece of paper placed over the magnet. When the paper is tapped, the filings exhibit "lines of force" around each pole of the magnet. The student proceeds to verify this observation in other situations, perhaps using other magnets and other kinds of metal objects. These observations, together with other knowledge, may lead the induction of the idea of a magnetic field of force surrounding each pole of the magnet. It is important to note in this example that the student has not been told of the magnetic field beforehand, nor given instruction in "how to induce." But this kind of mental operation is carried out.

Learning a cognitive strategy like induction, however, is apparently not done on a single occasion. Instead, this kind of capability develops over fairly long periods of time. Presumably, the learner must have a number of experiences with induction, in widely different situations, in order for the strategy to become dependably useful.

When a learner becomes capable of induction, it may obviously be used as a strategy in a great variety of other situations. Provided other requisite intellectual skills and information have been learned, an induction strategy may be used to arrive at an explanation of what makes smoke rise in the air, why pebbles in a stream are rounded and smooth, or what intention a writer has had in composing an editorial essay. In other words, the cognitive strategy of induction may be put to use in a great many situations of thinking and learning—situations which are enormously varied in their describable properties. In fact, the performances that the learner is able to exhibit in these situations may be seen to resemble each other only in the respect that they involve induction. And this, of course, is the basic reason for believing that such a cognitive strategy exists—it is by an act of induction that one arrives at the presence of the cognitive strategy of induction in other people.

The performance that a cognitive strategy like induction makes possible, as indicated in the final column of the table, is the efficient solution of a variety of practical problems. A variety of problems is necessary, because one cannot infer the capability of this cognitive strategy from one or even two problem solutions. Such instances may result from the simpler process of rule application, as would be observed if a student showed an ability to "solve" five algebraic equations of the same type one after another. However, if one can observe a student using induction to solve problems in mechanics, in plant growth, in governmental affairs, and in literature, one then feels relatively confident that the student has acquired and is employing this cognitive strategy.

Verbal Information   Students of science learn much verbal information, just as they do in other fields of study. They learn the properties of materials, objects, and living things, for example. A large number of "science facts" may not constitute a defensible primary goal of science instruction. Nevertheless, the learning of such "facts" is an essential part of the learning of science. Without information, learning in any subject could have no continuity, no "substance."

The example shown in Table 1 supposes that a student has learned the item of information "the boiling point of water is 100° C." One major function of such information is to provide the learner with directions for how to proceed in further learning. Thus, in learning about the change of state of materials from liquid to gaseous form, the learner may be acquiring an intellectual skill (that is, a rule) which relates atmospheric pressure to vaporization. In working with this relationship, a student may be asked to apply the rule to a situation which describes the temperature of boiling water at an altitude of nine thousand feet. At this juncture the *information* given in the example must be recalled in order to proceed with the application of the rule. One may be inclined to say this information is not particularly important—rather, the learning of the *intellectual skill* is the important thing. There is no disagreement about this point. However, the *information is essential* to these events. The learner must have such information available in order to learn.

Information may also be of importance for the transfer of learning from one situation to another. For example, a student of government may hit upon the idea that the persistence of a bureaucracy bears some resemblance to the growth of an abscess in the human body. If he or she has some information about abscesses, such an analogy may make it possible to think of causal relationships pertaining to bureaucracies which would not otherwise be possible. A variety of cognitive strategies and intellectual skills may now be brought to bear on this problem by the student, and new knowledge thereby generated. The initial transfer in such an instance is made possible by an "association of ideas," in other words, by the possession and use of certain classes of information.

Finding out whether students have learned some particular facts, or some particular organized items of information, is a matter of observing whether they can communicate them. The simplest way to do this, of course, is to ask for a statement of the information, either orally or in writing. This is the basic method commonly employed by a teacher to assess what information has been learned. In the early grades, assessing the communications children can make may require the use of simple oral questions. Pictures and objects that the child can point to and manipulate may also be employed.

Motor Skill   A motor skill is one of the most obvious kinds of human capabilities to observe. Children learn a motor skill for each printed letter they make with a pencil on paper. The function of the skill, as a capability, is simply to make possible the motor performance. Of course, these motor performances may themselves enter into the further learning of the students. For example, they employ the skill of printing letters when they are learning to make (and print) words and sentences. The acquisition of a motor skill can be reasonably inferred when the students can perform the act in a variety of contexts. Thus, if youngsters have acquired the *skill* of printing the letter *E* they should be able to perform this motor act with a pen, a pencil, or a crayon, on any flat surface, constructing letters with a range of sizes. Obviously one would not want to conclude that the skill has been learned from a single instance of an *E* printed with pencil on a particular piece of paper. But several *E*'s, in several different contexts, observably distinct from *F*'s or *H*'s, provide convincing evidence that this kind of capability has been learned.

Attitude   A student learns to have preferences for various kinds of activities; preferring certain people to others; showing an interest in certain events rather than others. One infers from a set of such observations that the student has *attitudes* toward objects, persons, or events which influence the choice of courses of action towards them. Naturally, there are many such attitudes that are acquired outside of the school, and many that schools cannot appropriately consider relevant to their instructional function. As one possibility, though, school instruction might have the objective of establishing positive attitudes toward subjects being studied (cf. Mager, 1968). Often, too, school learning is successful in modifying attitudes toward activities that provide esthetic enjoyment. The example of Table 3-1 is a positive attitude toward listening to music.

Considered as a human capability, an attitude is a persisting state that modifies the individual's choices of action. A positive attitude toward listening to music makes the student *tend* to choose such activity over others, when such choices are possible. Of course, this does not mean he or she will always be listening to music, under all circumstances. Rather, it means that when there is an opportunity for leisure (as opposed to other pressing concerns) the probability of a choice to listen to music is noticeably high. If one were able to observe the student over a reasonable period of time, one would be able to note that the choice of this activity was relatively frequent. From such a set of observations, it could be concluded that the student had a positive attitude toward listening to music.

In practice, of course, making such a set of observations about a single student, not to mention a class of students, would be an exceedingly time-consuming and therefore expensive undertaking. As a result, inferences about the possession of attitudes are usually made on the basis of "self-reports." These may be obtained by means of questionnaires which ask students what choices of action they would make (or in some cases, *did* make) in a variety of situations. There are of course technical problems in the use of such self-reports for attitude assessment. Since their intentions are rather obvious, students can readily make self-reports of choices which do not reflect reality. However, when proper precautions are taken, such reports make possible the inference that a particular attitude has been learned, or modified in a particular direction.

Thus, the performance that is affected by an attitude is the *choice of a course of personal action.* The tendency to make such a choice, towards a particular class of objects, persons, or events, may be stronger in one student than in another. A change in an attitude would be revealed as a change in the probability of choosing a particular course of action on the part of the student. Continuing the previous example, over a period of time, or as a result of instruction, the probability of choosing the activity "listening to music" may be altered. The observation of such change would give rise to the inference that the student's attitude toward listening to music had changed, that is, had become "stronger" in the positive direction.

Human capabilities as course goals

A single course of instruction usually has objectives that fit into several categories of human capability. The major categories, which cut across the "content" of courses, are the five we have described. From the standpoint of the expected outcomes of instruction, the major reason for distinguishing these five categories is that they *make possible different kinds of human performance.*

For example, a course in elementary science may foresee as general objectives such learning outcomes as these: (1) solving problems of velocity, time, and acceleration; (2) designing an experiment to provide a scientific test of a stated hypothesis; and (3) valuing the activities of science. Number one obviously names *intellectual skills* and therefore implies some performances involving intellectual operations which the student can show he can do. Number two pertains to the use of *cognitive strategies,* since it implies that the student will need to exhibit this complex performance in a novel situation, where little guidance is provided in the selection and use of rules and concepts he has previously learned. Number three has to do with an *attitude,* or possibly with a set of attitudes, which will be exhibited in behavior as choices of actions directed toward science activities.

The human capabilities distinguished in these five categories also differ from each other in another highly important way. They each require *a different set of learning conditions* for their efficient learning. The conditions necessary for learning these capabilities efficiently, and the distinctions among these conditions, constitute the subjects of the next two chapters. There, an account is given of the conditions of learning which apply to the acquisition of each of these kinds of human capability, beginning with intellectual skills and cognitive strategies, and following with the remaining three categories.

DESIGNING INSTRUCTION USING HUMAN CAPABILITIES

The point of view presented in this chapter is that instruction should always be designed to meet accepted educational goals. When goals are matched with societal needs, the ideal condition exists for the planning of a total program of education. Were such an undertaking to be attempted, the result would be, as a first step, a list of human activities, each of which would have associated with it an estimate of its importance in meeting the needs of the society.

When human activities derived from societal needs are in turn analyzed, they yield a set of *human capabilities.* These are descriptions of what human adults in a particular society ought to *know,* and particularly what they ought to *know how to do.* Such a set of capabilities would probably not bear a close resemblance to the traditional "subject-matter" categories of the school curriculum. There would, of course, be a relationship between human capabilities and the "subjects" of the curriculum, but it would probably not be a simple correspondence.

Most instructional design, as currently carried out, centers upon *course* planning and design. Such a framework is therefore accepted for the account to be given in this book. However, we shall continue to maintain an orientation toward the *goals* of instruction. Learning outcomes cannot always be well identified, it appears, by the topical titles of courses. They *can* be identified as the varieties of learned human capabilities which make possible different types of human performances. Accordingly, the present chapter has provided an introduction to the five major categories of capabilities, which will serve throughout the book as the basic framework of instructional design.

If the instructional designer thinks "These five categories are all well and good, but all that I'm *really* interested in is producing creative thinkers," he is engaging in a game of fooling himself. With the exception of motor skills, *all* of these categories are likely to be involved in the planning of any course. One cannot have a course without information, and one cannot have a course that doesn't affect attitudes to some degree. And most importantly, one cannot have a course without intellectual skills.

There are a couple of reasons why intellectual skills play a central role in designing the structure of a course of *study*. First, they are the kinds of capabilities which determine what the student can *do,* and thus are intimately bound up with the description of a course in terms of its learning outcomes. A second reason is that intellectual skills have a *cumulative* nature—they build upon each other in a predictable manner. Accordingly, they provide the most useful model for the sequencing of course structure. In the next chapter, we begin to look more closely at intellectual skills—what kinds are there, how can they be learned, and how does one know when they are learned?

SUMMARY

This chapter has shown that the defining of goals for education is a complex problem. In part this is because so much is expected of education. Some persons would wish that education emphasize the importance of understanding the past history of mankind; some would wish it to perpetuate the present culture or present academic disciplines; some would stress the need to help children and young adults adjust to a rapidly changing society; and others would hope that education can prepare students to become change-agents to improve themselves and the society in which they live.

One source of complexity in defining educational goals arises from the need to translate goals from very general ones to increasingly specific ones. Many "layers" of such goals would be needed to be sure that each topic in the curriculum actually moves the learner a step closer to a more distant goal. Probably this mapping has never been done completely for any curriculum. Thus there tend to be large gaps from general goals to the specific objectives for "courses" in the curriculum. A major problem then remains—the need to define "course objectives" in the absence of an entire network of connections between the most general goals and the specific course objectives.

Despite the involved nature of this problem, means are available for classifying course objectives into categories, which then make it possible to examine the scope of types of *human capabilities* the course is intended to develop. One purpose of such taxonomies (sets of performance categories) is to evaluate the objectives themselves in their entirety. The taxonomy presented in this chapter contains the following categories of learned capabilities:

1. Intellectual skills
2. Cognitive strategies

3. Verbal information
4. Motor skills
5. Attitudes

The usefulness of learning each of these types of capabilities has been discussed, and will be treated in greater detail in later chapters.

Uses of such a taxonomy, in addition to the evaluation of the variety of capabilities a course is intended to produce in the learner, include the following:

1. The taxonomy can help to group specific objectives of a similar nature together, and thus reduce the work needed to design a total instructional strategy.
2. The groupings of objectives can aid in determining sequence of segments of a course of study.
3. The grouping of objectives into types of capabilities can then be utilized to plan the internal and external conditions of learning estimated to be required for successful learning.

Each performance objective of a course defines a unique performance expected as an outcome of the instruction. By grouping objectives into the five categories of capabilities which have been described, one also can assess the adequacy of coverage in each category, while capitalizing upon the fact the conditions of learning are the same for each objective within that category. Identification of the conditions of learning for each type of human capability is the main topic of the next two chapters.

References

Bloom, B. S., Hastings, J. T., and Madaus, G. F. *Handbook on Formative and Summative Evaluation of Student Learning.* New York: McGraw-Hill, 1971.

Bruner, J. S., Goodnow, J. J. and Austin, G. A. *A Study of Thinking.* New York: Wiley, 1956.

Commission on the Reorganization of Secondary Education, *Cardinal Principles of Secondary Education.* Washington, D.C.: Department of the Interior, Bureau of Education, 1918 (Bulletin No. 35).

Fitts, P. M., and Posner, M. I. *Human Performance.* Belmont, Ca.: Brooks/Cole, 1967.

Gagné, R. M. *The Conditions of Learning,* 3d Ed. New York: Holt, Rinehart and Winston, 1977.

Krathwohl, D. R., Bloom, B. S., and Masia, B. B. *Taxonomy of Educational Objectives. Handbook II: Affective Domain.* New York: McKay, 1964.

Mager, R. F. *Developing Attitude toward Learning.* Belmont, Ca.: Fearon, 1968.

Mager, R. F. *Preparing Objectives for Instruction,* 2d Ed. Belmont, Ca.: Fearon, 1975.

Popham, W. J., and Baker, E. L. *Establishing Instructional Goals.* Englewood Cliffs, N.J.: Prentice-Hall, 1970.

Rothkopf, E. Z. Experiments on mathemagenic behavior and the technology of written instruction. In E. Z. Rothkopf and P. E. Johnson (ed.), *Verbal Learning Re-*

search and the Technology of Written Instruction. New York: Teachers College, 1971.

Singer, R. N. *Motor Learning and Human Performance,* 2d Ed. New York: Macmillan, 1975.

Skinner, B. F. *The Technology of Teaching.* New York: Appleton, 1968.

Womer, F. B. *What Is National Assessment?* Denver: Education Commission of the States, 1970.

chapter 4

Varieties of Learning:
Intellectual Skills and Strategies

When one begins to think about the application of learning principles to instruction, there is no better guide than to face the question, *what* is to be learned? We have seen that the answer to this question may in any given instance fall into one of the general classes (1) intellectual skills, (2) cognitive strategies, (3) information, (4) motor skills, or (5) attitudes. In this chapter, we intend to consider the conditions affecting the learning of *intellectual skills,* which are of central importance to school learning, and which in addition provide the best structural model for instructional design. It is a reasonable step to proceed then to a consideration of *cognitive strategies,* which are a special kind of intellectual skill deserving of a separate categorization. In the following chapter, consideration will be given to learning requirements for the remaining three classes of human capabilities.

An intellectual skill makes it possible for an individual to respond to his environment through symbols. Language, numbers, and other kinds of symbols represent the actual objects of the person's environment. Words "stand for" objects. They also represent relations among objects, such as "above," "behind," "within." Numbers represent the quantity of things in the environment, and various symbols are used to represent relations among these quantities (+, =, etc.). Other kinds of symbols are commonly used to represent spatial relations, like lines, arrows, and circles. The human individual communicates aspects of his experience to others by using such symbols. Symbol-using is one of the major ways the person remembers and thinks about the world in which he lives. We need to provide here an expanded description of these intellectual skills. What kinds of intellectual skills may be learned, and how are they learned?

TYPES OF INTELLECTUAL SKILLS

The intellectual skills learned by the individual during his school years are many, surely numbering in the thousands. One can appreciate this fact by thinking of a single domain—language skills. Even topics of instruction like oral reading, expressive reading, sentence composition, paragraph construction, conversing, and persuasive speaking contain scores of specific intellectual skills which must be learned. This is also true of skills of number and quantification within the various fields of mathematics. Many skills of spatial and temporal patterning form a part of such subjects as geometry and science. In dealing with intellectual skills, one must be prepared to look at the "fine-grain" structure of human intellectual functioning.

In whatever domain of subject matter they occur, intellectual skills can be categorized by *complexity*. This means the intricacy of the mental process that may be inferred to account for the human performance. For example, suppose that a learner is shown two novel and distinctive-looking objects, and told to learn how to tell them apart when they are brought back at a later time. The kind of mental processing required is not very complex. One can infer that what has been learned in this situation and can later be recalled is a "discrimination."

Quite a different level of complexity is indicated by the following example: Following instruction the learner is able to comprehend adjectives in the German language which he has never before encountered, constructed by adding the suffix "lich" (as with Gemüt—gemütlich). This kind of performance is often referred to as *rule-governed*, because the kind of mental processing it requires is "applying a rule." It is not necessary for the learner to state the rule, or even for him to be able to state it. He is, however, performing in a way that implies he must have learned an internal capability that makes his behavior regular, or rule-governed. What he has learned is called a *rule*. Obviously, such a process is more complex than the discrimination referred to in the previous paragraph.

Different levels of complexity of mental processing, then, make possible the classification of intellectual skills. Such categories cut across, and are independent of, types of subject matter (Gagné, 1964). How many levels of complexity of intellectual processing can be distinguished, or need to be? For most instructional purposes, the useful distinctions among intellectual skills are as shown in Figure 4–1.

Learning affects the intellectual development of the individual in the manner suggested by the diagram of Figure 4–1. In solving problems for which instruction has prepared them, learners are acquiring some *higher-order rules* (that is, *complex rules*). Problem solving requires that they recall some simpler, previously

PROBLEM SOLVING

(HIGHER-ORDER RULES)

|

requires as prerequisites

|

RULES

(including DEFINED CONCEPTS)

|

which require as prerequisites

|

CONCRETE CONCEPTS

|

which require as prerequisites

|

DISCRIMINATIONS

FIGURE 4–1 Levels of Complexity in Intellectual Skills

(Derived from R. M. Gagné, The Conditions of Learning, *3d Ed. New York: Holt, Rinehart and Winston, 1977).*

learned *rules.* In order to acquire these rules, learners must have acquired some *concrete concepts;* and in order to learn these concepts, they must have learned some *discriminations.* For example, the reader who is confronted with the problem of inferring the pronunciation of an unfamiliar printed word must bring to bear on this problem some previously learned rules ("decoding skills"), whose learning has in turn required the prerequisite of identifying printed letters (concepts). The child who is learning to identify a letter such as a printed E must have previously learned to distinguish three horizontal lines ══ from two ═══; that is, this discrimination must have been acquired as a prerequisite. Of course, the teacher who is concerned with instruction designed to get children to identify E may find it possible to assume that they already know two lines from three. If this assumption is not correct, it may be necessary to design instruction so that the learners "catch up" with specific capabilities that reflect the simpler forms of intellectual skills.

Discriminations

A discrimination is a capability of making different responses to stimuli which differ from each other along one or more physical dimensions. Examples in secondary and adult education may occur with stimuli encountered in art, music, foreign languages, and science. Instances of discrimination are often a regular part of instruction for the kindergarten and first grade. Here children are asked to distinguish two "pictures," one having vertical lines and another horizontal lines; or, one having a circle and the other a square. Matching to a sample is another variant form of the discrimination task; the child may be asked to match a red-colored block with another the same color in a group of blocks of various colors. In beginning music instruction, the child may be asked to learn to discriminate which of two tones is louder, or which of two tone-pairs contains tones that are "the same" or "different" in pitch.

A discrimination is a very basic kind of intellectual skill. Discrimination learning is encountered most frequently in young children, and also in mental retardates. So far as most school learning is concerned, discriminations are usually assumed to have been learned earlier in life. Every once in a while, however, one is surprised to realize that these elementary discriminations may not have been learned, and cannot be assumed. Does the learner of the French uvular and frontal *r* actually hear this distinction (that is, has he learned it as a discrimination)? Has the student microscopist actually seen the distinction (discriminated) between a bright and dark boundary which he will later learn to identify as a cell wall?

In describing the characteristics of a discrimination, as well as other types of intellectual skills to follow, we need to account for three components of the learning situation. These are:

1. The *performance* which is acquired, or to be acquired. What is it that the learner will be able to do after learning that he was not able to do before?
2. The *internal conditions* which must be present in order for the learning to occur. These consist of capabilities which are recalled from the learner's memory, and which then become integrated into the newly acquired capability.
3. The *external conditions* which provide stimulation to the learner. These may be visually present objects, symbols, pictures, sounds, or meaningful verbal communications.

For discrimination learning, these characteristics are described in the following paragraphs.

Performance   There must be a response which indicates that the learner can distinguish stimuli which differ on one or more physical dimensions. Often this is an indication of *same* or *different.*

Internal Conditions   On the sensory side, the physical difference must give rise to different patterns of brain activity. Otherwise, the individual must have available only the responses necessary to indicate that the difference is detectable, as in saying "same" and "different." The required responses may be as simple as pointing, making a checkmark, or drawing a circle around a pictured object.

External Conditions   The learning of discriminations involves external conditions reflected in some of the most generally applicable learning principles. *Contiguity* is necessary in that the response must follow the stimulus within a short time-span. *Reinforcement* is of particular importance to discrimination learning, and is made to occur *differentially* for right and wrong responses. A response indicating a correct distinction between "same" or "different" stimuli is followed by a pleasant familiar activity (for example, circling *other* figures of the same sort), whereas a response which is incorrect is not followed by such activity. When reinforcement occurs in this manner, the discrimination will soon be learned. *Repetition* also plays a particular role. The situation may need to be repeated several times, in order that the correct stimulus difference is selected. Sometimes this may happen in one trial, but often a few repetitions may be necessary in order to permit reinforcement to take its effect. Additional repetitions become necessary when *multiple* discriminations are being learned, as when several different object-shapes must be distinguished at one time.

Concrete concepts

A concept is a capability that makes it possible for an individual to identify a stimulus as a member of a class having some characteristic in common, even though such stimuli may otherwise differ from each other markedly. A concrete concept identifies an *object property* or object attribute (color, shape, etc.). Such concepts are called "concrete" because the human performance they require is recognition of a concrete object.

Examples of object properties are round, square, blue, three, smooth, curved, flat, and so on. One can tell whether a concrete concept has been learned by asking the individual to identify, by "pointing to," two or more members belonging to the same object-property class; for example, by pointing to a penny, an automobile tire, and the full moon as round. The operation of "pointing" may be carried out practically in many different ways; often, it is a matter of choosing, checking, circling, or grasping. Frequently, the operation of "pointing" is carried out by naming (labeling). Thus, the particular *response* made by the individual is of no consequence, so long as it can be assumed that he knows how to do it.

An important variety of concrete concept is *object position*. This can be conceived as an object property, since it can be identified by "pointing." It is clear, however, that the position of an object must be in relation to that of another object. Examples of object positions are above, below, beside, surrounding, right, left, middle, on, in front of. Obviously, one can ask that such positional characteristics be "pointed to" in some manner or other. Thus, object positions qualify as concrete concepts.

The distinction between a discrimination and a concept is easy to see. A young child may have learned to tell the difference between a triangle and a rectangle drawn on a piece of paper. That is, he may show that he sees these as different objects, by choosing, "pointing," or by responding differentially. Such a performance permits only the conclusion that the child can *discriminate* between these particular objects. To test whether he has the concept "triangle," however, one would need to ask him to identify several objects exhibiting this property—objects which otherwise differ widely in their other qualities such as size, color, border thickness, and so on. In other words, one must determine that the individual is capable of identifying the *class* of object properties, in order to conclude that he has acquired a concrete concept.

The capability of identifying concrete concepts is fundamentally significant for more complex learning. Many investigators have emphasized the importance of "concrete learning" as a prerequisite to "the learning of abstract ideas." Piaget (1950) made this distinction a key idea in his theory of intellectual development. The acquisition of *concepts by definition* (to be described next) requires that the learner be able to identify the referents of the words used in such definitions. Thus, to acquire the concept *rim* by way of the definition "the edge of a round thing," the learner must have as prerequisites the concrete concepts "edge" and "round." If he is not able to identify these concepts concretely, it will not be possible for him in any true or complete sense to "know the meaning" of *rim.*

Performance   Identifying a class of object properties, including object positions, by "pointing to" two or more members of the class. The "pointing" may be done in any of a number of ways (checking, circling, and so on) equivalent only in the sense that identification occurs.

Internal Conditions   In acquiring a concrete concept, discriminations must be recalled. Thus, an individual who is learning the concept *two* must be able to discriminate a variation in object quality like this: | | | from one like this: | |. The variation between *O* and other physical forms of O must have been discriminated, in order for the concept o to be learned.

External Conditions   Instances of the class are presented, varying as widely as possible in their nonrelevant characteristics, and the individual is asked to identify each by "pointing" or naming. For example, a concept like *two* may be identified by objects as vastly different in other characteristics as two dots on a page, two children, two buildings, or two baseballs. Negative instances are often of value as well. It may be that their function is primarily that of stimulating the recall of the necessary discriminations, as when / / (*two*) is distinguished from / / / (*not two*).

Defined concepts

An individual is said to have learned a defined concept when he can demonstrate the "meaning" of some particular class of objects, events, or relations. For example, consider the concept "alien", a citizen of a foreign country. An individual who has learned such a concept will be able to classify a particular person in accordance with the definition, by showing that that person is currently in a country of which he is not a citizen, and that he is a citizen of some other country. The demonstration may involve verbal reference to the definition, and this is an adequate demonstration when one assumes that the individual knows the meaning of the words "citizen," "other," and "country". Should it be the case that such knowledge cannot be assumed, it might be necessary to ask for the demonstration in other terms, perhaps involving "pointing to" pictures of people and maps of countries. *Demonstration* of the meaning is emphasized in order to establish a distinction between this kind of mental processing and the kind involved in memorized verbal information such as the statement "An alien is a citizen of a foreign country."

Many concepts can only be acquired as defined concepts, and cannot be identified by "pointing to" them, as can concrete concepts. Familiar examples are "family," "city," and abstractions like "justice." However, some defined concepts have corresponding concrete concepts which carry the same name and possess certain features in common. For example, many young children learn the basic shape of a triangle as a concrete concept. Not until much later in studying geometry do they encounter the defined concept of triangle, "a closed plane figure formed by three line segments which intersect at three points." The concrete and defined meanings of "triangle" are not exactly the same, yet they overlap considerably.

A simple example of a defined concept is *sidewalk,* the definition of which may be stated as "a walkway beside a street." Again, the defined concept must be demonstrated, in order for an external observer to know that it has been learned. Such a demonstration by the learner would consist, essentially, of (1) identifying a *walkway* (which might be done in this instance by a "pointing" operation, using a picture); (2) identifying a *street* (again possibly by "pointing"); and (3) demonstrating *beside* (by placing or drawing the two identified objects, walkway and street, in the correct spatial position).

Why doesn't one just ask the question, what does *sidewalk* mean? Why describe this elaborate procedure? The reason has been mentioned previously—only by insuring that the individual is capable of operations identifying the *referents* of the words can one be confident that the meaning of a defined concept has been learned. In practice, of course, the procedure of obtaining verbal answers to verbal questions is often used. But such a procedure is always subject to the ambiguity that the learner may be repeating a verbal chain, and that he doesn't know the meaning of the concept after all. It is for this reason that we use the phrase *demonstrate a concept* rather than a simpler phrase like *state a definition* or *define.* We want to imply that the learner has a "real understanding" of a defined concept, rather than the superficial acquaintance indicated by his reeling off a string of words.

Performance   The learner will demonstrate the concept by identifying instances of concepts which are components of the definition, and showing an instance of their relation to one another.

Internal Conditions   In order to acquire a concept by definition, the learner must recall all of the component concepts included in the definition, including the concepts which represent relations among them. (In the example of the sidewalk, *beside* is the relational concept.)

External Conditions   A defined concept may be learned by having the learner watch a demonstration. Most frequently, though, the concept is "demonstrated" by means of a verbally stated definition. Thus, the concept *scum* may be communicated by the statement "a filmy covering floating on a liquid." Provided the internal conditions are met, such a statement is sufficient to induce learning of the concept. What must be recalled are the concepts "filmy," "covering," "liquid," and "floating on"; not just the words.

Rules

A rule has been learned when it is possible to say with confidence that the learner's performance has a kind of "regularity" over a variety of specific situations. In other words, the learner shows that he is able to respond with a *class* of relationships among *classes* of objects and events. When a learner shows that he can sort cards marked X into a bin marked A, and cards marked Y into a bin marked B, this is insufficient evidence that his behavior is "rule-governed." (He may simply be exhibiting learning of the concrete concepts X and Y.) But suppose he has learned to put each X card into any bin two positions away from his last choice, and each Y card one position away from his last choice. In that case, he has learned a rule. He is responding to classes of objects (X and Y cards) with classes of relationships (one position away, two positions away). His behavior cannot be described in terms of a *particular* relation between the stimulus (the card) and his sorting response to a bin.

There are many common examples of rule-governed behavior. In fact, most behavior of human beings falls into this category. When we make a sentence using a given word such as *girl,* as in "The girl rode a bicycle," we are using a number of rules. For example, we begin the sentence with *The,* not with *girl,* employing a rule for the use of the definite article. The subject of the sentence is followed with a predicate, a verb coming next in order—that is, we say "The girl rode," and not "Rode the girl." The verb is followed in turn by the object "bicycle," which, according to one rule is placed in a particular order, and according to another is preceded (in this case) by the indefinite article *a.* Finally, we complete the sentence by bringing it to a close, which in written form involves a rule for the use of a period. Since we have acquired each of these rules, we are able to construct *any* sentence of the same structure, with *any* given words as subject and object.

Principles learned in science courses are exhibited by the learner as rule-using behavior. For example, we expect students who have learned Newton's second law, $F = ma$, to *apply* the rule embodied in this statement. A question such as the following may be asked: "What will be the acceleration of a body of 5 kilograms when acted on by a force of 3 Newtons?"

Obviously, possessing the capability called a *rule* does not mean being able to state it verbally. The student who can state "force equals mass times acceleration" cannot necessarily apply the rule to a specific concrete problem. The child performs the behavior of constructing oral sentences long before learning grammatical rules. The observer of learning behavior may have to "state the rule" being learned, in explanation of what is being talked about. There are many instances, however, in which learners are quite unable to state a rule, even though their performance indicates that they "know" it.

Now that we have indicated what a rule is, we can admit that a defined concept, as previously described, is actually not formally different from a rule, and is learned in much the same way. In other words, a defined concept is a particular type of rule whose purpose it is to classify objects and events; it is a *classifying rule*. Rules, however, include many other categories besides classifying. They deal with such relationships as equal to, similar to, greater than, less than, before, after, and many, many others.

Performance   The rule is demonstrated by showing one or more instances of the relation of the component concepts to one another; in other words, by applying the rule to some concrete instances. (The rule relating electrical resistance to cross-sectional area of a conductor could be exhibited by demonstrating a decrease in ohms when wire of larger diameter is selected for an electric circuit.)

Internal Conditions   In learning a rule, the learner must recall each of the component concepts of the rule, including the concepts that represent relations. It is assumed that these concepts have been previously learned and can be recalled. (In the example given, the learner must be able to recall such concepts as "cross section," "area," "conductor," and "decrease.")

External Conditions   Usually, the external conditions for learning rules involve the use of verbal communications. The rule may be communicated to the learner verbally, although not necessarily in a formally correct manner. The purpose of such verbal statements is to *cue* the arrangement of concepts in a correct order by the learner. They are not to teach the learner a formal verbal proposition representing the rule. Suppose, for example, a teacher intends to impart a particular rule in the decoding of printed words (the rule for pronouncing words having consonants followed by a final *e*). The teacher may say, "Notice that the letter a has a long sound when followed by a consonant, in a word that ends in *e.* This is true in words that you know like *made, pale, fate.* When the word does not end in *e,* the letter *a* has a short sound, as in *mad, pal, fat.* Now tell me how to pronounce these words which you may not have seen before: *dade, pate, kale.* "

The basic reasons for the verbal communication are two: (1) to remind the learner of component concepts to be recalled (such as "long vowel sounds," "consonants"); and (2) to get the learner to arrange component concepts in the proper order (that is, "consonant followed by final e," not "vowel followed by final consonant," nor "vowel followed by final e," nor "consonant followed by final vowel," nor any other incorrect ordering).

It is evident that the verbal communication used in rule learning may be more or less lengthy. Accordingly, more or less of the actual rule construction may be left up to the learner. Another way to say this is that the external conditions for instruction in a rule may provide different amounts of *learning guidance.* When minimal amounts of learning guidance are provided, instruction is said to emphasize *discovery* on the part of the learner (Bruner, 1961; Shulman and Keislar, 1966). Conversely, discovery is de-emphasized when the amount of learning guidance provided is large, as tends to be true in more detailed verbal communications. Studies of "discovery learning" suggest that small amounts of learning guidance have advantages for retention and transfer of the rules which are learned (cf. Worthen, 1968). Often techniques to bring about learning by discovery incorporate the use of pointed questioning of the learner. These questions lead to the discovery of proper ordering of component concepts.

Higher-order rules—problem solving

Sometimes, the rules which human beings learn are complex combinations of simpler rules. Moreover, it is often the case that these more complex, or "higher-order" rules are *invented* for the purpose of solving a practical problem or class of problems. The capability of problem solving is, naturally, a major aim of the educational process—most educators agree that the school should give priority to teaching students "how to think clearly." When students work out the solution to a problem which represents real events, they are engaging in the behavior of thinking. There are, of course, many kinds of problems, and an even greater number of possible solutions to them. In attaining a workable solution to a problem, students also achieve a new capability. They learn something which can be generalized to other problems having similar formal characteristics. This means they have acquired a new rule, or perhaps a new set of rules.

Suppose that a small car has been parked near a low brick fence, and is discovered to have a flat tire on one of its front wheels. No jack is available, but there is a ten-foot two-by-four, and a piece of sturdy rope. Can the front of the car be raised? In this situation, a possible solution might be found by using the two-by-four as a lever, the wall as a fulcrum, and the rope to secure the end of the lever when the car is in a raised position. This solution is invented to meet a particular problem situation. It is evident that the solution represents a "putting together" of certain rules which may not have been previously applied to similar situations in the past history of the individual who is solving the problem. One rule pertains to the application of force on an end of the car to achieve a lifting of that end. Another rule pertains to the use of the wall as a fulcrum which will bear an estimated weight. And still another, of course, is the rule regarding use of the two-by-four as a lever. All of these rules, in order to be used in an act of problem solving, must be recalled by the individual, which means they must have been previously learned. (Note once again that the rules we refer to cannot necessarily be verbalized by the problem solver; nor have they necessarily been learned in a physics course.) These previously acquired rules are then brought together by the individual to achieve the solution to the problem. And once solved, the individual has learned a new rule, more complex than those used in combination. The newly learned rule will be stored in the memory and used again to solve other problems.

The invention of a complex rule can be illustrated with a problem in mathematics. Suppose a student has learned to add monomials such as 2X and 5X, $3X^2$ and $4X^2$, $2X^3$ and $6X^3$. Now he is shown a set of polynomials, such as:

$$2X + 3X^2 + 1$$
$$2 + 3X + 4X^2.$$

The student is asked, "What do you suppose is the sum of these two expressions?" This question asks for the solution of a new problem, which (we assume) has not been previously encountered. Possibly, the student may make some false starts, which could be corrected. The chances are, however, that previously learned subordinate rules will permit him or her to think out the solution to this problem (for example, the rule that a variable a added to the variable a^2 results in the sum $a + a^2$; also the rule for adding monomials, such as $2a^2 + 3a^2 = 5a^2$. It is probably not a difficult problem for the student, therefore, to devise the complex rule: Add variables with the same exponents; express the sum as a set of terms connected by the $+$ sign. Again in this example, the problem solver has remembered and "combined" simpler rules into a more complex rule which is the solution to the problem.

The essential condition that makes this sort of learning a problem-solving event is the *absence* of any learning guidance, whether in the form of a verbal communication or in some other form. The solution has been "discovered," or invented. The learning guidance is provided by the problem-solver alone, not by a teacher or other external source. One may guess that some problem-solving *strategies* which may have been learned in quite different situations are probably brought to bear. But in any case, relevant rules are recalled and combined to form a new "higher-order" rule.

Performance The performance would require invention and use of a complex rule to achieve the solution of a problem which is novel to the individual. When the higher-order rule has been acquired, it should also be possible for the learner to demonstrate its use in other physically different, but formally similar, situations. In other words, the new complex rule which has been acquired exhibits transfer of learning.

Internal Conditions   In solving a problem, the learner must recall relevant subordinate rules and also relevant information. It is assumed that these capabilities have been previously learned.

External Conditions   The learner is confronted with an actual, or a represented, problem situation not previously encountered. Cues in the form of verbal communications are at a minimum, or may be absent entirely. The learner engages in "discovery learning"; he or she invents a solution.

COGNITIVE STRATEGIES

A very special kind of intellectual skill, of particular importance in problem solving, is called a *cognitive strategy.* In terms of modern learning theory, a cognitive strategy is a *control process,* an internal process by means of which learners select and modify their ways of attending, learning, remembering, and thinking (Gagné, 1977). A cognitive strategy is an *internally organized* skill which governs the learners' own intellectual processing. Several of Bruner's writings (1966, 1971) describe the operation and the usefulness of cognitive strategies.

A variety of studies have been concerned with the use of cognitive strategies such as those which control attention (Rothkopf, 1971) and encoding the learning of word pairs (Rohwer, 1975). In addition, a number of recent studies have been concerned with strategies of remembering in children (Flavell and Wellman, 1977). As for strategies of thinking, it is of interest to note that one can relate these to the theory of Piaget (1950) concerning intellectual development (cf. Flavell, 1963). Piaget's basic view is that the intellect of the child develops in identifiable stages, each of which represents the capability of using increasingly complex forms of logical operations. Thus, to Piaget, the capabilities which are here called cognitive strategies set limits to the kinds of problem solving children of various ages can successfully perform.

Within the framework of Piaget's theory, one can readily accommodate the learning of more specific intellectual skills such as are described in previous sections of this chapter. One can alternatively espouse a different theory: that cognitive strategies develop *out of* these more specific learned intellectual skills by a process of generalization (Gagné, 1968) rather than by simple maturation as the individual grows. The latter theoretical view is what leads us here to treat cognitive strategies as the crowning accomplishment of a great deal of specific learning, and accordingly to deal with them as a special variety of intellectual skill.

Often of particular interest in instructional design are those cognitive strategies which are called into play when the learner defines and thinks out a solution to a highly novel problem. While such strategies are usually of primary interest in educational programs, our knowledge of how to insure their learning is weakest (cf. Gagné, 1977, pp. 176–177). A number of strategies employed by adults in solving verbally stated problems are described by Wickelgren (1974). These include: (1) inferring transformed conceptions of the "givens;" (2) classifying action sequences, rather than randomly choosing them; (3) choosing actions at any given state of the problem which get closer to the goal ("hill climbing"); (4) identifying contradictions which prove that the goal cannot be attained from the givens; (5) breaking a problem up into parts; and (6) working backwards from the goal to new statements which imply the goal statement. Strategies like these are obviously applicable to "brain teaser" problems of an algebraic or geometric sort. Presumably, many real-life problems require even simpler cognitive strategies.

Learning cognitive strategies

A cognitive strategy is an internally organized skill that selects and guides the internal processes involved in defining and solving novel problems. In other words, it is a skill by means of which the learner manages his own thinking behavior. Notice that it is the *object* of the skill which differentiates cognitive strategies from other intellectual skills. The latter are oriented toward environmental objects and events, such as sentences, graphs, or mathematical equations. In contrast, cognitive strategies have as their objects the *learner's own thought processes*. Undoubtedly, the efficacy of an individual's cognitive strategies exerts a crucial effect upon the quality of his thought. They may determine, for example, how creatively he thinks, how fluently he thinks, and how critically he thinks.

Statements of educational goals often give highest priority to cognitive strategies. Many statements of goals for school learning give a prominent place to "teaching students how to think." While it would be difficult to find disagreement with the importance of such a goal, it seems wise to temper one's enthusiasm for it with a couple of facts pertaining to the feasibility of reaching it. First, one should realize that genetic factors, not amenable to the influence of education, are likely to play at least a large part in the determination of creative thought (cf. Tyler, 1965; Ausubel, 1978, Chap. 16). In other words, there are bound to be enormous differences in intellectual capacity among people, which can never be completely overcome by environmental influences such as education. Second, the internally organized nature of cognitive strategies means that the conditions of instruction can have only an indirect effect upon their acquisition and improvement. In the case of other types of intellectual skills, one can plan a sequence of learning events external to the learner which will insure the learning of those skills. But cognitive strategies require a more indirect control; one has to organize external events so as to increase the probability of certain internal events; and these in turn determine the learning of the cognitive strategy. Accordingly, the design of instruction for cognitive strategies has to be done in terms of "favorable conditions," and cannot be accomplished by specifying the "sufficient conditions." Generally, the favorable conditions are those which *provide opportunities for development and use* of cognitive strategies. In other words, in order to "learn to think," the student needs to be given opportunities to think.

Performance   The learner must originate novel solutions to problem situations, in which neither the class of solution nor the specific manner of solution are specified.

Internal Conditions   The learner needs to have available a variety of cognitive strategies of problem solution from which to make a selection. Obviously, too, if the learner is to arrive at a specific solution following such a selection, the intellectual skills involved in this solution must be available.

External Conditions   Novel problems need to be presented for which the class of solution required is not specified. If a learner is asked "What kinds of things would a man be able to do if he had two thumbs on each hand?" it is evident that the repertoire of cognitive strategies to attack the problem must be searched. Will the first thought be of the most unusual things two thumbs could do? Or will the learner carefully categorize the kinds of things thumbs can perform? Ultimately, both these approaches must probably be used. The particular way the learner attacks the problem is what is meant by cognitive strategy. Externally, what can be done is to insure that the problem presented is novel, and therefore that it represents a "favorable condition" for thought.

VARIETIES OF INTELLECTUAL SKILLS IN SCHOOL SUBJECTS

The range of human capabilities called intellectual skills, includes the varieties of discriminations, concrete concepts, defined concepts, rules, and the higher-order rules often acquired in problem solving. An additional category of internally organized skills is cognitive strategies, which govern the learner's behavior in learning and thinking, and thus determine its quality and efficiency. These varieties of learning are distinguishable (a) by the class of *performance* they make possible; (b) by the internal and external *conditions* necessary for their occurrence; and (c) by the *complexity* of the internal process which they establish in the individual's memory.

Any school subject may at one time or another involve any of these types of learned capabilities. However, the frequency with which they are encountered in various school subjects varies widely. Examples of discriminations can be found in such elementary subjects as printing letters and reading music. In contrast, there are few examples of this type, and many more of defined concepts, in a history course. However, quite a few examples of discriminations also occur in the beginning study of a foreign language, which may be undertaken in the ninth grade. In the same grade, the writing of compositions very frequently involves defined concepts and rules, but seems not to require the learning of discriminations or concrete concepts. In this case, the necessary learnings of these varieties have been accomplished years ago.

Any school subject *can* be analyzed to reveal the relevance of *all* of these kinds of learning. But this is not always a practical course of action, because the presentation of the subject in a particular grade may begin with the assumption that simpler kinds of learning have already been accomplished. Thus, discrimination of •• from • is certainly relevant to the study of algebra. But one doesn't begin the study of algebra with the learning of discriminations, because it is possible to assume these discriminations have been previously learned. In science, however, certain discriminations, such as those involved in using a microscope or spectrophotometer, may have to be newly acquired. Such simple skills must be learned before the student can progress to the concepts, rules, and problem solving which may represent the major aims of the course.

It should be evident that learning of the various types of capability is not related to age of the learner in any one-to-one sense. Human individuals do not learn all of their motor chains at age four, all of their discriminations at age five, and so on. Reasonable tasks of rule learning and problem solving are quite appropriate for four- and five-year-old children. Any learning tasks are "reasonable" ones when the particular skills that are prerequisite to them have been previously learned. It is true that, in the first grade, learning of discriminations is likely to occur with greater frequency than is the case in the sixth grade. In the tenth grade, one expects the learning of defined concepts and rules to occur with greater frequency than it does in the fourth grade. The general principle is that the kind of learning that may be required can be predicted, not from age, but only from the nature of the performance being sought as the objective of learning.

Is there, then, a *structure* of intellectual skills which represents the "path of greatest learning efficiency" for every subject in the curriculum? In theory, there is. Do we know what this structure is? Only vaguely, as yet. After all, teachers, curriculum specialists, and textbook writers *try* to represent structure in their lesson and curriculum plans, and have been trying for many years. Nevertheless, on the whole their efforts must be characterized as partial and inadequate. The purpose of this book is to describe a systematic method of approaching the problem, as free of culs-de-sac as possible. Such a method will also be subject to empirical verification, and to revision and refinement. The application of the method to be described can lead to descriptions of the "learning structure" of any subject taught in the school. This structure may be represented as a kind of *map* of the terrain to be covered in progressing from one point in human development to any other point.

The mapping of learning structures does not lead to "routinization" or "mechanization" of the process of learning. A map indicates starting points, destinations, and alternative routes in between; it does not tell how to make the journey. Making the "learning journey" requires a different set of internal events for each and every individual. In a fundamental sense, there are as many learning "styles" as there are individuals. Describing the learning structures for a progression of objectives within any school subject does not lead to prescribing how the individual student must learn. On the contrary, learning structures are simply descriptions of the accepted goals, or *outcomes* of learning, together with subordinate steps along the way.

SUMMARY

Starting with the need to identify goals as the desired outcomes of the educational system, Chapter 3 proposed that in attempting to design specific courses, topics, and lessons there is a need to classify performance objectives into broad categories: intellectual skills, cognitive strategies, verbal information, motor skills, and attitudes. Doing so, it was shown, facilitates (a) review of the adequacy of the objectives; (b) determination of the sequencing of instruction; and (c) planning for the conditions of learning needed for successful instruction.

The present chapter has begun the account of the *nature* of the performance capabilities implied by each of the five categories of learned capabilities, beginning with intellectual skills and cognitive strategies. For each of these two domains, this chapter has (a) presented examples of learned performances in terms of different school subjects; (b) identified the kinds of internal conditions of learning needed to reach the new capability; and (c) identified the external conditions affecting its learning.

For intellectual skills, several subcategories were identified: discriminations, concrete and defined concepts, rules, and the higher-order rules often learned by problem solving. Each represents a different class of performance, and each is supported by different sets of internal and external conditions of learning. Cognitive strategies were not broken down into subcategories, as intellectual skills were. Research in the future may suggest that this can and should be done.

The next chapter gives a corresponding kind of treatment to the remaining kinds of learned capabilities: information, attitudes, and motor skills. The purpose of Chapters 4 and 5 is to move one more step toward specification of an orderly series of steps to be used in the actual design of instruction for a lesson, a unit, a course, or an entire instructional system. Specifically, these chapters identify the appropriate internal and external conditions of learning for each kind of learned capability. They lead to suggestions of how to proceed with two aspects of instructional design: (a) how to take account of the *prior* learning that is assumed to be necessary for the learner before he can undertake the new learning to be attempted next; and (b) how to plan for the *new* learning in terms of the appropriate *external conditions* needed for the attainment of each type of learning outcome. In later chapters, these conditions will be translated into guidelines for instructional planning.

References

Ausubel, D. P., Novak, J. D., and Hanesian, H. *Educational Psychology: A Cognitive View.* 2d Ed. New York: Holt, Rinehart and Winston, 1978.

Bruner, J. S. The act of discovery. *Harvard Educational Review,* 1961, *31,* 21–32.
Bruner, J. S. *Toward a Theory of Instruction.* Cambridge, Mass.: Harvard University Press, 1966.
Bruner, J. S. *The Relevance of Education.* New York: Norton, 1971.
Flavell, J. H. *The Developmental Psychology of Jean Piaget.* Princeton, N.J.: Van Nostrand, 1963.
Flavell, J. H., and Wellman, H. M. Metamemory. In R. V. Kail and J. W. Hagen (ed.), *Memory in Cognitive Development.* Hillsdale, N.J.: Erlbaum Associates, 1977.
Gagné, R. M. Problem solving. In A. W. Melton (ed.), *Categories of Human Learning.* New York: Academic Press, 1964.
Gagné, R. M. Contributions of learning to human development. *Psychological Review,* 1968, *75,* 177–191.
Gagné, R. M. *The Conditions of Learning,* 3d Ed. New York: Holt, Rinehart and Winston, 1977.
Piaget, J. *The Psychology of Intelligence.* New York: Harcourt, 1950.
Rohwer, W. D., Jr. Elaboration and learning in childhood and adolescence. In H. W. Reese (ed.), *Advances in Child Development and Behavior,* Vol. 8. New York: Academic Press, 1975.
Rothkopf, E. Z. Experiments on mathemagenic behavior and the technology of written instruction. In E. Z. Rothkopf and P. E. Johnson (ed.), *Verbal Learning Research and Technology of Written Instruction.* New York: Teachers College, 1971.
Shulman, L. S., and Keislar, E. R. *Learning by Discovery: A Critical Appraisal.* Chicago: Rand McNally, 1966.
Tyler, L. E. *The Psychology of Human Differences,* 3d Ed. New York: Appleton, 1965.
Wickelgren, W. A. *How To Solve Problems.* San Francisco: Freeman, 1974.
Worthen, B. R. Discovery and expository task presentation in elementary mathematics. *Journal of Educational Psychology,* Monograph Supplement, 1968, *59,* No. 1, Part 2.

chapter 5

Varieties of Learning:
Information, Attitudes, Motor Skills

In this chapter, we need to continue our description of the varieties of human capabilities which may be learned. The courses and lessons that are designed for instruction are of course not always aimed at developing intellectual skills or cognitive strategies as discussed in the previous chapter. Furthermore, a topic or course of study, and even an individual lesson, may have more than one class of objective as a learning outcome. Instruction is typically designed to encompass several objectives in any given unit of instruction, and to achieve a suitable balance among them.

We shall be describing here the conditions applicable to the learning of three additional classes of learning outcomes: the learning of *information,* the establishment or changing of *attitudes,* and the acquisition of *motor skills.* As in the previous chapter, we need to consider three aspects of the learning situation, for each of these varieties:

1. The *performance* to be acquired as a result of learning.
2. The *internal conditions* that need to be present for learning to occur.

3. The *external conditions* which are established to bring essential stimulation to bear upon the learner.

INFORMATION AND KNOWLEDGE

A great deal of information is learned and stored in memory as a result of school instruction. Of course, an enormous amount is acquired outside of school as well, from the reading of books, magazines, newspapers, and by way of radio and television programs. From this very fact, it is apparent that special means of "instruction" do not have to be provided in order for a large amount of learning to occur. The communications provided by the various media are able to bring about learning in many people, provided of course that those who hear or see or read these communications possess the basic intellectual skills for interpreting them.

In school learning, however, there are many circumstances in which one desires greater certainty of learning than can ordinarily be expected from various extra-school communications. The literate individual may gain much information from a radio lecture on modern developments in chemistry. The amount of information learned by this means may vary greatly among different individuals, depending on their interests and previous experience. A formally planned course in chemistry, in contrast, may have the aim of teaching all students certain information deemed essential for further study of the subject, such as the names of elements, the states exhibited by compounds, and so on. Similarly, the purpose of a course in U.S. Government may be to teach all students the content of the articles of the United States Constitution. Planned instruction in school subjects is undertaken because of this need for certainty of learning particular bodies of information.

Two primary reasons exist for desiring a high degree of certainty in the learning of information. The first of these reasons has already been mentioned: Particular information may be needed in order for a learner to continue the learning of a topic or subject. Of course, some of the necessary detailed information may be looked up in a book or other source. A great deal of it, however, may need to be recalled and used again and again in pursuing study within a subject. Thus there is typically a body of information which is "basic" in the sense that future learning will be more efficiently conducted if it is acquired and retained.

A second reason for learning information is that much of its contents may be continually useful to the individual throughout life. All people need to know the names of letters, numerals, common objects, and a host of facts about themselves and their environment in order to receive and give communications. A great deal of such factual information is acquired informally without any formal planning. In addition, an individual may acquire unusual quantities of factual information in one or more areas of particular interest (a mass of facts about flowers, or automobiles, or the game of baseball). The problem faced in designing school curricula in any area is one of distinguishing between information that is more or less essential. Some may be used by the individual for communication throughout his lifetime. Other information may be personally interesting but not essential. The former category is one for which the standard of certainty of learning becomes the concern of formal education. There seems to be no reason to limit the information a person wishes to learn because of particular interests or desire for further learning.

When information is organized into bodies of meaningfully interconnected facts and generalizations, it is usually referred to as *knowledge*. Obviously, the information possessed by individuals within their own particular field of work or study is usually organized as a "body of knowledge." Thus we expect a chemist, for example, to have learned and stored a specialized body of knowledge about chemistry; and similarly, we expect a cabinetmaker to possess a body of knowledge about woods and joints and tools. Besides these masses of specialized knowledge, one must face the question of whether there is a value to acquiring knowledge that may be called *general*. It may be noted that most, if not all, human societies have answered this question affirmatively. In one way or another, means have been found to pass on the accumulated knowledge of the society from one generation to the next. Information about the origins of the society, tribe, or nation, its development through time, its goals and values, its place in the world, is usually considered a body of knowledge desirable for inclusion in the education of each individual.

In earlier years within our own society, there was a body of general knowledge, fairly well agreed upon, that was considered desirable for the "educated class" (those who went to college) to learn. It was composed of historical information about Western culture extending back to the early Greek civilization, along with related information from literature and the arts. Over a period of years, as mass education has progressively replaced class education, there has been an accompanying reduction in the amount of general cultural knowledge considered desirable for all students to learn. In recent years, there has been a growing emphasis upon an informal type of instruction involving student choices of what to learn. This development would seem to make it virtually impossible to identify a consistent body of knowledge that may be said to constitute general education. At most, such common cultural knowledge appears to be increasingly confined to the few courses in U.S. history and government required by law in many states. The desirability of this trend away from the learning of general cultural information appears open to serious question from the standpoint of societal stability.

What function does general cultural knowledge serve in the life of the individual? Evidently, such knowledge serves the purpose of communication, particularly in those aspects of life pertaining to citizenship. Knowing the facts about the community, the state, and the nation, and the services they provide, as well as the responsibilities owed them, enables the individual to engage in the communications necessary for the citizen's role. Cultural and historical knowledge may also contribute to the achievement and maintenance of the individual's "identity," or sense of self—awareness of his or her own origins in relation to those of the society to which the individual belongs.

A much more critical function of general knowledge can be conceived and speculated about, although evidence concerning it is incomplete. This is the notion that knowledge is the *vehicle* for thought and problem solving. In the previous chapter we have seen that thinking in the sense of problem solving requires certain prerequisite intellectual skills, as well as cognitive strategies. These are the tools individuals possess that enable them to think clearly and precisely. How does one think "broadly"? How can a scientist, for example, think about the social problem of the isolation of aged people? Or how can a poet capture in words the essential conflict of youthful rebellion and alienation? It is not unlikely that problem solution in both instances depends upon the possession by these individuals of bodies of knowledge which are not special to their fields, but which are shared by many other people. The thinking that takes place is "carried" by the associations, metaphors, and analogies of language within these bodies of knowledge. The importance of a "knowledge background" for creative thought has been discussed by many writers, and in recent years by Polanyi (1958).

In summary, it is evident that a number of important reasons can be identified for the learning of information, whether this is conceived as facts, generalizations, or as organized bodies of meaningful knowledge. Factual information is needed in learning the increasingly complex intellectual skills of a subject or discipline. Such information may in part be looked up, but is often more conveniently stored in memory. Certain types and categories of factual information must be learned because it is necessary for communication pertaining to the affairs of everyday living. Information is often learned and remembered as organized bodies of knowledge. Specialized knowledge of this sort may be accumulated by the individual learner while pursuing a field of study or work. General knowledge, particularly that which reflects the cultural heritage, is often considered desirable or even essential in making possible the communications necessary for functioning as a citizen of a community or nation. In addition, however, it seems likely that such bodies of general knowledge become the carriers of thought for the human being engaged in reflective thinking and problem solving.

THE LEARNING OF INFORMATION

Information may be presented to the learner in various ways. It may be delivered to his ears in the form of oral communications, or to his eyes, mainly in the form of printed words, with or without accompanying pictures. There are many interesting questions for research relating to the effectiveness of communication media (Bretz, 1971), and some of their implications for instructional design will be discussed in the next chapter. At this point, however, we wish to attend to a different set of dimensions, which cut across those of the communications media. Information that is presented for learning may vary in amount and organization.

Some variations along these dimensions appear to be more important than others for the design of school instruction. From this point of view, it seems desirable to distinguish three kinds of learning situations. The first concerns the learning of *labels,* or *names.* A second pertains to the learning of isolated or *single facts,* which may or may not be parts of larger meaningful communications. The third kind of situation to be discussed is the learning of *organized information,* or knowledge.

Learning labels

To learn a label simply means to acquire the capability of making a consistent verbal response to an object or object class in such a way that it is "named." The verbal response itself may be of almost any variety—"X–1," "petunia," "pocket dictionary," or "spectrophotometer." Information in this form is simply a short *verbal chain.* Reference to the substantial body of research on the learning of verbal "paired-associates" may be found in many texts (e.g., Hulse, Deese, & Egeth, 1975; Jung, 1968).

Learning the name of an object in the sense of a label is quite distinct from learning the *meaning* of that name. The latter phrase implies the acquisition of a *concept,* which has also been described previously. Teachers are well-acquainted with the distinction between "knowing the name of something" and "knowing what the name means." A student knows a label when he can simply supply the name of a specific object. To know that object as a concept (that is, know its meaning) he or she must be able to identify examples and non-examples that serve to define and delimit the class.

In practice, a name for a concept is often learned at the time the concept itself is learned, or just prior to that time. Although the task of name-learning may be easy for one or two objects at a time, difficulty increases rapidly when several different names for several objects or many names for many objects must be learned at once. Such a situation arises in school learning when students are asked to acquire the names of a set of trees, a set of leaves, or the set of members in a president's cabinet. Students engaged in such tasks may accurately be said to be "memorizing" the names, but there is scarcely harm in that, and students often enjoy doing it. In any case, label learning is a highly useful activity. Among its other uses, it establishes the basis for communication between the learner and the teacher, or between the learner and a textbook.

Learning facts

A fact is a verbal statement that expresses a relation between two or more named objects or events. An example is, "That book has a blue cover." In normal communication, the relation expressed by the fact is assumed to exist in the natural world. Thus, the words which made up the fact have *referents* in the environment of the learner. The words refer to those objects and to the relation between them. In the example given, the objects are "book" and "blue cover" and the relation is "has." It is of some importance to emphasize that a fact, as employed here, is defined as the *verbal statement* and not the referent or referents to which it refers. (Alternative meanings of a common word like "fact" may readily be found in other contexts.)

Students learn a host of facts in connection with their studies in school. Some of these are isolated in the sense of being unrelated to other facts or bodies of information. Others form a part of a connected set, related to each other in various ways. For example, children may learn the fact "the town siren is sounded at noontime," and this may be a fairly isolated fact which is well remembered, even though not directly related to other information. Isolated facts may be learned and remembered for no apparent reason; in studying history, a student may learn and remember that Charles G. Dawes served as vice-president in the administration of Calvin Coolidge, and at the same time learn the names of other vice-presidents. More frequently, though, a specific learned fact is related to others in a total set, or to a larger body of information. For example, a student may learn a number of facts about Mexico, which are related to each other in the sense that they pertain to aspects of Mexico's geography, economy, or culture. Such facts may also be related to a larger body of information including facts about the culture, economy, and geography of other countries, including the student's native country.

Whether isolated or connected with a larger set, learned facts are of obvious value to the student, for two major reasons. The first is that they may be essential to everyday living. Examples are: the fact that many stores and banks are closed on Sunday; or the fact that molasses is sticky; or the fact that the student's birthday is the tenth of February. The second and more obvious reason for the importance of learned facts to students is that they are used in further learning. In order to learn to find the circumference of a circle, for example, one needs to know the value of *pi.* In order to complete a chemical equation, the student may need to know the valence of the element sodium.

With regard to the function of facts as elements in the learning of skills or additional information, it is evident that such facts *can* be looked up in convenient reference books or tables, at the time this further learning is about to take place. There are many instances in which "looking-up" may be a proper and desirable procedure. The alternative is for the student to learn the facts, and store them in his memory, so that he may then retrieve them whenever he needs them. This alternative is often chosen as a matter of convenience and efficiency. Facts that are likely to be used again and again might as well be stored in memory— the student would likely find the constant looking-up a nuisance. The designer of instruction, however, has the obligation of deciding which of a great many facts in a given course are (1) of such infrequent usage that they had better be looked up; (2) of such relatively frequent reference that learning them would be an efficient strategy; or (3) of such fundamental importance that they ought to be remembered for a lifetime.

Performance   The performance that indicates a fact has been learned consists of stating a relation between two or more named objects or events. The statement may be made either orally or in writing.

Internal Conditions   For acquisition and storage, an organized context of information needs to be recalled, and the newly acquired fact must be related to it. For example, in order to learn and remember that Mount Whitney is the highest peak in the continental United States, a larger meaningful context of information (which may differ for each individual learner) needs to be recalled, such as classification of mountain peaks and ranges or a set of categories of mountains in the United States. A visual image of the range of mountains that includes Mount Whitney may also be an integral component of this information (cf. Rohwer, 1970). The new fact is associated by the learner with this larger information context.

External Conditions   Externally, a verbal communication, picture, or other cue is presented to stimulate the recall of the larger body of meaningful information. The new fact is then presented, usually by means of a verbal statement. The external communication may also suggest the association to be acquired, as in conveying the idea that Mount Whitney "sticks up highest" in the Sierra Nevada range. Time needs to be allowed for the rehearsal of the new fact or repetition of it in the form of a spaced review.

Learning bodies of knowledge

Larger bodies of interconnected facts, such as those pertaining to periods of history or to categories of art, science, or literature, may also be learned and remembered. Essentially the same conditions apply to such learning as to that of single facts. Larger bodies of knowledge are organized from smaller units so that they form meaningful wholes. A new factual unit is apparently learned by being related to or incorporated into another set of factual information, which then becomes stored in memory in a newly combined form.

The key to remembering bodies of information appears to be one of having them *organized* in such a way that they can be readily retrieved (Ausubel, 1968; Mandler, 1967). The periodic table of chemical elements, for example, besides having a theoretical rationale, also helps students of chemistry to remember the names and properties of a large number of elements. Similarly, students of U.S. history may have acquired a framework of historical "periods" into which many individual facts can be fitted for learning and remembering. The more highly organized is this previously acquired information, the easier it is for a student to acquire and retain any given new fact which can be related to this organized structure.

Performance   The substance of paragraphs or longer passages of connected prose appear to be learned and retained in a way that preserves their *meaning*, but not necessarily the detailed component facts contained in them (Reynolds and

Flagg, 1977). The more general ideas appear to be recalled better than the more specific ones (Meyer, 1975). Details are often "constructed" by the learner, apparently in accordance with a general "schema" (Bartlett, 1932) which represents the gist of a story or passage.

Internal Conditions   As in the case of individual facts, the learning and storage of larger units of organized information occurs within a context of a body of meaningful information previously stored in the learner's memory. The importance of this pre-existing set of organized knowledge has been emphasized by Ausubel (1968), who considers that newly learned information is *subsumed* into the larger meaningful structure. Some information-processing theories of memory conceive of new information being stored by *linking* with a network of propositions already in the learner's memory (for references, see Gagné, 1977, pp. 196–197).

External Conditions   The external conditions which favor the learning and retention of bodies of information pertain primarily to the provision of *cues.* Such cues enable the learner to search successfully for the information at a later time, and thus to retrieve it for use. Cues need to be as *distinctive* as possible, in order to avoid interference among stored verbal ideas. They also need to be of a sort which are *strongly linked* with the information to be recalled. The cues may be within the learner's environment, as when parts of a room are used to recall the sequence of ideas in a speech. More frequently, though, the cues are themselves retrieved from the learner's memory as words, phrases, or images.

Another external condition which plays a part in the retention of meaningful prose is the adoption of an attentional *strategy* by the learner. Suggestions of "what to look for" or "what to remember" may be made to a learner before learning begins; these may have the effect of activating a cognitive strategy for learning. A suggestion may be given directly, or indirectly via questions inserted in a text (cf. Frase, 1970). Another method involves the use of an *advance organizer* (Ausubel, 1968), a brief passage given before the text to be learned, which has the effect of orienting the learner to what is to be remembered in a subsequent passage.

Repetition has long been known to have a marked effect on the remembering of information, and this is true whether one is dealing with isolated facts or with larger bodies of information. The effective employment of repetition, however, is in providing *spaced* occasions for the learner to *recall* the information he has learned. The processes put into effect when information is retrieved from memory are apparently the most important factors in the remembering of such information.

LEARNING ATTITUDES

It would be difficult to overemphasize the importance of attitudes in school learning. In the first place, as is so evident to the teacher, the student's attitudes toward attending school, toward cooperating with his teacher and his classmates, toward giving attention to the communications presented to him and toward the act of learning itself, are all of great significance in determining how readily he learns.

A second large class of attitudes are those that the school aims to establish or change as a result of school learning. Attitudes of tolerance and civility towards other individuals are often mentioned as goals of education in the schools. Positive attitudes towards the seeking and learning of new skills and knowledge are usually stated as educational goals of far-reaching importance for the individual. More specific likings for the various subjects of the school curriculum, such as science, literature, or music, are often conceived as objectives of high value within each subject area. And finally, there are the attitudes of broad generality, usually called *values*, to which schools may be expected to contribute and to influence. These are attitudes pertaining to such social behaviors as are implied by the words fairness, honesty, charitableness, and a number of others.

Regardless of the great variety exhibited by the content of these types of attitudes, one must expect that they all resemble each other in their formal properties. That is to say, whatever the particular content of an attitude, it functions to affect "approaching" or "avoiding." In so doing, an attitude influences a large set of specific behaviors of the individual. It is reasonable to suppose, then, that there are some general principles of learning that apply to the acquisition and changing of attitudes.

Definition of attitude

Attitudes are complex states of human beings which affect their behavior towards people, things, and events. Many investigators have studied, and emphasized in their writings, the conception of an attitude as a system of beliefs (Fishbein, 1965), or as a state arising from a conflict or disparity in beliefs (Festinger, 1957). These views serve to point out the *cognitive* aspects of attitudes. Other writers deal with their *affective* components, the feelings they give rise to or which accompany them, as in liking and disliking. Learning outcomes in the "affective domain" are described by Krathwohl, Bloom and Masia (1964).

For a number of reasons, including practical ones, it seems desirable in the present context to give emphasis to the aspect of attitudes relating to *action*. Acknowledging that an attitude may arise from some complex of beliefs, and that it may be accompanied and invigorated by emotion, the important question would appear to be, what action does it support? The general answer to this question is that an attitude influences *a choice of action* on the part of the individual. A definition of attitude, then, is *an internal state which affects an individual's choice of action toward some object, person, or event.*

Portions of this definition require some comments. An attitude is an *internal state,* inferred from observations (or often, from reports) of the individual's behavior; it is not the behavior itself. If one observes an individual depositing a gum wrapper in a waste basket, he cannot infer from that single instance alone that the individual has a positive attitude towards disposing of personal trash, or a negative attitude towards pollution, and certainly not his attitude towards gum wrappers. A number of instances of behavior of this general class, however, may occur in a number of different situations. Such instances make possible the inference that this person has a positive attitude toward the disposal of personal trash, or a negative attitude toward littering. The inference is that some internal state affects a whole class of specific instances, in each of which the individual is making a *choice.*

The choice the individual makes and which is inferred to be affected by the attitude is of a *personal action.* Thus he may choose to throw away a gum wrapper or to hold it until a trash basket is handy. He may choose to vote for a presidential candidate or to vote against him—the choice indicates his attitude. A student may choose to speak in a friendly manner to a classmate of another race or not to speak to him—again, an indicator which may (along with other instances) reveal his attitude. In following this definition, one does not ask the question, "What is this person's attitude toward black Americans," because that is altogether too general a question to be answered sensibly. Instead, one asks, "What is this person's attitude toward *working with* black people, or *living near* black people or *sitting beside* a black person?" It is the choice of a personal action in each case that is affected by an attitude. In connection with school learning, one may be interested in a student's attitude toward *reading* books, *doing* scientific experiments, *writing* stories, or *constructing* an art object.

This definition implies that attitudes should be measured in terms of the choices of personal action taken by the individual. In some instances, such measurement can be done by observation over a period of time. For example, a teacher may record her observations of an elementary pupil over a weekly period, recording the number of times he helps his classmates as opposed to interfering with their activities. (cf. Mager, 1968). A proportion of this sort, recorded over several such periods, can serve well as a measure of "attitude toward helping others." Of course, such direct indicators of choice cannot always be obtained. For example, the teacher would find it difficult to obtain behavioral measures of "attitude towards listening to classical music," or "attitude towards reading novels," because many choices in these areas are made outside of the school environment. Attitude measures are therefore frequently based upon "self-reports" of choices in situations described in questionnaires. Typical questions, for example, may ask the student to check the probability of his choice on a ten-point scale, when asked a variety of questions such as: "When choosing a book from the public library to read on a summer afternoon, how likely are you to pick a novel about adventure on the seas?" This method of attitude measurement, emphasizing choices of action, has been described in the work of Triandis (1964).

Attitude learning

The conditions favoring the learning of attitudes and the means of bringing about changes in attitudes are rather complex matters, about which much is yet to be discovered. Certainly the methods of instruction to be employed in establishing desired attitudes differ considerably from those applicable to the learning of intellectual skills and verbal information (Gagné, 1972, 1977).

How does the individual acquire or modify an internal state that influences his choices in a particular area of action? One way that this is *not* done, according to a great deal of evidence, is solely by the use of persuasive communication (McGuire, 1969). Perhaps most adults would recognize the ineffectiveness of repeated use of such maxims as "Be kind to others," or "Learn to appreciate good music," or "Drive carefully." Even more elaborate communications, however, often have equally poor effects, such as those which make emotional appeals or those which are developed by a careful chain of reasoning. Apparently, one must seek more sophisticated means than these of changing attitudes, and more elaborately specified conditions for attitude learning.

Direct Methods There are direct methods of establishing and changing attitudes, which sometimes occur naturally and without prior planning. On occasion, such direct methods can also be employed deliberately. At least, it is worthwhile to understand how attitude change can come about by these means.

A conditioned response of the classical sort (cf. Gagné, 1977, pp. 76–80) may establish an attitude of approach or avoidance toward some particular class of objects, events, or persons. Many years ago, Watson and Rayner (1920) demonstrated that a child could be conditioned to "fear" (that is, to shrink away from) a white rat he previously had accepted and petted. This type of response was also made to other small furry animals. The unconditioned stimulus used to bring about this marked change in the child's behavior was a sudden sharp sound made behind the child's head, when the animal (the conditioned stimulus) was present. While this finding may not have specific pedagogical usefulness, it is important to realize that attitudes can be established in this way, and that some attitudes which students bring to school with them may be dependent upon earlier conditioning experiences. A tendency to avoid birds, or spiders, or snakes, for example, may be instances of attitudes having their origin in a prior event of conditioning. In theory, almost any attitude might be established in this way.

Another direct method of attitude learning having more usefulness for school situations is based upon the idea of arranging *contingencies of reinforcement* (Skinner, 1968). If a new skill or element of knowledge to be learned is followed by some preferred or rewarding activity, in such a way that the latter is contingent upon achieving the former, this general situation describes the basic prototype of learning, according to Skinner. In addition, the student who begins with a "liking" for the second activity (called a "reinforcer") will, in the course of this act of learning, acquire a liking for the first task. Following this principle, one might make a preferred activity for an elementary pupil, such as examining a collection of pictures, contingent upon his asking to see the pictures by means of a complete sentence ("May I look at the pictures?") as opposed to asking by blurting out a single word ("Pictures?"). Continuation of this practice in a consistent way and in a variety of situations will likely result in the child's using complete sentences when he makes a request. He will also come to enjoy the newly learned way of asking for things, because he has experienced success in doing so. In other words, his attitude toward "using complete sentences" will take a positive turn.

Generalizing somewhat from this specific learning principle of reinforcement contingencies, it may be said that *success* in some learning accomplishment is likely to lead to a positive attitude toward that activity. The child or young person acquires a definitely positive attitude toward ice skating when he achieves some success at it. The student develops a positive attitude toward listening to classical music when he realizes he is able to recognize the musical forms or themes it contains.

An Important Indirect Method A method of establishing or changing attitudes of great importance and widespread utility for school learning is called *human modeling* (Bandura, 1969). Here this method is referred to as indirect because the chain of events that constitute the procedure for learning is longer than that required for "direct" methods. Furthermore, as its name implies, this method operates through the agency of another human being, real or imagined.

A student can observe and learn attitudes from many sorts of human models. In his younger years particularly, one or both parents serve as models for actions which may be classified as instances of fairness, sympathy, kindness, honesty, and many others. Other members of the family such as older siblings may play this role. When he attends school, one or more teachers may become models for behavior, and this possibility remains true from kindergarten through graduate school. But the varieties of human modeling do not stop at the school. Public figures may become models, or prominent sports people, or famous scientists or artists. It is not essential that people who function as human models be seen or known personally—they can be seen on television or in movies. In fact, they can even be read about in books. This latter fact serves to emphasize the enormous potential that literature has for the determination of attitudes and values.

The human model must, of course, be someone whom the learner *respects;* or as some writers would have it, someone with whom he can *identify.* The model must be observed (or read about) performing the desired kind of behavior. He may be exhibiting kindness, rejecting drugs, or cleaning up trash. A teacher "model" may be dispensing praise consistently and impartially. Having perceived the action, whatever it may be, the learner also must see that such action leads to satisfaction or pleasure on the part of the model. This step in the process is called *vicarious reinforcement* by Bandura (1969). A sports figure may receive an award or display his pleasure in breaking a record; a scientist may exhibit his satisfaction in discovering something new, or even in getting closer to such a discovery. The teacher may show that she is glad to have helped a slow-learning child to acquire a new skill.

The essential conditions for learning attitudes by human modeling are summarized in the following paragraphs.

Performance An attitude is indicated by the choice of a class of personal actions. These actions can be categorized as showing positive-to-negative tendencies toward some objects, events, or persons.

Internal Conditions An attitude of respect for or identification with the human model must preferably be already present in the learner. If it is not, it needs to be established as a first step in the process. Intellectual skills and knowledge related to the behavior exhibited by the model must have been previously acquired, in order for this behavior to be imitated. (For example, one could not expect a learner to acquire a positive attitude towards solving differential equations unless he at least has learned what differential equations are!)

External Conditions These may be described as a sequence of steps, as follows:

1. Presentation (or continued presence) of the respected human model.
2. Demonstration by the model, or description by the model, of the desirable behavior.
3. Demonstration by the model of pleasure or satisfaction with some outcome of his behavior. This is the step which is expected to lead to vicarious reinforcement on the part of the learner.

Of course, modification of these steps is possible when the human model is not directly seen and when the desired performance cannot be directly observed. The essential conditions may still be present when the learner is viewing television or reading a book.

The modification of attitudes undoubtedly takes place all the time in every portion of the student's daily life. Adult models with whom the student comes in contact bear a tremendous responsibility for the determination of socially desirable attitudes in him. The teacher obviously needs to appreciate the importance of his role as a human model, if for no other reason than the large proportion of time the student spends in his presence. It is likely that those teachers the student later remembers as "good teachers" are the ones who have modeled positive attitudes.

MOTOR SKILLS

Sequences of unitary motor responses are often combined into more complex performances called *motor skills.* Sometimes these are referred to as "perceptual-motor skills" or "psychomotor skills," but these phrases appear to carry no useful added meaning. They imply, of course, that the performance of motor skills involves the senses and the brain as well as the muscles; however, this fact is known.

Characteristics of motor skills

Motor skills are learned capabilities that underlie performances whose outcomes are reflected in the rapidity, accuracy, force, or smoothness of bodily movement. In the school, these skills are interwoven throughout the curriculum at every age, and include such diverse activities as using pencils and pens, writing with chalk, drawing pictures, painting, using a variety of measuring instruments, and of course, engaging in various physical games and sports. Basic motor skills such as printing numerals on paper are learned in early grades and assumed to be present thereafter. One does not expect a course in fifth-grade arithmetic to be concerned with motor skills learning, even though the students' performances in such a course are in fact dependent upon the basic motor skills learned earlier. In contrast, a motor skill like tying a bowline knot may not previously have been learned by a fifth-grader, and so would conceivably constitute a reasonable objective for instruction at that age or later.

The increased precision of smoothness and timing which result from practice of a motor performance are considered by Adams (1977) to be dependent upon *feedback,* both internal and external. Internal feedback takes the form of stimuli from muscles and joints that make up a "perceptual trace," a kind of motor image which acts as a reference against which the learner assesses his own error on successive practice trials. External feedback is often provided by "knowledge of results," an external indication to the learner of his degree of error. As practice proceeds, improvement in the skill comes to depend increasingly upon the internal type of feedback, and to a lesser degree upon externally provided knowledge of results.

Usually, motor skills can be divided into part-skills that compose the total performance in the sense that they occur simultaneously or in a temporal order. Swimming the crawl, for example, contains the part-skills of foot flutter and arm stroke, both of which are carried out at the same time; and also the part-skill of turning the head to breathe, which occurs in a sequence following an arm stroke. Thus the total performance of swimming is a highly organized and precisely timed activity. Learning to swim requires the integration of part-skills of various degrees of complexity, some of them as simple as motor chains. The *integration* of these parts must be learned, as well as the *component part-skills* themselves.

Learning to integrate part-skills which are already learned (to some degree, at least) has been recognized by investigators of motor skills as a highly significant aspect of the total learning required. Fitts & Posner (1967) refer to this component as an *executive sub-routine,* using a computer analogy to express its organizing function. Suppose, for example, an individual learning to drive an automobile has already mastered the part-skills of driving backward, of turning the steering wheel to direct the motion of the car, and of driving (forward or backward) at minimal speed. What does such a person still need to learn in order to turn the car around on a straight two-lane street? Evidently, he needs to learn a procedure in which these part-skills are combined in a suitable order, so that by making two or three backward and forward motions, combined with suitable turning, the car is headed in the other direction. This procedure is the executive sub-routine. It is obviously an intellectual kind of process which "tells" the driver what to do next. Thus the internal process is not in itself "motor" at all.

Swimming provides an interesting comparison. It, too, has an executive sub-routine pertaining to the timing of flutter kicks, arm movements, and head-turning to breathe. But in this case, the smooth performance of these part-skills is usually being improved by practice at the same time that the executive routine is being exercised. Many studies have been performed to find out whether practicing the part-skills of various motor skills first is advantageous over practicing the whole skill (including the executive sub-routine) from the outset (Naylor & Briggs, 1963). No clear answer has emerged from these studies, and the best one can say is that it depends on the skill; sometimes part-skill practice is an advantage, and sometimes not. It is clear, however, that *both* the executive sub-routine and the part-skills must be learned. Practice on either without the other has many times been shown to be ineffective for the learning of the total skill. A collection of studies dealing with these questions has been assembled by Singer (1972).

The relatively simple motor skill of printing the capital letter A is a school task that illustrates these principles well. Instruction may be concerned at some point with the part-skills of drawing diverging lines downward from a point, and of drawing a horizontal line segment which meets these lines without crossing them. Learning must also include the executive sub-routine of which movement is executed first, which second, and which third. The total skill, comprising the three principal part-skills, is integrated by means of this executive sub-routine.

Learning motor skills

The learning of motor skills is best accomplished by repeated practice. There is no easy way of avoiding practice if one seeks to improve the accuracy, speed, and smoothness of motor skills. In fact, it is interesting to note that practice continues to bring about improvement in motor skills over very long periods of time (Fitts and Posner, 1967, pp. 15–19), as performers in sports, music, and gymnastics are well aware.

Performance The performance of a motor skill is reflected in an action of bodily movement involving muscular activity. The action is observed to meet certain standards of speed, accuracy, force, or smoothness of execution.

Internal Conditions Presumably, the prior learnings that must be recalled for the learning of part-skills are simply the individual responses or motor chains which compose them. For learning executive sub-routines, concrete concepts of relevant bodily movements or subordinate part-activities must be recalled. For example, the concepts of "backing" and "turning" in an automobile must be previously acquired and recalled in order to enter into the learning of the sub-routine of "turning the car around on a street."

External Conditions For the improvement of accuracy, speed, and quality of *part-skills,* the individual engages in practice, repeating the movements required to produce the desired outcome in each case. The provision of informative feedback to the learner, which tells him how good each try has been, is an important accompaniment to such practice. For the learning of the *executive routine,* several different kinds of communications to the learner have been successfully employed. Sometimes verbal instructions are used ("Bend your knee and put the weight on your left foot"). A "checklist" showing the sequence of movements of part-skills can be presented to the learner, with the expectation that he will memorize it as he practices. Pictures or diagrams may be used to show the sequence of movements required. Finally, the *total skill,* in which all the parts are correctly sequenced, is also improved by practice with the accompaniment of informative feedback to the learner (Singer, 1975).

SUMMARY

The present chapter has been concerned with a description of three different kinds of learning—information, attitudes, and motor skills. While they have some features in common, their most notable characteristic is that they are in fact different. They differ, first, in the kinds of outcome performances which they make possible:

1. information—verbally stating facts or generalizations
2. attitude—choosing a course of personal action
3. motor skill—executing a performance of bodily movement

As our analysis of the conditions of learning for each of these types of capability has shown, they differ from each other markedly in the conditions necessary for their effective learning. For information, the key condition is the provision of a *larger meaningful context.* For attitude, such a context is of no great help; instead, one must provide either a directly reinforcing event, or depend upon *human modeling* to bring about vicarious reinforcement of the learner. And for the learning of motor skills, besides the provision for both part-skills and an integrating skill, the important condition is *practice* with frequent informative feedback to the learner.

The kinds of performances associated with these capabilities and the conditions of effective learning are also obviously different from those described in the previous chapter pertaining to intellectual skills. The latter have their own distinguishable learning conditions and learning outcomes. Are the types of learning dealt with in this chapter in some ways less important than intellectual skills? In most ways, they are surely not less important. The recall of information may certainly be a legitimate and desirable objective of instruction for many instances of school learning. The establishment of attitudes is widely acknowledged to be a highly significant objective of many courses of study, and some would probably accord it highest importance of all. Motor skills, although they often appear to contrast with the schools' "intellectual" orientation, individually have their own justification as fundamental components of basic skills, of art and music, of science, and of sports.

The contrasting features of these kinds of learned capabilities, as compared with those of intellectual skills, do not reside in their differing importance for school programs of instruction. Instead, these capabilities differ with respect to the internal conditions which must be assumed, and the external conditions which must be arranged, in order for instruction to be effective. Included in these differences is the subordinate-superordinate relationships that intellectual skills have with each other, as described in the previous chapter, and which is not shared by the other varieties of learned capabilities covered in this chapter. This characteristic has particular implications for the determination of desirable *sequences of instruction,* as will be seen in Chapter 8.

The system of instructional design being developed in this book is one which makes intellectual skills the central planning components. That is, the fundamental structures of instruction are designed in terms of what the student will be *able to do* when learning has occurred, and this capability is in turn related to what he has *previously learned to do.* This strategy of instructional design leads to the identification of intellectual skills as a first step, followed by analysis and identification of their prerequisites. To this basic sequence may then be added, at appropriate points, the cognitive strategies which these basic skills make possible. Also to be added as components of total instructional sequences are the information, attitudes, and motor skills that need to be acquired in meeting the objectives of educational programs.

The next section of the book addresses itself directly to procedures for designing instruction. In a large part, the techniques are derived from the kinds of knowledge of learning varieties which have been described, and represent direct applications of this knowledge.

References

Adams, J. A. Motor learning and retention. In M. H. Marx and M. E. Bunch (ed.), *Fundamentals and Applications of Learning.* New York: Macmillan, 1977.

Ausubel, D. P., Novak, J. D., and Hanesian, H. *Educational Psychology: A Cognitive View.* 2d. Ed. New York: Holt, Rinehart and Winston, 1978.

Bandura, A. *Principles of Behavior Modification.* New York: Holt, Rinehart and Winston, 1969.

Bartlett, F. C. *Remembering.* New York: Cambridge University Press, 1932.

Bretz, R. *A Taxonomy of Communication Media.* Englewood Cliffs, N. J.: Educational Technology Publications, 1971.

Festinger, L. *A Theory of Cognitive Dissonance.* New York: Harper & Row, 1957.

Fishbein, M. A consideration of beliefs, attitudes, and their relationships. In I. D. Steiner and M. Fishbein (ed.), *Current Studies in Social Psychology.* New York: Holt, Rinehart and Winston, 1965.

Fitts, P. M., and Posner, M. I. *Human Performance.* Monterey, Calif.: Brooks/Cole, 1967.

Frase, L. T. Boundary conditions for mathemagenic behavior. *Review of Educational Research,* 1970, *40,* 337–347.

Gagné, R. M. *The Conditions of Learning,* 3d Ed. New York: Holt, Rinehart and Winston, 1977.

Gagné, R. M. Domains of learning. *Interchange,* 1972, *3,* 1–8.

Hulse, S. H., Deese, J., and Egeth, H. *The Psychology of Learning.* New York: McGraw-Hill, 1975.

Jung, J. *Verbal Learning.* New York: Holt, Rinehart and Winston, 1968.

Krathwohl, D. R., Bloom, B. S., and Masia, B. B. *Taxonomy of Educational Objectives. Handbook II: Affective Domain.* New York: McKay, 1964.

Mager, R. F. *Developing Attitude toward Learning.* Belmont, Ca.: Fearon, 1968.

Mandler, G. Organization and memory. In K. W. Spence and J. T. Spence (ed.), *The Psychology of Learning and Motivation,* Vol. 1. New York: Academic Press, 1967.

McGuire, W. J. The nature of attitudes and attitude change. In G. Lindzey and E. Aronson, *Handbook of Social Psychology,* 2d Ed., Vol. 3. Reading, Mass.: Addison-Wesley, 1969.

Meyer, B. J. F. *The Organization of Prose and its Effects on Memory.* New York: Elsevier, 1975.

Naylor, J. C., and Briggs, G. E. Effects of task complexity and task organization on the relative efficiency of part and whole training methods. *Journal of Experimental Psychology,* 1963, *65,* 217–224.

Polanyi, M. *Personal Knowledge.* Chicago: University of Chicago Press, 1958.

Reynolds, A. G., and Flagg, P. W. *Cognitive Psychology.* Cambridge, Mass.: Winthrop, 1977.

Rohwer, W. D., Jr. Images and pictures in children's learning: Research results and educational implications. *Psychological Bulletin,* 1970, *73,* 393–403.

Singer, R. N. *Psychomotor Domain: Movement Behavior.* Philadelphia: Lea & Febiger, 1972.

Singer, R. N. *Motor Learning and Human Performance,* 2d Ed. New York: Macmillan, 1975.

Skinner, B. F. *The Technology of Teaching.* New York: Appleton, 1968.

Triandis, H. C. Exploratory factor analyses of the behavioral component of social attitudes. *Journal of Abnormal and Social Psychology,* 1964, *68,* 420–430.

Watson, J. R., and Rayner, R. Conditioned emotional reactions. *Journal of Experimental Psychology,* 1920, *3,* 1–14.

PART THREE

DESIGNING INSTRUCTION

In this part of the book we move on from initial planning to the work of design itself. Once the goals of a course or curriculum have been determined, there follows a series of design steps directed toward the organization of courses into their major units or topics, and eventually into the form of statements of end-of-course performance objectives. These objectives are further analyzed in order to identify the essential prerequisite skills which must be learned before the target objectives can be mastered. Learning hierarchies are constructed to display the essential prerequisites for each intellectual skill objective. Objectives representing other domains of outcomes can then be integrated into the total plan for sequences of lessons or instructional modules.

Chapter 6 describes how analysis of major tasks to be learned can result in identification of two kinds of enabling objectives—the essential prerequisite skills and the supporting enabling objectives. Chapter 7 presents a method of defining performance objectives so as to be able to use them as unambiguous guides for the design of lessons and for the assessment of student performance following instruction.

Chapter 8 considers the problem of sequencing, and shows that such questions must be faced in four stages of design, from the order of major units or topics to the events within a single lesson. Chapter 9 deals with the events of instruction to be achieved. The following chapters indicate how these events are implemented when teams design instructional materials (Chapter 10), and when teachers design lessons (Chapter 11). Continuing the theme of objectives as an organizing principle, Chapter 12 considers methods for assessing student performance. Particular attention is given to assessment methods appropriate for each type of capability to be learned.

chapter 6

Analysis of the Learning Task

Designing instruction for a course or topic must surely begin with an idea of the purpose of what is being designed. The greatest clarity in conception of the outcomes of instruction is achieved when human performances are described. The question initially asked by the designer is not, "What will students be studying?" but rather, "What will students be doing after they have learned?" This means that design begins with a consideration of *instructional objectives.*

In describing a procedure for instructional design, it is difficult to decide whether *all* of the objectives (of a course or topic) should be specified as a first step, or only *some* of them. This difficulty arises because there are at least two kinds of instructional objectives involved in instructional design: (1) those to be attained at the end of a course study; and (2) those which must be attained during a course of study because they are prerequisites to the former type. The first kind may be called *target objectives,* and the second *enabling objectives.* In a course in reading, "comprehending prose paragraphs" is a target objective. Contributing to this objective in an enabling sense is the performance of "inferring the meaning of unfamiliar printed words from context."

The procedure adopted for description here is one that begins with the *target objectives* of a course or topic. It is these target objectives which are subject to *task analysis* as discussed in this chapter. A method of making precise descriptions of instructional objectives, both target and enabling, is contained in the next chapter. The ordering of these chapters reflects an important fact about the procedures of instructional design—instructional objectives must be *defined* clearly, and they must also be *analyzed.* It is difficult to say, for all cases, which of these procedures needs to be done first. This chapter deals with analysis, and assumes that the target objectives of a course or topic can be specified as indicated in the following chapter.

INITIAL APPROACHES TO DEFINING OBJECTIVES

As previous chapters have shown, there are several different kinds of human capabilities that reflect the outcomes of learning of educational programs. Any and all of them occur within each content area such as science, social studies, mathematics, language. How does one go about sorting these out in relation to the planning of any particular course of study? How does one tell whether a topic called "mixed numerical operations" or "composition of complex sentences" or "appraising the construction of building foundations" includes concepts, rules, information, or attitudes? We have seen that these types of intellectual processing make a difference in the planning of conditions for learning, including the determination of sequences in which they are learned. How can one find out, then, what human capabilities are included in a topic or a course?

The process of determining what capabilities are to be learned begins with the defining of *target objectives.* This is not necessarily an easy thing to do, and it needs to be approached in several stages. Most teachers believe they know what their objectives are, or what the objectives of any given lesson are. And in a general sense, they usually do. In order to be useful for instructional planning, however, objectives need to be defined in rather precise terms. The major reason is that language can be terribly misleading—commonly used words can mean very different things to different people. Carefully defined objectives, however, should have only a single meaning, and it should be the same meaning for all literate persons. Accordingly, they must have a somewhat *technical* meaning, conveying precise information about human performance.

Identifying course purposes

It seems desirable to begin the search for precisely stated objectives by attempting to identify the *purposes* of the course. At this point, one need not necessarily worry about achieving a truly communicable meaning—only one which satisfies the person who is trying to formulate the objectives. But even at this stage, there are some standards to be met and some pitfalls to be avoided. These are as follows:

1. The statement of the purpose of a course should be concerned with what the student will be like *after* the instruction, not what he is doing *during* the course. For example, a novice instructional designer might present the following as a statement of purpose: "to provide the student with experience in the identification of birds of the region." Now, obviously, this may be a statement of what is going to go on during the course—the student is going to "experience" birds and their identification. But the question is, what is the *purpose* of such experience? What does one expect of the student after the course? The chances are that the purpose might be expressed as "ability to identify common birds of the region." Notice the latter statement comes much closer to telling *what the student will be able to do following the instruction.*

2. The second tendency to avoid is that of stating purposes which are too far removed, too much in the future. Purposes should be stated in terms of the

expected current outcomes of instruction, not the more distant future ones. Here is an example of this kind of pitfall: "Students will acquire a lifelong respect for the importance of conserving natural wildlife." Now, perhaps one really does believe such a lifelong respect is valuable and desirable. But this does not make such a goal a legitimate purpose for a course. It is, in fact, quite presumptuous to think that such "lifelong respect" can be established by a single unit of instruction. If respect of this sort is going to be established, it will surely be the result of many influences. Accordingly, it is necessary to say to oneself, "That is all well and good, but in what way is the course going to contribute to that very general goal? Would the student acquire this lifelong respect just as readily *without* this course? If not, what, specifically, is being contributed by this course?" At this point, one is obviously brought back to the task of defining the purpose of the individual course in specific terms. Possibly it may turn out to be something like the following: "Students will be able to identify instances in which a lack of wildlife conservation has produced undesirable social consequences." Such a purpose would be quite appropriate for a course.

In summary, the initial try at defining objectives will probably be most sucessful if it is a statement of the *purpose* of a course. Such a statement should reflect what the student will be expected to be able to do following the course. The statement of purpose is grossly deficient if it states only some distant future goal (even though such a goal may itself be perfectly valid and desirable) without identifying the proximal expected outcome of the course. The purpose of instruction concerns what the student will be like *after* instruction, not what happens during instruction.

At this stage of developing a precise definition, the following kinds of statements appear to be quite acceptable as course purposes:

Understands the principle of commutativity in multiplication.
Is aware of tonal differences in the sounds of violin, viola, and cello.
Comprehends the idea of nationality.
Reads with enjoyment short stories with simple plots.

As will be seen in the next chapter, target objectives such as these can be given additional clarity by adding the details reflected in the following definitions:

Given numerical expressions of the form A $\times$ B, identifies them as equivalent to numerical expressions of the form B $\times$ A.
Given the presentation of a simple melodic passage of two bars, identifies the instrument as violin, viola, or cello.
Given positive and negative examples of named nationalities, classifies each in accordance with a definition.
Given a variety of prose items during an enforced waiting period, chooses to read short stories with simple plots.

In undertaking task analysis, the additional precision of meaning provide by such expanded statements is often necessary. Here, we shall assume that target objectives, even when stated more briefly as course purposes, can readily be transposed into their expanded form.

TYPES OF TASK ANALYSIS

Three different kinds of *analysis* may be performed on the target objectives of topics or courses. Each of these is undertaken for a different purpose, yet each serves the general aim of identifying and classifying the components of target objectives. The three kinds of analysis are as follows (Gagné, 1977b):

1. *Information-processing analysis.* Such analysis is carried out by identifying the sequence of decisions and associated actions involved in a performance that is a target objective. The resulting description provides a kind of flow-chart of the operations which make up the targeted performance, including the mental operations involved. Such a chart reveals components of the total performance which themselves must be treated as target objectives.
2. *Task classification.* Once target objectives have been identified, they can then be classified into one or more of the varieties of learning described in previous chapters—intellectual skill, cognitive strategy, information, attitude, or motor skill. The purpose of such classification is to indicate the necessary conditions for learning. In this case, it is not the target objectives that are being "analyzed"; rather, they are being classified to provide an analysis of instructional requirements.
3. *Learning task analysis.* Target objectives, including those which may have been revealed by an information-processing analysis, need to be further analyzed to reveal their prerequisites. These are the enabling objectives which enter into the planning of instruction in the sense that they imply instructional sequences.

On the whole, then, it is apparent that a good deal of analysis must be done for the purpose of instructional planning. Three different kinds of analysis are needed, each beginning with target objectives. From these analyses, one may expect to discover and delineate: (1) the component "steps" involved in the performances which have been identified as target objectives; (2) the kind of learning represented by the target objectives, which will indicate required conditions for learning; and (3) the prerequisites of the target objectives, which, since they must be previously learned, imply a sequence for instruction.

INFORMATION-PROCESSING ANALYSIS

Basically, an information-processing analysis of a target performance is simply a description of the sequence of steps involved in that performance. One can imagine making such a description for a very simple automatic act like eating ice cream, as follows:

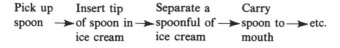

Actually, such an analysis would not be particularly revealing in the performance of a normal person more than five years old. It may be of more than passing interest, though, to note that such an analysis might indeed be useful in planning instruction for a young child, or for a mentally retarded older child. In such instances, the targeted skill of "eating ice cream" needs to be understood as containing the component steps of "picking up spoon," "inserting tip of spoon in ice cream," and so forth. Each of these components, as well as the total sequence, becomes a *target objective* in instructional planning.

A common performance like making sentences with indefinite pronouns as subjects may also be seen to comprise a series of steps such as the following:

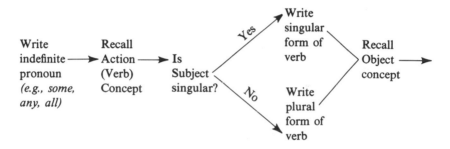

Such a sequence is a bit more complicated than that for eating ice cream, because it involves *choice,* and the *alternative actions* the choice implies. Information-processing analysis goes beyond the observed overt behavior (such as recalling a verb, and making a decision whether to use a singular or plural form). No doubt this accounts for the name of this method of analysis as "information-processing." The distinction between *choice* and *action* implies that a diagram of the resulting analysis needs to identify more than a series of steps—it needs to distinguish different kinds of steps. Thus, a more traditionally represented flow-chart would be one like that of Figure 6–1.

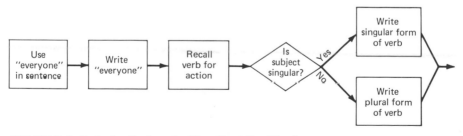

FIGURE 6–1   Beginning Portion of a Flow-Chart Resulting from an
Information-Processing Analysis of the Target Objective: Writing
Sentences with the Pronoun "Everyone" as Subject

Although the conventions of such flow-charts vary, the symbol of a trapezoid is often used to represent an *input,* a rectangle an *action,* and a diamond a choice or *decision.*

Some examples

A flow-diagram resulting from an information-processing analysis of the task of subtracting two-place numbers is illustrated in Figure 6–2.

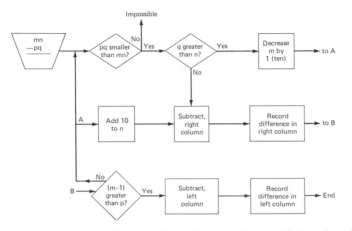

FIGURE 6–2   An Information-Processing Analysis of the Subtraction of Two-Place
Numbers

(From R. M. Gagné, Analysis of objectives. In L. J. Briggs (Ed.), Instructional Design. *Englewood Cliffs, N.J.: Educational Technology Publications, Copyright, 1977. Reproduced by permission of the copyright owner.*

Information-processing diagrams of a number of other tasks in mathematics learning are described by Resnick (1976) and by Greeno (1976). An analysis of reading, including both decoding and comprehension skills, has been made by Resnick and Beck (1977). The application of this type of analysis to the familiar task of balancing a checkbook has been described by Merrill (1971), and is shown in its initial stages in Figure 6–3.

Uses of information-processing analyses

Two primary kinds of information useful to instructional design are yielded by information-processing analyses. First, such an analysis and the diagram which results from it provide a clear description of the *target objective,* including the steps involved in the procedure. Figure 6–3, for example, describes the performance of checkbook balancing in a way that reveals its sequential steps. This is a description which conveys more information than the objective statement, "Given a set of cancelled checks and bank deposit slips, identifies correspondences and discrepancies in amounts shown in check stubs, to obtain a dollar and cent balance." A flow-chart of the procedure makes it possible for the instruc-

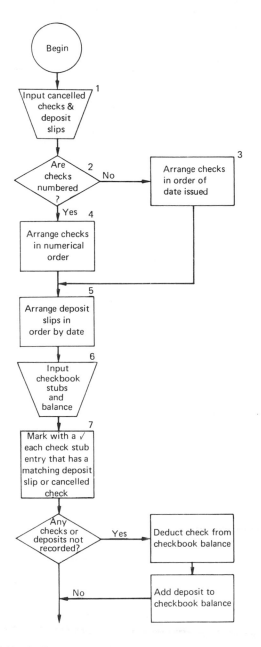

FIGURE 6–3 A Vertically Arranged Flow-Chart of Initial Steps in Reconciling a Bank
Statement with Checkbook Records

(Reproduced from Gagné, R. M. The Conditions Of Learning, *3d ed. New York: Holt, Rinehart and Winston, 1977. By permission of the copyright owner, Holt, Rinehart and Winston. Original drawing from P. F. Merrill,* Task Analysis: An Information Processing Approach. *Technical Memo No. 27. Tallahassee: Florida State University, CAI Center, 1971.)*

103

tional designer to specify the sequence of the target performance for presentation to the learner.

A second use of information-processing analysis arises from its revelation of individual steps that may not otherwise be obvious. This is particularly true of the decision steps, since they are, after all, instances of internal processing rather than of overt behavior. For example, the decisions indicated by the diagram of Figure 6–2 imply that the learner must be able to distinguish the larger from the smaller of two numbers, in order to carry out the task of subtraction. This is, then, a specific skill that must be acquired if it is not known already. It becomes one of the target objectives which make up the total task of subtracting two-place numbers.

2. CLASSIFYING TASKS

The instructional analysis that results in *task classification* begins with the target objectives of a lesson, topic, or course. These objectives may be derived simply from a list of course purposes, or in a more detailed fashion from an information-processing analysis, as described in the previous section. As implied by its name, task classification is not intended to make a finer-grained analysis of the performances which are identified as target objectives. Rather, it seeks to assign these performances to categories having distinctive implications for the conduct of instruction.

Categorizing tasks to be learned

The categories to which target tasks may be assigned for purposes of instructional planning are those described in previous chapters—intellectual skills, cognitive strategies, information, attitudes, and motor skills. The definitions of these categories, and examples of tasks corresponding to each, are given in Table 6–1. As Gagné (1977b, pp. 264–265) points out, overt behavior exhibited in a task does not determine the category to which it belongs. Instead, one must infer the type of *mental processing* required for the task, in accordance with the descriptions contained in Chapters 4 and 5, and as briefly summarized in the table.

Subordinate categories of *intellectual skills* are described in Table 6–1, beginning with discrimination and progressing through higher-order rules. It will be apparent that these subcategories, although clearly different, nevertheless all pertain to the kind of capability that makes it possible for the individual to demonstrate that he "knows how" to do something. In turn, these intellectual skills are quite different from such capabilities as stating something (*information*) or choosing a course of action (*attitude*).

Uses of task categories

The classification of tasks has a singular usefulness in the process of instructional design. The resulting categories, considered as capabilities to be learned, require different sets of *conditions* for their optimal learning, as described in

TABLE 6-1   Examples of Tasks Reflected in Target Objectives and the Learning
Categories They Represent

Task	Learning Category
Discriminates printed letters *g* and *p*	*Intellectual skill* (discrimination)—perceiving objects as same or different
Identifies *ovate* shape of tree leaves	*Intellectual skill* (concrete concept)—identifying an object property
Classifies *citizens* of a nation, by definition	*Intellectual skill* (defined concept)—using a definition to identify a class
Demonstrates instances of the rule relating pressure and volume of a gas at constant temperature	*Intellectual skill* (rule)—applying a rule to one or more concrete examples
Generates a rule predicting the inflationary effect of decreasing value of currency in international exchange	*Intellectual skill* (higher-order rule)—generating a more complex rule by combining simpler rules
Originates a written composition on the cybernetic features of a bureaucracy	*Cognitive strategy*—inventing a novel approach to a problem
States the main kinds of fire extinguishers and their uses	*Information*—communicating organized knowledge in a way that preserves meaning
Chooses reading novels as a leisure-time activity	*Attitude*—choosing a course of personal action toward a class of events
Executes the tightening of a lag screw with a socket wrench	*Motor skill*—carrying out a smoothly timed motor performance

Chapters 4 and 5. Accordingly, appropriate learning conditions can be used as a primary basis for the design of instruction.

The systematic knowledge we have about varieties of learning has direct implications for instruction. For example, we saw in the previous chapter that new *information* is learned by being related to a larger meaningful context of organized knowledge. When information is to be learned, the implications for instruction are that (1) provision needs to be made for either establishing or stimulating recall of the "meaningful context;" and (2) verbal or other cues need to be employed which will serve as "links" between the newly learned information and a previously acquired context of knowledge. The relation between learning conditions of various types of target objectives and the design of instruction is to be described and further elaborated in later chapters.

3. LEARNING TASK ANALYSIS

The target objectives that are identified for lessons or courses may be subjected to still another kind of analysis, called *learning task analysis*. This type is normally undertaken after the completion of one or both of the procedures previously described—information-processing analysis and task classification. Learning task analysis is of particular importance to instructional design, because it is the means of identifying *prerequisites* of what is to be learned. Thus one is able to progress from target objectives to *enabling objectives*. Both of these types of objectives must be incorporated into designed instruction.

In its most general meaning a *prerequisite* is a task which is learned prior to the learning of a target objective, and which then "aids" or "enables" that learning. Any given task may, of course, be a target objective for a particular lesson, and at the same time an enabling objective for a subsequent lesson, because it is a prerequisite of the task to be learned in the latter lesson. For example, the target objective of finding the diagonal distance across a rectangular piece of land obviously has as prerequisites the skills of (1) measuring the distances along the sides of the rectangle, and (2) applying the rule for computation of the hypotenuse of a right triangle. These two enabling capabilities may have been learned some years prior to the lesson designed to teach the target objective (finding the diagonal distance), or they may have been learned at an immediately prior time, as during the same lesson.

Types of prerequisites

An enabling objective may describe a prerequisite which is *essential,* as illustrated in the task just described. Alternatively, an enabling objective may designate a merely *supportive* prerequisite (Gagné, 1977b).

Examples of essential prerequisites may be found by analyzing the task of "supplying the definite article" for a noun in writing a sentence in the German language. In acquiring such a capability, a student must learn the prior tasks of (1) identifying gender, (2) identifying number (singular or plural), and (3) applying grammatical rules of case. Such capabilities may have been learned as a result of formal instruction, or in an incidental fashion by experience with the language. However, the latter possibility is not a relevant fact if one is concerned with the design of systematic instruction. What is relevant is that these "subordinate" capabilities are actually *part of* the total skill of supplying the definite article. This means that they are *essential* prerequisites, not merely helpful or supportive. These component skills must be learned if the total task of supplying the definite article is to be learned and performed correctly. Early or late in the course of instruction, they must be acquired *prior to* the learning of the objective.

An enabling objective (or prerequisite) may, in contrast, be simply supportive. This means that the prerequisite may aid the new learning by making it easier or faster. For example, a positive attitude toward learning to compose proper German sentences may have been acquired by the learner because of an anticipated visit to Germany. Such an attitude is likely to be helpful to the learner of the language. In other words, it is *supportive* of the learning, although not essential. Another example is provided by the possibility that the learner has previously acquired a *cognitive strategy* for remembering the gender of German nouns. Such a strategy might involve associating each newly encountered noun with a visual image representing, respectively, "masculine," "feminine," or "neuter." Again, such a strategy could be a *supportive* prerequisite because it makes learning easier or faster.

For each category of task (as identified by task classification), one can identify both essential and supportive prerequisites. However, these prerequisites are considerably different in character for each task category. Keeping these differences straight is important for instructional design. This is one of the major reasons for conducting task classification, and for determining such task categories before one attempts to identify prerequisites. In the following sections, our discussion of prerequisites begins with those that are essential, and proceeds to describe some that are supportive.

PREREQUISITES IN LEARNING INTELLECTUAL SKILLS

Intellectual skills, like other kinds of learning, are affected by both essential and supportive prerequisites. For this class of learning task, however, essential prerequisites are particularly evident, and also likely to be directly involved in the planning of individual lessons.

Essential prerequisites for intellectual skills

A target objective representing an intellectual skill can typically be composed of two or more "subordinate" and simpler skills. These latter skills are prerequisite to the learning of the target skill, in the sense that they must be learned first, before the target skill is "put together." The prior learning of prerequisites may have occurred some considerable time previously. Often, though, it occurs just prior to the learning of the target skill, within the same lesson.

An example of the meaning of essential prerequisites is provided by Gagné (1977a) for the task of *subtracting whole numbers.* Such a task may be represented by problems like the following:

(a) 473   (b) 2132   (c) 953   (d) 7204
     −342   −1715   −676   −5168

A commonly taught method of performing subtraction is by "borrowing," and we assume that is the method to be learned as part of the target skill. The four examples illustrate four prerequisite skills (rules) which are involved in the skill of subtracting whole numbers. Example (a), the simplest, is "subtracting one-place numbers in successive columns, without borrowing." Example (b) is "subtracting when several borrowings are required, in nonadjacent columns." Example (c) may be described as "successive borrowing in adjacent columns;" borrowing must be done in the first column on the right, so that 6 can be subtracted from 13, and again in the next column, so that 7 can be subtracted from 14. Example (d) is the prerequisite skill "borrowing across zero."

Each of these prerequisite skills represents a rule that is involved in the total skill of subtracting whole numbers. The latter task cannot be learned in any complete sense without the prior learning of these subordinate skills. They therefore deserve to be called *essential* prerequisites.

Other examples of prerequisites for intellectual skills may be found by examining the results of the information-processing analyses described earlier in this chapter. The analysis of subtraction, of course, includes the "borrowing" skill which is comparable to Example (a). Balancing a checkbook (Figure 6–2) may be seen to require the prerequisite skills of (a) arranging numbered slips in sequential order; (b) arranging dates in sequential order; (c) subtracting dollars and cents; and (d) adding dollars and cents. When the objective is writing sentences with the subject "everyone," the essential prerequisites indicated by the diagram of Figure 6–1 are (a) identifying verb names for actions and (b) using rules to make verbs singular or plural.

Hierarchies of prerequisite skills   While learning task analysis is often concerned with the prerequisites of a target skill, the analysis may be applied to the enabling skills as well, since these skills themselves have prerequisites. Accordingly, it is possible to continue the learning task analysis until a point is reached at which the skills identified are quite simple (and perhaps assumed to be known by all students).

When a learning task analysis is carried out on successively simpler components of a target skill, the result is a *learning hierarchy* (Gagné, 1977b). This outcome may be displayed as a diagram containing "boxes" describing the successively identified subordinate skills (i.e., essential prerequisite skills). Figure 6–4 is an example of a learning hierarchy for the target objective of "subtracting whole numbers." At a first "level" of analysis, this learning hierarchy incorporates the four prerequisite skills involved in subtracting, as described in the previous section (numbered VII, VIII, IX, and X). Proceeding from that point, analysis makes possible the identification of the simpler skill VI, "subtracting when a single borrowing is required, in any column." This can readily be perceived as an essential prerequisite to the more complex skills of "borrowing" (VIII, IX, and X). Skill VI, however, may also be analyzed to reveal the prerequisites described in the boxes labeled IV and V. The process may be continued to the level of simple subtraction "facts" (I).

The learning hierarchy produced by a learning task analysis displays a pattern of progressively simpler intellectual skills. These skills are enabling objectives for a given target objective (which is also an intellectual skill). Furthermore, any particular skill, which may itself be an enabling objective for a target skill, is composed of other subordinate skills.

When instructional design interest centers upon an intellectual skill as an objective, the enabling skills of primary relevance are the immediate prerequisites. Thus, the most important questions to be answered by a learning task analysis come from only two adjacent "levels" of the learning hierarchy. Is there, then, any usefulness to the display of the entire pattern of enabling skills, involving several "levels"? The main uses for a fully worked-out learning hierarchy are (1) as a guide in the design of a sequence of instruction (Cook and Walbesser, 1973), and (2) as a guide for student and teacher in the planning of instructional

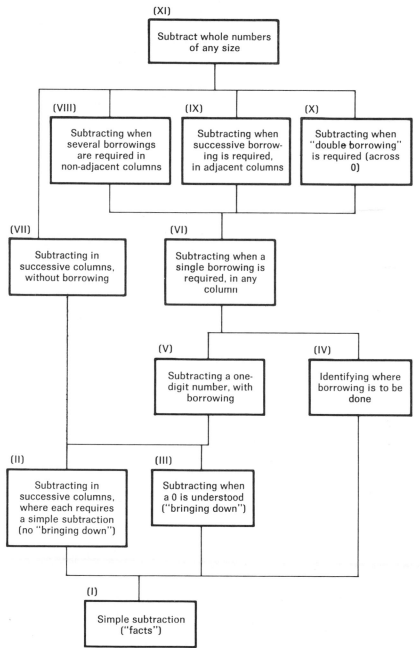

SUBTRACTION

(XI)
Subtract whole numbers of any size

(VIII)
Subtracting when several borrowings are required in non-adjacent columns

(IX)
Subtracting when successive borrowing is required, in adjacent columns

(X)
Subtracting when "double borrowing" is required (across 0)

(VII)
Subtracting in successive columns, without borrowing

(VI)
Subtracting when a single borrowing is required, in any column

(V)
Subtracting a one-digit number, with borrowing

(IV)
Identifying where borrowing is to be done

(II)
Subtracting in successive columns, where each requires a simple subtraction (no "bringing down")

(III)
Subtracting when a 0 is understood ("bringing down")

(I)
Simple subtraction ("facts")

FIGURE 6–4 A Learning Hierarchy for Subtracting Whole Numbers

assignments (Glaser, 1976). Both of these uses are to be described more fully in Chapter 8.

Conducting a Learning Task Analysis for Intellectual Skills   Intellectual skill analysis is carried out by "working backwards" from a target skill. Obviously, the purpose of the analysis is to reveal the *simpler component skills* which comprise the target skill. Often there is a correspondence at the first level of analysis between the component "steps" resulting from an information-processing analysis and the component "skills" revealed by a learning task analysis. But the distinction between sequential steps and subordinate skills should be carefully maintained. The steps are what an individual *does* in sequence when exhibiting a target performance, the capability of which has been learned. In contrast, the subordinate skills are what the individual must *learn,* in a sequence beginning with the simplest.

Subordinate skills are derived by asking the question of any given intellectual skill: "What simpler skill(s) would a learner have to possess in order to learn this skill?" (Gagné, 1977b, pp. 271–273). Once the first set of subordinate (enabling) skills is identified, the process may be repeated by addressing the same question to each of these. Of course, the subordinate skills so generated become simpler and simpler. Normally, the process stops at a point which is determined pragmatically. One decides, on the basis of knowledge about student characteristics, that the skills at the lowest "level" of the hierarchy are already known and do not have to be learned. Naturally, this "stopping point" varies with the educational background of the students. A learning hierarchy on grammatical rules in a foreign language, for example, would have many more "levels" for students who had learned few grammatical rules of their native language, than for students who had learned many of these rules.

Supportive prerequisites for intellectual skills

A number of kinds of learning, when undertaken on a prior basis, may be *supportive* in the acquisition of an intellectual skill. This means that the previously acquired capabilities may be helpful, although not essential, for the learning of a target skill.

Verbal information, for example, is often useful to the learner in acquiring intellectual skills, presumably because it facilitates the verbal communications which are a part of instruction. Some good examples of the relation of verbal information to the learning of an intellectual skill occur in a study by White (1974). White developed and validated a learning hierarchy for the intellectual skill "finding velocity at a prescribed point on a curved graph relating position (of an object) and time." In its initially derived form, the trial hierarchy included capabilities of the *information* sort, such as "states that the slope of a p–t graph is velocity," and "states units of slope in units labeling axes." The results of White's investigation showed that while these capabilities may have been helpful for intellectual skill learning, they did not reveal themselves as being *essential.* In this, they contrasted markedly with other subordinate components of the intellectual skill category. Further verification of the supportive nature of information, contrasting with prerequisites that are essential, is provided in a study by White and Gagné (1978).

The instructional designer may find it desirable to take into account several kinds of supportive prerequisites. Depending on other circumstances, these may be introduced into a single lesson, or they may be given a place in the sequence of a topic or course. The major possibilities of supportive prerequisites for intellectual skill learning would appear to be as follows:

Information as Supportive Prerequisites   As our previous example illustrates, information may support the learning of intellectual skills by aiding the communication of instruction. Often, examples of this function take the form of *labels* for the concepts involved in rule learning. Another possible function of verbal information is as a *context* providing cues for retrieval of the intellectual skill (Gagné, 1977b, pp. 200–201). Normally, when intellectual skills are being learned, a fair amount of information is included at the same time (see, for example, any typical science textbook). Presumably, a supportive function is being performed by the latter sort of material. The circumstance to be avoided in design is not the "mixing" of intellectual skills and information during instruction, but the potential confusion of these two types of learning as target objectives.

Cognitive Strategies as Supportive Prerequisites   The learning of intellectual skills may be aided in a supportive sense by the use of cognitive strategies. For example, if learners of "adding positive and negative integers" have available the cognitive strategy of imagining a "number line," their learning of the requisite rules may be facilitated. Generally speaking, cognitive strategies may speed the learning of intellectual skills, make them easier to recall, or aid their transfer to novel problems. While these actions of cognitive strategies have broad acceptance, it must be said that empirical evidence on the effectiveness of their support is as yet scanty, and is still sorely needed.

Attitudes as Supportive Prerequisites   The supportive effect of positive attitudes on the learning of intellectual skills is widely recognized. Presumably, the attitudes a learner has toward a subject of study strongly influences the ease with which the subject is learned, retained, and put to use (Mager, 1968). The relation between positive attitude and learning may often be readily observed in students' conduct toward a subject like mathematics. Evidence concerning the effects of "affective entry characteristics" on achievement in school subjects is reviewed by Bloom (1976).

LEARNING TASK ANALYSIS AND OTHER LEARNING TYPES

The rationale of learning task analysis can also be brought to bear on learning tasks other than intellectual skills—on the learning of cognitive strategies, information, attitudes, and motor skills. The purpose of analysis remains unchanged, that is, the identification of both essential and supportive prerequisites. However, the picture that emerges in considering these applications is surely different, and also less clear. Capabilities like information and attitude are not learned by "putting together" subordinate parts, as is the case with intellectual skills. Consequently, prerequisites for these other types of learning tend to be of a supportive rather than an essential nature.

A table prepared by Gagné (1977a) summarizes the essential and supportive prerequisites resulting from analysis of five types of learning, and is reproduced here as Table 6–2.

TABLE 6–2   Essential and Supportive Prerequisites for Five Kinds of Learning Outcome[a]

Type of Learning Outcome	Essential Prerequisites	Supportive Prerequisites
Intellectual Skill	Simpler Component Intellectual Skills (rules, concepts, discriminations)	Attitudes Cognitive Strategies Verbal Information
Cognitive Strategies	Specific Intellectual Skills (?)	Intellectual Skills Verbal Information Attitudes
Verbal Information	Meaningfully Organized Sets of Information	Language Skills Cognitive Strategies Attitudes
Attitudes	Intellectual Skills (sometimes) Verbal Information (sometimes)	Other Attitudes Verbal Information
Motor Skills	Part-skills (sometimes) Procedural Rules (sometimes)	Attitudes

[a]*From Gagné, R. M. Analysis of objectives. In L. J. Briggs, (ed.),* Instructional Design. *Englewood Cliffs, N. J.: Educational Technology Publications, 1977, p. 141. Reproduced by permission of the copyright owner, Educational Technology Publications.*

Prerequisites: cognitive strategies

Presumably, the prerequisites for cognitive strategies of learning, remembering, and thinking are some very basic (and perhaps very simple) mental abilities. For example, an effective cognitive strategy for remembering a list of items may be to generate a different mental image for each item. The essential prerequisite in such a case must be the *ability to have visual images,* which surely must be considered a very basic ability. Again, an often effective cognitive strategy in solving complex mathematical problems is breaking the problem into parts and seeking the solution to each part. What prerequisite ability is involved in such a strategy? Evidently, an *ability to divide a verbally described situation into parts.* This, too, seems to be a fundamental kind of ability of a rather simple sort.

Whatever the essential prerequisites of cognitive strategies may be, there is disagreement concerning how much they depend upon innate factors (which develop through maturation) and how much they are learned. A discussion of these issues has been presented by Case (1978), and more briefly by Gagné (1977a). The factor of maturation plays a prominent role in the developmental theory of Piaget (1970). In contrast, Gagné (1977b) proposes that cognitive strategies are generalizations from learned intellectual skills. It is interesting to note, however, that either of these processes (maturation or learning) takes its effect over a considerable period of time, viewed from the standpoint of intellectual development.

Supportive prerequisites for the learning of cognitive strategies include the *intellectual skills* which may be useful in learning the particular material or solving the particular problems presented to the learner. Relevant *verbal information* may also play this supportive role. Just as in learning other kinds of capabilities, favorable *attitudes* toward learning are likely to be helpful.

Prerequisites: information

In order to learn and store information, the learner must have some *basic language skills.* A number of learning theories propose that information is stored and retrieved in the form of propositions. If this is the case, then the learner must already possess the essential prerequisite skills of forming propositions (sentences) in accordance with certain rules of syntax. These skills, of course, are likely to have been learned fairly early in life.

Information, whether of single items or longer passages, appears to be most readily learned and retained when it occurs within a *larger context of meaningful information.* This context may be learned immediately before the new information to be acquired, or it may have been learned a long time previously. The provision of this meaningful context has been described as a learning condition in Chapter 5, and deserves to be classified as a supportive prerequisite of information learning.

Attitudes support the learning of information in much the same way as they do other kinds of learning tasks. A number of differing *cognitive strategies* have been found to be supportive of the learning of word lists (cf. Gagné, 1977b, pp. 1969–172; Rohwer, 1973). Presumably, it should be possible to identify particular strategies which aid the retention of prose passages, as in remembering the "gist" of a textbook chapter.

Prerequisites: attitudes

The acquiring of particular attitudes may require the prior learning of particular *intellectual skills* or particular sets of *information.* In this sense, then, these learned capabilities may be essential prerequisites to attitude learning. For example, if an attitude toward choosing "truth in labeling" of packaged foods is to be acquired, the learner may need to have (1) the intellectual skills involved in comprehending the printed statement on the label, and (2) a variety of information about food ingredients.

As Table 6–2 indicates, attitudes may have a mutually supportive relation to each other. Thus, *related attitudes* may be supportive of the acquisition of a given attitude. For example, preference for a political candidate makes it easier for a person to prefer also the political views of that candidate's party. In a more general sense, the degree to which a human model is respected affects the readiness with which the attitude he presents is adopted.

Besides its essential role in a specific sense, *information* also has a supportive function in connection with the establishment of attitudes. Knowledge of the situations in which the choice of personal action will be made contributes to the ease of attitude acquisition. For example, an attitude such as "don't drive after drinking" will likely be more readily acquired if the individual has knowledge about the various social situations in which the temptation to drive after drinking will occur.

Motor Skills   As described in Chapter 5, motor skills are often composed of several *part-skills.* It is sometimes the case that the most efficient learning comes about when part-skills are practiced by themselves and later combined in practice of the total skill. In such instances, the part-skills may be said to function as essential prerequisites for the learning of the total skill.

Another component of a motor skill which has this role is the *executive sub-routine* (Fitts and Posner, 1967), which is sometimes learned as an initial step in the acquiring of a motor skill. Swimming the crawl, for example, involves an executive sub-routine that selects a sequence of movements for arms, legs, body, and head. Even before the total skill is practiced very much, the swimmer may receive instruction in the correct execution of this sequence. In Table 6–2, these sub-routines are referred to as "procedural rules." When learned separately and prior to the skill itself, they may be classed as essential prerequisites.

Positive *attitudes* toward the learning of a motor skill, and toward the performance it makes possible, are often supportive prerequisites of some significance.

SUMMARY

Task analysis refers to several different, though interrelated, procedures which are carried out to yield the systematic information needed to plan and specify the conditions for instruction. The three procedures described in this chapter are: (1) *information-processing analysis;* (2) *task classification;* and (3) *learning task analysis.* The first two of these techniques may be carried out in any order, or simultaneously. The third, learning task analysis, depends upon information yielded by (1), or (1) and (2) together. All three types of analysis begin with target objectives for lessons or courses.

Information-processing analysis describes the steps taken by the human learner in performing the task he has learned. Included in these steps, in the typical case, are (1) input information, (2) actions, and (3) decisions. Of particular importance is the fact that this type of analysis usually reveals mental operations which are involved in the performance, but which are not directly observable as overt behavior. Together, the various steps in the performance may be shown in a flow-chart. The results of the analysis exhibit (or imply) capabilities which must be learned as components of the performance described as the *target objective.*

These components are themselves instructional objectives, called *enabling objectives,* which support the learning of the target objective. In addition, they may need to be analyzed further (in the manner of learning task analysis) to reveal additional enabling objectives.

Task classification has the purpose of providing a basis for designing the conditions necessary for effective instruction. The objectives of instruction are categorized as intellectual skills, cognitive strategies, information, attitudes, or motor skills. As indicated in previous chapters, each of these categories carries different implications regarding the conditions necessary for learning, which can be incorporated into the design of instruction.

Learning task analysis has the purpose of identifying the *prerequisites* of both target and enabling objectives. Two kinds of prerequisites are distinguished— *essential* and *supportive.* Essential prerequisites are so-called because they are components of the capability being learned, and therefore their learning must occur as a prior event. Other prerequisites may be supportive in the sense that they make the learning of a capability easier or faster.

Target objectives of the intellectual skill variety may be analyzed into successive "levels" of prerequisites, in the sense that complex skills are progressively broken down into simpler ones. The result of this type of analysis is a *learning hierarchy,* which provides a basis for the planning of instructional sequences. Prerequisites for other categories of learning objectives do not form learning hierarchies, since their prerequisities do not relate to each other in the manner of intellectual skills.

A number of kinds of supportive prerequisites may be identified for particular types of target objectives. For example, task-relevant information is often supportive of intellectual skill learning. Positive attitudes toward lesson and course objectives are also an important source of learning support. Cognitive strategies of attending, learning, and remembering may be brought to bear by the learner in supporting these processes.

References

Bloom, B. S. *Human Characteristics and School Learning.* New York: McGraw-Hill, 1976.

Case, R. Piaget and beyond: Toward a developmentally based theory and technology of instruction. In R. Glaser (ed.), *Advances in Instructional Psychology,* Vol. 1. Hillsdale, N.J.: Erlbaum Associates, 1978.

Cook, J. M. and Walbesser, H. H. *How To Meet Accountability.* College Park, Md.: University of Maryland, Bureau of Educational Research and Field Services, 1973.

Fitts, P. M., and Posner, M. I. *Human Performance.* Monterey, Cal.: Brooks/Cole, 1967.

Gagné, R. M. Analysis of objectives. In L. J. Briggs (ed.), *Instructional Design.* Englewood Cliffs, N.J.: Educational Technology Publications, 1977a.

Gagné, R. M. *The Conditions of Learning,* 3d Ed. New York: Holt, Rinehart and Winston, 1977b.

Glaser, R. Cognitive psychology and instructional design. In D. Klahr (ed.), *Cognition and Instruction*. Hillsdale, N.J.: Erlbaum Associates, 1976.

Greeno, J. G. Cognitive objectives of instruction: Theory of knowledge for solving problems and answering questions. In D. Klahr (ed.), *Cognition and Instruction*. Hillsdale, N.J.: Erlbaum Associates, 1976.

Mager, R. F. *Developing Attitude toward Learning*. Belmont, Ca.: Fearon, 1968.

Merrill, P. F. *Task Analysis: An Information-Processing Approach*. Technical Memo No. 27. Tallahassee: Florida State University, CAI Center, 1971.

Piaget, J. Piaget's theory. In P. Mussen (ed.), *Carmichael's Manual of Child Psychology*, Vol. 1. New York: Wiley, 1970.

Resnick, L. B. Task analysis in instructional design: Some cases from mathematics. In D. Klahr (ed.), *Cognition and Instruction*. Hillsdale, N.J.: Erlbaum Associates, 1976.

Resnick, L. B., and Beck, I. L. Designing instruction in reading: Interaction of theory and practice. In J. T. Guthrie (ed.), *Aspects of Reading Acquisition*. Baltimore: The Johns Hopkins Press, 1977.

Rohwer, W. D., Jr. Elaboration and learning in childhood and adolescence. In H. W. Reese (ed.), *Advances in Child Development and Behavior,* Vol. 8. New York: Academic Press, 1973.

White, R. T. The validation of a learning hierarchy. *American Educational Research Journal*, 1974, *11,* 121–136.

White, R. T., and Gagné, R. M. Formative evaluation applied to a learning hierarchy. *Contemporary Educational Psychology,* 1978, *3,* 87–94.

chapter 7

Defining Performance Objectives

The procedures of task analysis lead to the identification of what must be learned, given certain lesson and course purposes. These procedures also emphasize that up to this point, instructional design continues to be concerned with the *outcomes* of learning, and not yet with the events that bring about learning itself. The classification of these outcomes, both target and enabling objectives, makes possible the planning of instruction in terms of events relevant to learning, as well as the sequencing of occasions for learning. Before proceeding with such planning, however, it is desirable to give some further consideration to the defining of objectives.

ACHIEVING PRECISION IN OBJECTIVES

We have seen that statements of course purposes, as they are frequently given, are not models of precision. They do not manage to reduce ambiguity to the level usually needed for instructional design. "Being aware" of tonal differences in the sounds of musical instruments may mean one thing to one teacher, and something quite different to another. "Comprehending" the idea of nationality may mean "stating a definition of nationality" to one teacher; it may mean "distinguishing nationality from birthplace" to another. It is the existence of this ambiguity which has led several writers to attempt to describe ways of overcoming it in the defining of objectives (cf. Mager, 1975; Popham and Baker, 1970).

Greater precision in the definition of objectives meets two needs: the need for *communication* of the purposes of instruction, and the need for *evaluation* of instruction. Objectives which are precisely defined provide a common technical basis for meeting both of these needs. One wants to communicate the intended outcomes of instruction to students, teachers, and parents (when appropriate). While these communications usually differ from each other in the ways they are stated, one nevertheless wants all of them to express the *same idea*. This goal can best be achieved by having available a technically complete definition of the objective. Likewise, one wants the observations (or tests) used in evaluating the outcome of learning to reflect the commonly understood idea of this outcome. Again, this can best be achieved by reference to a technically adequate definition of the outcome. Precise definitions of objectives become the specifications for "domains" from which items for achievement testing are drawn (Popham, 1975). Objective definitions thus insure that what is evaluated and what is communicated as an intended learning outcome have a common meaning.

Overcoming ambiguity in objective statements

As has often been suggested, the procedure for overcoming the ambiguity of course purpose statements and thus achieving greater precision, runs somewhat as follows: "All right, I will accept this statement as reflecting one of the purposes of the course. The question now is, *how will I know* when this purpose has been achieved?"

How will one know that the student "understands the principle of commutativity"?

How will it be known that the student "appreciates allegory in 'A Midsummer Night's Dream' "?

How can it be told that the student "comprehends spoken French"?

How will one tell that the student "reads short stories with enjoyment"?

Statements of course purposes may be quite successful in communicating general goals to fellow teachers, yet they are often not sufficiently precise for unambiguous communication of the *content* and *outcomes* of instruction. The key to their ambiguity is simply that they do not tell another person how he could *observe* what has been accomplished without being present during the lesson itself. Being able to make such an observation may be of interest to another teacher who accepts the general purpose of the course and wishes to know how to tell when it has been accomplished. It may be of interest to a parent who may not know exactly what "commutativity" means but wishes to assure himself that his son or daughter can in fact use this principle in performing arithmetic operations. It is likely to be of interest to the student, who wants to be able to tell when his own performance reaches the goal that the teacher or textbook had in mind.

An objective is precisely described when it communicates to another person what he would have to do to *observe* that a stated lesson purpose has in fact been accomplished. The statement is inadequately precise if it does not enable the other person to think of how he would carry out such an observation. Consider the following instances:

1. "Realizes that most plant growth requires sunshine." Such a statement doesn't say or imply how such an outcome would be observed. Does it mean that the teacher would be satisfied with the answer to a question such as "Is the sunshine necessary for the growth of most plants?" Evidently not. How, then, would such an objective be observed?

2. "Demonstrates that sunshine affects plant growth." This statement implies that the teacher must observe instances in which the student shows that he knows the relation between sunshine and plant growth. The observation might be made in various ways (by using actual plants, pictures, or verbal statements). The main point is, it tells in a general way what sort of observation is required.

The criterion of "being able to observe" the proposed outcome of a lesson is often referred to as an *operational* criterion; and statements of objectives having this characteristic may be called *operationally defined objectives*. When defined in this precise way, definitions of objectives communicate to another person the "operations" he must carry out in order to observe the achievement of the objective.

What is observed when a second person undertakes to convince himself that an objective has been achieved? Obviously, he is observing the *performance* of a student in a situation. Accordingly, statements of objectives having this "operational" characteristic are also called *performance objectives*. In achieving precision in stating objectives, one is said to be "defining objectives in terms of human performance (or human behavior)." Basically, then, these terms "operationally defined objectives," "behaviorally defined objectives," "objectives defined in terms of performance" all mean the same thing. When objectives are so stated, they communicate to another person what he would have to do to observe the achievement of the course's purpose or purposes.

Components of operational descriptions of objectives

Precisely described objectives are those which make observations of another person possible. They need to include a number of components. They must, first, describe the action that the student is taking. Obviously, too, an objective must describe the situation in which that action takes place. Something must usually be said about the limits within which the performance of the student will be expected to occur. And most important of all, the objective must indicate what kind of human performance is involved. This means objectives must describe what kind of human capability is to be inferred from the performance that is under observation.

Our description of the components of operational definitions of objectives is not widely different from that given by other authors (Mager, 1975; Popham and Baker, 1970; Briggs, 1970), and is not intended to differ from them in any crucial respect. There are differences in emphasis, however, resulting from our attempt to make some distinctions which other authors have not highlighted. Particularly, we distinguish verbs for *action* from verbs used to identify the *learned capability* implied by the behavior under observation.

An initial example, which will be expanded later, comes from the lesson purpose "types a letter." Such a goal might be found in a course in typing designed to establish skills for employment as typist.

The incompleteness of the description "types a letter" may be indicated by the following comments:

1. *Action.* The statement is obviously most adequate with respect to this component. An observer would be able to judge that the performance had been carried out *by typing.*

2. *Object.* The object of the performance is similarly clear—the individual is expected to produce a *letter.*

3. *Situation.* What is the situation faced by the student when asked to type a letter? Is he given the components of the letter in longhand copy? Does he produce the letter from an auditory message, or from notes? Obviously, what the student actually does is highly dependent on the situation. An objective must specify the features of this situation.

4. *Tools and Other Constraints.* The main question here is *how* must the required performance be carried out? This depends on what tools are available, or what other limits are set to the performance. Does the student use an electric typewriter? Does he make a carbon? How long is the letter? Quite different limits might be set for a lesson intended for a beginning student and one for a fully trained student.

5. *Capability To Be Learned.* Here is the most important omission of all. The statement "types a letter" does not really tell the nature of the learned capability that can be inferred from the student's performance. "Types a letter" might mean "*copies* a letter," or it might mean the quite different performance, "*composes a letter.*" Something must be done, therefore, to represent the *kind* of performance the student is expected to exhibit. This means one must state the inferred kind of human capability involved.

Let us see, then, what a total and precise definition of the objective "typing a letter" might be. Suppose that the task set for the typist is that of answering a piece of correspondence concerned with orders and shipping, without help from anyone concerning what the contents of the letter should be. One would need to describe the total performance somewhat as follows:

Given a received letter inquiring about the shipping of an order,	(Situation)
generates	(The learned capability, implying a problem-solving process)
a letter in reply	(Object)
by typing,	(Action)

using an electric typewriter, making one carbon of a one-page letter.	(Tools and other constraints)

It is difficult to pin down what may be the "important" parts of this objective statement, since each part serves a different function. Can any be left out? No, not if one wants a truly precise and complete definition, free of ambiguities. It is worth noting, however, that the *verb denoting the learned capability* is the part that brings about the major differentiation of the performance from that of a contrasting performance, that of copying a letter from a longhand original. The latter kind of activity may be described as follows:

Given a written longhand letter,	(Situation)
executes	(The learned capability, a motor skill)
a copy	(Object)
by typing,	(Action)
using an electric typewriter, making one carbon of a one-page letter.	(Tools and other constraints)

Obviously, although the implements used are the same, this is a very different kind of human activity from that given in the previous example.

The situation reacted to is different, and in particular the *learned capability* is quite a different one. "Executes" is an acceptable word for this process, implying a learned motor skill, something which is quite different from that implied by the "generates" of the other example.

Here is another example of an objective with its components, taken from elementary mathematics:

Given two "missing factor" equations, using a X sign and an = sign,	(Situation) (Learned capability, a rule)
demonstrates	
supplying the missing factor in one equation from the known factor in the other equation	(Object) (Action)
by writing the missing factor,	
using the commutative property of multiplication.	(Tools and other constraints)

Again it is apparent that, although all parts of the objective contribute to the description, the *learned capability* is surely one of the most important components. In this case it tells us that the individual is "demonstrating" the application of a rule (the commutative rule of multiplication).

Still another example may be given, this time pertaining to a language skill basic to beginning reading:

Given orally presented words of	(Situation)
single syllables, beginning with	(Learned capability, concrete
consonants,	concepts)
identifies	
the beginning consonant of each	(Object)
word,	(Action)
by printing	(Tools and other constraints)
in appropriate blanks.	

This is of course a fairly simple skill, and it is therefore rather readily described. Again in this instance, it may be seen that a major contribution to precise meaning is carried by the verb "identifies," used to describe the learned capability. Notice, for example, how inappropriate a verb like "demonstrate" or "solve" would be in this case.

Choosing action words

The choice of verbs in the definition of an objective is a matter of critical importance. The primary reason is, of course, the avoidance of ambiguity. One wishes the statement of an objective to *reliably communicate,* in such a way that two different literate people will agree that any specific instance of an actually observed performance is or is not an example of the described objective. As a number of writers have pointed out (e.g. Mager, 1975; Popham and Baker, 1970) verbs like "knows," "understands," "appreciates," do not communicate reliably. Thus, while such verbs are appropriate for stating general purposes of a course of study, by themselves they do not yield the reliable communication necessary to an objective statement. They must usually be followed by a line of thought such as the following: "I have said 'the student will understand'. Now, how will I be able to tell that 'he understands'? What kind of performance could I point to which would convince me, and also my colleague Mr. Jones, that the student 'understands'? Well, I would be convinced he 'understands' if he could show me how to do it. Do what? Well, if he could actually supply the missing factor in an equation, for example. Let me see if I can express that action so that Mr. Jones could also agree with me, that is, so that he could identify the same performance that I have in mind. If I can do that, I shall have a defined performance objective."

Such reasoning is basic to the formulation of an objective, and leads to the choice of verbs which accomplish the primary purpose of reliable communication. There is, however, one additional distinction about the use of verbs that remains to be described. As shown by previous examples, there are two kinds of verbs in a complete definition of an objective. The verb denoting *Action* is likely to be thought of first. While it may come second in thought, the verb which identifies the *Learned Capability* is, however, probably of even greater importance in its implications for instructional design.

Verbs for Action   Verbs denoting action are not difficult to find. Common ones are: writes, draws, states orally, selects, matches, names, groups, collects, applies, employs, verifies. There are, of course, synonyms for these, and there are many others as well. Action verbs are unambiguous when they reliably communicate observable performances to another person. Beyond this criterion, no further distinctions or classifications appear feasible. After all, there are many verbs in our language; and from the total set, there are also many which communicate action rather precisely.

In the objective statement, the *action* verb normally appears in its "ing" form. (This is true in the models we are describing. It is, of course, not an absolute rule, since objective statements may be organized in a number of ways.) Here are some examples of objectives in which the role of the verb ending in "ing" is shown:

1. Given an appropriate question, states the provisions of the First Amendment, in *writing.*
2. Given a beaker of water, ringstand, Bunsen burner, and thermometer, demonstrates that water changes state at 100°C., by *recording* several temperature readings.
3. Given a passage of poetry, classifies the similes contained in it by *checking* the words compared.

By using this form, we mean to emphasize that the action verb, while essential for completeness of communication, is not necessarily the most important verb in the objective definition. The major verb is, instead, that which denotes the learned capability. In Mager's (1975) expression, the major verb conveys the *main intent.* It may be noted that an action verb like "writing" does not in itself identify the intellectual skill involved in the performance, as previous examples have shown. In exhibiting the action of "writing a sentence," for example, a first-grade student might be copying a sentence given in his workbook; a fifth-grade student might be assembling a sentence from a subject, verb, and object supplied by the teacher; an eighth-grade student might be composing a sentence to describe a pictured scene. All are *writing,* yet each is exhibiting a different kind of learned capability—a different instructional outcome.

It may be noted that the capability verb represents a new competency to be attained, while the action verb often refers to some action the learner already knows how to perform. For example, when young children are learning to *discriminate* (capability verb) circles from rectangles, they may be asked to *point to* a drawing which matches a standard. It is assumed that pointing is an action children already know how to do. This known ability is used as an indicator that the discrimination has been learned.

Describing human capabilities

The purpose of the major verb of the objective statement is to communicate the *kind of human capability* one expects to be learned, as may be observed in some performance exhibited by the student. We undertake to identify in this section the words that can be used for description of the capabilities.

Verbs for Intellectual Skills   Our account of the choices of verbs to describe performances implying learned capabilities begins with the types of intellectual skills described in Chapter 3. We need to be concerned with the categories of (1) discriminations; (2) concrete concepts; (3) defined concepts; (4) rules; and (5) higher-order rules.

If five categories of intellectual skills describe learning outcomes in this general domain, it should follow that *these may be described by five verbs.* This is exactly what we propose. We have chosen the verbs with considerable care, so that each denotes an intellectual skill as distinctively as possible. At the same time, these verbs have a degree of abstractness at least one degree greater than verbs for action. This, too, is deliberate, since verbs for intellectual functioning should not be confused with those that simply describe observable actions. The former require an *inference* about behavior, whereas the latter merely permit the observable aspects of the performance to be identified.

The five verbs which can be used to describe intellectual skills in definitions of performance objectives are shown in the first portion of Table 7–1. The final column of the table provides examples of phrases (not complete statements) for objectives, illustrating their use.

The statements that result when these verbs are used have a formal character that sometimes makes them seem unduly cumbersome. For example, it may often seem better, in a literary sense, to simply state that the student "finds values of specified variables in algebraic equations," rather than to state, "demonstrates, by transforming algebraic equations, solving to obtain the value of a specified variable." But the latter statement makes clear that the expected performance *requires the use of rules,* whereas the former does not necessarily make this clear. One can imagine a situation in which the student could "find" the value of a specified variable without using such rules; as, for example, in the equation $x=3$.

Another example of the apparent formal complexity of statements using these verbs may be shown with the verb *classify.* Suppose that, instead of the complete phrase shown in Table 7–1, one were to be satisfied with "states and gives an example of the definition of 'family'." Neither of these verbs implies an unambiguous meaning for the intellectual skill involved. "States," may very well apply to "stating information," as might be the case if the student repeats the definition "a group consisting of the head of a household and all persons living therein related to him." Further, "giving an example" might be done by identifying one or more family groups by name or in pictures. To convey the full meaning of the desired objective, *classifies* must be included to indicate that the student is ex-

TABLE 7–1   Standard Verbs to Describe Human Capabilities, with Examples of Phrases
Incorporating Action Verbs

Capability	Capability Verb	Example (Action Verb in Italics)
Intellectual Skill		
Discrimination	DISCRIMINATES	discriminates, by *matching* French sounds of *"u"* and *"ou"*
Concrete Concept	IDENTIFIES	identifies, by *naming*, the root, leaf, and stem of representative plants
Defined Concept	CLASSIFIES	classifies, by *using a definition*, the concept "family"
Rule	DEMONSTRATES	demonstrates, by *solving* verbally stated examples, the addition of positive and negative numbers
Higher-order Rule (Problem Solving)	GENERATES	generates, by *synthesizing* applicable rules, a paragraph describing a person's actions in a situation of fear
Cognitive Strategy	ORIGINATES	originates a solution to the reduction of air pollution, by *applying model* of gaseous diffusion
Information	STATES	states orally the major issues in the presidential campaign of 1932
Motor Skill	EXECUTES	executes *backing* a car into driveway
Attitude	CHOOSES	chooses *playing golf* as a leisure activity

pected to show the meaning of the concept "family," including distinguishing it from other concepts.

Perhaps it should also be pointed out that we propose these five verbs, not because we feel wedded to them as words (some surely have approximate synonyms), but because we consider that there are *five necessary distinctions to be made*. Using these five words as verbs for intellectual skills has the desirable effect of preserving these distinctions. Trying to achieve a better "literary" style for statements of objectives can easily add confusion where there should be as little as possible. If one is inclined to prefer other verbs, their equivalence or lack of equivalence to these should be clearly stated.

Verb for Cognitive Strategy   The next entry in the table shows the suggested major verb of the description of a cognitive strategy, which is *originates.* This verb implies the kind of intellectual process presumed to be involved in tasks requiring thinking or problem solving. When confronted with a truly novel task, without a familiar context, we suppose that the learner must search for applicable rules and applicable information. He then, in effect, formulates a general type of solution, and checks to see how such a solution applies to one or more specific instances. This whole sequence of mental operations is implied by the verb "originate." Actually, there may be more than one cognitive strategy involved in a problem-solving process of this sort. However, as previously mentioned, we are unable to identify these strategies more precisely at present. Perhaps someday it will be possible to describe as many or more sub-types of cognitive strategies as is currently possible for intellectual skills.

The example suggests a description for a problem-solving activity in which the learner originates a solution to the problem of reducing air pollution by bringing to bear on this problem a model (that is, a set of complex rules) of gaseous diffusion which he has previously learned. This is, of course, a hypothetical example.

A comment may be in order concerning the difference between the acquiring of a higher-order rule by problem solving, and the application of a cognitive strategy to a problem-solving task. For the former, the suggested phrase is "generate a solution," whereas for the latter it is "originate a solution." The difference is not one we can describe with utter confidence, because additional study of these complex mental processes is badly needed. We speculate, however, that the difference lies in the necessity to reach "out of context" for a solution that is truly a matter of originating. One may, for example, imagine a problem-solving situation in which some higher-order rule must be invented, that is, generated for a mathematical principle, based upon a combination of previously learned mathematical rules. Such a "generating" process remains within the context of mathematics. In contrast, however, would be an instance in which a thinker came to "see" the applicability of some model of physical science to the occurrence of a social phenomenon such as inflation or population growth. The original set of rules used in such a solution would be "out of context." They would need to be searched for in the individual's memory, and the problem would need to be formulated before its solution could be tested. Thus, to a greater extent, one would expect that "originating a solution" calls upon the internally organized capabilities called cognitive strategies. (Interesting discussions of originating performances are to be found in Bruner, 1971, pp. 52–97.)

Verb for Motor Skill   The major verb suggested for descriptions of motor skill is *executes.* The performance used to illustrate the use of this verb is backing an automobile into a driveway. Obviously, the verb denoting action in this instance is "backing." But we use the verb "executes" to imply the capability of a highly organized skill which is observed by means of a performance possessing appropriate characteristics of smoothness and efficiency.

Verb for Attitude   As seen in the preceding chapter, an attitude is a human capability that influences an individual's choice of some personal action. The major verb for a statement of an attitudinal objective, then, is not difficult to find. It is *chooses.* In Table 7–1, the example used is one which supposes that the student chooses playing golf when given the opportunity of selecting a leisure-time pursuit. Under proper circumstances, it may be supposed that the observation of such a performance (or the self-report of it) can lead to the inference of a positive attitude toward this activity. As is true with other types of objectives, the action verb can be of various sorts, such as "by signing up for golf," or "by selecting golf from a list of sports."

Statements of Objectives and Criteria of Performance

Instructional objectives describe the *class* of performances that may be used to determine whether the implied human capability has been learned. However, they do not state in quantitative terms what *criteria* will be used to judge whether any particular performance class has been learned. That is to say, the objective statements themselves do not describe how many times the student is to "demonstrate the addition of mixed numbers," or how many "errors" will be permitted. They do not state what will be needed for the observer to be confident that the designated capability has been learned. There are two very good reasons why the criterion of performance should not be included in a statement of an instructional objective. First, the necessary criteria are likely to be different for each type of human capability, and it is highly desirable to avoid the error of thinking they can be the same. Second, the question of criteria of performance is a question of "how to measure," and is intimately bound up with the techniques of performance assessment. At the point in instructional planning, when objectives are being described, it is confusing to become concerned with assessment procedures. Such procedures are described in a later chapter of this book.

Statements of objectives prepared in the manner described here *always* imply "mastery" (cf. Bloom, 1971). But what is the criterion of mastery, that is, how is it to be measured? This is a question which needs to be separately decided in connection with specific assessment methods. Sometimes, it is perfectly clear that mastery means that the student will exhibit the performance 100 percent of the time (minus some small percent for "measurement error"). For example, if the objective is defined as "given two or more mixed numbers, demonstrates their addition by writing the sum," one expects the performance of the student to indicate the achievement of this objective for any or all mixed numbers. Such a conclusion might be reached by asking the student to perform a large number of examples of adding mixed numbers, or as few as two or three. The conclusion sought—that the student has or has not mastered this task—is the same in either case.

On other occasions, as when information is being measured, it may be desirable to specify some portion of ideas to be correctly stated, such as three out of five, or four out of six. But this is more appropriately a matter of assessment, rather than a portion of the objective statement itself. For example, the statement implying mastery might be, "states in writing three major economic factors contributing to inflation." For such an objective, an assessment technique must be chosen which specifies a decision concerning what conclusion can be drawn if the student can state only two of three factors, or one of three. Regardless of this latter decision, the objective statement continues in unchanged form to imply mastery.

An exception to the principle of mastery occurs in the case of attitudes. Because of the nature of this kind of human capability, which is one of *modifying* choices, one cannot conceive of an attitude as being "mastered." Instead, attitudes make choices more or less probable. The assessment of attitudes, therefore, although derived from the objective statements, implies only a conclusion concerning the *relative strength* of an attitude. In other words, one does not expect to be able to draw the conclusion from assessment based on an attitudinal objective that "a positive attitude has been mastered," but only that "an attitude has been changed in the positive (or negative) direction."

In the case of intellectual skills, the mastery implied by the statement of the objective has an important theoretical significance. Its function is accounted for in the theory of *learning hierarchies* (Gagné, 1977, pp. 142–147). According to this theory, the learning of any particular intellectual skill is important because it supports the learning of more complex skills. This support by previously learned intellectual skills, however, occurs only when they are readily accessible in memory at the moment the new learning occurs (or is about to occur). In an operational sense, "mastery" means *readily accessible to recall at the time of learning* of the more complex skill. Strictly speaking, therefore, the measurement of mastery must be so designed as to predict the "readily accessible recall" of the intellectual skill which has been learned. From this theoretical view, it is not possible to predict in precise terms how "mastery" should be measured. Nor is it wise to adopt some arbitrary standard like "five out of six correct responses." The criterion of mastery will vary with what is being learned, and needs to be determined as a part of the assessment process.

PREPARING STATEMENTS OF INSTRUCTIONAL OBJECTIVES

Having described the components of complete statements of objectives, we return now to the procedure for preparing these statements.

An example from science

Suppose that the instructional designer has in mind, or formulates in a written statement, the purposes to be accomplished by a course of instruction. If the lesson is one in science, the following purposes might be considered. These have been abstracted from a list of objectives for junior high school science instruction prepared by the Intermediate Science Curriculum Study (1973).

1. Understanding the concept of an electric circuit.
2. Knowing that a major advantage of the metric system in science is that its units are related by factors of ten.
3. Taking personal responsibility for returning equipment to its storage places.

Objective No. 1—The Concept of an Electric Circuit This is a fairly straight-forward purpose for instruction. The first question to be asked by an instructional designer is: "What kind of capability am I looking for here?" Do I mean by "understanding" something like "stating what an electric circuit is"? No, that would not be convincing, since it might merely indicate that the student had acquired some verbal information which he could repeat, perhaps in his own words. Do I mean "distinguishing an electric circuit from a non-circuit when shown two or more instances"? No, I cannot be sure that the student has the understanding I wish in this case, because he may simply be able to pick up the cue of an open wire in the instances shown him and respond on that basis. What I actually want the student to do is to *show me that he can use a rule for making an electric circuit* in one or more specific situations. The rule concerned has to do with the flow of electric current from a source through a connected set of conductors and back to the source. The student could be asked to exhibit this performance in one or more different situations.

The result of this line of reasoning is an objective statement which puts together the necessary components as follows:

> [Situation:] Given a battery, light bulb and socket, and pieces of wire [major verb for capability:] demonstrates [object:] the making of an electric circuit [action:] by connecting wires to battery and socket and testing the lighting of the bulb.

Objective No. 2—Knowing Something about the Metric System The statement of purpose in this instance implies that some information is to be learned. Again, the first question to be asked by the instructional designer is, "What do I mean by 'knowing' this fact about the metric system? What will convince me that the student 'knows'?" In this instance, the designer may readily come to the conclusion that "knowing" means *being able to state* the particular fact about the metric system. Accordingly, the identification of the required capability as *information* is fairly straightforward.

> The resulting objective can then be constructed as follows: [Situation:] Given the question: "What major advantage for scientific work do the units of the metric system have?" [major verb for capability:] states [object:] that its units are related by factors of ten [action:] by writing, in his own words.

Objective No. 3—Taking Responsibility for Equipment In thinking over this instructional purpose, the designer will immediately realize that it is not concerned with whether the student is able to put equipment back in its place, but rather with whether he *tends to do so* on all appropriate occasions. The word "responsibility" implies that the actions of the student may occur at any time, and are not expected to result from any specific direction or question. The designer must ask himself, "What would convince me that the student is 'taking responsibility' of this sort?" The answer to this question implies that the objective in this case deals with choices of personal action, in other words, with an *attitude.*

The standard method of constructing the objective would therefore take this form:

> [Situation:] Given occasions when laboratory activities are completed or terminated [major verb for capability:] chooses [object:] courses of action [action:] returning equipment to its storage places.

An example from English

A second example of the procedure for constructing statements of objectives comes from a hypothetical course in English, concerned with the study of literature. Suppose that a set of lessons in such a course had the following purposes:

1. Identifying the major characters in *Hamlet.*
2. Understanding Hamlet's soliloquy.
3. Being able to recognize a metaphor.

Objective No. 1—Identifying the Major Characters in *Hamlet* This objective, according to our model, involves using definitions to *classify.* In this case the student is being asked to classify characters in *Hamlet* in accordance with their functions within the plot of the play. Under most circumstances, it would be assumed that his doing this by way of verbal statements would be convincing. That is, the student answers a question like: "Who was Claudius?" by defining Claudius as the king of Denmark, Hamlet's uncle, who is suspected by Hamlet of having killed his father. The objective can be constructed as follows:

> [Situation:] Given oral questions about the characters of *Hamlet,* as "Who was Claudius?" [major verb for capability:] classifies [object:] the characters [action:] by defining their relationships to the plot.

Objective No. 2—Understanding Hamlet's Soliloquy Here is a much more interesting, and presumably a more important instructional purpose. The instructional designer needs to ask himself, "How will I know if the student 'understands' this passage?" In all likelihood, the answer he will find to this question is "ask the student to express the thoughts of the passage in words that simplify or explain their meaning." (An example would be explaining that "to be, or not to be" means "to remain living or not.") To accomplish such a task, the student must solve a series of problems, bringing a number of intellectual skills to bear upon them such as rules for using synonyms, rules for defining, and concepts of figures of speech. In sum, what he will be asked to do is to *generate* a paraphrase of the soliloquy. It is, then, a *problem-solving* task, or more precisely a whole set of problems, in which subordinate rules must be applied to the generation of higher-order rules. The latter cannot be exactly specified, of course, since one does not know exactly how the student will solve each problem.

As a result of this analysis, the following objective might be composed:

> [Situation:] Given instructions to interpret the meaning of Hamlet's soliloquy in simple terms [major verb for capability:] generates [object:] an alternative communication of the soliloquy [action:] by writing sentences of simple content.

Objective No. 3—Recognizing Metaphors   Even in its expression, this objective has the appearance of representing a somewhat less complex purpose than No. 2. It may be evident, also, that if a student is able to generate a paraphrased soliloquy, he must be able to detect the metaphoric meaning of such phrases as "to take arms against a sea of troubles." In this simpler example of a purpose, then, the question for the instructional designer is, "What will convince me that the student can 'recognize' a metaphor?" Obviously, a metaphor is a concept, and since it is not something that can be denoted by pointing, it must be a *defined concept.* The performance to be expected of the student, then, will be one of *classifying a metaphor in accordance with a definition.*

The resulting objective might be stated as follows:

> [Situation:] Given a list of phrases, some of which are metaphors and some not [major verb for capability:] classifies [object:] the metaphors [actions:] by picking out those that conform to the definition, rejecting those that do not.

An alternative objective (and possibly a better one) for this instructional purpose would be:

> [Situation:] Given a phrase containing a verb participle and an object (as, "resisting corruption") [major verb for capability:] classifies [object:] a metaphor [action:] by giving an example which accords with the definition (as, "erecting a bulwark against corruption").

An example from social studies

A course in social studies in junior high or high school might have the following purposes:

1. Knowing terms of office for members of the two houses of Congress.
2. Interpreting bar charts showing growth in agricultural production.
3. Applying knowledge of the "judicial review" process of the Supreme Court.

Objective No. 1—Terms of Office for Congress   The intended outcome in this case is information. It is, of course, rather simple information, and therefore something that might be learned in grades before high school. As an objective, this purpose may be stated as follows:

> [Situation:] Given the question, "What terms of office do members of both houses of Congress serve?" [major verb for capability:] states [object:] the terms for House and Senate members [action:] orally.

Objective No. 2—Interpreting Bar Charts   Often an important kind of objective in social studies is an intellectual skill. Interpreting bar charts is a rule-using skill. There may be several such skills of increasing complexity to be learned.

Consequently, particular attention has to be paid to the description of the situation. More complex charts may require more complex intellectual skills, or a combination of them. This objective may be illustrated by the following example:

> [Situation:] Given a bar chart showing production of cotton bales by year during the period 1950–1960 [major verb for capability:] demonstrates [object:] the finding of years of maximal and minimal growth [action:] by checking appropriate bars.

Objective No. 3—Applying Knowledge of "Judicial Review" The statement of this goal is somewhat ambiguous. It might best be interpreted as one of solving problems pertaining to the Supreme Court's judicial review function, and exhibiting knowledge by so doing. Such an objective might be stated in the following way:

> [Situation:] Given the statement of an issue of constitutionality contained in a fictitious Act of Congress, and reference to the constitutional principle to be invoked [major verb for capability:] generates [object:] a proposed judicial opinion [action:] in written form.

USING OBJECTIVES IN INSTRUCTIONAL PLANNING

When instructional objectives are defined in the manner described here, they reveal the fine-grained nature of the instructional process. This in turn reflects the fine-grained characteristic of what is learned. As a consequence, the quantity of individual objectives applicable to a course of instruction usually numbers in the hundreds. There may be scores of objectives for the single topic of a course, and several for each individual lesson.

How does the instructional designer employ these objectives in his development of topics, courses, or curricula? And how does the teacher use objectives? Can the teacher, as the designer of an individual lesson, make use of lengthy lists of objectives? Many such lists are available, it may be noted, for a variety of subjects in all school grades.*

Objectives and instruction

The instructional designer, or design team, faces the need to describe objectives as part of each individual lesson. Typically, there will be several distinct objectives for a lesson. Each may then be used to answer the question, "What *kind* of a learning outcome does this objective represent?" The categories to be determined are those corresponding to the major verb indicating capability. That is, the objective may represent information, an intellectual skill in one of its sub-varieties, a cognitive strategy, an attitude, or a motor skill. Having determined the categories of a lesson's objectives, the designer will be able to make decisions about the following matters:

*Lists of objectives may be obtained on order from the Instructional Objectives Exchange, Box 24095, Los Angeles, California, 90024.

1. whether an original intention about the lesson's purpose has been overlooked, or inadequately represented;
2. whether the lesson has a suitable "balance" of expected outcomes; and
3. whether the approach to instruction is matched to the type of objective in each case.

The Balance of Objectives The objectives identified for each lesson are likely to represent several different categories of learning outcome. First of all, it may be possible to identify a *primary* objective, one without which the lesson would seem hardly worthwhile. In addition, however, there are necessarily bound to be some *supportive prerequisites,* as described in the previous chapter. Thus, the lesson which has an intellectual skill as its primary objective is likely to be supported by other objectives classifiable as cognitive strategies, information, attitudes. As an example, one might expect a lesson having as its primary objective the intellectual skill of "demonstrating chemical equations for the oxidation of metals" to include, as well, objectives pertaining to information about common metallic oxides, and to favorable attitudes toward possessing knowledge about metallic oxides. How to reflect these several objectives in lesson design is a subject for later chapters. The first step, however, is to see that a reasonable balance of the expected outcomes is attained.

Designing Instruction Clearly, then, the systematic design of lessons making up a topic or course will result in the development of a sizeable collection of statements of objectives. This collection will grow as lessons are developed and assembled into topics. Decisions about the correspondence of these objectives with original intentions for the topic and course, and about the "balance" of objectives, can also be made with reference to these larger instructional units. As in the case of the individual lesson, these decisions are made possible by the categorization of objectives into types of capabilities to be learned.

The teacher's design of the single lesson also makes use of individual statements of objectives and the classes of capabilities they represent. The instructional materials available to the teacher (textbook, manual, or whatever) may identify the objectives of the lesson directly. More frequently, the teacher may need to (1) infer what the objectives are; and (2) design the lesson so that the objectives represented in the textbook are supplemented by others. For purposes of planning effective instruction, the determination of categories of expected learning outcomes is as important to the teacher as it is to the design team. The teacher, for tomorrow's lesson, needs to make decisions about the adequacy with which the lesson's purpose is accomplished, and about the relative balance of the lesson's several expected outcomes.

Objectives and assessment

Fortunately, the lists of individual objectives which are developed in a systematic design effort have a second use. Descriptions of objectives, as we have said, are descriptions of what must be observed in order to verify that the desired learning has taken place. Consequently, statements of objectives have direct implications for *assessing* student learning.

The teacher may use objective statements to design situations within which student performance can be observed. This is done to verify that particular outcomes of learning have in fact occurred. Consider the objective: "Given a terrain map of the United States and information about prevailing winds, demonstrate the location of regions of heavy rainfall by shading the map" (applying a rule). This description more or less directly describes the situation which can be used by a teacher to verify that the desired learning has taken place. A student, or a group of students, could be supplied with terrain maps, prevailing wind information, and asked to perform this task. The resulting records of their performances would serve as an assessment of their learning of the appropriate rule.

With comparable adequacy, statements of objectives can serve as bases for the development of teacher-made tests. These in turn may be employed for formal kinds of assessment of student performance, when considered desirable by the teacher. Alternately, they can be used as "self-tests" which students employ when engaging in individual study or self-instruction.

The classes of objectives described in this chapter constitute a *taxonomy* which is applicable to the design of many kinds of assessment instruments and tests. A somewhat different, although not incompatible, taxonomy of objectives is described in the work of Bloom (1956), and of Krathwohl, Bloom, and Masia (1964). The application of this latter taxonomy to the design of tests and other assessment techniques is illustrated in many subject-matter fields by Bloom, Hastings, and Madaus (1971). This work describes in detail methods of planning assessment procedures for most areas of the school curriculum. Further discussion of methods for developing tests and test items based on the categories of learning outcomes described in this chapter is contained in Chapter 9.

SUMMARY

The identification and definition of performance objectives is an important step in the design of instruction. Objectives serve as guidelines for developing the instruction, and for designing measures of student performance to determine whether the course objectives have been reached.

Initially, the aims of instruction are frequently formulated as a set of *purposes* for a course. These purposes are further refined and converted to operational terms by the process of defining the performance objectives. These describe the *planned* outcomes of instruction, and they are the basis for evaluating the success of the instruction in terms of its intended outcomes. It is recognized, of course, that there are often unintended or unexpected outcomes, judged, when later observed, to be either desirable or undesirable.

This chapter has presented a five-component guide to the writing of performance objectives. The five elements named were:

1. Situation
2. Learned Capability
3. Object
4. Action
5. Tools or other constraints

Examples are given, showing how these components can be used to result in unambiguous statements of objectives for different school subjects. The examples chosen also illustrate objectives for various categories of learned capabilities.

Special attention is called to the need for care in choosing action verbs suitable for describing both the learned capability inferred from the observed performance, and for describing the nature of the performance itself. Table 7–1 presents a convenient summary of *major* verbs and *action* verbs.

The kinds of performance objectives described for the various categories of learned capabilities play an essential role in the method of instructional design presented in this book. Precisely formulated definitions of objectives within each category serve as a technical base from which unambiguous communications of learning outcomes can be derived. Different communications of objectives, conveying approximately a common meaning, may be needed for teachers, students, and parents. At the same time, precisely defined objectives relate the same common meanings to the construction of tests for evaluation of student performance, as will be indicated later in Chapter 12.

References

Bloom, B. S. (ed.) *Taxonomy of Educational Objectives. Handbook I: Cognitive Domain.* New York: McKay, 1956.

Bloom, B. S. Learning for mastery. In B. S. Bloom, J. T. Hastings, and G. F. Madaus (eds.), *Handbook on Formative and Summative Evaluation of Student Learning.* New York: McGraw-Hill, 1971.

Bloom, B. S., Hastings, J. T., and Madaus, G. F. *Handbook on Formative and Summative Evaluation of Student Learning.* New York: McGraw-Hill, 1971.

Briggs, L. J. *Handbook of Procedures for the Design of Instruction.* Pittsburgh, Pa.: American Institutes for Research, 1970.

Bruner, J. S. *The Relevance of Education.* New York: Norton, 1971.

Gagné, R. M. *The Conditions of Learning,* 3d Ed. New York: Holt, Rinehart and Winston, 1977.

Intermediate Science Curriculum Study. *Individualizing Objective Testing.* Tallahassee, Florida: ISCS, Florida State University, 1973.

Krathwohl, D. R., Bloom, B. S., and Masia, B. B. *Taxonomy of Educational Objectives. Handbook II: Affective Domain.* New York: McKay, 1964.

Mager, R. F. *Preparing Objectives for Instruction,* 2nd Ed. Belmont, Ca.: Fearon, 1975.

Popham, W. J., and Baker, E. L. *Establishing Instructional Goals.* Englewood Cliffs, N.J.: Prentice-Hall, 1970.

Popham, W. J. *Educational Evaluation.* Englewood Cliffs, N.J.: Prentice-Hall, 1975.

chapter 8

Designing Instructional Sequences

Learning directed toward the goals of school education must necessarily take place on a number of occasions over a period of time. The learning of any single performance objective is preceded by the learning of prerequisite objectives, and is followed by other occasions for learning directed toward more complex objectives.

A course or curriculum must require decisions about the sequencing of objectives, since not all objectives can be taught at once. It is reasonable, then, to seek sequences which promote effective learning. One key to effectiveness rests upon the building of sequences which hold learners' interest because the total context of the sequence is meaningful, and because elements within the sequence build from simple (prerequisite) skills to more complex (target) skills which take longer to accomplish.

As will be seen, the question of sequencing is encountered at several "levels" of curriculum and course design, and the issues are somewhat different among levels. But basically, the matter of effective sequences of instruction is closely related to the matter of course organization. While there is no very systematic body of knowledge relating to how major parts of a course should be organized and sequenced, there is a reason to try to organize it "from the top, downward" —to go from more general to more specific objectives.

In Chapter 2 we indicated that once the objectives or goals are specified for a given curriculum or course, it is desirable to next identify major "course units," each of which may require several weeks of study. Under each such unit, one may next identify "terminal objectives" to be reached by the end of the unit or by the end of the course. These terminal objectives are then broken down into enabling objectives, each of which may in turn have several subordinate objectives.

Intellectual skill objectives are usually the starting point for consideration of the sequencing of instruction; objectives from other domains of learning outcomes are then woven into the overall sequence wherever they best support intellectual skill objectives, or vice versa. The integration of intellectual skill objectives with those from other domains of outcome may then be represented as "instructional maps" for various levels of course organization (cf. Wager, 1977). Ultimately, individual lessons are planned to integrate related skills into an overall "lesson," which may of course require more than a single period of instruction.

There is no standard number of "levels" to be employed in organizing a course, hence the number of levels at which sequencing decisions must be made is also a matter of considerable variation.

Briggs (1977, Chap. 4) has suggested that after a needs analysis has resulted in goals for a curriculum in a given subject, each year of instruction be considered a course. Then, for each such course, objectives would be derived for the following levels:

1. Life-long objectives, which imply the continued future use of what is learned, after the course is over.
2. End-of-course objectives, which state the performance expected immediately after instruction is completed for the course.
3. Unit objectives, which define the performances expected on clusters of objectives having a common purpose in the organization of the total course.
4. Performance objectives, which are the specific outcomes expected, and which are likely to be at the appropriate level for task analysis.
5. Enabling objectives, which support the learning of performance objectives either because they are essential prerequisite skills required to learn target objectives or because they facilitate such learning. The construction of *learning hierarchies* (Chapter 6) identifies the essential prerequisites, while empirical evidence may be sought in identifying other enabling objectives.

AN EXAMPLE OF COURSE ORGANIZATION

Considering the nature of the content of this book it is perhaps not inappropriate to illustrate the levels of course organization for a graduate course in "the design of instruction." This course is a part of a doctoral program in instructional systems design. Related courses in the curriculum pertain to learning theory, research methods, statistics, varieties of instructional design, design theories, and models of instructional delivery. Students entering the course typically have master's degrees, often in an area of teaching such as science education, or in fields such as educational media or educational administration. Most of them have completed an introductory course in the theory base for systems models for the design of instruction.

Students are taught to design their own courses based on some identified instructional need or goal. Following the "general to specific" basis for course design, students are asked to state their course objectives at several levels.

The levels of objectives for the graduate course in the design of instruction may be illustrated as follows:

1. Life-long Objective After completion of this course, the students will continue to add to their course design skills by (a) enrolling for other design courses, (b) seeking a variety of opportunities to apply design skills in circumstances which require them to modify learned models or to originate new models. Students will choose to employ or originate systematic course design procedures based on theory, research, and consistent rationales; they will choose to use empirical data to improve and evaluate their designs.

2. End-of-course Objective By the end of the course, the student will have demonstrated the ability either to perform or to plan each step in a systems model of instructional design, from needs analysis to summative evaluation. (In this course, efforts are concentrated on Stages 4 through 9, as listed in Table 2–1).

3. Unit Objectives Students will complete four successive "assignments" by completing states of design representing the following course units:

Unit A: The student will generate a course organization showing life-long objectives, end-of-course objectives, unit objectives, and specific performance objectives, with accompanying measures of learner performance for whatever levels of objectives at which the learners' work is to be evaluated.

Unit B: The student will generate, in writing, a learning hierarchy for an intellectual skill objective, and will devise an instructional map to show how the prerequisite skills in the hierarchy are to be sequenced in relation to each other and in relation to objectives in other domains of outcomes.

Unit C: The student will generate, in writing, either a lesson plan or a module of instruction, showing a rationale for media selection and prescriptions for instruction to be prepared for each medium selected.

Unit D: The student will generate a written script which implements the media prescriptions made in Unit C.

4. Specific Performance Objectives (for Unit C, above)

a. State the objective(s) or enabling objective(s) for the lesson being planned.
b. Classify the objective(s) by domain (and sub-domain, if appropriate).
c. List the instructional events to be employed, and give a rationale for use or non-use of each of the nine events.
d. List the type of stimuli for each event.

e. List the media choices appropriate for each event.
f. Identify the theoretically best medium for each event.
g. Make the final medium selection for each event.
h. Give a rationale for decisions in **d** through **g**.
i. Write the prescriptions (to the media producers) for each event.

Specific performance objectives for all four units of this course, along with criteria appropriate for evaluating students' work in the course, are listed in detail elsewhere (Briggs, 1977, pp. 464–468). Many of the prerequisite objectives supporting the specific performance objectives for the course are represented in the form of practice tests and exercises (Briggs, 1970) that students take to test their readiness to write each of the four "assignments" listed previously as course units.

Note that the students' work is evaluated at the level of *unit objectives.* They are expected to master the specific objectives and associated prerequisite skills by learning from: (a) group sessions with the instructor; (b) readings; (c) self-tests and practice exercises; (d) conferences with the instructor; (e) written feedback from the instructor after each assignment is completed; and (f) critique of their own work, using the published criteria for evaluation of each assignment. In a similar course for less sophisticated students it might be appropriate to evaluate student performance for each specific performance objective, or even for each enabling objective.

The levels of objectives previously described may be taken as one way to express the "organization of a course." Note that this organization itself stops at the level of objectives for individual lessons. However, the materials prepared for the course are targeted to the enabling objectives and to those instructional events thought necessary for inclusion in students' materials. The materials which are successful for graduate students may not be entirely successful for other learners. For the latter, modified versions might need to incorporate greater precision in events for various prerequisite objectives. Five other examples of this method of expressing the organization of a course are presented by Briggs (1972, 1977) for different subject areas and ages of learners.

The sequencing of the four course units follows the design stage sequence shown in Table 2–1 (Chapter 2). While *learning* presumably could take place in other sequencing arrangements, in this case it appeared reasonable to have the *learning sequence* follow the sequence that an experienced designer would employ in practice. On the other hand, there is often reason to have the learning sequence *different* from the on-the-job sequence. It may be further noted that the sequence of activities for learners in the classroom is often different from either the sequence in which the teacher acquired classroom management skills or the sequence in which designers of materials employ their skills (Briggs, 1977, p. 12).

Another example of sequence planning may be illustrated by the levels of a curriculum in English writing for the junior high school. The sequence problem obviously arises here at the total course level. Or, there may be a problem to be solved for the single course topic, such as "writing descriptive paragraphs." A third and critically important level of the "sequence question" concerns the sequence of skills within the individual lesson, such as "constructing sentences with dependent clauses." And finally, there is the matter of the sequence of events which does occur or is planned to occur, to bring about the acquisition of an individual learning objective, such as "identifying initial letters of sentences as capitalized letters." These four different levels of the sequence problem are illustrated in Table 8–1.

It is important to distinguish among these four levels of the "sequence question," since quite different considerations apply to each one. As will be apparent from the contents of this chapter, we are mainly concerned here with Levels 1 and 2, and will be dealing again in the next three chapters with the questions posed by Levels 3 and 4.

Sequence of the course and curriculum

It is difficult to find a basis for correct sequencing of the entire set of topics for a course or set of courses other than a kind of "common-sense" logical ordering. Presumably, one wants to insure that prerequisite intellectual skills and verbal information that are necessary for any given topic have been previously learned. For example, the topic of adding fractions is introduced in arithmetic after the student has learned to multiply and divide whole numbers, because the operations required in adding fractions include these "simpler" operations. In a science course, one is concerned that a topic like "graphically representing relations between physical variables" has been preceded by a topic such as "measuring physical variables," because these are the measures which will be represented on the graph. Similarly, one attempts to insure that a social studies topic on "comparison of family structures across cultures" has been preceded by a topic on "the family" and one on "What is a culture?"

TABLE 8–1   Four Different Levels of the Problem of Instructional Sequence

	Unit	Example	Sequence Question
Level 1	Course or Course Sequence	Essay Composition	How shall the topics of "achieving unity," "paragraph arrangement," "writing the paragraph," "summarizing," etc., be arranged in sequence?
Level 2	Topic	Writing the Paragraph	How shall the sub-topics of "topic sentence," "arranging ideas for emphasis," "expressing a single idea," etc., be arranged in sequence?
Level 3	Lesson	Composing a topic sentence	How shall the subordinate skills in composing a topic sentence be presented for learning in sequence?
Level 4	Lesson Component	Constructing a complex sentence	How shall the communications and other events in the learner's environment be arranged in a sequence resulting in learning of the desired single capability?

Presumably, the primary basis for the design of such topic sequences within courses or sets of courses rests upon judgments of *how much* can be accomplished within any single topical unit. If the conceived subject is "small" (such as "Roman numerals"), it can be planned as a single topic. If it is large, this means it will take more time, and therefore must be designed as a succession of topics, or possibly as a sequence of common "threads" within a succession of topics.

Course and curriculum sequences are typically represented in *scope and sequence charts,* which name the topics to be studied in a total course or set of courses and lay them out in matrices, often indicating the topics suggested for each grade level. More elaborate methods for representing both topics and lessons have been attempted, notably by *Science—A Process Approach* (AAAS Commission on Science Education, 1967). The chart which accompanies this elementary science curriculum not only suggests a set of topics and a sequence of lessons within each, but also indicates the set of prerequisite relationships which may be presumed to exist among them.

It may be that some theoretical basis will one day be proposed to replace the "common-sense logic" which now underlies the design of sequences of topics for courses. The idea of the "spiral curriculum" (Bruner, 1960, p. 52), for example, proposes that content topics be systematically reintroduced at periodic intervals. Two purposes are served by such a scheme. First, the previously learned knowledge of the topic is given a review, which tends to improve its retention. And second, the topic may be progressively elaborated when it is reintroduced, leading to broadened understanding and transfer of learning. The conception of the spiral curriculum has not as yet been explicated in detail, but it appears to hold much promise for future curriculum design efforts.

Sequence of the topic

Designing a sequence of instruction within a topic is a problem on which some systematic techniques can be brought to bear. Initially, it may be recognized that a topic can, and often does, have several components—several different purposes. A topic on "the family," for example, is likely to include purposes like (a) "understanding the definition of 'family'," (b) "knowing differences in the characteristics of families of different cultures," and (c) "appreciating cultural differences in families." It may be noted that we use the word "purpose" to represent the aims of a topic. This word is used to imply an instructional unit of intermediate size—a size which is typical in the planning of topics. Note also that statements of purpose are not usually phrased in terms of human performance, as are the unitary objectives described in the previous chapter.

A mathematics topic, such as "understanding the addition of integers," may likewise have more than one purpose. One may be "finding the sum of positive and negative numbers," while another within the same topic may be "deriving the properties of a number system from basic axioms." Further, the designer of instruction for such a topic may even have in mind the purpose of "appreciation of the precision of mathematical reasoning."

The probability is high that when differing purposes (stated in terms similar to those employed in these examples) can be identified as part of a single topic, one must be prepared to deal with different kinds of *learning outcomes* (that is, different types of *learned capabilities*). Unfortunately, though, the existence and number of different learning outcomes cannot be established with certainty simply by stating more than one purpose for a topic. The difficulty lies in the ambiguities of language. Thus, a statement like "appreciation of family differences" may imply one, two, or even three different kinds of learned capabilities, when examined more thoroughly.

Analyzing Goal Statements to Determine Learning Outcomes   To overcome the difficulty of language ambiguity in statements of topic purposes, one must move toward *performance objectives*. It is often recommended that the entire process of stating a total set of performance objectives, including those for each lesson in the topic, be carried out. Such an effort would likely yield a fairly large number of specific performance objectives, such as "classifies the functions of a mother" (for a topic on the family), and many equally specific others. This manner of proceeding is surely not incorrect in any basic sense. The specific objectives can then be grouped and categorized into types of learned capabilities, which is the desired outcome.

However, it may be recognized that, although correct, the method of defining an entire set of performance objectives may be inconvenient at this stage of the game. The designer of instruction within a topic may well not want to be bothered with the details of performance objectives in order to plan the various component lessons on which his attention is focused. He wishes to answer the question, "What lessons are needed?" rather than, "What objectives are to be contained within each lesson?" He therefore is likely to search for a shortcut.

How can one "move in the direction of performance objectives" without actually stating all of them in detail? One possible answer is to attempt to analyze each topic purpose in terms of some *representative* performance objectives, rather than all of them. "Appreciation of family differences"—what does that mean in terms of human performance? It might mean "classifying the characteristics which make families differ, from one culture to another"—a reasonably good performance objective. Or, it might mean "generating a definition of family which accounts for cultural differences"—a different but equally good performance objective. At this point it may be clear to the designer that there is still another possibility latent in this topic statement. This is "choosing not to make prejudicial statements about families or members of families from different cultures"—again, a reasonably good performance objective.

When analyses of this sort are carried out and yield objectives in performance terms, even if only representative examples, the process of identifying learning outcomes becomes quite clear. With just a little thought, one can readily identify the kind of learned capability which is being demanded, as follows:

"classifying the characteristics which make families differ from one culture to another"	type of capability—an intellectual skill, more specifically, a defined concept
"generating a definition of family which takes account of cultural differences"	type of capability—a different intellectual skill, namely, problem-solving
"choosing not to make prejudicial statements about families or members of families from different cultures"	type of capability—an attitude

It is evident from this example, then, that statements of topic purposes are simply too ambiguous to be dealt with in analytical fashion. They may serve a satisfying purpose for the person who enunciates them (who may, of course, be a parent or school-board member). The instructional designer, however, cannot work with such ambiguity. He must find at least representative examples of the performance objectives which reflect the single or multiple meanings of the topic statement. In this way, the designer will readily be able to categorize them as types of capabilities to be learned.

The previously stated mathematics example, "understanding the addition of integers," can be analyzed as readily to yield types of learning outcomes as follows:

"finding the sum of positive and negative numbers"	type of capability—intellectual skill (rule)
"deriving the properties of a number system from basic axioms"	type of capability—(1) intellectual skill (problem solving) and (2) cognitive strategy
"preference for using the precision of mathematical reasoning"	type of capability—attitude

Identifying the Lessons Required for a Topic   Once the learning outcomes have become clear, it is possible to proceed with planning the lessons required for the topic. Often, one tries to have a single lesson deal with a single learning outcome. The reason for this procedure, of course, is that each type of learning outcome (motor skill, verbal information, intellectual skill, cognitive strategy, attitude) requires a different set of critical learning conditions, as described in Chapters 4 and 5. However, a hard-and-fast rule should probably not be suggested, since in many instances the designer may think it better to include more than one type of learning outcome in each lesson, or even to shift back and forth between different types of outcomes. The implication is that planning for lessons within a topic should be done in terms of learned capabilities. These are likely to be the stable elements in the total plan, rather than the lessons themselves.

The components of the topic, then, can be planned as sets of lessons (if relatively lengthy instruction is implied), individual lessons (if instruction is of moderate length), or parts of lessons (if small). In any case, these components of the topic need to be conceived as *differentiated types of learning outcomes,* each of which requires a different set of critical conditions in order for the desired learning to occur. Of course, it is possible that a topic might have only one type of capability to be learned; but it not uncommon for several types to be present within a given topic.

Sequencing Lessons in Topics   Now it is possible to return to the main subject of this section, which is the sequencing of lessons within topics. In view of the fact that different learning outcomes may be involved, this is not an entirely simple matter, and again, it is one in which common sense plays a part.

Table 8–2 summarizes the major considerations regarding the sequential arrangement within a topic for each of the types of learned capability. The middle column of the table indicates sequencing principles applicable to the particular kind of capability which represents the central focus of the learning. The right-hand column lists sequence considerations relevant to this learning, but arising in other domains.

TABLE 8–2   Desirable Sequence Characteristics Associated with Five Types of
Learning Outcome

Type of Learning Outcome	Major Principles of Sequencing	Related Sequence Factors
Motor Skills	Provide intensive practice on part-skills of critical importance and practice on total skill.	First of all learn the executive routine (rule).
Verbal Information	For major sub-topics, order of presentation not important. Individual facts should be preceded or accompanied by meaningful context.	Prior learning of necessary intellectual skills involved in reading, listening, etc. is usually assumed.
Intellectual Skills	Presentation of learning situation for each new skill should be preceded by prior mastery of subordinate skills.	Information relevant to the learning of each new skill should be previously learned or presented in instructions.
Attitudes	Establishment of respect for source as an initial step. Choice situations should be preceded by mastery of any skills involved in these choices.	Information relevant to choice behavior should be previously learned or presented in instructions.
Cognitive Strategies	Problem situations should contain previously acquired intellectual skills.	Information relevant to solution of problems should be previously learned or presented in instructions.

Sequencing Lessons for Motor Skills   In the case of motor skills, there is evidence which implies that the learning of an executive routine (Fitts and Posner, 1967, p. 11) is of critical importance to total learning. Such a routine represents the "procedure" of the motor performance and governs the sequence of actions involved in it. The executive routine is actually a rule, the intellectual-skill component of a motor skill. For example, in learning to put the shot, the performer must learn to follow the sequence of taking some running steps, stopping at a line, taking a stance with the shot, and then ejecting the shot. In carrying out these actions in order, the performer is following a rule, that must be learned as an early part of the total learning task, perhaps first of all. The more specific motor components must then be practiced. Generally, the evidence does not indicate that the total skill will always be more quickly or readily learned if the components are practiced as "parts" before being put together into the total skill (Bilodeau, 1966, p. 398). Highly complex motor skills appear to be best learned when practiced as "wholes." However, in some instances there may be an advantage to providing intensive practice on some part-skill which plays a particularly critical role in determining good performance in the whole skill. An example is the intensive practice of the "flutter-kick" by swimmers who are aiming at competitive swimming of the "crawl."

Sequencing Lessons for Information   When outcomes of information learning are intended, sequence is not of outstanding importance. For example, in order to learn the political events leading up to the election of President Lincoln, it is not of great importance that these events be discussed in a strict temporal order, so long as this order is indicated (cf. Payne, Krathwohl, and Gordon, 1967). The presentation of these facts within a meaningful context, however, is an important consideration for effective learning. Ausubel (1968) suggests that the meaningful context in the form of an "advance organizer" should come first, and he has obtained evidence to this effect (Ausubel, 1960; Ausubel and Fitzgerald, 1961).

Sequencing Lessons for Intellectual Skills   When the topic or subtopic requires the learning of *intellectual skills,* sequence, in the sense of the mastery of prerequisite skills, becomes a most important consideration, as we have seen in Chapter 6 (cf. Gagné, 1977, pp. 142–150). The learning of each skill representing a lesson objective will occur most readily when the learner is able to bring to bear those recalled, previously acquired skills which are relevant to the new task. The learning of such tasks also requires information, which may either be recalled or presented as a part of instructions for the learning task. For example, if the intellectual skill being acquired involves the balancing of a chemical equation, the learner may need either to recall, or to be told by instructions, such facts as the valence of hydrogen (H^+), sulfur (S^-), and other elements.

Sequencing Lessons for Attitudes   The learning of attitudes seems to best occur under circumstances in which a respected "source" (that is, a person) makes a verbal communication to the learner regarding desirable choices of action, or perhaps displays these choices directly. For example, by his behavior the model may indicate a preference for counting to ten before losing his temper. To be effective, however, it is clear that the person acting as the model must be admired, respected, or otherwise well thought of. Of course, respect for the model may already be present in the learner, as when that person is a teacher, a parent, or a friend. If such respect is not present, for example, when the source is not well-known to the learner, it must be established as a first step in the sequence of events leading to attitude learning or change.

The desired attitude may involve choosing some action which in turn requires intellectual skills. Again, the implication is that such skills must have been previously learned; and if they were not, they should be acquired before the learning of the attitude is undertaken. For example, the desired learning may concern a consumer attitude governing the tendency to compare prices of packaged foods in terms of ratios, or cost per ounce. But such an attitude will not be successfully established, regardless of how well the other conditions of instruction may be arranged, if the learner has not acquired the capability of forming ratios to obtain comparative costs. In a similar manner, it may be determined that information relevant to the desired course of action is needed. Such information may be recalled from prior learning, or may be presented as part of the learning situation, usually before the communication which centers on the attitude to be learned.

Sequencing Lessons for Cognitive Strategies   In the learning of cognitive strategies, problem situations that require self-management skills of organizing, analyzing, and thinking are presented to the learner. In arranging such problem situations within a topic, one is often concerned that they be designed with suitable variety, so that the strategy being learned will become generalizable to many new situations in the future. Variations in successively presented problems need not occur in any particular sequence so far as is now known. However, it would seem best to avoid variations which appear too extreme, which have the effect of making the problem too "difficult" and scare the learner away. Even more important, the designer of instruction must avoid presenting problems which actually *are* too difficult—demanding intellectual skills or information which the learner does not possess. For instance, a geometrical problem may challenge the learner to engage in the kind of thinking which improves certain of his cognitive strategies; but if he fails to solve the problem because he is missing some component skill or piece of information about a particular geometrical relationship, the learning will not be effective, and the occurrence may contribute to the learner's discouragement. Prior learning of both relevant intellectual skills and relevant information (when not supplied by instructions) accordingly becomes a matter of consequence to the design of sequences for the learning of cognitive strategies.

Opportunities for application of cognitive strategies to varied problem situations are important to the learning of this kind of capability. Such varied "practice" appears to be essential for acquiring strategies which are broadly generalizable. In addition, success in solving problems has the effect of establishing and maintaining positive attitudes toward this kind of activity. In successfully solving novel problems, the learner may be acquiring confidence in his own capabilities. Thus he may be increasingly ready to trust his resources of cognitive strategies in meeting new problems.

Sequence of components within the lesson

The principles governing the design of sequences of instruction within lessons are essentially similar to those for various kinds of learning outcomes as they occur in topics, and as shown in Table 8-2. These types of learned capabilities typically appear as smaller "chunks" in lessons than they do in topics. Sometimes, of course, a particular "chunk" may require more than one time period, and thus need two or more lessons for complete coverage.

As we have seen, more than one type of learning outcome—intellectual skill, cognitive strategy, information, motor skill, or attitude—may occur within a lesson. Each of these kinds of outcome implies certain prerequisite learnings, and therefore an instructional sequence. Following the procedure we have outlined previously, the designer of a lesson will be placing emphasis on what the student can *do* as a result of instruction. Usually this means that the designer will need to make a somewhat detailed analysis of the *intellectual skills* involved in a lesson. The planning of a lesson can often best be undertaken by making intellectual skills the major organizing factor. In any case, the method of analyzing these skills to reveal the requirements of sequencing needs to be described in greater detail.

Table 8-2 indicates, for intellectual skills, that each new skill should be preceded by prior mastery of subordinate skills. The way this influences the planning of events of a lesson is described in the following chapter. Before reaching that point, however, it may be desirable to review some of the implications of the notion of *essential prerequisites* (discussed in Chapter 6) for the sequencing of instruction.

LEARNING HIERARCHIES AND INSTRUCTIONAL SEQUENCE

The nature of intellectual skills makes it possible to design effective conditions for their learning with considerable precision. When a proper sequence of prerequisite skills is established, the learning of intellectual skills becomes a process which is easy for a teacher to manage. In addition, the process of learning becomes highly reinforcing for the learner, because he frequently realizes that with apparent and satisfying suddenness he knows how to do some things that he didn't know before. Thus the activity of learning takes on an excitement for him which is at the opposite pole from "drill" and "rote recitation."

As described in Chapter 6, the learning hierarchy which results from a learning task analysis is the arrangement of intellectual skill objectives into a pattern which shows the prerequisite relationships among them. An additional example of a learning hierarchy, this time for a skill in kindergarten mathematics, is shown in Figure 8–1.

Here the lesson objective (for a preschool or kindergarten child) is one of dividing a group of objects into halves, and a similar group of objects into thirds. In order to learn to perform such a task correctly, the child must have some prerequisite skills, which are indicated on the second "line" of the hierarchy. Specifically, he or she must be able (1) to look at a set of objects which the teacher has divided into halves and be able to identify them (as by pointing) as "halves," and similarly for a set of objects divided into thirds. Also, the child must be able (2) to make subsets of objects which are equal by a one-to-one pairing process. These two prerequisite skills, then, are considered to be essential for the learning of the skill represented by the target objective with which the hierarchy was begun. Each of these prerequisite skills (1) and (2) has its own prerequisites, which are indicated on the next "line" of the hierarchy.

What is meant by a prerequisite? Evidently, a prerequisite is a "simpler" intellectual skill, but such a characterization is quite inadequate to identify it properly, since one could name many intellectual skills pertaining to sets of

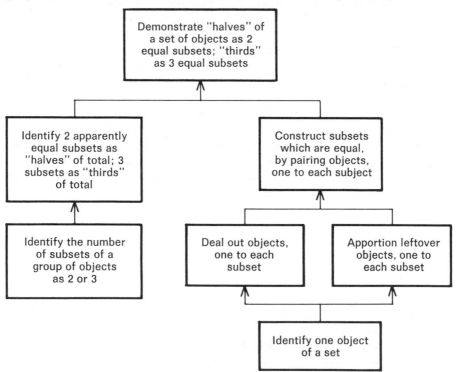

FIGURE 8–1   A Learning Hierarchy for a Task in Elementary Mathematics

(Adapted from Resnick and Wang, 1969.)

objects which are simpler than the lesson objective described in the figure. A prerequisite skill is *integrally related* to the skill which is superordinate to it, in the sense that the latter skill cannot be done if the prerequisite skill is not available to the learner. Consider what the child is doing when "demonstrating 'halves' of a set of objects as two equal subsets." He or she makes a physical separation of the objects, on a table top. But the child must know that to achieve "halves" there must be *two* subsets; this is prerequisite (1). And he or she must be able to make these two subsets equal, in the sense that each contains exactly the same number of members; this is prerequisite (2). If the child *fails* to do either of these things, he or she will not be able to perform the milestone objective. Now turn this idea around: If the child *already knows* how to do each of these subordinate things, learning to do the lesson objective will be easy and straightforward. The likelihood is that (once asked) the child will learn to do it rapidly, and even with the kind of immediacy implied by the word "discovery."

The general form of question one needs to ask about any skill, in order to identify its prerequisites, is "What would the learner have to know how to do in order to learn this (new) skill, assuming I simply told him or her what was wanted?" (cf. Gagné, 1968). In other words, prerequisite intellectual skills are those that are critically required to be recalled by the learner, if the learning of the new skill is to proceed most rapidly and without problems. There is a way of checking whether one's first attempt to answer the preceding question has been successful. This is to think out what the to-be-learned performance requires of the learner, and identify "how the learner could go wrong." Applying this to the lesson objective of Figure 8–1, one can see that a child who is attempting to "demonstrate halves of a set of objects" might fail if he or she didn't divide the set into two parts—this is prerequisite (1); or, the child might fail if he or she didn't make these two parts equal—this is prerequisite (2). Thus the specification of prerequisite skills should provide a complete description of those previously learned skills needed by the learner in order to acquire the new skill most readily.

Incidentally, the fact that prerequisite skills may be checked by considering ways in which the learner can fail serves to emphasize the direct relevance of learning hierarchies to the teacher's task of *diagnosis*. If one finds a learner who is having trouble acquiring a new intellectual skill, the first diagnostic question should probably be, "What prerequisite skills has this person failed to learn?" The contrast between such a question and those of, "What genetic deficiency does this person have?" or "What is the person's general intelligence?" will be apparent. The latter questions may suggest solutions which merely serve to remove the learner from the learning environment by putting him or her in a special group or class. Responsible diagnosis, in contrast, attempts to discover what the learner needs to learn. The chances are high that this will be a prerequisite intellectual skill, as indicated by a learning hierarchy. If it is, suitable instruction can readily be designed to get the learner "back on the track" of a learning sequence which continues to be positively reinforcing.

SUMMARY

This chapter opens with an account of how the organization of a total course relates to questions about the sequencing of instruction. Four levels of sequencing decisions are identified.

Ways are suggested of deciding upon instructional sequences at the levels of the course and the topic. Course planning for a sequence of topics is typically done by a kind of "common-sense" logic. One topic may precede another because it describes earlier events, or because it is a component part, or because it provides a meaningful context for what is to follow.

In proceeding from course purposes to performance objectives, it may not always be necessary to describe all the intermediate levels of planning in terms of complete lists of performance objectives for the topic. The method suggested here involves choosing representative samples of objectives within each domain of learning outcomes. It may be noted, however, that the more complete procedure can be followed and may sometimes be desirable as is illustrated in Briggs (1972, 1977).

The designing of sequences for intellectual skills is based upon learning hierarchies which are derived by "working backwards" from target objectives to analyze the sequences of skills to be learned in an order suggested by their arrangement, as described in Chapter 6. The learning of a new skill will be accomplished most readily when the learner is able to recall the subordinate skills which compose it. When an instructional sequence has been designed for an intellectual skill, related learning of other capabilities may be interjected at appropriate points, as when the learning of information is required or the modification of an attitude is desired. In other instances, instruction aimed at other capabilities may come before or after the intellectual skill represented in the learning hierarchy.

Designing sequences for other types of learned capabilities also requires an analysis of prerequisite learnings. Examples were given to illustrate how such prerequisites may be identified and incorporated into sequences of instruction.

The following three chapters describe how the plans for instructional sequence are carried into the design of a single lesson or lesson component. It is in the latter context that the "events of instruction" are introduced. These events pertain to the external supports for learning provided by the teacher, the course materials, or by the learner himself. They depend upon the prior learning which has been accomplished in accordance with a planned sequence.

References

AAAS Commission on Science Education. *Science—A Process Approach.* Hierarchy Chart. New York: Xerox, 1967.

Ausubel, D. P., Novak, J. D., and Hanesian, H. *Educational Psychology: A Cognitive View.* 2d. Ed. New York: Holt, Rinehart and Winston, 1978.

Ausubel, D. P. The use of advance organizers in the learning and retention of meaningful verbal material. *Journal of Educational Psychology*, 1960, *51*, 267–272.

Ausubel, D. R., and Fitzgerald, D. The role of discriminability in meaningful verbal learning and retention. *Journal of Educational Psychology,* 1961, *52,* 266–274.

Bilodeau, E. A. *Acquisition of Skill.* New York: Academic Press, 1966.

Briggs, L. J. *Handbook of Procedures for the Design of Instruction.* Pittsburgh: American Institutes for Research, 1970.

Briggs, L. J. *Student's Guide to Handbook of Procedures for the Design of Instruction.* Pittsburgh: American Institutes for Research, 1972.

Briggs, L. J. (ed.). *Instructional Design: Principles and Applications.* Englewood Cliffs, N.J.: Educational Technology Publications, 1977.

Bruner, J. S. *The Process of Education.* Cambridge, Mass.: Harvard University Press, 1960.

Fitts, P. M., and Posner, M. I. *Human Performance.* Belmont, Ca.: Brooks/Cole, 1967.

Gagné, R. M. Learning hierarchies. *Educational Psychologist,* 1968, *6,* 1–9.

Gagné, R. M. *The Conditions of Learning,* 3d Ed. New York: Holt, Rinehart and Winston, 1977.

Payne, D. A., Krathwohl, D. R., and Gordon, J. The effect of sequence on programmed instruction. *American Educational Research Journal,* 1967, *4,* 125–132.

Resnick, L. B., and Wang, M. C. *Approaches to the Validation of Learning Hierarchies.* Pittsburgh, Pa.: Learning Research and Development Center, University of Pittsburgh, 1969.

Wager, W. Instructional technology and higher education. In L. J. Briggs (ed.), *Instructional Design.* Englewood Cliffs, N.J.: Educational Technology Publications, 1977.

The Events of Instruction

Planning a course of instruction makes use of the principles described in the preceding chapters: determining what the outcomes of instruction are to be, defining performance objectives, and deciding upon a sequence for the topics and lessons which make up the course. When these things have been done, the fundamental "architecture" of the course is ready for more detailed planning in terms of both teacher and student activities. It is time to give consideration to the bricks and mortar of the individual lesson.

Supposing, then, that the course of instruction has been planned so that the student may reasonably progress from one lesson to the next. How does one insure that he or she takes each learning step, and does not falter along the way? How is the student coaxed along during the lesson itself? How does one, in fact, *instruct* the student?

THE NATURE OF INSTRUCTION

In designing the "architecture" for the course, we have said virtually nothing about how instruction itself may be done. During a lesson there is progress from one moment to the next as a set of events acts upon and involves the student. This set of events is what is specifically meant by *instruction*.

The instructional events of a lesson may take a variety of forms. They may require the teacher's participation to a greater or lesser degree; and they may be determined by the student to a greater or lesser degree. In a basic sense, these events constitute a set of *communications to the student*. Their most typical form is as verbal statements, whether oral or printed. Of course, communications may be made to young children which are not verbal, and which instead use other media of communication such as gestures or pictures. But whatever the medium, the essential nature of instruction is most clearly characterized as a set of communications.

The communications which make up instruction have the sole aim of aiding the process of learning—that is, of getting the student from one state of mind to another. It would be wrong to suppose that their function is simply "to communicate" in the sense of "to inform." Sometimes it appears that teachers are inclined to make this mistake—they "like to hear themselves talk," as has sometimes been said. There is perhaps no better way to avoid the error of talking too much than to keep firmly in mind that communications during a lesson are to facilitate learning, and that anything beyond this is mere chatter. Much of the communicating done by a teacher is essential for learning. Sometimes a fairly large amount of teacher communication is needed; on other occasions, however, none may be needed at all.

Self-instruction and the self-learner

Any or all of the events of instruction may be put into effect by the learner himself when he is "self-instructing." Students engage in a good deal of self-instruction, not solely when they are working on "programmed" materials, but also when they are studying textbooks, performing laboratory exercises, or completing projects of various sorts. Skill at self-instruction may be expected to increase with the age of the learners, as they gain in experience of learning tasks. Events of the lesson, designed to aid and support learning, require teacher activities to a much greater extent in the first grade than they do in the tenth. As learners gain experience and continue to pursue learning activities, they acquire more and more of the characteristics of "self-learners." That is, they are able to use skills and strategies by which they manage their own learning.

The events of instruction to be described in this chapter, therefore, should not be viewed as being invariably required for every lesson and every learner. In practice, a judgment must be made concerning the extent of self-instruction the learner is able to undertake. A more extensive consideration of self-instruction in systems of individualized instruction is contained in Chapter 14.

Instruction and learning

The purpose of instruction, however it may be done, is to provide support to the processes of learning. It may therefore be expected that the kinds of events that comprise instruction should have a fairly precise relation to what is going on within the learner whenever learning is taking place. In order to undertake instructional design at the level of the individual learning episode, it appears necessary to derive the desirable characteristics of *instructional events* from what is known about *learning processes.*

While we are unable within the confines of this book to describe modern theoretical notions of learning processes in detail, it appears worthwhile to provide a brief account of learning theory, which the reader may wish to supplement by reference to other works. In particular, we are concerned with establishing a sound basis in learning theory for the derivation of instructional events. Each of the particular events that make up instruction functions to aid or otherwise support the acquisition and the retention of whatever is being learned. These functions of external events may be derived by consideration of the internal processing which makes up any single act of learning. The kinds of internal processing referred to are those varieties involved in modern cognitive learning theories (cf. Estes, 1975; Klatzky, 1975).

The sequence of processing envisaged by cognitive theories of learning is approximately as follows (Gagné, 1974, 1977b). The stimulation which affects the learner's receptors produces patterns of neural activity which are briefly "registered" by *sensory registers*. This information is then transformed into a form which is recorded in the *short-term memory,* where prominent features of the original stimulation are stored. The short-term memory has a limited capacity in terms of the number of items that can be "held in mind." The items that are so held, however, may be internally "rehearsed," and thus maintained. An important transformation, called "semantic encoding," takes place when the held information enters the *long-term memory* for storage. As its name implies, in this kind of transformation information is stored according to its meaning. (In the context of cognitive learning theory, information has a general definition which includes the five kinds of learned capabilities distinguished in this book.)

When learner performance is called for, the stored information or skill must be searched for and "retrieved." It may then be transformed directly into action, by way of a *response generator*. Frequently, the retrieved information is recalled to the *working memory* (another name for the short-term memory), where it may be combined with other incoming information to form new learned capabilities. Learner performance itself sets in motion a process that depends upon external *feedback,* which involves the familiar procedures of *reinforcement.*

In addition to the learning sequence itself, cognitive theories of learning and memory propose the existence of *executive control* processes. These are processes which select and set in motion certain cognitive strategies relevant to learning and remembering. Control processes of this sort modify the other information-flow processes of the learner. Thus, they may exercise control over attention, over the encoding of incoming information, and over the retrieval of what has been stored.

The *kinds of processing* that are presumed to occur during any single act of learning may be summarized as follows:

1. *Attention*—determines the extent and nature of reception of incoming stimulation
2. *Selective perception*—transforms this stimulation into the form of object-features, for storage in short-term memory
3. *Rehearsal*—maintains and renews the items stored in short-term memory
4. *Semantic encoding*—the process which prepares information for long-term storage

5. *Retrieval,* including *search*—returns stored information to the working memory, or to a response generator mechanism
6. *Response organization*—selects and organizes performance
7. *Feedback*—an external event which sets in motion the process of *reinforcement*
8. *Executive control processes*—select and activate cognitive strategies; these modify any or all of the previously listed internal processes.

A diagram indicating the relation between the structures involved in cognitive theories of learning and memory, and the processes associated with them, is shown in Figure 9–1.

Instructional events

The processes involved in an act of learning are, to a large extent, activated internally. That is to say, the output of any one structure (or the result of any one kind of processing) becomes an input for the next, as Figure 9–1 indicates. However, these processes may also be influenced by *external* events, and this is what makes instruction possible. Attention, for example, may obviously be affected by particular arrangements of external stimuli. The features of a picture of text organized by selective perception may be influenced by highlighting, underlining, bold printing, and other measures of this general sort. The particular kind of semantic encoding which is done in learning may be specified or suggested by meaningful information provided externally.

From these reflections on the implications of learning theory, one can derive a definition. Typically, *instruction is a set of events external to the learner which are designed to support the internal processes of learning* (Gagné, 1977b). The events of instruction are designed to make it possible for a learner to proceed from "where he is" to the achievement of the capability identified as the target objective. In some instances, these events occur as a natural result of the learner's interaction with the particular materials of the lesson; as, for example, when the beginning reader comes to recognize an unfamiliar printed word as something familiar in his or her oral vocabulary, and thus receives *feedback.* Mostly, however, the events of instruction must be deliberately arranged by an instructional designer or teacher. The exact form of these events (usually, communications to the learner) is not something that can be specified in general for all lessons, but rather must be decided for each learning objective. The particular communications chosen to fit each set of circumstances, however, should be designed to have the desired effect in supporting learning processes.

The functions served by the various events of instruction in an act of learning are listed in Table 9–1, in the approximate order in which they are typically employed (Gagné, 1968, 1977a). Thus, the initial event of *gaining attention* is one which supports the learning event of *reception* of the stimuli and the patterns of neural impulses they produce. Another very early instructional event, *informing the learner of the objective,* is presumed to set in motion a process of executive

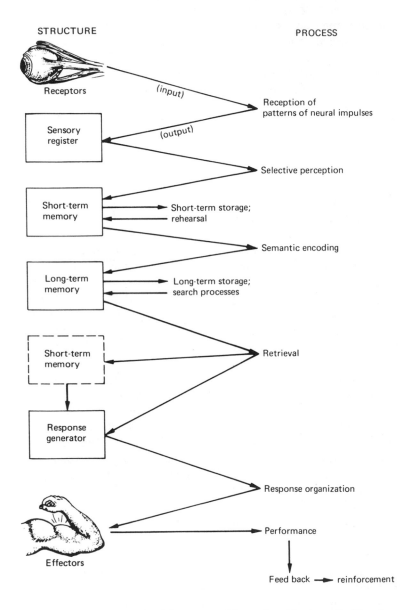

STRUCTURE   PROCESS

Receptors

(input)

Reception of
patterns of neural impulses

Sensory
register

(output)

Selective perception

Short-term
memory

Short-term storage;
rehearsal

Semantic encoding

Long-term
memory

Long-term storage;
search processes

Short-term
memory

Retrieval

Response
generator

Response organization

Effectors

Performance

Feed back ➤ reinforcement

FIGURE 9–1   The Postulated Structures of Some Cognitive Learning Theories, and the
             Processes Associated with Them

*(From Gagné, R. M. The Conditions of Learning, 3d Ed. New York: Holt, Rinehart and
Winston, 1977, Figure 3.2. By permission of the copyright owner, Holt, Rinehart and
Winston).*

156

control by means of which the learner maintains his orientation to the learning task and its expected outcome. The events which follow in Table 9–1 can each be related to the learning processes shown in Figure 9–1.

It should be realized at the outset that these events of instruction do not invariably occur in this exact order, although this is their most probable order. Even more important, by no means are all of these events provided for every lesson. Sometimes, one or more of them may already be obvious to the learner, and therefore may not be needed. Also, one or more of these kinds of communication are frequently provided by the learner himself, particularly when the learner is a sophisticated self-learner.

Gaining Attention   Various kinds of events are employed to gain the learner's attention. Basic ways of commanding attention involve the use of stimulus change, as is often done in moving display signs or in the rapid "cutting" of scenes on a television screen. Beyond this, a fundamental and frequently used method of gaining attention is to appeal to the learner's interests. A teacher may appeal to some particular child's interests by means of a verbal question such as "Wouldn't you like to know what makes a leaf fall from a tree?" in introducing a lesson dealing with leaves. One child's interest may be captured by such a question as, "How do you figure a baseball player's batting average?" in connection with a lesson on percents. Naturally, one cannot provide a standard content for such questions—quite to the contrary, since every student's interests are different. Skill at gaining attention is a part of the teacher's art, involving insightful knowledge of the particular students involved.

Communications which are partially or even wholly non-verbal are often employed to gain attention for school lessons. For example, the teacher may present

TABLE 9–1   Events of Instruction, and Their Relations to Processes of Learning

Instructional Event	Relation to Learning Process
1. GAINING ATTENTION	*Reception* of patterns of neural impulses
2. INFORMING THE LEARNER OF THE OBJECTIVE	Activating a process of *executive control*
3. STIMULATING RECALL OF PREREQUISITE LEARNINGS	*Retrieval* to working memory
4. PRESENTING THE STIMULUS MATERIAL	Emphasizing features for *selective perception*
5. PROVIDING "LEARNING GUIDANCE"	*Semantic encoding*
6. ELICITING THE PERFORMANCE	Activating a *response organization*
7. PROVIDING FEEDBACK ABOUT PERFORMANCE CORRECTNESS	Establishing *reinforcement*
8. ASSESSING THE PERFORMANCE	Activating *retrieval*; making *reinforcement* possible
9. ENHANCING RETENTION AND TRANSFER	Providing cues and strategies for *retrieval*

a demonstration, perhaps exhibiting some physical event (a puff of smoke, an unexpected collision, a change in color of liquid) which is novel and appeals to the student's interest or curiosity. Or, a motion picture or television scene may depict an unusual event and thus command attention.

A good preplanned lesson provides the teacher with one or more options of communications designed to gain attention. When instruction is individualized, the teacher is able to vary the content and form of the communication whenever necessary, in order to appeal to individual student interests.

Informing the Learner of the Objective   In some manner or other, the learner should know the kind of performance which will be used as an indication that learning has, in fact, been accomplished. Sometimes this aim of learning is quite obvious, and no special communication is required. For example, it would be somewhat ridiculous to make a special effort to communicate the objective to a novice golfer who undertakes to practice putting. However, there are many performance objectives which may not be initially obvious to students in school. For example, if the subject under study is the Preamble to the United States Constitution, being able to recite it verbatim is not at all the same objective as being able to state its major ideas. If decimals are being studied, is it obvious to the student during any given lesson whether he or she is expected to learn to (1) read decimals, (2) write decimals, or perhaps, (3) add decimals? The student should not be required to guess what is in the instructor's mind. The student needs to be told (unless, of course, he or she already knows).

On the whole, it is probably best not to take the chance of assuming that the student knows what the objective of the lesson is. Such a communication takes little time, and may at least serve the purpose of preventing the student from "getting entirely off the track." Communicating the objective also appears to be an act consistent with the frankness and honesty of a good teacher. In addition, the act of verbalizing the objective may help the teacher to stay "on target."

Of course, if objectives are to be communicated effectively, they must be put into words (or pictures, if appropriate) that the student can readily understand. For a six-year-old, an objective like "given a noun subject and object, and an active verb, formulate a correct sentence" must be translated into a communication which runs somewhat as follows: "Suppose I have the words 'boy,' 'dog,' and 'caught.' You could make them into a sentence, like 'The boy caught the dog.' This is called 'making a sentence,' and that's what I want you to do with the words I point to." Performance objectives, when used to describe a course of study, are typically stated in a form designed to communicate unambiguously to teachers or to instructional designers. The planning of instruction for a lesson, however, includes making the kind of communication of the lesson's objective which will be readily understood by students.

It is sometimes speculated that communicating an objective to students may tend to keep them from trying to meet still other objectives which they may formulate themselves. No one has ever seen this happen, and the chances are it is a highly unlikely possibility. When one communicates a lesson's objective to students, they are hardly inclined to think that such a statement forbids them from giving further thought to the subject at hand. Working with an objective of "reading decimals," for example, it is not uncommon for a teacher to ask the question, "What do you suppose the sum of these decimals might be?" Thus still another objective is communicated, which the students are perfectly free to think about, while making sure that they have achieved the first-mentioned objective. Naturally, one also wants the students to develop in such a way that they will think of objectives themselves and learn how to teach them to themselves. Nothing in the communication of a lesson's objectives carries the slightest hint that such activities are to be discouraged. The basic purpose of such communication is simply to answer the student's question, "How will I know when I have learned?"

Stimulating Recall of Prerequisite Learned Capabilities   This kind of communication may be critical for the essential event of learning. Much of new learning (some might say, all) is, after all, the combining of ideas. Learning a rule about *mass* (Newton's Law) involves a combination of the ideas of *acceleration* and *force,* as well as the idea of *multiplying.* In terms of modern mathematics, learning the idea of *eight* involves the idea of the *set seven,* the *set one,* and *joining.* Component ideas (concepts, rules) must be previously learned if the new learning is to be successful. At the moment of learning, these previously acquired capabilities must be highly accessible in order to take part in the learning event itself. Their accessibility is insured by having them recalled just before the new learning takes place.

The recall of previously learned capabilities may be stimulated by a communication which asks a recognition, or better a recall, question. For example, when children are being taught about rainfall in relation to mountains, the question may be asked, "Do you remember what the air is like in a cloud which has travelled over land in the summer?" (The air is warm.) The further question may then be asked, "What is the temperature of the land on a high mountain likely to be?" (Cold.) This line of questioning recalls previously learned rules, and obviously leads to a strand of learning which will culminate with the acquisition of a new rule concerning the effects of cooling on a warm, moisture-laden cloud.

Presenting the Stimulus Material   The nature of this particular event is relatively obvious. The stimuli to be displayed (or communicated) to the learner are those involved in the performance which reflects the learning. If the learner must learn a sequence of facts, such as the events of history, then these are facts which must be communicated, whether in oral or printed form. If the learner is engaged in the task of pronouncing aloud printed words, as in elementary reading, then the printed words must be displayed. If the student must learn to respond to oral questions in French, then these oral questions must be presented, since they are the stimuli of the task to be learned.

Although seemingly obvious, it is nevertheless of some importance that the proper stimuli be presented as a part of the instructional events. For example, if the learner is acquiring the capability of answering questions delivered orally in French, then the proper stimuli are *not* English questions, nor printed French questions. (This is not to deny, however, that such tasks may represent subordinate skills which have previously been used as learning tasks.) If the learner is to acquire the capability of using positive and negative numbers to solve verbally stated problems, then the proper stimuli are verbally stated problems, and not something else. If one neglects to use the proper stimuli for learning, the end result may be that the learner acquires the "wrong" skill.

Stimulus presentation often emphasizes *features* that determine selective perception. Thus, information presented in a text may contain italics, bold print, underlining, or other kinds of physical arrangements designed to facilitate perception of essential features. When pictures or diagrams are employed, important features of the concepts they display may be heavily outlined, circled, or pointed to with arrows. In establishing discriminations, distinctive features may be emphasized by enlarging the differences between the objects to be distinguished. For example, in programs of reading readiness, large differences in shapes (such as those of a circle and triangle) may be introduced first, followed by figures exhibiting smaller differences. Distorted features of a *b* and a *d* may be initially presented, in order that the smaller differences of these letters will eventually be discriminated.

Stimulus presentation for the learning of concepts and rules requires the use of a *variety of examples.* When the objective is the learning of a concept such as "circle," it is desirable to present not only large and small circles on the chalkboard or in a book, but also green circles, red ones, and ones made of rope or string. One might even have the children stand and join hands to form a circle. For young children, the importance of this event can hardly be over-emphasized. The failure to provide such a variety of examples accounts for the classic instance related by William James in which a boy could recognize a *vertical* position when a pencil was used as the test object, but not when a table knife was held in that position.

Comparable degrees of usefulness can be seen in the use of variety of examples as an event for rule learning. To apply the formula for area of a rectangle, $A = x \cdot y$, the student must not only be able to recall the statement which represents the rule, but he must know that A means area; he must understand what area means; he must know that x and y are the dimensions of two non-parallel sides of the rectangle, and he must know that the dot between x and y means multiply. But even when all these subordinate concepts and rules are known, the learner must do a variety of examples to insure that he understands and can use the rule. Retention and transfer are also likely to be enhanced by presenting problems stated in words, in diagrams, and in combinations of the two, over a period of time.

Once such rules are learned, groups of them need to be selectively recalled, combined, and used to solve problems. Employing a variety of examples in problem solving might entail teaching the learner to break down odd-shaped figures into known shapes, like circles, triangles, and rectangles, and then to apply rules for finding the area of these figures as a way to arrive at the total area of the entire shape.

In the learning of both concepts and rules, one may proceed either inductively or deductively. In learning concrete concepts, like circle or rectangle, it is best to introduce a variety of examples before introducing the definition of the concept. (Imagine teaching a four-year-old the formal definition of a circle before exposure to a variety of circles!) But for the older learners who are learning defined concepts, a simple definition might best come first, such as: "A root is the part of a plant below the ground." Assuming the learner understands the component concepts that are contained in the statement, this should be a good start, perhaps followed at once by a picture.

Providing Learning Guidance   Suppose one wishes a learner to acquire a rule (or it might be called a defined concept) about the characteristics of prime numbers. He might begin by displaying a list of successive numbers, say, 1 through 25. He then might ask the learner to recall that the numbers may be expressed as products of various factors; $8 = 2 \times 4 = 2 \times 2 \times 2 = 8 \times 1$, etc. The learner could then be asked to write out all the factors for the set of whole numbers through 30. What is wanted, now, as a learning outcome, is for the learner to discover the rule that there is a certain class of numbers whose only factor (or divisor) other than the number itself is 1.

The learner may be able to "see" this rule immediately. If not, he may be led to its discovery by a series of communications in the form of "hints" or questions. For example, such a series might run somewhat as follows: "Do you see any regularities in this set of numbers?" "Do the original numbers differ with respect to the number of different factors they contain?" "In what way are the numbers 3, 5, and 7 different from 4, 8, and 10?" "In what way is the number 7 like the number 23?" "Can you pick out *all* the numbers which are like 7 and 23?"

These communications and others like them may be said to have the function of *learning guidance*. Notice that they do not "tell the learner the answer"; rather, they suggest the line of thought which will presumably lead to the desired "combining" of subordinate concepts and rules so as to form the new to-be-learned rule. Again, it is apparent that the specific form and content of such questions and "hints" cannot be spelled out in precise terms. Exactly what the teacher or textbook says is not the important point. It is rather that such communications are performing a particular function. They are stimulating a direction of thought and are thus helping to keep the learner "on the track." In performing this function, they contribute to the efficiency of learning.

The amount of learning guidance, that is, the number of questions and the degree to which they provide "direct or indirect prompts," will obviously vary with the kind of capability being learned (Wittrock, 1966). If what is to be learned is an arbitrary matter such as the name for an object which is new to the learner (say, a pomegranate), there is obviously no sense in wasting time with indirect hinting or questioning in the hope that somehow such a name will be "discovered." In this case, "just telling the student the answer" is the correct form of guidance for learning. At the other end of the spectrum, however, are cases where less direct prompting is appropriate, because this is a logical way to discover the answer, and such discovery may be more permanent than being told the answer.

The amount of questioning or hinting needed will also vary with the learner. Some learners require less learning guidance than do others in most situations. They simply "catch on" more quickly. Prior learning can never reduce such individual differences to the zero point. For this reason, learning guidance needs to be adapted to the individual learner. Too much of it may seem condescending to the quick learner, whereas too little of it can simply lead to frustration on the part of the slow learner. The best practical solution would seem to be to apply learning guidance a little at a time, and allow the student to use as much as he needs. Only one "hint" may be necessary for a fast learner, whereas three of four may work better with a slower learner. In memorizing a poem, one would give the actual word which the learner cannot recall, but in learning a principle one might just supply a hint.

In the learning of attitudes, a *human model* may be employed, as indicated in Chapter 5. Models themselves, as well as the communications they deliver, may be considered to constitute the learning guidance in attitude learning. Thus the guiding communication in this case takes a somewhat more complex form than is the case with the learning of information or intellectual skills. The same function of semantic encoding is being served, however.

Eliciting the Performance   Presumably, having had sufficient learning guidance, the learners will now be carried to the point where the actual internal "combining" event of learning takes place. Perhaps they look less confused, or some indication of pleasure has crossed their faces. They have "seen" how to do it! We must now ask them to *show* that they know how to do it. We want them not only to convince us, but to convince themselves as well.

Accordingly, the next event is a communication that in effect says "show me," or "do it." Usually, this first performance following learning will use the same example (that is, the same stimulus material) with which the learners have been interacting all along. For example, if they have been learning to make plurals of words ending in *ix,* and have been presented with the word *matrix,* the first performance is likely to be production of the plural *matrices.* In most instances, the instructor will follow this with a second example, like *appendix,* in order to make sure the rule can be applied in a new instance.

Providing Feedback   Although in many situations it may be assumed that the essential learning event is concluded once the correct performance has been exhibited by the learner, this is not universally the case. One must be highly aware of the aftereffects of the learning event and their important influence on determining exactly what is learned. In other words, as a minimum, there should be feedback concerning the correctness or degree of correctness of the learner's performance. In many instances, such feedback is automatically provided—for example, an individual learning to throw darts can see almost immediately how far away from the bull's eye the dart lands. Similarly, a child who has managed to match a printed word with one in his or her oral vocabulary, and which at the same time conveys an expected meaning, receives a kind of immediate feedback which has a fair degree of certainty. But, of course, there are many tasks of school learning which do not provide this kind of "automatic" feedback. For example, in practicing using the pronouns *I* and *me* in a variety of situations, is the student able to tell which are right and which are not? In such instances, feedback from an outside source, usually a teacher, may be an essential event.

There are no standard ways of phrasing or delivering feedback as a communication. In an instructional program, the confirmation of correctness is often printed on the side of the page or on the following page. Even standard textbooks for such subjects as mathematics and science customarily have answers printed in the back of the book. When the teacher is observing the learner's performance, the feedback communication may be delivered in many different ways—a nod, a smile, or a spoken word. Again in this instance, the important characteristic of the communication is not its content but its function: providing information to the learners about the correctness of their performance.

Assessing Performance   The immediate indication that the desired learning has occurred is provided when the appropriate performance is elicited. This is, in effect, an assessment of learning outcome. Accepting it as such, however, raises the larger questions of *reliability* and *validity* which relate to all systematic attempts to assess outcomes or to evaluate the effectiveness of instruction. These are discussed in a later chapter, and we shall simply state here their relevance to the single learning event.

When one sees the learner exhibit a single performance appropriate to the lesson objective, how does the observer or teacher tell that he or she has made a *reliable* observation? How does that person know the student didn't do the required performance by chance, or by guessing? Obviously, many of the doubts raised by this question can be dispelled by asking the learner to "do it again," using a different example. A first-grader shows the ability to distinguish the sounds of *mat* and *mate.* Has he or she been lucky, or can the child exhibit the same rule-governed performance with *pal* and *pale?* Ordinarily, one expects the second instance of the performance to raise the reliability of the inference (concerning the student's capability) far beyond the chance level. Employing still a third example should lead to higher probability so far as the observer is concerned.

How is the teacher to be convinced that the performance exhibited by the learner is *valid?* This is a matter which requires two different decisions. The first is, does the performance in fact accurately reflect the objective? For example, if the objective is "recounts the main idea of the passage in his or her own words," the judgment must be made as to whether what the student says is indeed the *main* idea, not just any old idea. The second judgment, which is no easier to make, is whether the performance has occurred under conditions which make the observation *free of distortion.* As an example, the conditions must be such that the student could not have "memorized the answer," or remembered it from a previous occasion. The teacher must be convinced, in other words, that the observation of performance reveals the learned capability in a genuine manner.

Obviously, the single, double, or triple observations of performance that are made immediately after learning may be conducted in quite an informal manner. Yet they are of the same sort, and part of the same piece of cloth, as the more formally planned assessments described in a later chapter. There need be no conflict between them, and no discrepancies.

Enhancing Retention and Transfer   When information or knowledge is to be recalled, the existence of the meaningful context in which the material has been learned appears to offer the best assurance that the information can be reinstated. The network of relationships in which the newly learned material has been embedded provides a number of different possibilities as cues for its retrieval.

Provisions made for the recall of intellectual skills often include arrangements for "practicing" their retrieval. Thus, if defined concepts, rules, and higher-order rules are to be well retained, course planning must make provision for systematic *reviews* spaced at intervals throughout weeks and months. The effectiveness of these spaced repetitions, each of which requires that the skill be retrieved and used, contrasts with the relative ineffectiveness of repeated examples given directly following the initial learning (Reynolds and Glaser, 1964).

As for the assurance of transfer of learning, it appears that this can best be done by setting some *variety* of new tasks for the learner—tasks which require the application of what has been learned in situations that differ substantially from those used for the learning itself. For example, suppose that what has been learned is the set of rules pertaining to "making the verb agree with the pronoun subject." Additional tasks which vary the pronoun and the verb may have been used to assess performance. Arranging conditions for transfer, however, means varying the entire situation more broadly still. This might be accomplished, in this instance, by asking the child to compose several sentences in which he himself supplies the verb and the pronoun (rather than having them supplied by the teacher). In another variation of the situation, the student may be asked to compose sentences using pronouns and verbs, to describe some actions shown in pictures. Ingenuity of the teacher is called for in designing a variety of novel "application" situations for the purpose of insuring transfer of learning.

Variety and novelty in problem-solving tasks are of particular relevance to the continued development of cognitive strategies. As has previously been mentioned, the strategies used in problem solving need to be developed by the systematic introduction of occasions for problem solving interspersed with other instruction. An additional event to be especially noted in the presentation of novel problems to the student is the need to make clear the general nature of the solution expected. For example, "practical" solutions may be quite different from "original" solutions, and the student's performance can easily be affected by such differences in the communication of the objective (cf. Johnson, 1972).

Instructional events and learning outcomes

The events of instruction may be appropriately employed for each of the five kinds of learned capabilities described in Chapters 3 and 4. In the case of some events, such as gaining attention, the particular means employed to bring about the event does not have to be different for intellectual skill objectives, say, and for attitude objectives. However, the event employed to represent learning guidance for these two kinds of outcomes is likely to be very different indeed. As we have seen in the previous section, the encoding of an intellectual skill is usually aided by verbal instructions, as by communicating to the learner a verbal statement of a to-be-learned rule. In contrast, effective encoding of an attitude often requires a complex event which includes observation of a human model.

A summary of appropriate events of instruction for each type of learned capability is contained in Table 9–2. The nine instruction events listed in the first column are followed by columns containing brief descriptions of the conditions of learning appropriate for intellectual skills, cognitive strategies, information, attitudes, and motor skills.

As inspection of the table will show, the particular form taken by the instructional event depends, naturally enough, upon the capability to be learned. For example, when an intellectual skill is to be learned, the stimulation of recall pertains to the retrieval of prerequisite concepts or rules; whereas if information is to be learned, the recall of a context or organized information is required. Similar specific differences in the form of the event may be noted throughout the table. The single exception is the event of gaining attention. The stimulus or sensory modality change employed to gain attention often is unrelated to the anticipated learning outcome.

THE EVENTS OF INSTRUCTION IN A LESSON

In using the events of instruction for lesson planning, it is apparent that they must be organized in a flexible manner, with primary attention to the lesson's objectives. What is implied by our description of these events is obviously not a standardized, routine, set of communications and action. The invariant features of the single lesson are the functions which need to be carried out in instruction. Even these functions are adapted to the specific situation, the task to be accomplished, the type of learning represented in the task, and the students' prior

TABLE 9–2 Instructional Events and the Conditions of Learning They Imply for Five Types of Learned Capabilities

Instructional Event	Type of Capability				
	Intellectual Skill	Cognitive Strategy	Information	Attitude	Motor Skill
1. Gaining Attention	Introduce stimulus change; variations in sensory mode				
2. Informing learner of objective	Provide description and example of the performance to be expected	Clarify the general nature of the solution expected	Indicate the kind of verbal question to be answered	Provide example of the kind of action choice aimed for	Provide a demonstration of the performance to be expected
3. Stimulating recall of prerequisites	Stimulate recall of subordinate concepts and rules	Stimulate recall of task strategies and associated intellectual skills	Stimulate recall of context of organized information	Stimulate recall of relevant information, skills, and human model identification	Stimulate recall of executive sub-routine and part-skills
4. Presenting the stimulus material	Present examples of concept or rule	Present novel problems	Present information in propositional form	Present human model, demonstrating choice of personal action	Provide external stimuli for performance, including tools or implements
5. Providing learning guidance	Provide verbal cues to proper combining sequence	Provide prompts and hints to novel solution	Provide verbal links to a larger meaningful context	Provide for observation of model's choice of action, and of reinforcement received by model	Provide practice with feedback of performance achievement
6. Eliciting the performance	Ask learner to apply rule or concept to new examples	Ask for problem solution	Ask for information in paraphrase, or in learner's own words	Ask learner to indicate choices of action in real or simulated situations	Ask for execution of the performance
7. Providing feedback	Confirm correctness of rule or concept application	Confirm originality of problem solution	Confirm correctness of statement of information	Provide direct or vicarious reinforcement of action choice	Provide feedback on degree of accuracy and timing of performance
8. Assessing performance	Learner demonstrates application of concept or rule	Learner originates a novel solution	Learner restates information in paraphrased form	Learner makes desired choice of personal action in real or simulated situation	Learner executes performance of total skill
9. Enhancing retention and transfer	Provide spaced reviews including a variety of examples	Provide occasions for a variety of novel problem solutions	Provide verbal links to additional complexes of information	Provide additional varied situations for selected choice of action	Learner continues skill practice

learning. But each one of these functions should be specifically considered in lesson planning.

It is now possible to consider how these events are exemplified within an actual lesson. We have chosen as a model a first-grade lesson in elementary science, entitled *Linear Measurement,* from *Science—A Process Approach* (AAAS Commission on Science Education, 1967). The objective of this exercise is "demonstrating a procedure for finding the length of an object in units on an agreed-upon scale." The following columns show, on the left, the suggested activity for the lesson; and on the right, a description of the instructional event being served by each of these activities.

LESSON ACTIVITIES AS GIVEN IN SCIENCE—A PROCESS APPROACH, PART B, MEASURING 2—LINEAR MEASUREMENT

INSTRUCTIONAL EVENT

A large cardboard box is placed on one side of the room, a table on the other. Children are asked how they could tell, without moving box or table, whether the box would fit under the table. Suggestions are asked for, discussed, and verified.

Gaining attention by introducing a novel situation, appealing to children's motive for mastery of their environment.

Children in groups are given "measuring sticks" varying in length from 5 to 100 cm. They are asked to think about how they could use the sticks to measure the height of the box.

Stating the objective.

Measurements obtained by different groups of children are found to be different. The suggestion is made that different "units" be given different names. A table is made of measurements obtained by children, reporting the number of units they obtained in measuring a designated length.

During this activity, there is *recall* of a previously learned capability, in which lengths of unit sticks are ordered from shortest to longest. In addition, the children are being asked to *recall* the counting of numbers, in reporting how many units are contained in the length they measure. They are learning to select shorter or longer units and to place them end-to-end, both subordinate skills which will be readily *recalled* in the next activity.

Children are asked to measure strips of tape placed on the floor (a little over 1.5 meters long); and also to measure the length of new pencils. Different groups of children have

The *stimulus materials* for the learning are presented: the sticks and the lengths to be measured.

The "tries" made by the children,

different-sized measuring units (5 cm. to 100 cm.). The children discuss the appropriateness of different lengths being measured.

Finally, they are asked to compare the suitability of 15 cm. sticks and the 100 cm. sticks in measuring the tapes on the floor. The 15 cm. sticks and the 100 cm. sticks are laid end-to-end on each side of the tapes, and the children are asked which units are more suitable.

Following the learning, additional appraisal is carried out by marking different chalk-lengths on the floor, and asking the children to select appropriate unit sticks to report their measurements in number of stick-lengths.

A "generalizing experience" is suggested, consisting of measurements of the span of the child's outstretched arms, and also his height. The children must choose the "stick units" and make the measurements.

which are more or less successful, depending on the units they work with, provide for discussions in which some amount of *learning guidance* is given.

The *performance* sought is elicited by the question "Which is more suitable for measuring these tapes?" The selection of appropriate units is the objective in this case.

Feedback is given for selection of units that result in more successful and less successful measurement attempts.

Assessment of the learning has been carried out in an immediate sense, in this lesson, by asking for the measurement of (1) pencils, and (2) tapes on the floor. The assessment is continued, in order to increase confidence in its reliability, by the additional "appraisal" portion of the exercise.

Transfer of learning is the functional aim of this and other measurements which might be employed. Note the intention of using varied situations for these additional activities.

Retention is provided for in these materials by scheduling review in a subsequent lesson. For example, Measurement 4 is entitled "Linear Measurement Using Metric Units."

It is evident, then, that this lesson in elementary science has been carefully planned in the sense that it reflects each of the instructional events described in this chapter. Of course, it should be understood that the lesson itself has only been summarized here; the reader who wishes to gain a fuller understanding of its suggested procedures should refer to the original source. Obviously, it is an exercise in which the teacher's art has considerable opportunity to flourish, within the framework of events which generate confidence for the desired learning to be accomplished.

Comparison with Lessons for Older Students   As instruction is planned for middle and higher grades, one can expect the events of instruction to be increasingly controlled by the materials of a lesson, or by the learners themselves. Thus, when units of instruction which make up a course of study are structurally similar, as may be the case in mathematics or beginning foreign language, for example, the objectives for each succeeding unit may be evident to students, and therefore may not need to be communicated. For reasonably well-motivated students, it is often unnecessary to make any special provisions for controlling attention, since this event, too, may be appropriately managed by the learners themselves. This circumstance clearly contrasts with that prevailing in, say, a classroom of seventh-graders, where special provisions for obtaining attention often need to be made.

Homework assignments, such as those which call for learning from a text, depend upon the learners to employ cognitive strategies available to them in managing instructional events. The text may aid selective perception by its inclusion of bold printing, topic headings, and other features of this general sort. The text may, and often does, include a context of meaningful material which provides for semantic encoding by relating new information to organized knowledge already in learners' memories. An important part of "studying," however, is the necessity for practicing appropriate performance, whether this is a matter of stating information in the learner's own words, applying a newly learned rule to examples, or originating solutions to novel problems. For these events of self-instruction, as well as for the judgment of correctness which gives an immediate sort of feedback, learners frequently must depend upon cognitive strategies available to them.

SUMMARY

This chapter is concerned with the events that make up instruction for any single performance objective, as they may occur within a lesson. These are the events that are usually external to the learner, supplied by the teacher or text, or by other media with which the learner interacts. When self-instruction is undertaken, as is to be more frequently expected as the learner's experience increases, instructional events may be brought about by the learner himself. However they originate, the purpose of these events is to activate and support the internal processes of learning.

The general nature of supporting external events may be derived from the information-processing (or "cognitive") model of learning and memory, which is employed in one form or another by many contemporary learning investigators. This model proposes that a single act of learning involves a number of stages of internal processing. Beginning with the receipt of stimulation by receptors, these stages include (1) a brief *registration* of sensory events; (2) *temporary storage* of stimulus features in the short-term memory; (3) a *rehearsal* process which may be employed to lengthen the period of short-term storage and to prepare information for entry into long-term memory; (4) *semantic encoding* of information for long-term storage; (5) *search* and *retrieval* to recall previously learned material; and (6) *response organization* producing a performance appropriate to what has been learned. Most theories include, either implicitly or explicitly, the process of (7) *reinforcement* as brought about by external feedback of the correctness of performance. In addition, this learning model postulates a number of (8) *executive control processes* which enable the learner to select and use cognitive strategies which influence other learning processes.

As derived from this learning model, instructional events are given as follows:

1. Gaining attention
2. Informing the learner of the objective
3. Stimulating recall of prerequisite learnings
4. Presenting the stimulus material
5. Providing "learning guidance"
6. Eliciting the performance
7. Providing feedback about performance correctness
8. Assessing the performance
9. Enhancing retention and transfer.

These events apply to the learning of all of the types of learning outcomes we have previously described. Examples are given to illustrate how each is planned for and put into effect.

The order of these events for a lesson or lesson segment is approximate, and may vary somewhat depending upon the objective. Not all of them are invariably used. Some are made to occur by the teacher, some by the learner, and some by the instructional materials. An older, more sophisticated learner may supply most of these events by his own study effort. For young children, the teacher would arrange for most of them to occur.

As these events apply to the various kinds of capabilities being acquired, they take on different specific characteristics. This is a matter to be expanded upon in the following chapter. For example, *presenting the stimulus* (Event 4) for the learning of discriminations requires conditions in which the differences in stimuli become increasingly fine. Concept learning, however, requires the presentation of a variety of instances and non-instances of the general class. Conditions of *learning guidance* (Event 5) required for the learning of rules include examples of application; whereas these conditions for information learning are prominently concerned with linking to a larger meaningful context. For attitude learning, this event takes on an even more distinctive character when it includes a human model and the model's communications. The following chapter deals more fully with ways in which the events of instruction reflect these different conditions for the support of learning.

References

AAAS Commission on Science Education. *Science—A Process Approach, Part B.* New York: Xerox, 1967.

Estes, W. K. (ed.) *Handbook of Learning and Cognitive Processes,* Volume 1. *Introduction to Concepts and Issues.* Hillsdale, N.J.: Erlbaum Associates, 1975.

Gagné, R. M. Learning and communication. In R. V. Wiman and W. C. Meierhenry (ed.), *Educational Media: Theory into Practice.* Columbus, Ohio: Merrill, 1968, pp. 93–114.

Gagné, R. M. *Essentials of Learning for Instruction.* New York: Holt, Rinehart and Winston, 1974.

Gagné, R. M. *The Conditions of Learning,* 3d Ed. New York: Holt, Rinehart and Winston, 1977a.

Gagné, R. M. Instructional programs. In M. H. Marx and M. E. Bunch (ed.), *Fundamentals and Applications of Learning.* New York: Macmillan, 1977b.

Johnson, D. M. *A Systematic Introduction to the Psychology of Thinking.* New York: Harper & Row, 1972, pp. 272–338.

Klatzky, R. L. *Human Memory: Structures and Processes.* San Francisco: Freeman, 1975.

Reynolds, J. H. and Glaser, R. Effects of repetition and spaced review upon retention of a complex learning task. *Journal of Educational Psychology,* 1964, *55,* 297–308.

Wittrock, M. C. The learning by discovery hypothesis. In L. S. Shulman & E. R. Keislar (eds.), *Learning By Discovery: A Critical Appraisal.* Chicago: Rand McNally, 1966.

chapter 10

Selecting
and Using Media

One of the essential decisions that must be made in instructional design is what medium to employ as a vehicle for the presentation of the stimulation which makes up the events of instruction. There are possible choices of media to deliver the communications, or for other kinds of stimulation of which instruction is composed.

In this chapter we intend to describe the problem of media selection which confronts designers of instructional programs and also teachers who design means of delivery of instruction in lesson planning. Some of the common features of media selection "models" will be described as well as the factors to be taken into account in selecting media. A method of media selection will then be outlined, which indicates ways of incorporating desirable features. Some limitations of this method will be noted in comparison with other models.

SELECTION VERSUS DEVELOPMENT OF MEDIA PRESENTATIONS

When instructional design is developed from the very beginning one expects that media presentations will be part of the design. The term media, however, is employed here in a very broad sense. Instructional delivery may be accomplished by means of the verbal speech of a teacher, or by a printed text, as well as by way of vehicles of more complex technical material such as sound and video recordings. Often, however, existing media presentations are *selected* as part of a larger instructional plan, rather than being separately *designed* and *developed*. Teachers, as well as teams of instructional designers, may carry out a comprehensive design of instruction which depends upon the selection of media.

Teachers as instructional designers

Teachers often select and use a great variety of both print and non-print media materials. Only infrequently do teachers develop such materials or media presentations themselves. In conventional procedures, teachers select materials which will enable learners to master the desired objectives. This selection function can be thought of as a part of lesson planning. Briggs (1977) has suggested that a completed lesson plan can contain the following ingredients:

(1) a statement of the objectives of the lesson;
(2) a list of the instructional events to be included in the lesson;
(3) a list of media, materials, and activities by which each event is to be accomplished; and
(4) notes on necessary teacher roles and activities, and directions to be given to the learners.

It will be recalled from earlier chapters that we view the purpose of instructions as providing the desired instructional events for each lesson. Most of these events are needed for lessons in all the domains of learning outcomes commonly sought in education. Accordingly, one must choose *some* medium of instruction for each event. The media chosen may be the teacher's voice, or a film, or a book, or the learner's own study effort.

In selecting media and materials, the teacher is likely to discover immediately that available materials and media presentations are not *indexed* or *catalogued* according to objectives and instructional events. It is therefore suggested that the teacher make decisions about media in the process of lesson planning based on the two following questions:

1. What medium would I like to use for each instructional event?
2. Where will I find the specific materials, prepared in that medium?

Actually, of course, there is a third question affecting the teacher's decisions, and that is how the selected materials will be used. But this chapter deals primarily with media selection, while Chapter 11 focuses on media utilization.

While available materials will often contain much of the desired content (thus providing the desired instructional stimulus), they may not provide for other instructional events. For example, a film may deliver desired content, but it may not present the objective, or guide semantic encoding, or contain pauses for student response and feedback. In that case the teacher must either create such events separately from the film, or stop the film at points so that questions and feedback can occur. Other media, such as programmed instruction booklets, may furnish all the desired events for a lesson.

Most often, then, the teacher is faced with having to select media and materials that were not specifically designed for the exact objectives that have been adopted. Furthermore, the materials available often do not provide all the desired instructional events. Many materials are carefully organized to present information in a logical order but do not cover each instructional event appropriate for specific objectives. As a result the teacher cannot make all the media selection from catalogs; the actual media materials must be previewed before final selection is made. Subsequently, the teacher's lesson plans are designed to indicate how the selected materials will be used, and to note how the events not presented by the materials are to be accomplished.

On the brighter side, publishers and other suppliers of media are providing modules of instruction with increasing frequency. Such modules often give directions to both teachers and learners on how the materials and exercises can be used to reach the objectives, as well as how to know that they have been reached. While such modules may not always be designed around the specific set of instructional events described in this book, they usually have been designed to implement a systematic strategy of instruction. Some modules contain the actual materials to be used, while others just list them. As the use of such modules becomes more widespread, teachers should experience fewer difficulties in lesson planning and in selecting media and materials.

To summarize to this point, in the past teachers have had to spend considerable effort in locating and selecting appropriate media and materials. It has not always been easy to locate materials appropriate for a particular lesson objective. Thus, teachers have had to function both as designers and as managers of instruction. Owing to time limitations and other concerns, they have had to design by *selecting* from available materials. They were not able to undertake the development of more highly suitable materials. With the advent of *designed modules,* teachers have been relieved of much of the burden of design, making it possible for them to concentrate their time and energies upon the management of instruction.

Later portions of this chapter discuss how to go about media selection. But first we must consider how teams function as designers of modules and entire delivery systems as well.

Teams as designers

The modules that are available for selection and utilization by teachers have, of course, been designed by others. This may have been done by individuals working alone, but more often the modules are probably the product of a team effort. Sometimes modules are provided for single instructional objectives for which no materials previously existed. As new educational needs are identified, entirely new modules and materials are also required. Some modules are prepared to improve the quality or efficiency of instruction for long-recognized needs. Still other modules are parts of entire courses or curricula. It is beyond the scope of this book to discuss how teams are organized and managed, but the design procedures they use in their work will be described here. Basically, the principles of media selection and the design of materials are the same for design teams as for teachers, although the relative balance of responsibility for design and for implementation is different in the two cases. Both teachers and design teams need to select media of instruction, although only designers have the major responsibility for developing media materials. In short, both teachers and teams are designers; teachers are usually the managers of instruction.

DELIVERY SYSTEMS AND MEDIA

In the context of the total set of instructional system design stages outlined in Table 2–1 and discussed in Chapter 2, we need to relate delivery systems to media of instruction. As previously defined, a delivery system is the total of all components necessary to make an instructional system operate as intended. Media represent one component of delivery systems.

Since the term, *media,* has no entirely standardized meaning, we pause here to clarify our meaning of the term in relation to other terms to which it may be related:

sensory mode—the sense organ stimulated by an instructional message (the eye, the ear, and so on)

channel of communication—the sensory mode used in a communication (visual, auditory, tactile, kinesthetic, olfactory, and so on)

type of stimulus—the means but not the mechanism of communication, that is, the spoken word (whether by live voice or a recording), the printed word (whether presented in a book or on a chalkboard), motion pictures (whether presented by videotape or films)

media—the physical means of communication (books, printed modules, programmed texts; computers; slide/tape presentations; films, videotapes, and so on.)

Although the usages of these terms are somewhat arbitrary, they are presented because at least a few people use *media* to mean *all* of the above. Even with these definitions, students sometimes ask whether media refer to "hardware" or "software." According to our usage they could be either. We consider a motion picture projector as hardware, but we would classify the film (the medium) as software. Thus when both hardware and software are involved one would need to specify which is referred to: for example, the computer or the program presented by it, the projector or the film in it. In these cases the software carries the instructional stimuli, even though the hardware is necessary to present them. Among the previous distinctions, that between *type of stimulus* and *media* is most relevant to the method of media selection to be presented in this chapter.

Since no standard list of delivery systems has yet emerged in the literature Table 10–1 has been prepared to clarify the issue. It conveys the intended relationship of delivery systems to media, and relates both to kinds of learner activity, teaching methods, and teacher roles. This list of combinations of these five components of instruction is obviously not all-inclusive, but it does convey many examples to illustrate our usage of these terms.

It may be noted that a particular instructional system may utilize more than one delivery system. In fact, most major curricula or instructional systems may be expected to include more than one delivery system. For example, most individ-

TABLE 10–1 Relationships Among Some Components of an Instructional System

Delivery System	Possible Media	Learner Activity	Methods, Teacher Roles
Group instruction	Books, other reading materials	Reading	Lectures
	Charts, chalkboard, displays	Listening	Discussions
	Teacher	Observing demonstrations	Demonstrations
	Guest speakers	Manipulating objects	Oral quizzing
	Real objects, models, laboratory equipment, plants, animals	Visits	Corrects papers
	Overheads	Taking written tests	Scores tests
	Movies	Home study	Prepares reports to parents and administrators
	Field trips	Exercises and projects	
Individualized instruction (in school settings)	Programmed texts	Reading	Placement testing
	Books	Responding	Diagnostic testing
	Modules	Self-pacing	Monitors pupil progress
	Audio-visual devices for learner-control	Self-checking	Remedial instruction
	Peer tutoring	Completing exercises	Forming small groups which change frequently
	Self-check tests	Working with a peer	Keeps records
	Placement and progress tests	Taking tests	Monitors pupil use of materials and tests
	Diagnostic tests	Completing individual projects	Finds peer tutors to help pupils
	Learning centers and associated equipment and materials		Supervises available teacher aids
			Prepares reports to parents and administrators
Small group instruction	Books	Reading to each other	Assesses level of pupil progress
	Exercises	Performing joint laboratory exercises	Forms small groups for specific lessons or exercises
	Laboratory materials	Discussion	Assesses progress of individuals and small groups
	Slide/tape presentations	Watching presentations together	Keeps records
	Sound recordings	Completing team assignments	Assists in locating materials, using equipment
			Introduces new projects to small groups

176

	Materials	Student activities	Faculty functions
Independent study	Books Libraries Reading lists Laboratories Learning centers and associated equipment and materials Lists of objectives or exercises Final examinations	Reading and independent study Conducting library searches and laboratory experiments Writing papers Conferring with faculty members Taking written and oral examinations Writing major papers, thesis, or dissertation	Advisor performs guidance function Suggests or assigns tasks, papers, books, etc. Confers with student upon request or as scheduled Conducts examinations and evaluations of progress Conducts dissertation defense Certifies completion of specified units of work for credits or degrees Forms advisory committees to assist in above functions
Work-study programs	Any or all of the above for study portion of program Work at specified community locations involves variety of persons and equipment as media	Any or all of the above for study portion of program Any assigned work function, under supervision	Any or all of the above for study portion of program Coordinates work assignments with study portion of program
Home study (correspondence courses)	Books Exercises Tests Communications with instructor Programmed texts Modules Inexpensive viewers used with external lighting	Home study by reading, completion of exercises, taking tests, and corresponding with instructor	Assigns materials, exercises, and tests Answers questions by mail Scores tests and certifies completion of course May prepare and mail supplementary materials to those needing it

ualized instruction programs actually include, as a minimum, the kinds of media shown in Table 10–1 for group instruction, for small group instruction, and for individualized instruction. Table 10–1 clearly shows that several media usually are used together in a single delivery system. Similarly, in a single lesson or module it is common to find several media used. Our model of media selection requires consideration of alternative media for each instructional event in a lesson which could conceivably lead to the choice of a different medium for each event in a lesson. But more frequently, even for this model, the final plan suggests the use of one medium for several events in a lesson or module.

MEDIA SELECTION PROCEDURES

A number of different models of media selection have been prepared, which may first be described in terms of their distinctive features. Following this account, we proceed to discuss factors to be considered in making media selections, and then to outline our preferred model. While all these matters are of some interest to teachers who *select and utilize* media, they may be of special interest to design teams that plan the *development* of media presentations, including those using both print and non-print materials.

Features of media selection models

Media selection models have many features in common. For example, virtually all models call for consideration of the kind of objective being dealt with, the characteristics of the intended learners, and a host of practical factors such as size and composition of the group to be served, the range of viewing and hearing distances, and the like. Since separate summaries of the features of each model would be redundant, we will begin by listing some features common to the models, and then focus the discussion on the features of the models which differ.

Most writers on media selection models would initially agree that there is no one medium which is universally superior to all others for all types of desired outcomes and for all learners. This conclusion is also supported by research on media utilization (Briggs, Campeau, Gagné, and May, 1966; Briggs, 1968, 1970; Aronson, 1977). Most writers also agree that one cannot identify media which are particularly effective for a single school subject for a single grade level. Rather, careful design work and the results of media research both suggest that media are best selected for specific purposes within a single lesson. Thus, a motion picture may be an effective way to portray historical events in history lessons, but the teacher may be left to inform the learner of the objective, offer learning guidance, and provide feedback. It is not that a specially designed film could not provide all these events but rather that most available films do not do so. Films can also be used to portray theoretical events such as atomic particles in motion, or for enlarging, condensing, speeding up or slowing down the portrayal of observable activities in nature or in manufacturing processes. Other examples of media usage, along with a listing of some advantages and limitations of various media, have been described by Briggs (1970).

Media research and experience in media selection thus offer no simple answers about media selection which can be applied in a "cookbook" manner. Rather, thoughtful analysis is to be recommended, in considering the factors to be enumerated in a later section of this chapter. We turn first, however, to a consideration of distinctive differences among various media selection models.

Open vs. Closed Models There are two major ways of approaching media selection. In the "closed" approach, one decides which medium is to be used, and then proceeds to select or develop that medium. This approach may be used because of personal preferences for particular media, or because the resources are available for developing or using some media but not others. Given the same set of objectives, different designers with much experience in developing instruction, each in a different medium, may tend to overuse that medium when some objectives (or parts of them) *could* be better taught by other media. There is often a tendency for designers to make the same medium selection for large units of instruction, or even for an entire course.

Under an "open" model, one senior designer typically makes the media selections, and then assigns the development work to persons with appropriate media capabilities. This open model, in our opinion, is likely to lead to better media selections for small units of instruction; hence it is more analytical and more fine-grained than the closed model approach.

Several difficulties would arise in attempting to undertake research to verify or refute these opinions. It would be difficult to be sure that the same level of expertise was applied in developing the same instruction in different media. That is to say, success in finding comparable skill levels in script writing and production for several media would be difficult to demonstrate and measure. Also, the same content may or may not be conveyed in the parallel forms of the lesson, since different types of stimuli and sense modalities may not convey exactly the same message. With all the difficulties apparent in comparing media for a single lesson, comparing models in an effort to achieve generalizable results would appear to be an almost impossible task. This being the case, attention may best be directed to theoretical analysis of the distinctive features of the various models.

Size of "Chunk" Users of the closed model are likely to make media decisions for very large segments of instruction, while those applying an open model may make decisions for much smaller units of instruction. The closed model encourages use of intuitive rather than analytical rationales, and hence tends toward course-grained rather than fine-grained analyses and rationales.

Intuitive vs. Analytical Rationales If one asks designers how they go about selecting media the replies are likely to indicate that some have only an intuitive basis for choice, others use analytical rationales in varying degrees of detail, while still others apparently have no media selection model.

Among analytical rationales, the concept of the "cone of experience" explicated by Dale (1969) would appear to be analytic in its treatment of learner variables, and not analytic with respect to task variables. Dale's cone is applicable in practice to whatever size of instructional chunk the user chooses. Further discussion of Dale's rationales will be presented later in the chapter, where it is shown how his work can be combined with our own preferred set of procedures for media selection.

Factors in media selection

Task Variables   When media selections are being made, most designers consider the type of performance expected of learners as a result of instruction. Some media lend themselves more readily to the incorporation of immediate oral recall of the substance of information just received. Other media are more convenient when demonstration of skills is required of the learner. In general terms this means that some media lend themselves better than others to the incorporation of the desired conditions of learning. To help proceduralize this kind of analysis, we suggest noting the general kind of stimulus desired (printed or spoken words, real objects, or pictures) and the kind of responding desired, before further decisions affecting selection are made.

The following list indicates how the identification of type of stimuli presented in a lesson implies certain options of media choice.

Type of Stimuli	*Media Options*
1. Printed words	books; programmed instruction; handouts; charts; slide projectors; posters; chalkboard; checklists;
2. Spoken words	teacher; tape recording;
3. Still pictures and spoken words	slide tapes; voice slide; lecture with posters;
4. Motion, spoken words, and other sounds	motion pictures; television; live demonstration;
5. Pictoral portrayal of theoretical concepts	animated motion pictures; puppets and props.

In short, careful attention to the nature of the learning task (as given by its objective, or desired outcome) is a part of any analytical model of media selection.

Learner Variables   Nearly all designers would agree that the characteristics of learners must be considered when selecting media. There is not uniform agreement, however, on *which* characteristics are important. An area of research on the "trait-treatment interaction problem" seeks to identify which learner characteristics can be matched to specific features of the instruction, including the media used. Much more research will apparently be needed before we can hope for a practical guide to aid a designer in matching media to learners. Many educators are convinced that different learners, because of their different "learning styles," could benefit most from media which match those styles. Just what those learning style differences are, and whether they may be differentially effective with different media, is now largely unknown. Even if the styles were known, it might not be feasible or economical to provide enough parallel media packages for each lesson to accommodate all significant person-media interactions.

There are, however, some crude indicators of person variables which are useful in media selection. Obviously if it is known that the learners cannot read, print materials (for purposes other than learning to read) would be ruled out for initial instruction. Somewhat finer distinctions than this have shown some promise in research studies relating to learner variables and media (Briggs, 1968).

Given normal progression in reading skills for groups of learners, the learner's age is a useful matter to consider in media selection. In this connection, Dale's (1969) "cone of experience" is a useful tool. Dale listed twelve categories of media and exercises, in a somewhat age-related fashion. Thus, at Level 1, "Direct purposeful experience," it is proposed that a child come into physical contact with objects, animals, and people, using all the senses to "learn by doing." As one goes up the age scale, pictorial and other simulated substitutes can be employed for some of the experiences. At the top of the cone is the use of "verbal symbols," which suggests learning by reading, an efficient method for sophisticated learners. When dealing with cognitive objectives—information, intellectual skills, and cognitive strategies—a rule of thumb previously suggested by Briggs (1972) is: "Go as low on the scale as you need to in order to insure learning for your group, but go as high as you can for the most efficient learning." By considering the opposing factors of "slow but sure" (time-consuming direct experience) and "fast but risky" (typically occurring when learners are not skillful readers), one may decide just where on the scale is the best decision point for media selection.

Dale's categories are as follows:

12. Verbal symbols
11. Visual symbols—signs; stick figures
10. Radio and recordings
9. Still pictures
8. Motion pictures
7. Educational television
6. Exhibits
5. Study trips
4. Demonstrations
3. Dramatized experiences—plays, puppets; role-playing
2. Contrived experiences—models; mock-ups; simulation
1. Direct purposeful experience

For attitude objectives, Wager (1975) has suggested that Dale's age/media relationship becomes inverted, as compared to the relationship for cognitive objectives. Thus, while a young child benefits from direct experience with real objects for cognitive objectives, he may acquire an attitude by hearing verbal statements from people he respects, as discussed in Chapter 5. Attitudes may be formed by listening to statements from respected "models." Wager goes on to say that *changing* an already established attitude, on the other hand, may require real life experiences for both children and adults. Briggs (1977) describes attitude formation and change as it takes place at various age levels by various methods: (a) classical conditioning, (b) hearing persuasive communications, and (c) human modeling. Clearly different media would be involved in these different methods.

Some educators have sought to identify kinds of family backgrounds which are related to effectiveness of various media. Such factors may indeed be related to entering competencies and attitudes of pupils toward school learning, but it is not clear at present whether such data would be more useful in checking on the entering competencies of pupils in order to decide what they need to be taught or for selecting the media which relate to how they should be taught. However, a few indirect media selection implications are fairly likely. For example, children from homes where parents do not or cannot read are less likely than other children to have acquired a love for reading and skill in reading, other factors being equal.

The Assumed Learning Environment   Another set of factors in media selection is based upon administrative considerations rather than technical ones. The practicality of use of media varies with such features of the learning environment as: (1) size of school budget; (2) size of class; (3) capability for developing new materials; (4) availability of radio, television, and other media equipment; (5) teacher capabilities and availability for an instructional design effort; (6) availability of modular materials for individualized, performance-based instruction; (7) attitudes of principal and teachers towards innovations; and (8) school architecture.

Many of the decisions related to these factors may have been made early in the instructional design process, as discussed in Chapter 2. However, these early decisions are intended to match the total use or non-use of various delivery systems and media for specified school environments. Also, some of the factors clearly suit the situation where a retrofit is being made—where an established curriculum is being re-designed piecemeal as a gradual change strategy. These decisions are not at the same level of detail as media selection for specific lessons and instructional events within lessons.

The Assumed Development Environment   Obviously, it would be useless to plan to design a delivery system (and the attendant media) if the design and development resources were not adequate for the task. That is, the time, budget, and personnel available will influence the probability of success in designing specified delivery systems. The kinds of personnel available, for example, will determine the kinds of media that can be developed successfully. Beyond this, the personnel available will determine the kind of design model that is feasible for the situation. Carey and Briggs (1977) have discussed further how budgets, time, and personnel influence not only what instruction can be developed, but also what *design models* and what *team management* systems are appropriate to the task.

The Economy and the Culture   In designing an instructional system, one will wish to choose media which are acceptable to the users and are within the budget and technology resources available. Attitudes toward various media may differ between urban and rural people or among ethnic or socioeconomic subgroups. Some countries or regions would not have the technological skills or the electric power to utilize radio and television, while these media would be practical and acceptable in other countries or regions. There may even be religious or cultural attitudes which help determine local reactions to various media. Print media may carry high prestige in one area, while radio and television have greater favor in another. All these factors should be considered if the media selected for a delivery system are to find acceptance.

Within boundaries of acceptance for various media, further consideration can then be given to cost-effectiveness. Under one circumstance, cost may be the overriding factor, while under another circumstance a required level of effectiveness may be determined first, after which costs are considered. For example, designers of military training often separate those objectives which must be completely mastered at any cost because they are critically important from those objectives which are less critical in importance. For the latter, lower performance levels may be acceptable when time and money can be saved in training.

In regard to all the factors relating to economy and culture, designers will need to ascertain the intended user's status and intentions, in order to avoid selecting media which may be unacceptable or impractical. There are many ways of gathering such information, including visits to the users and the use of questionnaires. Perhaps the best way is to arrange to have some of the users become members of the design team. This practice may not only help assure acceptance of the media chosen but also enhance the effectiveness of the total instruction designed.

Designers who serve as education consultants to other countries become aware of the need to avoid recommending a "United States solution" to problems in countries which cannot adopt some solutions which serve well in the United States. This refers not only to media selection but also to the total instructional approach which must be designed for the intended user. Even the translations of instructional materials or of rather straightforward directions (as in teachers' guides) must be carefully reviewed to insure clarity for the user. The importance of this point may be appreciated by recalling that even when designing materials for our own students we are not sure that the communications are understood until they are tested in use by those students. In short, what is perfectly clear to the writer may be very confusing to the reader.

Practical Factors   Assuming that the media under consideration for an objective are acceptable to the intended users and are within their capabilities for use in the learning environment, a number of detailed practical factors remain to be considered in order to try to select convenient and effective media. A general discussion of such factors for each of several media is found in books on media selection and utilization. One such discussion contains a useful summary, by William Freeman, of the advantages and limitations of lectures, discussion, demonstrations and practice, and programmed instruction (in Briggs, 1970, pp. 148–152). Another relevant item (Briggs, 1970, pp. 153–155) is an analysis by John G. Wilshusen, Jr. and Richard Stowe of how a number of media relate to size of group, type of learner response desired, type of stimulus presentation, simplicity of physical classroom arrangements, requirements for lighting or darkness in the room, and other environmental conditions. This analysis indicates the suitability of each medium for various combinations of these conditions.

Some of the practical factors to be considered in media selection are:

1.   What size of group must be accommodated in one room at a single occasion?
2.   What is the range of viewing and hearing distance for the use of the media?
3.   How easily can the media be "interrupted" for pupil responding or other activity and for providing feedback to the learners?
4.   Is the presentation "adaptive" to learners' responses? Can it be "reprogrammed" quickly to adjust to learners' responses?
5.   Does the desired instructional stimulus require motion, color, still pictures, spoken words, or written words?
6.   Is sequence fixed or flexible in the medium? Is the instruction repeatable (replicable) in every detail?
7.   Which media provide best for incorporating most of the conditions of learning appropriate for the objective?
8.   Which media provide more of the desired instructional events?
9.   Do the media under consideration vary in probable "affective impact" for the learners?
10.   Are necessary hardware and software items obtainable, accessible, and storable?
11.   How much disruption is caused by using the media?
12.   Is a "backup" easily available in case of equipment failure, power failure, film breakage, etc.?
13.   Will teachers need additional training?
14.   Is a budget provided for spare parts, repairs, and replacement of items which become damaged?
15.   How do costs compare with probable effectiveness?

The reader may be able to think of many items which could be added to this list of practical factors in media selection. Most teachers can report instances in which a burned-out bulb or a broken film has made necessary a sudden change in plans. Equally disruptive is the selection of a medium unsuitable for the size of the group, which means that many persons cannot see or hear. These practical factors are thus no less important than other kinds of factors discussed earlier. Having a backup plan or an alternate lesson is one way to minimize the negative reaction when something "goes wrong" in the classroom.

A METHOD OF MEDIA SELECTION

Previous chapters have shown that there are many design steps to be taken prior to media selection, at least when following the general design model presented in this book. Some of these prior steps are: analysis of objectives; defining the objectives; classifying the objectives by domain of learning outcome; designing instructional sequences. Chapter 9, dealing with the events of instruction, has prepared the reader to apply those events to planning instruction for the specific objectives or enabling objectives which represent the purposes of single lessons.

As conceived here, two major steps in lesson planning are the specification of the needed instructional events and the selection of a medium of instruction for each instructional event. The purpose of this section is to outline a systematic method of media selection which begins with the lesson objective (and its classification as to type of learning outcome) and ends with a prescription of how the selected media will be produced in such a way as to apply the conditions of learning relevant for that category of outcome. As seen in Table 9–2, some of the conditions of learning can be associated directly with specific instructional events, so that the conditions help determine just how to provide for that event. Other conditions are applicable across all categories of outcomes, such as conditions for gaining attention and for stimulating recall of prerequisites; this is, however, uncharacteristic of most of the conditions which vary according to domain of outcome. Table 9–2 summarizes the relationships existing among these three important concepts; (1) Categories of Learning Outcomes, (2) Instructional Events, and (3) Conditions for Learning. In that table, the *column headings* show the types of learning outcomes; the *row headings* list the instructional events which are common for all categories of outcomes, and the intersection of a column and a row lists a condition of learning, which usually varies across the categories of learning (even for the same instructional event).

A schematic aid

Figure 10–1 represents a schematic aid or format found useful in recording choices and rationales related to media selection. This format has been presented, with examples, elsewhere (Briggs, 1970, 1972). When used by a designer working alone as both designer and teacher, this format may be employed as one step in lesson planning, that is, to make media selections which guide the search for on-the-shelf media presentations to be employed for the lesson. When used by a team of designers who develop new materials rather than select from available materials, this format represents a way to arrive at prescriptions for the media presentations to be developed.

The purposes of each numbered component shown in Figure 10–1 are described in the following paragraphs.

1. Objective to be analyzed. This may be a target objective, but more frequently it will be an enabling objective representing an essential prerequisite, or an information objective, related to the learning of a more comprehensive intellectual skills objective. In any event, an objective small enough to be learned in a single lesson is preferred. The format could also be used for an objective requiring a greater amount of learning time (in the case of more sophisticated learners). The objective for the lesson might represent a single enabling skill in a learning hierarchy (Chapter 6) or it could merely be chosen from a planned sequence of lessons (Chapter 8).

2. Classification of the objective. Following the statement of the lesson objective comes the classification of the objective in terms of the domain of learning outcome represented. In appropriate instances, the classification would show only the domain, for example, *attitude.* In other cases, both domain and subdomain would be shown, such as, *intellectual skill—concrete concept.*

3. Listing instructional events. Here one lists those instructional events to be accomplished during the lesson (Chapter 9). In a lesson for young children, one might well plan specifically for all of these events. For older learners, one might show fewer events to be furnished by the materials and the teacher, on the assumption that the learners can supply some of the events in their own study efforts. In the case of graduate students, for example, one might provide only the objective and a model of a successful performance, supply an instructional stimulus such as a book or module, and then provide feedback to a performance or a product of the learner. For younger learners, there might be several cycles of (a) presenting the stimulus, (b) guiding the learning, (c) eliciting a response, and (d) providing feedback, within a single lesson.

The selection of events to be employed as a part of the functions of the media and the teacher should be adjusted to the complexity of the objective and the capabilities of the learners.

4. Selecting type of stimuli. This is a more general and basic decision than media selection. Often the choice is between written words or spoken words as types of stimuli, taking into consideration the objective and the age of the learner. Once the choice of printed words is made, for example, the later media selection decision is whether to use programmed instruction, a book, or a printed handout. If spoken words become the stimulus choice, one later decides whether this means a live lecture by the teacher or a tape recording. If moving pictures are the stimulus choice, the media available are films, videotape, etc. Other stimulus choices, such as still pictures or simulations, also offer many media alternatives. Consideration of the age, reading ability, and other learner characteristics can help determine the type of stimulus to be used for each instructional event. Referral to Dale's "cone of experience" may be helpful at this point.

1. Objective or enabling objective being analyzed.
2. Domain and/or type of learning represented.

3. Instructional event	4. Type of stimulus	5. Candidate media	6. Theoretically best (or tentative) media choices	7. Final media selection
a.				
b.				
c.				
d.				
e.				

8. Rationale for media selected: (How well can the student Develop effective instructional strategies (Reasons for decisions made # 3 → # 7

9. Prescriptions for media producer:

FIGURE 10–1 A Format for Prescribing Media to be Developed

The nature of the performance called for by the objective is also an important consideration. If the learner is expected only to list a series of steps in a procedure, printed words may be an appropriate type of stimulus. However, if the learner is to actually carry out the steps in the performance, a series of still pictures might be appropriate for one of the events of instruction.

Type of stimulus needs also to be considered in terms of the specific instructional events being planned. Choice of stimuli may vary considerably even within a single lesson for a group of learners. Some typical stimulus choices for various instructional events might be as follows:

Instructional Event	*Type of Stimulus*
a. Gaining attention	Unusual sounds; startling visuals
b. Information about objective	Spoken words; real objects
c. Guiding learning	Spoken or written words; demonstration; sample products or performance
d. Providing feedback	Spoken or written words
e. Enhancing retention and transfer	Variety of media and examples

In summary of this step, in selecting type of stimuli, one needs to consider the nature of the objective, the nature of the learner, and the particular instructional event being planned. Each type of stimulus leaves various *media* of instruction open to further consideration.

5. Listing candidate media. Once the type of stimulus for an event has been selected, it is useful to list a variety of media, all of which can convey the selected type of stimulus. It may even be useful for the novice designer to list media which are non-candidates—that is, those media which cannot convey the selected type of stimulus. Note that the purpose of this step is not to make the medium selection for the event, but to *consider* a range of media from which one will later select a medium that is effective, practical, and provides variety without undue inconvenience or distraction. One reason for listing several candidate media is that often no one of them is better than any other, generally speaking. But one medium may be more suitable for the particular learners or the particular objective.

Toward the end of the analysis, the designer will seek a limited number of media for the entire lesson. In reviewing the media selections for the entire series of events, one can substitute, reduce, or enlarge the variety of media by noting the range of candidate media listed. To be sure, an experienced designer may do much of this analysis "in his head" rather than on paper. But for the person first learning this method of media selection, doing these steps on paper provides a mechanism for learning and for feedback from an instructor or colleague. And in team efforts, this explicit format enhances communication and coordination of work among team members. The format thus becomes a control tool for the project director.

From the examples given previously, which concern selecting types of stimuli for various instructional events, we may now note some candidate media for the types of stimuli:

Type of Stimuli	Candidate Media
a. Unusual sounds; visuals	Teacher, tape recorder; pictures
b. Spoken words; real objects	Teacher, tape recorder; various objects
c. Demonstration; sample products	Teacher, films, videotape, visiting experts; sample themes written by students
d. Spoken or written words	Teacher, tape recorder, books, chalkboard
e. Varieties for generalization	Real objects of varying color, size, shape, etc., pictures of objects, verbal problem situations

In selecting candidate media for an event in a lesson, the aim is to reject marginal or poor uses of media. For example if *spoken words* is the stimulus selected, it would be wasteful, if not distracting, to show a person talking in a videotape recording. An inexpensive tape recording would do as well or better. It is not always effective to use both spoken words and moving pictures at the same time. Either the audio or the visual channel may interfere with rather than support the "message" carried by the other channel. Of course if the content is carefully designed, the two channels may be made to support each other.

6. Selecting theoretically best media. It is often useful in taking this step in the analysis to assume that the designer has the capability to use any medium desired, regardless of the resources required to develop and use it. This may indeed violate the limits of resources actually available to the designer and the user. But it affords an excellent opportunity to decide *why* there is a theoretically best medium for this event of this lesson for the intended learners. Your rationale on your choice of the medium to be entered in this column may be the key to eventually choosing *another* medium (which is within your capability) in a creative way.

For example, suppose the choice is Computer Assisted Instruction, and more specifically the PLATO system, because it is able to present visual displays of the kind needed, and because it can give different feedback to different students, depending upon their specific responses. Hence "CAI-PLATO" is entered in the events "present the stimulus," "elicit student responding," and "providing feedback." But then the designer may remind himself that the user has no PLATO resources, and cannot plan to acquire any. Further reflection may lead to the decision that there are many ways to present the desired visual displays—as still pictures, as drawings accompanied by explanatory statements, or in motion picture sequence or videotaped sequence (if there is any portion of the sequence or lessons in which motion is really needed). Any of those media could be adapted to the purpose. The still pictures could be used along with a coordinated audio tape to give explanations, pose questions, allow time gaps for student responding, and taped feedback (perhaps containing feedback to responses that sample students have made). The drawings could be arranged as a branching programmed text in order to provide appropriate feedback to a variety of responses. If a videotaped sequence is constructed, it can easily be stopped at points, with the teacher providing questions and feedback. Even motion picture films can pose questions, pause for responding, and provide feedback. Perhaps these substitute media are less efficient or less flexible than PLATO, but the major reasons for preferring PLATO might lead to good adaptations of other media.

In conventional entertainment films or TV programs, there are no pauses provided for viewer responses to questions, and for subsequent feedback, although instructional designers and researchers have shown that such features are feasible and effective. By specifying the desired functions to be performed by a theoretically best medium, a line of thinking may be started which leads to a creative presentation in a substitute medium, when such a substitution is necessary.

In some cases, there may appear to be no theoretically best medium—all the candidate media are suitable to present the kind of instructional event desired. In that case, the space may be left blank, or one of the candidate media may be entered as a "tentative" medium choice as part of a plan to make a final choice after considering media for other events of the lesson. If all the candidate media appear equally attractive for the desired event, the final choice can rest on ease of transition—thus, if adjacent events are already planned for a medium that is one of the candidate media for the event under consideration, then the choice could be made on that basis.

The purpose of this step, then, is not to force an unjustified decision that there actually is one best medium among the candidate media, nor to encourage development of media the user cannot put into practice, but to insure that the features of successful accomplishment of the event are specified, in order that the medium finally chosen is utilized more effectively.

For example, if only one event (or part of a lesson) requires the learners to see objects in motion, it would be wasteful to produce a 40-minute motion picture film for the entire lesson when it is only necessary to show objects in motion for two minutes. If single-concept film equipment is not available for the motion sequence, a live demonstration or brief videotape might serve for that portion of the lesson.

7. *Final media selections.* Up to this point in the analysis, each instructional event is dealt with in isolation from the others in order to make the determination on how each event might be best accomplished. There now comes the point at which all events must be brought together to make up a successful lesson. The designer now considers the practicality of using all the theoretically best media recorded in the previous column. The designer visualizes the instructional environment to determine whether so many media are used that they may create

management problems in the classroom, or so few that they may produce monotony for the learners. Surely one would not wish to change media for each instructional event in the series, nor to allow attention to lag because of an overuse of one medium.

It is at this point that the designer considers the practical factors (listed earlier in this chapter), as well as the nature of the learners and the nature of the lesson's objective. An easily managed, smoothly flowing sequence of events is sought, in which the media changes may be motivating but not distracting. In making this series of decisions, the designer aims: (1) to stay within the resources and constraints of both the media developers available and the classroom environment, (2) to use a medium long enough for efficiency but to aim for interest and effectiveness, and (3) to make good use of the capabilities of the media.

8. *Rationale for media choices.* When the format of Figure 10–1 is used in the training of designers, the Rationale section often reveals how well the student can develop effective instructional strategies. This part of the form is used to show the reasons for the decisions recorded in columns 3 through 7. It is also at this point that student designers may reveal their ability to apply learning theory, instructional theory, and research findings to develop the overall strategy for the lesson (or module). Their familiarity with the capabilities of the media are indicated, as well as their understanding of how to select events appropriate for intended learners.

This section of the form can aid an instructor in a design course: (1) to evaluate his students' ability to apply theory to practice, (2) to determine their knowledge of media, (3) to note their grasp of practical factors and the task and learner characteristics important in designing instruction, and hence, (4) to identify areas of needed further study.

Following the form presented in Figure 10–1, one sheet is used for each lesson. For a more detailed analysis, it is useful to prepare a separate sheet for each event of the lesson. An example of this sort, prepared by a student in an instructional design course, is described by Ackerman (1977). Still other variations are often possible, for example, to plan a lesson for several groups of learners having different characteristics, or to plan a lesson for different delivery systems (Briggs, 1970, 1972).

9. *Writing prescriptions for media production.* This step is, of course, the culminating one, in that the designer's principal responsibility may stop here. In other cases, the designer may continue to work with the media developers and producers, and with subject-matter experts. In this section of the form, the designer may employ knowledge of theory, ingenuity, and creativity. In a sense, this is the synthesis phase, following a long series of different kinds of analysis.

In writing the prescription for each instructional event, the designer attempts to incorporate communications to the learner which effect the conditions of learning relevant for the type of outcome implied by the lesson objective. Reference may be made again to Table 9–2 at this point. The prescription itself is a condensed statement of the display or other communication to be prepared in the chosen medium.

A team leader can review the prescriptions for adequacy with respect to the following criteria:

1.   Do they utilize appropriate conditions of learning?
2.   Do they describe the communication to be prepared in sufficient detail to enable script writers and media production personnel to do their work?
3.   Will the prescriptions adequately provide for each instructional event?
4.   Will the entire lesson, as planned, be adequate for the intended learners?
5.   Are the media selected appropriate for the intended learners?
6.   Does the type of response required of the learners represent progress toward the end performance expected when the lesson is completed?
7.   At the completion of the lessons will the learners be able to perform adequately on an appropriate assessment test?
8.   Will the total lesson "move" so that learner interest and attention are maintained?
9.   Is the development of the lesson within resources available, and will the management of the lesson be within the resources of the user?
10.   Will the media and prescriptions find acceptance by learners and teachers when the lesson is presented in its final form?

With respect to the instructional content described in the prescriptions, there is a gray area where prescriptions end and script writing begins. Prescriptions could be written in such detail that they are the scripts. It is desirable that designers, media specialists, subject-matter experts and teachers all have a role in developing prescriptions and scripts. Such persons will need to form mutually supportive relationships with each other.

In small design efforts, of course, a single person may fill his or her own prescriptions. Student designers can learn much by writing scripts from the prescriptions even though they may lack the skills to actually produce materials in some of the media chosen for the lesson.

In the process of writing prescriptions the designer may make frequent reference to Table 9–2, which summarizes the conditions of learning for each instructional event for the various domains of learning outcome. Student designers can also check their own prescriptions by referring to that table (which summarizes information about learning conditions described more thoroughly in Chapters 4 and 5).

10. Script writing. In a final usable form, the content of materials to be developed in media form is often called a *script.* While there are "production notes" included in the final scripts for the various media to help members of the production crew to perform their functions, a draft script can be prepared simply by making two columns on sheets of paper, one column headed AUDIO and the other VIDEO. Under the video column, the script writer either describes the still pictures or actions to be shown in slides, videotape, film, or an artist may make sketches to illustrate the still or moving visuals to be developed. Under the audio column, the script writer presents, verbatim, the dialog or narration to be prepared.

It may often be desirable for the designer or subject-matter expert to prepare a first draft of the script from the prescriptions, after which the media production specialists comment on any difficulties in producing the script in the desired media, or on any changes which may lead to better utilization of the particular media.

If one wishes to distinguish the stages of design, development, and production, it would be possible to consider the writing of the *prescription* as the end of the design phase. Development and revision of scripts could be considered the development or production planning phase, while the actual preparation of the presentations could be considered as the production phase. The many details involved in the latter two phases will not be further discussed in this book.

The materials to be developed by the design process described to this point next need to be subjected to formative evaluation (Chapters 12 and 15).

We have used the terms *prescriptions* and *scripts* here to emphasize the dual nature of the design model presented in this book—a model of lesson planning in which materials are *selected,* and a model of materials *development* by team efforts. For this reason, we have avoided the vocabularies of specific medium developments, such as "treatment," "storyboard," etc. Teachers select materials and media, and they design lesson plans to guide the utilization of materials selected, along with group and individual learning activities. Teams design the prescriptions for new materials. The prescriptions are more specific than the terms synopsis or treatment used in the media production industry. Prescriptions are roughly equivalent to storyboards. The term *script* is used here with much the same meaning that it has in media production.

ADAPTING THE MODEL TO PROJECT CIRCUMSTANCES

This chapter has presented a method of media selection and prescription writing that may be described as fine-grained and analytical. Emphasis is placed on making media decisions separately for each instructional event in a lesson, as a first step. Then the tentative (or theoretically best) choice for each event is reconsidered in relation to media for all events of the lesson.

The format presented here for media selection and utilization (Figure 10-1) may appear excessively detailed. The format has proved to be an excellent learning aid for trainees in the design model. The use of the format clearly makes use of fundamental components of the design approach presented throughout this book. Emphasis is placed upon performance objectives and their classification by use of a taxonomy of learning outcomes; upon instructional events; and upon conditions of learning. Thus, explicit use of theory and research is provided for in the format, and subsequent empirical formative and summative evaluations are assumed.

The model of media selection and utilization presented here is therefore systematic, internally consistent, and related directly to the major theoretical orientation of this book. Nevertheless, some users will point out that the format presented here is laborious, time-consuming, and somewhat tedious. This may be so; but learning to do systematic design requires disciplined effort. Designers trained by use of this model will have the detailed skills from which they can design simpler models to fit the resources and constraints of specific design projects. Carey and Briggs (1977) have shown that the skilled design team leader must not only adopt, adapt, or design a new design model to fit the project budget and personnel available, but must also develop time periods for specific tasks, make personnel assignments, and monitor the entire management plan. Some techniques for performing these team leader functions have also been specified, but will not be further discussed here. A design model must be developed (or adapted) to fit the circumstances of the project relative to: budget; time; personnel; facilities; equipment; supplies; and institutional characteristics of the developing agency and the using agency.

Carey and Briggs (1977) point out that the media selection format (that is presented in this chapter) would be overwhelming if the personnel also had to be trained to produce the designed products in a short time period, as in a summer's workshop for example. One would choose a simpler model in such a case—a model which necessarily sacrifices some of the analytical power of the present model. As a minimum, such a simpler design model can continue to emphasize the use of performance objectives to guide both the development of the instruction and the assessment of learner performance. Probably the concept of instructional events could also be retained, but a shortcut taken in media selection.

It is not known which aspects of the design model presented in this book could be eliminated with the least loss in learning effectiveness. But surely every loss in consideration of how learning takes place would result in a weaker model. Experienced designers, of course, may not only adapt models to circumstances, but they may do much of the analysis "in their heads," just as a mathematician needs to record fewer steps in problem solution than students.

SUMMARY

This chapter begins with a brief account of how teachers design instruction, in part by *selecting* materials. Design teams usually *develop* new materials. Much of the theorizing involved in the two functions, however, can be the same, according to the design model presented in this book.

A distinction is made between media and delivery systems, the latter referring to collections of media. Both have effects on teacher and pupil roles.

Media selection models are described, first in terms of their similarities, and next with respect to their differences. The differences are described as variations in (1) the size of segment in which media choices are made, (2) the extent to which media are predetermined rather than resulting from a detailed analysis, and (3) the extent to which the rationales for media choices are made explicit.

Factors to be considered in media selection have been discussed under the following headings: task variables; learner variables; the assumed learning environment; the economy and the culture; and practical factors.

A model of media selection and prescription writing was presented and discussed in terms of the format presented in Figure 10–1. The steps to be taken in this method of media selection are:

1. Statement of the objective of the lesson
2. Classification of the objective
3. Selection of instructional events
4. Determining type of stimuli for each event
5. Listing the candidate media for each event
6. Listing the theoretically best media for the events
7. Making final media choices
8. Writing a rationale for the decisions made
9. Writing a prescription for each event
10. Writing a script for the prescriptions

Agreeing that this method of media selection is a demanding one, requiring much time, effort, and theory-using, the need for team leaders to design simpler models or adaptations is recognized. Research is needed in ways to simplify the model with the least loss in theoretical power and empirical effectiveness.

References

Ackerman, A. S. Income tax preparation. In Briggs, L. J. (ed.), *Instructional Design: Principles and Applications.* Englewood Cliffs, N.J.: Educational Technology Publications, 1977.

Aronson, D. Formulation and trial use of guidelines for designing and developing instructional motion pictures. Ph.D. dissertation, Florida State University, 1977.

Briggs, L. J. Learner variables and educational media. *Review of Educational Research,* April 1968, *38,* 160–176.

Briggs, L. J. *Handbook of Procedures for the Design of Instruction.* Pittsburgh, Pa.: American Institutes for Research, 1970.

Briggs, L. J. *Student's Guide to Handbook of Procedures for the Design of Instruction.* Pittsburgh, Pa.: American Institutes for Research, 1972.

Briggs, L. J. (ed.). *Instructional Design: Principles and Applications.* Englewood Cliffs, N.J.: Educational Technology Publications, 1977.

Briggs, L. J., Campeau, P. L., Gagné, R. M., and May, M. A. *A Procedure for the Design of Multimedia Instruction.* Pittsburgh, Pa.: American Institutes for Research, 1966.

Carey, J., and Briggs, L. J. Teams as designers. In Briggs, L. J. (ed.), *Instructional Design: Principles and Applications.* Englewood Cliffs, N.J.: Educational Technology Publications, 1977.

Dale, E. A. *Audiovisual Methods in Teaching,* 3d Ed. New York: Holt, Rinehart, and Winston, 1969.

Wager, W. Media selection in the affective domain: A further interpretation of Dale's Cone of Experience for cognitive and affective learning. *Educational Technology,* July 1975, *15*(7), 9–13.

chapter 11

Designing the Individual Lesson

Goals of instructional programs, and the objectives derived from them, need to be defined at several different levels. In previous chapters we have described techniques for planning goals and objectives for courses, for topics or units within courses, and for particular kinds of learning objectives within a unit or topic. Instruction itself must also be planned at correspondingly different levels. Prior chapters have provided a groundwork of principles and strategies for the planning of courses and topics. Chapter 9 was increasingly specific, introducing those events of instruction which ultimately must be incorporated into the planning of the day-to-day process of teaching, in other words, into the design of the *individual lesson.* Chapter 10 has shown a method of utilizing these same instructional events when a team of designers specify media to be produced to "carry" much of the instruction. The media presentations may be planned either for use in group instruction or for an individualized instructional delivery system.

In the context of the present chapter, instruction is to be designed with reference to performance objectives and the prerequisite capabilities they imply. Often the lesson has only a single objective, which itself may represent a single capability subordinate to a more inclusive objective. Thus the *lesson* is the level at which instruction is designed in detail. In planning for individualized instruction the level of planning comparable to the lesson is the *module* (see Chapter 14). Designing instruction at this level concerns the moment-by-moment events of instruction.

Most of the characteristics of human capabilities which have been discussed earlier are used as a basis for planning the lesson. So, too, are the events of instruction described in Chapter 9. These events apply to the design of all kinds of lessons, no matter what the domain of the learning outcome intended. In this chapter, we emphasize the variations among lessons which are introduced to correspond with *different* domains of learning outcomes. These variations are first considered in terms of their implications for designing *sequences* of instruction, and later with respect to the establishment of *effective learning conditions* for the different domains.

In designing a lesson one needs first to insure that the general events of instruction are provided for. In addition it is necessary to classify the lesson as having a particular type of learning objective. Once this step has been accomplished, it will then be possible (1) to place the lesson properly in a sequence relating it to its prerequisites, and (2) to incorporate into the instructional events of the lesson the conditions for effective learning appropriate to the domain of its intended outcome. These events are brought about by whatever media are selected as most appropriate for the purpose.

LESSON PLANNING AND MODULE DESIGN

Chapter 10 opened with a discussion emphasizing that teachers design lessons so as to *select* the most suitable instructional materials available, since teachers normally do not actually *develop* such materials. Teachers also do not normally have the planning time to design an entire course in detail before the actual instruction begins. So, in practice, teachers often "design as they teach"—that is, they may design sequences of lessons in advance, but perhaps not all lessons for the course are designed before the teaching begins.

These practical circumstances also tend to force teachers to plan each lesson only in sufficient detail to be "ready" for each lesson; they are able to improvise some of the details as the lesson progresses. This is not an entirely unfortunate state of affairs, since it leaves the teacher free to "redesign on the spot"—that is, to adjust procedures to the responses of the learners in ways that could not be entirely foreseen in advance even with more time for planning.

As is shown in Chapter 13, the nature of instruction in large groups results in less precision of control of instruction than is possible in small groups. Thus the unpredictability of student response in a large group, coupled with restricted planning time, mean that instruction is often planned and carried out with only a moderate degree of precision.

Utilization of small group or individualized instruction modes which allow more adaptive instruction increase the precision of instruction. Increased levels of adaptation to individual entering competencies and rates of learning are possible with instruction which permits self-pacing and self-correction for each learner; these functions, in turn, are made possible in tutoring or small group modes and with materials which allow *branching* by the student to the most needed and helpful exercises contained in the materials. Such branching is made possible by some learning modules in the form of programmed instruction, computer-assisted instruction, or by frequent use of self-tests which enable the learner to use the module in an adaptive manner.

Some increases in the precision of the instruction are therefore possible with the use of individualized instruction for large groups, as described in Chapter 14; the maximum precision, however, lies in the tutoring mode discussed in Chapter 13. Some increases could be achieved by more time for lesson planning by teachers, and other increases may be achieved by teams in the development of modules, as described in Chapter 10.

In summary, teachers of large groups have limited planning time, so they plan only parts of courses at a time and with only the degree of detail for each lesson that time permits. While handicapped by the limits to precision typical of large group instruction, skill in "redesigning on the spot" may result in relatively efficient instruction.

Designers of modules, working usually in teams, are often able to design in more detail than teachers can in their lesson planning. Thus some details of the "model" for instructional design, as presented in this book, have been modified to fit the two different circumstances. In Chapter 10, a very detailed, "fine-grained" method of design of instructional materials, by team effort, was described. This degree of detail is feasible when time and money are available and when specially trained design personnel do the work. Instruction so designed has the potential for high precision when sufficient tryouts and revisions are possible and when adaptive features help adjust the instruction to individual differences among the learners. The procedures described in Chapter 10, then, represent the "detailed model" appropriate for the well-supported team effort, in which new materials (for carefully chosen media to be employed largely in an individualized instruction mode) are to be developed. This chapter presents the less detailed form of our model for the design of instruction; this form is appropriate for the usual circumstances when the individual teacher is the designer of the instruction.

Both forms of our model, however, retain the emphasis we have consistently placed on these central themes:

1. The importance of classifying objectives by use of some taxonomy of learning outcomes, such as the five domains discussed in Chapters 3, 4, and 5.
2. The importance of the sequencing of instruction at several levels; this discussion began in Chapter 8, and is continued in this chapter.
3. The importance to attending to the events of instruction which apply to all domains of outcomes (Chapter 9).
4. The importance of incorporating into the events of instruction the particular conditions of learning relevant to the domain of the objective of the lesson (Table 9–2 and this chapter).

We now turn to further discussion of the sequencing of instruction and then to instructional events and conditions of learning. The chapter concludes with a discussion of steps in lesson planning and an example of a lesson plan which incorporates the less detailed form of the model which would usually be adopted by an individual teacher who designs and conducts the instruction.

ESTABLISHING A SEQUENCE OF OBJECTIVES

A lesson objective can usually be analyzed to reveal a desirable teaching sequence. Lesson objectives can often specify the learning of fairly complex skills, which require the prior learning of simpler skills in order for instruction to be effective. This is particularly true if one begins lesson planning with an objective representing an intellectual skill such as a defined concept, rule, or a problem-solving task. The skills to be learned in such tasks typically suggest a preceding sequence of objectives for simpler skills and related information. The sequences implied for lesson objectives representing information, motor skills, and attitudes present quite a different picture, as Chapter 5 has indicated. Yet each of these kinds of learned capability has its own prerequisites, and accordingly its own implications for instructional sequence.

Planning a sequence for intellectual skill objectives

We begin our account of lesson sequence planning with objectives representing *intellectual skills.* The subordinate skills required to attain an objective of this sort can be derived as a learning hierarchy. Suppose that one does indeed want to establish the skill of subtracting whole numbers of any size, as diagrammed in Figure 6-4. The learning hierarchy for this objective, as shown in Chapter 6, lists ten essential prerequisites, shown as "boxes" in the hierarchy. Let us assume that box I, simple subtraction facts, represents learning already accomplished earlier by the pupils. The teacher now needs to design a lesson, or perhaps more likely, a sequence of lessons, to enable the learners to subtract any whole numbers they may encounter. While there are several sequences of teaching the skills shown in boxes II through X that might be successful, the implication of the hierarchy is that the bottom row of boxes should be taught first, then the next higher row, and so on. It may also be inferred that a sequence going in order from box II to X might be the most effective sequence.

In summary, hierarchies are so arranged that there may be options in a sequence of boxes within a horizontal row, but there are not options concerning going from the bottom row, upwards, at least when we wish to adopt a single sequence for all learners in the group.

This is not to say that *no* student could learn the task by a sequence which violates the above rules of thumb. But if a student did learn by such a "non-hierarchical" sequence, it might be because the student already could perform the skills in some of the boxes, or because he or she had sufficient cognitive strategies to discover some of the rules without having received direct instruction in their application.

Determining a Starting Point Continuing with the example of learning to subtract whole numbers, it is possible that some students in a group may have already learned some of the prerequisite skills in some of the boxes. One child may already be able to perform the skills in boxes II and III; another may be able to perform II through V. Obviously one needs to begin the instruction at a point which takes up the sequence "where each child is." This is conveniently done in individualized instruction programs, as described in Chapter 14, but it can be done also with a group by arranging other activities for children who do not need some of the instruction planned for the group. An alternative, of course, is for children to "sit through" some of the instruction as a "review," although this may not always be the best solution. A review of earlier skills may be needed at the beginning of each lesson to be sure there is ready recall when the new learning is undertaken. Generally speaking, however, intellectual skills once learned, are recalled well, as compared to the recall of facts or labels, for example.

Specifying a Sequence of Lessons A teacher must decide "how much" should be included in each lesson, as well as the sequencing of the lessons, following the implications for sequencing, discussed earlier. It might often be convenient to teach some "boxes" as single lessons; other boxes may be combined within one lesson.

The hierarchy, then, implies several possible effective lesson sequences. The skill relationships which indicate essential prerequisites need to be maintained in planning such sequences—otherwise no particular sequence is implied, and the teacher may choose to insert instruction relating to other domains of outcome into the sequence. Often a sequence of lessons is built around an intellectual skill objective in such a way as to include instruction concerning information objectives, attitudes, and cognitive strategies (Wager, 1977).

Achievement of Skills in Sequence The planning of lessons designed to attain the final skill, XI, contains the assumption that each student will display *mastery* of prerequisite skills before being asked to learn the next higher skill. For example, before tackling skill X, requiring "double borrowing" across a column containing a zero, it must be ascertained that the learner can do skills VI and VII, requiring subtracting in successive columns without borrowing, and borrowing in single columns and multiple columns.

The notion of mastery must be taken with complete seriousness when one is dealing with intellectual skills. The lessons must be so designed that each prerequisite skill can be performed with perfect confidence by the learner before attempting to learn more complex skills in the hierarchy. Any lesser degree of learning of prerequisites will result in puzzlement, delay, inefficient trial and error at best, and in failure, frustration and termination of effort toward further learning at the worst.

Provisions for Diagnosis and Relearning   Lesson planning which utilizes the hierarchy of intellectual skills may also provide for diagnosis of learning difficulties. If it is found that a student has difficulty learning any given skill, the most probable diagnostic indication is that he cannot recall how to perform one or more prerequisite skills. Any given lesson may provide for diagnosis by requiring that prerequisite skills be recalled. If one or more cannot be recalled, then relearning of these prerequisites must be undertaken. Thus the assessment of mastery for any given skill, occurring as a part of a lesson on that skill, may be followed by further diagnosis of prerequisite skills, in case mastery is *not* achieved. Following this, provision should be made for a "relearning loop" in the sequence of lessons, which gives the student an opportunity to relearn and to display mastery of the necessary prerequisites before proceeding.

Sequence in relation to cognitive strategies

The use of cognitive strategies by a learner is indicated by his or her solution of one or more novel problems with answers of greater or lesser quality. In such problems, however, there are many "right" answers, not just one. Accordingly, one cannot specify a particular sequence of prior learning leading up to the presentation of a problem situation. What must be recognized, nevertheless, is that novel problem solution depends upon previously learned information and intellectual skills. To the extent that relevant capabilities are unavailable to the learner, he or she will be restricted in the variety of adequate solutions that can possibly be invented.

Planning for a sequence of instruction designed to improve the quality of problem solving (and the inferred effectiveness of the learner's thinking strategies) usually takes the form of *repeated opportunities* for problem solving. Such occasions may be interspersed with instruction having other intended outcomes, and typically are made to recur over relatively long periods of time. In this way, it is expected that gradual improvement in cognitive strategies will be possible. However, it does not seem likely that observable amounts of improvement in this type of capability can occur within the space of a single lesson or two.

Planning a sequence for information learning

As indicated in Chapter 5, the most important prerequisite for the learning of information is the provision of a meaningful context within which the newly learned information can be "subsumed," or with which it can be in some meaningful sense "associated." The principles applicable to sequencing differ somewhat depending on whether the objective concerns learning a set of names (labels), learning an isolated fact, or learning the sense of a logically organized passage.

Names or Labels   The learning of a set of names (such as the names of a number of trees) is facilitated by the use of previously learned organized structures which the learner has in his memory. A variety of structures may be used by the learner to "encode" the newly acquired information. The encoding may take the form of a simple association, as when a new French word "la dame" is associated with the English word "dame," which thus becomes a somewhat humorous association for "lady." Sometimes, encoding may involve the use of a sentence, such as that which associates "starboard" with "right," in "the star boarder is always right." Frequently, too, the method of encoding may involve the use of visual images, as would be the case if the learner associated an image of a crow with a person's name "Crowe." The imagery employed for encoding may be quite arbitrary, as when a learner uses the shops on a well-known street as associates for newly acquired names of things having nothing to do with the shops themselves (cf. Crovitz, 1970).

It is clear, then, that the learning of new names or labels calls upon previously learned entities stored in the learner's memory. Yet, in this kind of information learning, it does not seem reasonable that a *specific* sort of previous learning, implying a sequence of instruction, can be recommended. While it is possible to facilitate the learning of new labels by prescribing some particular "codes" for the learner to use, such a procedure is generally found to be less successful than permitting the learner to use an encoding system of his or her own. What the learner mainly needs to have learned previously, aside from the various meaningful structures which he may have in his memory, is "how to encode." This would be a particular kind of *cognitive strategy.* The possibilities of long-term instruction designed to improve such a strategy have not been explored. The lesson designer, therefore, typically assumes that both the strategy and the encoding structures have been previously learned, and makes no specific provision for them in the lesson sequence.

Individual Facts   The learning of individual "facts," as they may occur, for example, in a chapter of a history test, also involves an encoding process. In this case, the encoding is usually a matter of relating the facts to larger meaningful structures—larger organized "bodies of knowledge" which have been previously learned.

Two kinds of procedures are available for instructional sequencing when one is dealing with factual information. Both of them should probably be employed, with an emphasis determined by other factors in the situation. The first is the prior learning (in a sequence) of what Ausubel (1968) calls "organizers." If the learner is to acquire facts about automobiles, for example, an "organizing passage" may first be presented which informs the learner about the major distinctive categories of automobile description—body style, engine, frame, transmission, and so on. The specific facts to be learned about particular automobiles then follow.

The second procedure, not entirely unrelated to the first, involves the use of questions or other statements to identify the major categories of facts for which learning is desired (cf. Frase, 1970; Rothkopf, 1970). Thus, if the learning of the names of persons described in a historical passage is the most important information to be learned, prior experience with questions about such names in a "sample" passage will facilitate the learning and retention of names. Should the lesson have the objective of stating dates, then dates could be asked about in a prior passage.

Organized Information   Most frequently, an objective in the category of information states an expectation that the learner will be able to state a set of facts and principles in a meaningful organized manner. For example, an objective in social studies might be to trace the steps involved in the passage of a bill by the United States Congress. The learning of organized information of this sort is also subject to an encoding procedure which calls upon previously learned structures in the student's memory. However, the existence of such prior information, as well as relevant language skills, is usually assumed by the lesson designer, rather than being specifically provided in an instructional sequence. Sometimes, the learning of new information can take advantage of the prior learning of a related class of information. An example is cited in the work of Ausubel (1968); he speaks of the process of "correlative subsumption," occurring when information about Buddhism is acquired following the learning of information about a different religion, Zen Buddhism.

Planning a sequence for a motor skill

The capabilities that constitute prerequisites for the learning of a motor skill are the part-skills that may compose the skill to be learned, and the executive sub-routine (the complex rule) which serves to control their execution in the proper order. Of course, the relative importance of these two kinds of prerequisites depends largely upon the complexity of the skill itself. To attempt to identify part-skills for dart-throwing, for example, would not be likely to lead to a useful sequencing plan; but in a complex skill such as swimming, practice of part-skills is usually considered a valuable approach.

Typically, the learning of the executive sub-routine is placed early in the sequence of instruction for a motor skill, before the various part-skills have been fully mastered. Thus, in learning to put the shot, the learner may at an early stage acquire the executive sub-routine of approaching the line, shifting his weight, bending his arm and body, and propelling the shot, even though at this early stage his performance of the critical movements is still rather poor.

The learning of particular part-skills may themselves have important prerequisites. For example, in the skill of firing a rifle at a target, the concrete concept of a correct sighting "picture" is considered to be a valuable subordinate skill to the execution of the total act of target shooting. Accordingly, a plan of instruction for a motor skill must provide not only for the prior practice of part-skills, when this is appropriate, but also on some occasions for a sequence relevant to the individual part-skills themselves.

Planning a sequence for attitude learning

As is true for other kinds of learned capabilities, the learning or modification of an attitude calls upon previously acquired entities in the learner's memory. A positive attitude toward reading poetry, for example, could scarcely be established without some knowledge of particular poems on the learner's part, or without some of the language skills involved in interpreting the meaning of poetic writing. Thus, for many attitudes with which school learning is concerned, the planning of an instructional sequence must take into account these kinds of prerequisite learning.

The basis for an instructional sequence aimed at establishing an attitude is to be found in the particular information and intellectual skills that become a part of the personal action expected to be chosen by the learner, following instruction. If the learner is to have a positive attitude, for example, toward associating with people of races different from his own, such an attitude must be based upon information concerning what these various "associations" (playing games with, working with, dining with, etc.) are about. Or, if the learner is to acquire a positive attitude towards the methods of science, this must be based upon some capabilities (skills) of using some of these methods.

An instructional sequence for learning an attitude, then, often begins with the learning of intellectual skills and information relevant to that attitude. It proceeds then to the introduction of a procedure involved in establishing the "positive" or "negative" tendency which constitutes the attitude itself, as described in Chapter 5.

When the method of human modeling is employed for attitude modification, another prerequisite step in the sequence may be necessary, depending on the circumstances. Since the "message" which represents the attitude needs to be presented by a respected source (usually a person), it may in some instances be necessary to establish or to build up respect for the source. "A famous scientist" is likely not to command the respect that a particular scientist, such as Lavoisier, does; and Lavoisier as a pictured person is more likely to be respected if the learner knows of his accomplishments. In contrast, a living "famous person," perhaps a sports hero, may not require a "build-up."

LESSON PLANNING FOR LEARNING OUTCOMES

The sequence of capabilities exemplified by the learning hierarchy (for intellectual skills) or by a set of identified prerequisites (for other types of outcomes) is used as a basis for planning a *series* of lessons. The implication it has for the design of a *single* lesson is that one or more prerequisite capabilities need to be available to the learner. Obviously, though, there is more than this to the planning of each lesson. How does the student proceed from the point of having learned some subordinate knowledge or skills to the point of having acquired a new capability? This interval, during which the actual learning occurs, is filled with the kinds of instructional events described in Chapter 9. These events include the actions taken by the students and by the teacher, in order to bring about the desired learning.

Effective learning conditions for instructional events

The most general purpose for what we have called the events of instruction is that of arranging the external conditions of learning in such a way as to insure that learning will occur. Instructional events, as described in Chapter 9, are typically incorporated into the individual lesson. In a general sense these events apply to all types of lessons, regardless of their intended outcomes. Just as we have found it necessary to describe particular sequencing conditions that pertain to different lesson outcomes, we also recognize a need to give an account of the particular events that affect the learning effectiveness of lessons having different kinds of outcomes. This makes it possible to recall the *conditions of learning* for various classes of learning outcomes, as described in earlier chapters, and to apply these principles to the arrangement of effective learning within a lesson.

Tables in the following sections are intended to consolidate several ideas which influence lesson design. First, they assume the general framework of instructional events described in Chapter 9, without developing these ideas further. Second, they describe procedures for implementing optimal learning conditions that are specifically relevant to each class of learning objective. These have been referred to in Chapters 4 and 5 as the *external conditions* of learning. And third, they take account of the problem of lesson sequencing by representing the recall of prerequisite capabilities appropriate for each kind of learning outcome as *internal conditions.*

The result of this integrating exercise is a kind of checklist of distinctive conditions for effective learning which need to be incorporated into the general framework of instructional events in order to accomplish particular learning objectives.

Lessons for Intellectual Skill Objective   Effective learning conditions for the varieties of intellectual skills that may be reflected in planning the events of a lesson, are given in Table 11–1. Each list of conditions given in the second column begins with a statement designating the recall of a previously learned capability, often from a previous lesson in a sequence. The list then proceeds with conditions which are to be reflected in other instructional events (such as those of presenting the stimulus, providing learning guidance, eliciting the student performance, etc.). In interpreting the information in this column, the reader may find it useful to review the statements of internal and external conditions of learning for these types of objectives, as described in Chapters 4 and 5.

Lessons for Cognitive Strategy Objectives   Conditions designed to promote effective learning for cognitive strategies are listed in the beginning portion of Table 11–2. The list pertains particularly to the learning of strategies of produc-

TABLE 11–1   Effective Learning Conditions for Incorporation into Lessons Having
Intellectual Skill Objectives

Type of Lesson Objective	Learning Conditions
Discrimination	Recall of S-R connections ("responses") Repetition of situations presenting "same" and "different" stimuli, with feedback Emphasis on distinctive features
Concrete Concept	Recall of discrimination of relevant object qualities Presentation of several concept instances, varying in irrelevant object qualities Identification of concept instances by student
Defined Concept	Recall of component concepts Demonstration of the components of the concept, *or* verbal statement of the definition Demonstration of concept by the student
Rule	Recall of component concepts or subordinate rules Demonstration or verbal statement of the rule Demonstration of rule-application by student
Higher-Order Rule	Recall of relevant subordinate rules Presentation of a novel problem Demonstration of new rule in achieving problem solution

tive thinking and problem solving. External and internal conditions for learning cognitive strategies have been previously discussed in Chapter 3.

Lessons for Objectives of Information, Attitudes, Motor Skills   The design of instructional events for lessons having objectives of the classes of outcome designated as Information, Attitudes, and Motor Skills needs to take into account the particular conditions for effective learning shown in the corresponding portions of Table 11–2. These lists are derived from the fuller discussion of internal and external conditions of learning contained in Chapter 4.

STEPS IN LESSON PLANNING

Assuming that a teacher has organized a course into major units or topics, and has further planned sequences of lessons for each, how does that teacher proceed with the design of a single lesson?

Following our emphasis upon providing for the events of instruction, including the incorporation of effective learning conditions for the domain represented in the objective of the lesson, we suggest that teachers employ a *planning sheet* that will contain the following elements:

1. A statement of the objective of the lesson and its classification as to domain of outcome.
2. A list of the instructional events to be employed.

3.   A list of the media, materials, and activities by which each event is to be accomplished.

4.   Notes on teacher roles and activities, and directions to be given to the learners.

Such a planning sheet could list the objective at the top, with a column for each of the other three items just identified. After the planning sheet is completed, a description of the procedures for the lesson could be given in two columns, as in the example of a lesson design given in the closing section of this chapter.

Some varieties of circumstances related to the mentioned four elements of the planning sheet will now be discussed, in turn.

The objective of the lesson

As noted earlier, some lessons may have a single objective, while others may provide some instruction concerning several related objectives. For example, one lesson may be concerned with teaching a single enabling objective which appears in a learning hierarchy for a more complex intellectual skill objective. In the same lesson, however, the teacher may also incorporate one or more related information objectives, and the total lesson may be intended to move the student a little

TABLE 11–2   Effective Learning Conditions for Incorporation into Lessons Having Objectives of Cognitive Strategies, Information, Attitudes, and Motor Skills

Type of Lesson Objective	Learning Conditions
Cognitive Strategy	Recall of relevant rules and concepts
	Successive presentation (usually over an extended time) of novel problem situations with class of solution unspecified
	Demonstration of solution by student
Information	
Names or Labels	Recall of verbal chains
	Encoding (by student) by relating name to image or meaningful sentence
Facts	Recall of context of meaningful information
	Performance of reinstating fact in the larger context of information
Knowledge	Recall of context of related information
	Performance of reinstating new knowledge in the context of related information
Attitude	Recall of information and intellectual skills relevant to the targeted personal actions
	Establishment or recall of respect for "source" (usually a person)
	Reward for personal action either by direct experience or vicariously by observation of respected person
Motor Skill	Recall of component motor chains
	Establishment or recall of executive sub-routine (rules)
	Practice of total skill

closer to a longer-term attitude or cognitive strategy objective. In this sense, the instruction is "finished" in one lesson only for the enabling objective and for the information objectives; it is not finished for the others. If some learners have not mastered the first two kinds of objectives by the conclusion of the lesson, it is not "finished" for them until further learning takes place.

Often it is useful to draw "instructional maps" (Wager, 1977) in the process of planning sequences of lessons. These maps may be drawn at several levels, corresponding to the four levels at which the question of sequencing arises in the design of a course, as described in Chapter 8. Such maps may serve as a checklist of objectives in various domains so that none are omitted inadvertently in a series of lessons when the teacher becomes involved in the details of planning for a single objective.

Given a lesson with several objectives, as in the above example, it is easy to see that the teacher would not blindly present all nine instructional events for the enabling objective, then another nine events for each information objective, and so on for each objective represented in the lesson. Rather, the teacher might decide to gain attention and present the several objectives in a single brief statement. Then recall of prerequisites for the enabling objective only might be stimulated, after which a stimulus appropriate for all the lesson objectives might be presented. Following that, there may be cycles of two other events, eliciting response and providing feedback, one cycle for each objective, or perhaps cycles which combine two objectives at a time.

By such means, flexibility is sought in how the overall model of instructional design is utilized. Often the best applications of the model omit some of the events or combine them for two or more objectives. Also, there are often cycles of some events within a lesson.

Listing the instructional events

As shown in this chapter and in Chapter 9, the events of instruction are not all invariably found in a lesson, nor do they always appear in a fixed linear order. A teacher considers the sophistication of the learners as self-directing learners and the nature of the objective(s) of the lesson.

Note also that under some circumstances, an entire "period" may be taken for a single instructional event. Often a teacher will wisely spend an entire hour in attempting to establish motivation for a series of lessons or a task to be undertaken by the learners. Or, an hour may be required to present a complex objective to the students, including a discussion or a demonstration of its subordinate parts, each of which the learners are to respond to in some prescribed manner. Recall, for example, from Chapter 8, the graduate course in instructional design, for which "objectives" are written at the "unit" level, not at the "lesson" level. Since there are only four such "unit objectives" for the entire course, and since students submit written materials to demonstrate their competency only for these four objectives, it is reasonable to spend an hour or more for clarifying the exact nature of the expected performance for each unit before the actual instruction for the unit is undertaken. This might not be a reasonable procedure, of course, for other learners or other kinds of course organization.

Thus, while the events of instruction represent a crucial element in the design model presented in this book, it is evident that the manner in which such events are planned must reflect the best estimate of the capabilities and entering competencies of the students. The example of a lesson for first grade children given in Chapter 9 and the example given later in this chapter for high school students, employ the events and their associated conditions of learning for the domains of outcomes in a more fine-grained manner than in the example for graduate students.

Choosing media, materials and activities

It is at this step in instructional design that the greatest difference may be noted between our "fine-grained" form of the model for design teams and the less detailed form of the model for teachers as designers. Note in Chapter 10 that even the choice of the media of instruction involves four distinct steps for each instructional event of a lesson; these steps are followed by three others (rationale, prescriptions, and scripts) before the production of instructional materials is begun.

Of course the model for design teams can be more complex because of the capabilities of teams and because production of new materials is a part of the plan.

On the other hand, teachers need only to select and plan the use of the materials. Even this task, however, is complicated by the fact that available materials are not usually indexed by objective and certainly not by instructional event. Teachers must not only search among topical titles in catalogs of materials, but often they also must actually preview the materials before their suitability for the planned lesson may be determined. Beyond this, in our model of lesson planning, teachers must next analyze the materials to determine which of the planned lesson events can be brought about by the learners' interaction with the materials, so that remaining events can be planned for accomplishment by the teacher or by the learners themselves.

Sometimes teachers will, in effect, utilize another step, choosing the theoretically best media found in the model for design teams. That is, when considering, for example, the event "gaining attention" for an objective in a genetics unit in science for young children, the teacher might think: "I wish I could find a 16mm. film showing various species of animals whose distinctive features are so exaggerated as to make them comical. I could use this to lead up to the objective about how genes determine these differences." (Note how this thought of the teacher utilizes a condition of learning for "gaining attention" in Table 9–2.) Of course, such a film may not be found; in that case the teacher would devise another way to accomplish the event.

It may be noted that the media frequently chosen for instructing young children include real objects, such as rocks, plants, animals, boxes, bottles, and so on —things which can be seen, felt, moved, and otherwise employed for "direct purposeful experiences" (Dale, 1969). Also frequently used are pictures of objects presented with or without recorded narratives. Teachers make much use of challenging questions to hold the interest of their young charges, and they encourage oral interchanges to enhance skills in communication and social interaction.

As reading skills are developed, increasing use is made of print materials, although non-print materials presented by various media continue to be used to provide variety, interest, and learning support for the less skilled readers.

Textbooks often not only provide the central core for many lessons, but they also may facilitate the sequencing of lessons. If a textbook can be found which is clearly sequenced in the way the teacher wishes to organize the course, lesson planning may be facilitated, and the teacher may not need to search catalogs for other materials so often. A particular book or book chapter may be used for a great variety of objectives. That is, a specific body of "content" may be read by students for a variety of purposes; the teacher may need only to specify the desired purpose as an objective that the students can understand.

Sometimes, of course, the content of a book chapter is arranged so as to constitute a "lesson" in itself. That is, there may be a list of chapter objectives and a related list of exercises or questions. Marginal notes may guide thinking, and the text itself may stimulate recall of prior learning. More typically, perhaps, the text "presents the stimulus material," leaving it to the teacher to decide the use which the information is to serve in reaching determined objectives. Often a "Foreword" or a separate teachers' guide suggests alternative uses for the book. Generally textbooks are probably more widely adapted if they do not seem to restrict the teacher to only one mode of use or only one form of course organization.

Teacher and learner activities

Instructional media and materials may be viewed separately from the activities which characterize their use in a course of instruction. They are physical entities in themselves—items available on the market. To the teacher, however, these items have value only in terms of the learning activities they may stimulate, and the outcomes so produced. Therefore, for best use of the materials, we recommend that the teacher study them carefully to note the instructional events which they do not appear to address, so that he or she can plan how the missing events will be accounted for in the lesson plan.

In this sense, the choice of materials may largely define the roles the teacher needs to fill, with due regard for the assumed learners' roles. As stated earlier, the planned instructional events need to be explicitly allocated among materials, teacher, and learners in order that none be overlooked. Some notes may be made in the lesson plan so that all *planned* events occur.

Teachers may plan to obtain the greatest use of materials by selecting those which present both the desired "content" and contain the stimulation for a large proportion of the desired events. In this case, the course may be classified as "materials dependent"; the teacher may then help with guidance, evaluation, and enhancing transfer and generalization. Other teachers of similar courses may design a "teacher dependent" course, making less use of materials. Still other teachers may design a "learner dependent" course, in which students may select many of their own objectives and largely locate their own learning resources under guidance of the teacher and the librarian.

The nature of lesson plans would clearly differ in the various approaches just mentioned, but all could reflect a *systematic plan* as to how the instructional events are assumed to be accounted for.

During the course of lesson planning, teachers and other designers may make frequent reference to Table 9–2 and to Tables 11–1 and 11–2. These three tables summarize, in different fashions, the conditions of learning to be incorporated into instructional events for lessons directed toward the various domains of outcomes. Another way of showing the relationship among (a) conditions of learning, (b) instructional events and (c) the domains and sub-domains of outcomes is found elsewhere (Briggs, 1977, pp. 275–277).

Consistent and frequent reference to these tables can lead designers to "sharpen" their instructional strategies when designing lessons or instructional materials. While experienced teachers may "intuitively" employ some of the conditions of learning summarized in this book and presented in more detail elsewhere (Gagné, 1977), their planning can be checked by reference to the tables mentioned to improve the plans and to see that no relevant principle is overlooked.

An example of lesson design

An example of lesson design to be described here is a condensed and modified version of a plan by Carol Robb, which is presented in full detail elsewhere (Briggs, 1972, pp. 140–177).

This lesson is intended as a part of a high school course sequence in journalism, defined as "the work of gathering news, writing news reports, editing, and publication of a newspaper." The course, "Introduction to Journalism," is a prerequisite for students who wish to work on the school newspaper. A required entering competency is the ability to type well enough to present the student's own news story to an editor or printer. Speed is not essential, but accuracy and neatness are.

The *course objective* is as follows: "The student will be able to gather news, write it in acceptable form, and edit the copy for publication. He will employ standard practices in newspaper layout and placement of stories according to their 'newsworthiness.' He will be able to differentiate between news and feature stories. He will be able to write headlines; to avoid libel; and to formulate a philosophic position of a newspaper in our society. He can identify the duties of each position in a standard newspaper organization."

As might be expected from the above course description, an early topic of the course deals with the following capabilities: "The student will be able to view an event, decide whether it is newsworthy, record the pertinent facts, write an acceptable news story based on the 'who, what, when, where, why?' criteria, and edit his copy and type it for setting into type." Components of this topic are expressed in performance terms as topic purposes, including:

1. Observing and taking notes on an actual event or a simulated event (motion picture or videotape);
2. Deciding newsworthiness, and if such criteria are met, recording necessary facts and checking their accuracy;
3. Using the notes to write a news story;
4. Editing in a form to be sent in for typesetting.

For topic purpose 3, a learning hierachy was constructed which contained, among others, the following performance objectives:

a. Given notes on a newsworthy event, demonstrates the writing of a good lead.
b. Given notes and a lead, demonstrates the organization of the story in "pyramid" form.
c. Given (a) and (b), generates the story, using standards of brevity and reader interest.

It is evident that the writing of a good lead requires the component capability of classifying a "lead," and distinguishing it from the remainder of the story. In this case, the designer indicated the form of a single lesson for the subordinate objective *"given a news story, classifies the 'lead' by underlining."* In other words, this particular lesson was designed for the learning of the defined concept "lead." Keeping in mind the events of instruction, and the conditions of learning appropriate to such an objective (Table 9–2), the following events of the lesson were arranged:

(1) State the objective of the lesson

(1) The teacher explains that the class will learn what a "lead" is. The ultimate goal is to *write* leads; but for now the students need only to *recognize leads.*

(2) Inform the learner of the objective by providing a model of performance

(2) The teacher projects a slide containing a short news story. The sentences which are underlined constitute the lead. Students are told that at the end of the lesson they will be asked to underline the lead in other news stories.

(3) Learning guidance

(3) The teacher asks the class to try to explain why the underlined part of the slide is the "lead." They speculate on what lead means in this context; some attempt to define "lead."

(4)	Learning guidance: providing a verbal definition	**(4)**	The teacher now defines the lead as the *first part* of a news story which gives a *skeleton outline* of the *entire story* in the *fewest possible words.*
(5)	Learning guidance: providing a variety of examples	**(5)**	The teacher next projects several other slides and hands out some one-page news stories.
(6)	Present the stimulus, and elicit performance	**(6)**	The teacher asks the students to identify leads to "practice" stories. The students respond by pointing on the screen or by underlining on paper.
(7)	Provide feedback	**(7)**	The teacher provides confirmation and corrective feedback as needed.
(8)	Assess attainment of objective	**(8)**	A group of three short news stories is given. Students underline the lead as a performance test over the lesson.

Discussion of the example

It is clear that this sample lesson could have been presented somewhat differently, without departing from its objectives as the learning of a defined concept. Some teachers might spend much time on Step 3, expecting that the students will "discover" the definition of a lead. This plan permits such an approach. It provides, however, that in case the student discussion is not adequate, the teacher next gives the verbal definition as a timesaving step in the lesson.

The use of a variety of examples is usually important for such a lesson, in which one wishes to insure that the learned capability can be applied to new situations. It is conceivable, of course, that the verbal definition alone might be enough to enable some students to apply the rule consistently.

An alternate version of the lesson is somewhat more prescriptive, depending upon the application of *formal criteria* for identifying an acceptable lead. In this alternate plan, one would insert, after Step 2, the event "stimulate recall of prior learning." Here the teacher would elicit recall of the six criteria: who, what, when, where, why, and how. The teacher would suggest that a good lead must contain most of these or all of them. Formal criteria for a lead are listed in the designer's plan for this form of the lesson (Briggs, 1972, p. 173).

It may be noted that since the objective of this lesson is "classifying the lead of a story in accordance with a definition," the assessment requires an appropriate performance, not just the statement of a definition of a lead. The latter statement could be learned as an item of information, and would not meet the objective of the lesson. Nowhere in the lesson are the learners asked to state the definition; but they are asked to identify several "practice" leads before their performance is assessed.

SUMMARY

This chapter has dealt with lesson planning as the accomplishment of two major activities: (1) planning for sequences of lessons within a course unit or topic, and (2) design of individual lessons in such a way that effective conditions of learning can be incorporated into the instructional events of each lesson.

Up to the point of lesson planning, all the stages of instructional design can be similar whether a team is designing an entire curriculum or a teacher is designing a course. At the point of lesson design, however, teachers are offered a simpler form of our model, while a more detailed form of the model was offered in Chapter 10 for teams developing modules and other instructional materials and media. In spite of the differences between selecting materials as a part of lesson design by teachers, and developing materials by design teams, the purpose of both designs is the same—to incorporate effective conditions of learning into the instructional events for all lessons and modules.

The matter of establishing sequences of lessons was discussed separately for each domain of outcomes. The use of learning hierarchies was shown to be of central importance in design of sequences of lessons for intellectual skill objectives. Other considerations govern the sequencing decisions for other domains of outcomes.

It was shown that to make each instructional event in the lesson successful the conditions of learning relevant to the outcome (represented by the lesson objective) must be incorporated into the lessons. While intuition, ingenuity, creativity and experience are all valuable when planning lessons, reference to relevant conditions of learning can sharpen instruction and prevent the overlooking of some of the functions of instruction. Two tables in this chapter, and Table 9–2, summarize the conditions to be designed into the events of instruction for lessons directed toward various domains of outcomes.

Four steps in lesson planning were discussed. These include:

1. Listing the objective of the lesson.
2. Listing desired instructional events.
3. Choosing materials and learning activities.
4. Noting roles for teachers and learners.

An example of a lesson plan for a high school course in journalism showed that the results of the above four steps in lesson planning may be recorded in a two-column format, one listing the instructional events, and the other describing how each event is accomplished.

References

Ausubel, D. P., Novak, J. D., and Hanesian, H. *Educational Psychology: A Cognitive View.* 2d. Ed. New York: Holt, Rinehart and Winston, 1978.

Briggs, L. J. *Student's Guide to Handbook of Procedures for the Design of Instruction.* Pittsburgh, Pa.: American Institutes for Research, 1972.

Briggs, L. J., (ed.). *Instructional Design: Principles and Applications.* Englewood Cliffs, N.J.: Educational Technology Publications, 1977.

Crovitz, H. E. *Galton's Walk.* New York: Harper & Row, 1970.

Dale, E. A. *Audiovisual Methods in Teaching,* 3d Ed. New York: Holt, Rinehart, and Winston, 1969.

Frase, L. T. Boundary conditions for mathemagenic behaviors. *Review of Educational Research,* 1970, *40,* 337–347.

Gagné, R. M. *The Conditions of Learning,* 3d Ed. New York: Holt, Rinehart, and Winston, 1977.

Rothkopf, E. Z. The concept of mathemagenic behavior. *Review of Educational Research,* 1970, *40,* 325–336.

Wager, W. Media selection in the affective domain: A further interpretation of Dale's Cone of Experience for cognitive and affective learning. *Educational Technology,* July 1975, *15*(7), 9–13.

Wager, W. Instructional technology and higher education. In L. J. Briggs (ed.), *Instructional Design.* Englewood Cliffs, N.J.: Educational Technology Publications, 1977.

chapter 12

Assessing Student Performance

Instruction is designed to bring about the learning of several kinds of capabilities. These are evidenced by improved performance on the part of the student. While much learning goes on outside the school, and much results from the student's own effort, the responsibility of the school is to organize and provide instruction directed toward specific goals—goals which might not be achieved in a less organized manner.

The outcomes of this planned instruction consist of student performances which show that various kinds of capabilities have been acquired. Five domains of such capabilities have been identified and discussed in previous chapters: intellectual skills, cognitive strategies, information, motor skills, and attitudes. Performance objectives in these categories, applicable to a course of instruction, may be further analyzed to discover the prerequisites on which their learning depends. These in turn can form a basis for deciding upon a sequence of individual lessons, and for the design of the lessons themselves.

Both the designer of instruction and the teacher need a way to determine how successful the instruction has been, in terms of the performance of each student, and in terms of entire groups of students. There is a need to assess student performance to determine whether the newly designed instruction has met its design objectives. Assessment may also be done to learn whether each student has achieved the set of capabilities defined by the instructional objectives. Both these purposes can be served by the development of procedures for assessing student performance, which is the topic of this chapter.

PURPOSES OF PERFORMANCE MEASURES

In Chapter 2, it was pointed out that measures of student performance may have as many as five different specific purposes. These are briefly discussed in the following sections.

Pupil placement

When children return to school after each summer vacation, they will have forgotten some skills learned the previous year, and they will have acquired new information, skills, and attitudes. Even in the unlikely event that the members of a group left school the previous year with highly similar capabilities, they will not all be at the same "starting point" in respect to the new sequence of skills to be learned in a new school year.

Placement tests are often used to determine just which skills in a sequence each pupil has learned and can recall at the time the tests are administered (soon after the opening of a new school year). The results of such tests show the pattern of each child's areas of mastery and non-mastery, so that appropriate exercises are identified as the starting point for instruction. Programs of individualized instruction (Chapter 14) are well designed for this purpose; under group instruction, the teacher will need to arrange some activities for the majority of the group, while providing other activities for pupils who need to "catch up" or work ahead of the majority. The more suitable provisions are made for each learner, the more precision the instruction will have and the more likely the students are to experience success.

Diagnosis of difficulties

Diagnostic tests may be constructed to measure the separate prerequisite skills in learning hierarchies drawn to represent the essential parts of total skills (Chapter 6). These tests are especially helpful when some learners are seen to be "falling behind." A probable reason for falling behind, especially in large-group instruction, is that earlier skills in a sequence were not *mastered,* thus making it difficult to learn superordinate skills. Based on the results of a diagnostic test, the learner can be given remedial instruction back at the point he or she failed to master a skill. In some instances, of course, the remedial instruction may need to employ methods and materials different from those originally used, in order to avoid a second failure at the same trouble point in a sequence of lessons.

Checking pupil progress

Performance tests are often administered after each objective in a sequence of lessons has been presented in order to insure that each child is mastering each objective. Teachers learn to use such tests less often when an entire group consistently progresses well, and to use them more often when a number of learners are experiencing difficulties. Of course some progress checking is done informally by the teacher, in making "spot checks" with a few learners on each occasion. But in individualized instruction programs (Chapter 14) these tests are typically a part of each "module"; testing of this frequent sort shows right away that a learner is falling behind. By keeping progress checks brief, consistent with the adequacy of the assessment, the learner can receive reassurance that he is progressing well. The results of such tests also represent dependable information for the teacher to use in planning the next steps in the instruction.

For advanced learners, as in universities and colleges, progress checks are usually made less often, as by "midterm" examinations. Some college instructors give weekly tests, while others may use only final examinations in their courses.

Reports to parents

The use of performance measures not only assures both learners and teachers that all is well, but it constitutes a dependable basis for reporting progress to parents and administrators. The results of accumulated progress checks also provide a basis for promotion and for admission to higher institutions of learning.

Evaluation of the instruction

A final purpose of performance tests is to improve and evaluate the instruction itself. In recent years materials for instruction have often undergone *formative evaluations*—tryouts and subsequent revisions of the materials with individuals, with small groups, and with large groups in field test situations. For this purpose the total scores earned by each pupil on performance measures are, of course, of interest to indicate the overall degree of success attained. Even more important for purposes of revising the instruction are item analyses showing which items are passed or failed by a majority of pupils. These item scores are particularly useful in deciding where the instruction needs to be improved. Techniques for formative evaluations are further discussed in Chapter 15 (see also Dick, 1977a).

Performance tests are also used in conducting *summative evaluations* of the instruction. These evaluations are conducted after course revisions have been accomplished, and after the resulting form of the course has been used for other groups of learners. Procedures for summative evaluation are also discussed further by Popham (1975), by Dick (1977b), and in Chapter 15.

The principles of preparing performance measures are similar whether one wishes to construct tests for each prerequisite skill in a learning hierarchy, or to construct a test for an entire objective or for a larger unit of study. In the remainder of this chapter we discuss tests in terms of their validity for measuring performance on a single objective. However, the single objective could be considered as a course objective, a unit objective, a single lesson objective, or an enabling objective.

DEVELOPMENT PROCEDURES FOR OBJECTIVE-REFERENCED ASSESSMENT

The term *objective-referenced assessment* is used with a literal meaning in the context of this book. It is intended to imply that the way to assess student learning is to build tests or other assessment procedures which directly measure the human performances described in the objectives for the course. Such measures of performance make it possible to infer that the intended performance capability has indeed been developed as a result of the instruction provided. Similar tests can be administered before the instruction is given (pretests), and provisions made to allow students to bypass instruction which they do not need. Normally, a teacher tests only for the "assumed entering capabilities" before introducing the instruction, and assesses performance on the objective itself only following instruction (that is, by a post-test). A convenient compromise practice may be for the teacher to permit any student who thinks he has mastered the objective before instruction to take the test reflecting that objective as a pretest, and to excuse the student from that portion of the instruction if he passes it.

The performance objective is the keystone in planning assessment of performance. We have indicated the critical importance of the *verbs* in the statement for correctly describing the objective (Chapter 7). The verbs are equally crucial as a basis for planning the performance assessment. Such verbs tell what the student should be asked to *do* when taking the performance-assessment test. Note that the *capability* verb refers to the capability that is *inferred* to be present in the student's repertoire, when the student has successfully performed as stated in the *action* verb in the objective. The capability verb is the *intent* of the objective; the action verb is the *indicator* that the intent has been achieved by the learner.

Congruence of objective and test: validity

The objective-referenced orientation to assessment greatly simplifies the concept of *validity* in performance measurement. This approach to assessment results in a direct rather than an indirect measure of the objective. Thus it eliminates the need to relate the measures obtained to a criterion by means of a correlation coefficient, as must usually be done when indirect measures are used, or when tests have been constructed without reference to any explicit performance objectives. Accordingly, one can address the matter of test validity by inspection to obtain an answer to this question: "Is the performance required during assessment the same performance as that described in the objective?" If the answer is a clear "yes," then the test is valid. In practice, it is desirable for more than one person to make this judgment, and for consistency to be attained among these judges.

Validity is assured when the assessment procedure results in measurement of the performance described in the objective. This occurs when the test and the objective are *congruent* with each other. A caution may be interjected here, however. This method of determining validity assumes that the statement of the objective is itself valid, in the sense that it truly reflects the purposes of the topic or lesson. The procedures described for defining objectives in Chapter 7 are intended to insure that this is the case. Nevertheless, there may be an additional need to recheck the consistency of specific objectives and more broadly stated purposes. Sometimes, inconsistencies become apparent when statements of objectives are transformed into tests of student performance.

It should be recognized that the word "test" is used here in a generic sense to mean any procedure for assessing the performance described in an objective. Thus the use of this word can cover all forms of written and oral testing as well as procedures for evaluating student products such as essays, musical productions, constructed models, or works of art. We choose the term "assessment" to refer to the measurement of student performance, rather than the alternative of "achievement testing." The latter term is often associated with norm-referenced measurement, which will be the subject of a later discussion in this chapter. At this point, however, *test* and *assessment* are used to refer to objective-referenced performance measurement.

Some of the performance objectives given in Chapter 7 can be used to illustrate how judgments about test validity may be made. Initially, we shall be concerned primarily with two of the five parts of an objective statement, the two verbs which describe the *capability* to be learned, and the *actions* the student takes in demonstrating this capability. Later on, other parts of the objective will be related to performance assessment.

First, consider the example of *generating* a letter by typing. The word "generate" is the clue that in the test situation the student must compose his own letter, rather than typing a different form of a letter composed by someone else. It is clear that the learner must use his capability of generating a particular kind of letter within the constraints of the situation described in the objective. In the alternative objective relating to typing, the learner receives a written longhand letter composed by someone else. These two objectives relating to business letters are very different. One requires only the skill of typing a letter already composed, while the other requires also the problem-solving capability of composing the letter. Thus two domains (motor skills and intellectual skills) are sampled.

In a second example drawn from Chapter 7, the student must *demonstrate* the use of a rule by supplying the missing factor in an equation. Simply copying the missing value from a book, or remembering the value from having seen the problem worked before, would not constitute a valid test for this capability. In designing a test, care must be taken to use different examples for testing than those used for teaching, so as to minimize the chance that the correct response can be supplied by any means other than the intended intellectual process.

In any example of demonstrating mastery of a concept, the learner may *identify* the concept by printing the first letter of the concept (name) in a blank. This is not the same as either copying the first letter, or spelling the name of the concept. It is also different from the performance of explaining how the concept may be used. Any or all of these latter instances may be useful performances, but they do not reflect the intent of the objective, either as to the capability required or the action which signifies that the capability is present.

Exercises on judging the validity of test items by comparing them with the corresponding performance objectives are given by Briggs (1970, Chapter IV).

Designing the test situation

The form of performance objectives described in Chapter 7 serves as the basis from which the test situation can be derived. It will be recalled that the five components of an objective statement are given as: (1) situation; (2) learned capability; (3) object; (4) action; and (5) tools and constraints. Such a statement also provides a description of the situation to be used in testing.

For certain types of objectives and for learners who are not too young, the change of only a few words may convert the objective statement to a test. For example, one could give the objective on generating and typing a letter to the learner as "directions for taking the test." All that would be needed in addition would be to supply the "received letter," and to provide an electric typewriter, typing paper, and carbon paper. The person administering the test would further be instructed to insure a favorable (monitored) test environment, and to record and call "time." For the objective of demonstrating the substitution of factors from one equation to another, about all the test administrator (teacher) would need to do would be to supply two equations of the proper form and make clear whether the student was expected to write his answers on the same page or on a separate answer page. The objective itself should be communicated so that the learner understands how he is to solve the "problems," that is, by using the commutative property of multiplication.

It is clear, then, that the more closely objectives are prepared to follow the outline given in Chapter 7, the fewer decisions remain to be made in planning the test, and the fewer "directions" must be given to the student. Statements of objectives as prepared for the use of the instructional designer or teacher also are used to define most of the test situation for the student. Of course, both objectives and test items derived from them have to be presented in simpler terms for young children, either for communicating the purpose of the lesson to them or for testing their performance after the lesson is completed.

Some Cautions   In using objectives to plan tests, a few cautions should be noted. The more incomplete the statements of objectives are, the more these cautions may be needed, because more must be "filled in" in moving from the objective to the test situation.

1. Substitute verbs which change the meaning of either the *capability* or the *action* described in the objective should be avoided. When synonyms or more simple explanations are needed to translate the objective into a test, these restatements must be reviewed for agreement with the intent of the objective. Particular care should be taken not to change from an answer the student must somehow construct or develop for himself, to an answer he must merely choose, select, or recall. If an objective says "generate a position and a defense for the position," he can only do this orally or in writing—not by selecting answers from a multiple-choice test. Avoidance of ambiguity in "guessing at" what vague verbs mean in poorly stated objectives can be achieved by using the standard verbs from Table 7-1. But careful attention needs to be given to deciding upon unambiguous

meanings for verbs such as "summarize," "describe," "list," "analyze," "complete," except as *"ing"* verbs denoting the particular action expected. Review of an objective in these terms sometimes reveals that the objective itself needs to be changed. In that case, it should be changed before planning the instruction, and before using the statement either as a lesson objective or as a part of the directions for a test.

2. Changes in other elements of the objective should be avoided, except when needed to simplify directions to the student as to how to take the test. That is, unless a deliberate change is intended, the situation, the object, and the tools and other constraints, as well as the two verbs denoting the capability and the action, should be congruent between the objective and the test. It is possible that changes might be so great as to make the test call for capabilities the students have not yet been taught. In a "worst possible" mismatch between objective and test, capabilities in different domains of learning outcomes might be specified in the objective and in the test. In such a situation, if the teaching were to be directed to an objective in still a third domain, there would be maximum non-congruence among the three anchor points. A revealing instance pertaining to this caution might be obtained by asking teachers or designers, on three separate occasions, to produce their "objectives," their "examinations," and their "lesson plans." Is it an inconceivable finding that the objectives might call for "appreciate," while the teaching contains "facts," and the examination calls for "use of concepts and rules"?

3. Tests should not be made either more "easy" or more "difficult" than the objectives. These terms need not enter into testing of the objective-referenced variety. The aim is one of accurately representing the objective, rather than one of estimating how to make tests sufficiently difficult.

4. The test should not try to achieve a large range in scores or a "normal" distribution of scores. The aim of such testing is not that of "discriminating" among the students. That is to say, testing does not have the purpose of finding that student A scores higher or lower than student B. Rather, its purpose is to discover which objectives both students have learned.

THE CONCEPT OF MASTERY

The introduction of the idea of *mastery* of learning outcomes (Bloom, 1968) requires a change in viewpoint towards the conduct of instruction, as well as towards its assessment. In conventional instruction, both the teacher and the students expect that only a few students will learn so well as to receive an *A* in the topic or course. The rest will either do fairly well, as represented by a *C*, for example, or they will "fail." When test scores are plotted as frequency distributions, a "normal curve" is formed, and certain percentages of students are assigned to various letter grades.

In commenting on the impact of this system of assessment, Bloom, Hastings, and Madaus (1971, p. 43) observe that the expectations so established tend to fix the academic goals of teachers and students at inappropriate low levels, and thus reduce both teacher and student motivation. The particular educational practice which produces these effects is "group-paced" instruction, in which all students must try to learn at the same rate and by the same mode of instruction. When both pace and mode are fixed, the achievement of each student becomes primarily a function of his aptitude. But if both mode and rate of instruction can vary among learners, the chances are that more students can become successful in their learning.

It is easier to set up means by which *rate* of learning is allowed to vary among learners than it is to predict the *mode* of learning which will benefit each student the most. And of course there are economical and other limits—one cannot provide a different mode for every single student. Modularized, individualized instruction can largely take care of the rate problem, and to some extent (when alternate materials or modes are available) the problem of learning "style" as well. The diagnostic features of individualized assessment also make it possible to help a student redirect his efforts properly.

Mastery learning means essentially that if the proper conditions can be provided, perhaps 90 to 95 percent of the students can actually master most objectives to the degree now only reached by "good students." Thus the mastery learning concept abandons the idea that students merely learn more or less well. Rather, an effort is made to find out why students fail to reach mastery, and to remedy the situation for such students. The resolution of a learning problem by a student usually requires one of the following measures: (a) more time for learning, (b) different media or materials, or (c) diagnosis to determine what missing prerequisite knowledge or skills he must acquire to master the objective. Within this context, the personal knowledge of the teacher can be added to form decisions concerning students whose performance is exceptional even when these methods have been fully utilized. The general aim implied by the notion of mastery includes the resolution to provide materials and conditions by means of which most learners can be successful at most tasks, in a program that is reasonable for each individual.

Determining criteria for mastery

How can it be known when a student has performed satisfactorily, or attained mastery, on a test applicable to any particular objective? The student needs to be told he was successful, so that he can then move on to work toward achieving the next objective he chooses or has assigned to him. In case he has not been successful in attaining the objective, the teacher needs to determine what remedial instruction is needed.

A remedial decision for an objective in the intellectual skill domain can best be made by administering a diagnostic test over the capabilities subordinate to the objective. In other instances, the teacher may use oral testing methods to find out where in the teaching sequence the failure to learn first began. When instruction is individualized, the individual lessons often include such diagnostic tests on subordinate capabilities. For a known slow-learner, such "diagnostic" tests of subordinate competencies may be used as "assessments of performance" so that the learner is known to have mastered each capability before he goes on to the next. This procedure detects "small failures" before they accumulate into "large failures" of entire lessons, topics, or courses. Certainly consistent use of frequent testing could often prevent the "year-after-year" failures, or at least alert the school earlier than usual to a need to reappraise the program for a particular student.

When "mastery" is defined for a test assessing performance on an objective, this also defines the "criterion of success" for that objective. The first step is to define *how well* the learner must perform on the test to indicate success on that objective. Then a record is made of *how many* students have reached the criterion (mastery). This makes it possible to decide whether the instruction over that objective has reached its design objective. Later, at the end of an entire course, the percentage of students who reached the criterion of mastery on all the objectives (or any specified percentage of the objectives) can be computed. From such data, one can determine whether the course-design criterion has been met. A frequently used course-design criterion is that 90 percent of the students achieve mastery of 90 percent of the objectives, but other percentages than these may of course be used. Sometimes three design criteria are set, with one to indicate minimal acceptable success, while the others represent higher degrees of success. In general, this means of representing course-design criteria can be used to give *accountability* for the performance of students following instruction.

The administration of tests applicable to course objectives, and the definition of "mastery level" for each objective, provide the means for evaluating both the course itself and the performance of individual students. Thus students can be "promoted" on the basis of such tests, and the test results can be used in the *formative evaluation* of the course, showing where revisions are needed, if any (see Chapter 15). This built-in capability for course improvement is compatible not only with "fair promotion standards" for students, but also with the individualization of instruction, and with the development and evaluation of entire instructional systems.

While the action of defining mastery on each objective, when objective-referenced tests are employed, is intended primarily for the purpose of monitoring student progress and for discovering how successful the course is, data from the same tests can be used for "assigning grades" when that is required by the school.

CRITERIA FOR OBJECTIVE-REFERENCED ASSESSMENT

The question next to be addressed concerns the matter of deciding upon criteria of mastery for each kind of learning objective. Typical procedures for each domain of learning outcomes are described in the following section.

Intellectual skill objectives

Problem solving   As an illustration of criteria for assessing performance for this type of learning outcomes, we begin with the objective for the learning of a *higher-order rule (problem-solving),* briefly described in Table 7-1 (p. 125). The statement of this objective is "generates, by synthesizing applicable rules, a paragraph describing a person's actions in a situation of fear."

To "score" such a paragraph as acceptable, a list of features the paragraph should include would be prepared. In this case no "verbatim key" is possible, and mechanical scoring is out of the question (at least with technology currently available). Since no grammatical requirements are reflected in this abbreviated statement of the objective, it may be assumed that an adequate description of a case of fear need only be "descriptive" and not necessarily error-free in grammar and punctuation. If several teachers are using the same objective, they might work together to define assessment criteria more precisely, and to agree upon *how many actions* must be described and how to judge that they describe a *fearful reaction* of the person. The minimum number of rules to be "synthesized" in developing the description could be agreed upon. The application of some rules might be mandatory, and some optional, in a satisfactory paragraph.

As in many appropriate tests, the test for this objective is not to be judged simply as "8 out of 10 questions right." The criteria to be looked for may be both qualitative and quantitative in nature. Whatever the checklist for scoring may contain, its application will require judgment, not a clerical checking of an answer with an "answer key." Consequently, degree of agreement among teachers in applying the checklist to determine "acceptable" or "not acceptable" paragraphs is a relevant factor in determining the reliability of the measure of performance obtained. The criteria employed for judging such a performance might be (a) expression, (b) one action of the large muscles, and (c) two statements of rules governing emotional expression in behavior.

Rule learning   For the learning of a *rule,* the example given in Table 7-1 is "demonstrates, by solving verbally stated examples, the addition of positive and negative numbers." In order to examine the matter of performance criteria more exactly, one needs to begin with an expanded version of this objective, which is: "Given verbally stated examples involving physical variables which vary over a range of positive and negative values, demonstrates the addition of these values by writing appropriate mathematical expressions yielding their sum." Obviously, this more complete statement adds to the specification of the situation, and therefore to the adequate formulation of a test item. Such an item, for example, might say, "The temperature in Greenland on one day was 17°C. during the day and decreased by 57° during the night. What was the nighttime temperature?"

Thus the "situation" part of the objective statement defines the class of situations from which particular test items are to be drawn. Suppose the objective is: "Given a verbal statement defining values of length and width of a rectangularly shaped face of an object, finds the area of the face." From such a statement, an item such as the following could readily be derived: "A box top is 120 cm. in length and 47 cm. in width; what is its area?" It may be noted that the statement of the objective in this case implies that the performance will be measured in a situation including a verbal statement of the problem. A different statement beginning "Given a diagram of a rectangle with values of length and width indicated . . ." would of course imply a different form of test item.

A remaining decision pertaining to the criterion of performance measurement has to do with the question of how many items to employ. Obviously, the aim is to achieve measurement to which the ideas of "mastered" versus "not mastered" can be applied. It may need to be determined empirically how many items must be used in order to make such a decision correctly. By convention, ten or twenty items might be considered necessary as a number of examples for a test of the learning of an arithmetic rule. While there is no strong argument against this practice, except for the time required, it is difficult to see why more than three or four examples are needed. The aim in using multiple examples is primarily one of avoiding "errors of measurement" which may arise because of one or more undesirable idiosyncratic features of a single item.

Defined Concepts   To derive an illustration of performance criteria for the measurement of a *defined concept,* the following example of an objective may be used: "Given a picture of an observer on the earth and the sky above him, classifies the zenith as the point in the sky vertically above the observer." Again it is apparent that the situation described in this statement may be directly represented in the form of a test item. For example, such an item might first depict (in a labeled diagram) the earth, the sky, and an observer standing on the earth. Going on, it could say: "Show by an angular diagram the location of the *zenith.*" For answer, the student would draw a vertical line pointing from the observer to the sky, indicate that it made a 90° angle with the earth's surface at the point at which the observer was located, and label the point in the sky to which the line was directed as the "zenith."

An item of this type would not be highly dependent on the verbal abilities of the student, and might be a desirable form of measurement for that reason. Alternatively, providing verbal facility of the student could be assumed, an item might be based upon a differently stated objective, as follows: "Asked to define, classifies zenith as the point in the sky vertically (or 90° to the surface) above an observer on the earth, by stating a definition orally." It is evident that measurement in this case is subject to distortion. Unless one is entirely convinced that the student has mastered the subordinate concepts (earth, sky, observer, 90°), the resulting response of the student may have to be interpreted as a memorized verbal chain. Nevertheless, it is noteworthy that verbal statements are often employed as criteria for assessment of defined concepts.

Concrete Concepts   The assessment of *concrete concept* learning involves the construction of items from an objective statement like the following: "Given five common plants and asked to name the major parts, identifies for each the root, leaf, and stem, by pointing to each while naming it." For such an assessment to be made, the child would be provided with five plants laid out on the table. In response to the teacher's question, he or she would point to and name the root, leaf, and stem for each plant. Of course, an objective with a somewhat different statement of the "situation" would lead to a corresponding difference in the test item. For example, the objective statement: "Given pictures of five common plants, identifies the root, leaf, and stem of each by placing labels bearing these names opposite the appropriate part," implies a specifically different kind of test item. Whereas the previous example assumes only that the oral responses "root," "leaf," and "stem" can be made without error, the latter example requires the assumption that the labels containing these words can be read.

A very simple example of assessment for a concrete concept is provided by the task of identifying a common geometrical shape, as it may occur in an early grade. The objective statement might read: "Given a set of common geometrical shapes, and oral directions 'show me the circles,' identifies the circles by pointing." From this statement may be derived an assessment item which involves giving the child a piece of paper on which appear figures such as the following:

$$\bigcirc \square \triangle \bigcirc \circ \square \bigcirc \square \bigcirc \triangle \bigcirc$$

Upon being given the oral directions, "Point to each one that is a circle," the child would make the appropriate response to each circular figure, in order to be counted as having attained the concept.

Verbal and Motor Chains   Measuring *verbal* or *motor chains* requires a fairly self-evident process. In the case of a verbal chain, for example, one might simply say, "Recite 'Old Ironsides.' " Decisions would need to be made as to whether hesitations or promptings would be acceptable for criterion performance. A time limit might be set for hesitations; and the learner should be informed whether enthusiasm, voice inflection, gestures, or aspects of performance other than the correct verbal chain itself are to be expected. Such criteria should preferably be known before practice starts, as well as at the time of the test.

Shorter verbal chains often are tested as an incidental part of a test whose aim is primarily a more complex form of learning. Having a student work with chemical equations without reference to a listing of symbols of any kind would constitute an example.

Motor chains have for many years been evaluated by "comparison with standards," as in the case of handwriting. Many years ago, a familiar scene in the elementary school room was the Palmer Scale for grading handwriting. A sample of the pupil's writing was compared with ideal samples on a board containing various degrees of "correct" penmanship, each having a numeral such as 90, 80,

70, etc., indicating the "standard" for each level of skill in writing. This was a "criterion-referenced" form of grading in that standards were stable and always meant the same thing; and also in the sense that teachers could say that 60 was "passing" at the third grade, 70 at the fourth grade, and so on.

Cognitive strategies

While it would seem desirable to extend the notion of mastery learning to all domains of instructional objectives, its application to the measurement of cognitive strategies cannot readily be achieved. Since such strategies as we deal with them here are primarily relevant to performances of novel problem solving, it is apparent that the *quality* of the mental process is being assessed, and not simply its presence or absence. Sometimes, novel problems have many solutions, rather than a single solution. In such instances, cognitive strategies will have been used by the student in achieving the solution, whatever it may be. Accordingly, assessment becomes a matter of judging how good the solution is, and it is unlikely that a "pass-fail" decision will be made.

It is noteworthy that standards of originality and inventiveness are applied to the assessment of such student products as theses and dissertations in university undergraduate and graduate education. Besides being thorough and technically sound, a doctoral dissertation is expected to make "an original discovery or contribution" to a field of systematic knowledge. Exact criteria or dimensions for judging this quality are typically not specified. Varying numbers of professionally qualified people usually arrive at a consensus concerning the degree of originality exhibited by a dissertation study, and its acceptability as a novel contribution to an area of knowledge or art.

Productive Thinking   The measurement of productive thinking, and by inference the cognitive strategies that underlie such thinking, has been investigated by Johnson and Kidder (1972) in psychology classes at the undergraduate level of education. Students were asked to invent novel hypotheses, questions, and answers in response to problem statements which go beyond the information obtained from lectures and textbook. The problems employed included (1) predicting the consequences of an unusual psychological event; (2) writing an imaginative sentence incorporating several newly learned (specified) concepts; (3) stating a novel hypothesis related to a described situation; (4) writing a title for a table containing behavioral data; and (5) drawing conclusions from a table or graph. When items such as these were combined into tests containing 10 to 15 items, reasonably adequate reliabilities of "originality" scores were obtained. Quality was judged by two raters whose judgments were found to agree highly after a short period of training.

Assessments of originality can presumably be made of students' answers, compositions, and projects at precollege levels. In fact, such judgments are often made by teachers incidentally, or at any rate informally, concerning a variety of projects and problems undertaken by students in schools. It seems evident that systematic methods of assessment can be applied to cognitive strategies at these lower levels of the educational ladder, although this has not as yet been done.

It should be pointed out that the assessment of cognitive strategies, or the originality of thought, as an *outcome* of learning does not necessarily have the same aim, nor use the same methods, as those employed in the measurement of creativity as a *trait*. Creativity has been extensively studied in this latter sense (Torrance, 1963; Guilford, 1967; Johnson, 1972), and the findings go far beyond the scope of the present discussion. When assessment of the quality of thought is to be undertaken as a learning outcome, two main characteristics must be sought. First, the problem (or project) that is set for the student must require the utilization of knowledge, concepts, and rules which have been recently learned by the student, rather than calling upon instances of skills and information which may have been acquired an indeterminate number of years previously. Second, it must be either assumed, or preferably shown, that students have in fact learned relevant prerequisite information and skills, before the assessment of "originality" is undertaken. This condition is necessary to insure that all students have the same opportunity to be original, and that their solutions are not handicapped by the absence of necessary knowledge and intellectual skills.

Information

In this domain, the concept of mastery must be related to a predetermined set of facts, generalizations, or ideas, an acceptable number of which the student can state in acceptable form or degree of completeness and accuracy. The conventional "norm-referenced" measurement is often closely related to assessment of information. The fundamental distinction to be held in mind, however, is that of *objective* versus *content-referenced* measurement. The aim of assessment is to determine whether certain objectives have been attained, rather than to discover whether some content has been "covered."

Objective-referenced assessment may be achieved for the information domain of learning outcomes by specifying what information is to be learned as a minimum standard of performance. Objectives pertaining to information should state clearly *which* names, facts, and generalizations should be learned. They thus differentiate the core content of information to be recalled, from the incidental information which may be in the book and which some students may be able to recall, but which represents learning beyond the required level.

It would be a mistake to make the objectives in the information domain so exhaustive as to leave no time for objectives in other domains. Instead, one should deliberately seek out and identify those informational outcomes which are likely to contribute most to the *attainment of objectives in other domains*. While masses of information should be acquired over years by the well-educated person, this goal should not be allowed to interfere with the attainment of objectives in the areas of intellectual skills and problem-solving strategies.

When students are provided with information objectives (names, facts, or generalizations and condensed substance to be learned), it is possible for them to undertake the learning of these objectives with the same confidence applied to learning objectives in other domains, *simply because they know what they are expected to learn.* When the possibility of doing this is recognized, the testing of students for information can become as fair and humane as are tests on intellectual skills.

Examples of Information Items   Some typical items for information assessment are as follows:

1. Describe at least three of the causes of the Revolutionary War, as discussed in the textbook.
2. Tell briefly what was the role of each of these men in the affair at West Point. (This statement to be followed by names of the men, and further identification of the affair as Benedict Arnold's treason).
3. State the chemical symbols for the following compounds.
4. Write a paragraph summarizing how a president is elected when the electoral college fails to elect.
5. Show in one page or less the major advantages of objective-referenced measurement, by simply *listing* them.
6. Name any 15 of these 20 animals from seeing their pictures.
7. What is the boiling point of water?
8. Read this report and write a summary of the four main themes developed in the report.

As these examples indicate, objective-referenced testing of information requires the exact identification of what information is to be learned and retained. If the listing of names or dates is to be acquired, this should be made clear. Alternatively, if the substance of a passage is to be recounted, this objective should be made equally apparent to the student. These procedures make learning for mastery feasible, and also fair and reasonable.

Attitudes

As Chapter 5 has indicated, attitudes vary in the intensity with which they influence the choice of personal actions. Since the strength of attitudes is what one wishes to assess, it is evident that "mastery" cannot be identified. The assessment of strength of an attitude toward or against a class of action choices may be obtained in terms of the proportion of times the person behaves in a given way in a sample of defined situations. For example, attitude toward using public transportation might be assessed by observing the likelihood of a student's choosing various forms of public (rather than private) transportation in the various situations in which such choices are made. The observed incidents would be the basis for inferring the degree to which the person *tends* to use or not to use public conveyances.

In assessing an attitude like "concern for others," it is evident that no "pass-fail" criterion of mastery can be set. However, a teacher might adopt the objective that all her second-grade pupils will improve in the positive direction of this attitude during a year's period. In addition, it would be possible to adopt the standard that each child will exhibit concern for others, either in verbal expression or overt actions, more times per month in May than during the previous October. Anecdotal records may be kept recording such actions, and reports of "improved" or "not improved" made at the end of the school year. Such reports can be quantified in terms of number of positive actions and in terms of proportion of positive to total (positive plus negative) actions. Behaviors representing neither kind of action would simply not be recorded, in recognition of the fact that some of the child's time is spent in study periods offering little opportunity for behaving either way toward other people.

The following examples suggest some actions which might be recorded in relation to such an attitude as "concern for others": any act or word directed to comforting a child who is upset; expression of condolence for illness or other misfortune; helping locate lost articles; suggesting that the class write letters to an ill classmate; offering encouragement to any child experiencing a difficulty whether relating to learning or otherwise; offering to tutor a child who missed work due to absence or failure; offering to share a discovery about materials or methods for learning; helping to obtain first aid for a playground injury.

Attitudes are often measured by obtaining "self-reports" of the likelihood of actions, as opposed to direct observations of the actions themselves. As is well known, the most serious limitation in the use of questionnaires for this purpose is the possibility of bias resulting from students' attempts to answer questions in ways that will win approval, as opposed to a manner that reflects their choices accurately. There appears to be no simple solution to the problem of obtaining truly accurate information from self-reports, although many investigations have been carried out with this purpose (cf. Fishbein, 1967). Best results appear to be achieved when students are first assured that the assessment being done is not intended as an "adversary" process; that is, when they are relieved of the anxiety of reporting only what will (they think) be approved. When questionnaires are administered to groups, the additional precaution is frequently taken to insure that responses are anonymously recorded.

Motor skills

Assessment of motor skills, like that for information, typically requires the setting of certain standards of performance. Usually such standards refer to the *precision* of the performance, but often also to its *speed*. Since motor skills are known to improve in either or both of these qualities with extended practice, it is unrealistic to expect that mastery can be defined in the sense of "learned" or "not-learned." Accordingly, a standard of performance must be decided upon in order to determine whether mastery has been achieved.

Typing skill provides a good example of assessment methods in this domain. A number of different standards of performance are set at progressively higher levels for practice which has extended over increasingly long periods of time. Thus a test standard of 30 words per minute with a specified minimum number of errors may be adopted as a reasonable standard in a beginning course, while 40 or 50 words per minute may be expected for an advanced course after more time has been given for additional practice.

Reliability of objective-referenced measures

Choosing criteria for items and tests designed to accomplish objective-referenced measurement requires the selection of standards of performance which are appropriate to the stated objective, as the preceding discussion has shown. In addition, the items employed for assessment need to yield measurement which is *dependable.* This latter feature of the assessment procedure is referred to as *reliability,* and it has two primary meanings.

Consistency   A first meaning of reliability is *consistency* of measurement. It is necessary to determine that the student's performance in answering or completing one particular item designed to assess his performance on an objective is consistent with his performance on other items aimed at the same objective. A pupil in the second grade may be asked by one item to demonstrate his mastery of an arithmetic rule by means of the item: $3M + 2M = 25$; $M = ?$ Obviously, the purpose of assessment is to discover whether he is able to perform a *class* of arithmetic operations of this type, not simply whether he is able to do this single one. Accordingly, additional items belonging to the same class (for example, $4M + 3M = 21$; $5M + 1M = 36$) are typically employed in order to insure the dependability of the measurement.

In informal testing situations, as when the teacher "probes" by asking questions of one student after another, single items may be employed to assess performance. However, it is evident that no measure of consistency is available in such situations. On any single item, a student may make a successful response because he happens to have seen and memorized an "answer." Alternatively, his response may be incorrect because he has inadvertently been misled by some particular characteristic of the item. The single item does not make possible a confident conclusion that the student has mastered the performance implied by the objective.

In those instances in which the class of performances represented by the objective is well defined (as in the arithmetic example previously given) the procedure of selecting additional assessment items of the same class is fairly straightforward. It is essential to bear in mind that the conclusion aimed for is not "how many items are correct?" but rather "does the number correct dependably indicate mastery?" While two items are obviously better than one, they may yield the puzzling outcome, half right–half wrong. Does this mean that the student has attained mastery, or does it mean he got one item right only because he somehow managed to memorize an answer? Three items would seem to provide a better means of making a reliable decision about mastery. In this case, two out of three correctly answered leads to a certain confidence that reliability of measurement has been achieved. More items can readily be employed, but three seems a reasonable minimum on which to base a reliable assessment of mastery.

When cognitive strategies are the aim of assessment, the "item" selected for the purpose of assessment may actually be a rather lengthy problem-solving task. For example, such a task might be to "write a 300-word theme on a student-selected topic, within one hour." Assessing performance consistently may require several items, since it is necessary to disentangle the prior learning of information and intellectual skills from the quality of original thought. A number of occasions must be provided on which the student can display the quality of his performance within this domain of learning outcome. The aim is to make it unlikely that a student could meet the criteria set for such tasks without possessing a genuine, generalizable capability of writing original themes on other topics.

Temporal Dependability   The second meaning of reliability is dependability of the measurement on temporally separated occasions. One wishes to be assured that the student's demonstration of mastery of the objective as assessed on Monday is not different from what it would be on Tuesday, or on some other day. Is his performance an ephemeral thing, or does it have the degree of permanence one expects of a learned capability? Has his performance, good or bad, been determined largely by how he felt that day, by a temporary illness, or by some adventitious feature of the testing situation?

Reliability of measurement in this second meaning is usually determined by a second testing separated from the first by a time interval of days or weeks. This is the test-retest method, in which good reliability of the tests is indicated by a high degree of correspondence between scores obtained by a group of students on the two occasions. Often this procedure is used in the formative evaluation of the test, but it may also be employed in practical assessment to determine whether what has been learned has a reasonable degree of stability.

NORM-REFERENCED MEASURES

Tests designed to yield scores which compare each student's performance with that of a group, or with a norm established by group scores, are called *norm-referenced*. Characteristically, such tests are used to obtain assessments of student achievement over relatively large segments of instructional content, such as topics or courses. They differ from objective-referenced tests in that they typically measure performance on a *mixture* of objectives, rather than being confined to assessment of single, clearly identifiable objectives. Thus, a norm-referenced test is more likely to have the purpose of assessing "reading comprehension" than it is to measure the attainment of the individual skills involved in reading, considered as specific objectives.

Because of this characteristic of comprehensive coverage, norm-referenced tests are most useful for *summative* kinds of assessment and evaluation (see Chapter 15). They provide answers to such questions as, "How much American history does a student know (compared to others at his grade level)?" "How well is the student able to reason using the operations of arithmetic?" "What proficiency does the student have in using grammatical rules?" Obviously, such assessment is most appropriate when applied to instruction extending over reasonably long periods of time, as in mid-course or end-of-course examinations.

At the same time, the characteristics of norm-referenced measures imply some obvious limitations, as compared with objective-referenced tests. Since their items usually represent a mixture of objectives, often impossible to identify singly, they cannot readily be used for the purpose of diagnostic testing of prerequisite skills and knowledge. For a similar reason, norm-referenced tests typically do not provide direct and unambiguous measures of what has been learned, when the latter is conceived as one or more defined objectives.

Often a norm-referenced test presents questions and tasks which require the student at one and the same time to utilize learned capabilities of intellectual skills, information, and cognitive strategies. In so doing, they make possible assessments of student capabilities which are "global" rather than specific to identifiable objectives. For this reason they are particularly appropriate for assessing outcomes of learning in a set of topics or in a total course. Since the scores obtained are also representative of a group (a single class, or a larger "referenced" group such as ten-year-old children), the score made by each student may conveniently be compared with those of others in the group. Percentile scores are often used for this purpose; the score of a student may be expressed, for example, as "falling at the 63d percentile."

Teacher-made tests

Tests constructed by teachers are sometimes of the norm-referenced variety. The teacher may be interested in learning how well students have learned the content of a course, which may represent a number of different objectives and several categories of learning outcome. Mid-course and end-of-course examinations often have this characteristic of mixed purposes of assessment. These may also be conceived as being aimed at testing the student's "integration" of the various skills and knowledges he is expected to have learned.

At the same time, a norm-referenced test makes possible the comparison of student's performances within a group, or with a referenced group (such as last year's class). Often, such tests are refined over periods of years, using methods of item analysis to select the most "discriminating" items (cf. Wood, 1960; Payne, 1968). This means that items which do not discriminate—those that many students answer correctly and those that few answer correctly—are progressively discarded. Tests refined in this manner tend increasingly to measure problem-solving and other cognitive strategies. They may also, in part, measure "intelligence," rather than what has been directly learned. While this may be a legitimate intention when the aim is to assess the total effects of a course of study, it is evident that this quality of norm-referenced tests makes them very different from objective-referenced tests.

When assessment is aimed at the outcomes of individual lessons or parts of lessons, little justification can be seen for the use of norm-referenced tests. When such tests are used to assess student performance resulting from the learning of defined objectives, they are likely to miss the point of assessment entirely. When instruction has been designed so as to insure the attainment of objectives, tests should be derived directly from the definition of the objectives themselves, as indicated in the earlier portion of this chapter. Unless objective-referenced tests are used for this purpose, two important purposes of assessment will likely be neglected: (1) the assessment of mastery of the specific capabilities learned; and (2) the possibility of diagnostic help for students in overcoming particular learning deficiencies by retrieving missing prerequisite skills and knowledges.

Standardized tests

Norm-referenced tests intended for broad usage among many schools within a school system, a region, or in the nation as a whole, may have norms that are *standardized.* This means that the tests have been given to large samples of students in specified age (or grade) groups, and that the resulting distributions of scores obtained become the standards to which the scores of any given student or those of any class of students, may be compared. Sometimes the standard norms are expressed as percentiles, indicating what percent of the large sample of students attained or fell below particular scores. Often, too, such standards are expressed as grade-equivalent scores, indicating the scores attained by all children in the group who were in the first grade, the second grade, and so on. Procedures used in the development and validation of standardized tests are described in many books on this subject (cf. Cronbach, 1970; Thorndike and Hagen, 1969; Tyler, 1971).

Standardized tests are generally norm-referenced tests—the development of objective-referenced tests has not yet proceeded to the point of availability for a variety of objectives and for a variety of "levels" of instruction. Accordingly, standardized tests typically exhibit the characteristics previously described. They are usually mixed in their measurement of particular objectives, since their items have not been directly derived from such objectives. Their items are selected to produce the largest possible variation in scores among students, and thus their scores tend to be rather highly correlated with intelligence, rather than with particular learning outcomes. With few exceptions, they fail to provide the identification of missing subordinate capabilities which is essential to diagnostic aims.

Obviously, then, standardized tests are quite inappropriate for use in the detailed assessment of learning outcomes from lessons having specifiable objectives. Their most frequent and most appropriate use is for the purpose of summative evaluation of total courses or of several years of instruction. When employed for these purposes, standardized tests can provide valuable information about the long-term effects of courses and of larger instructional programs.

SUMMARY

Up to this point, we have been concerned primarily with goals and performance objectives, with the domains of learning they represent, and with the design of lessons which employ instructional events and conditions of learning suitable for the chosen objectives. In this chapter we turn our attention to the assessment of student performance on the objectives. Thus we proceed from the *what* and the *how* to the *how well* aspect of learning.

For the purpose of assessing student performance on the planned objectives of a course, *objective-referenced tests employing a criterion-referenced interpretation* constitute the most suitable procedure. Such tests serve several important purposes:

1. They show whether each student has mastered an objective, and hence may go on to study for another objective.
2. They permit early detection and diagnosis of failure to learn, thus helping to identify the remedial study needed.
3. They provide data for making improvements in the instruction itself.
4. They are "fair" evaluations in that they measure performance on the objective that was given to the student as an indication of what he was supposed to learn. This kind of testing is consistent with the honesty of the relation of teacher to learner.

Objective-referenced tests are direct rather than indirect measures of performance on the objectives. They deal with each objective separately, rather than with very large units of instruction, such as an entire year of study. For this reason they have diagnostic value, as well as value for formative evaluation of the course.

The *validity* of objective-referenced tests is found by determining the congruence of test with objective. *Reliability* is obtained by measuring the consistency of the performance assessment, and its dependability over time. The concept of *mastery* is relevant for objective-referenced tests in the domains of intellectual skills, motor skills, and information. For these types of learning outcomes, mastery levels can be defined as error-free performances. In the case of cognitive strategies and attitudes, since assessments deal with "how well" or "how much," the use of criteria of mastery is less clearly applicable. Examples are given of how criteria of performances can be chosen for each learning domain.

Another type of test is called *norm-referenced*. Such tests do not measure separate, specific objectives of the course. Rather, they measure mixtures or composite sets of objectives, whether these are identified or not. When a norm-referenced test is a standardized test, it has been carefully designed and revised to yield high variability of scores. The interpretation of the scores is made by reference to norms, which represent performance on the test for large groups of learners. Such tests permit comparison of a score of one pupil with that of others; they also permit comparing the average score for a group with the scores of a larger norm group.

References

Bloom, B. S. Learning for mastery. *Evaluation Comment,* 1968, *I,* No. 2.

Bloom, B. S., Hastings, J. T., and Madaus, G. F. *Handbook on Formative and Summative Evaluation of Student Learning.* New York: McGraw-Hill, 1971.

Briggs, L. J. *Handbook of Procedures for the Design of Instruction.* Pittsburgh, Pa.: American Institutes for Research. 1970.

Cronbach, L. J. *Essentials of Psychological Testing,* 3d. Ed. New York: Harper & Row, 1970.

Dick, W. Formative evaluation. In L. J. Briggs (ed.), *Instructional Design: Principles and Applications.* Englewood Cliffs, N.J.: Educational Technology Publications, 1977a.

Dick, W. Summative evaluation. In L. J. Briggs (ed.), *Instructional Design: Principles and Applications.* Englewood Cliffs, N.J.: Educational Technology Publications, 1977b.

Fishbein, M. A. (Ed.). *Attitude Theory and Measurement.* New York: Wiley, 1967.

Guilford, J. P. *The Nature of Human Intelligence.* New York: McGraw-Hill, 1967.

Johnson, D. M. *A Systematic Introduction to the Psychology of Thinking.* New York: Harper & Row. 1972.

Johnson, D. M., and Kidder, R. C. Productive thinking in psychology classes. *American Psychologist,* 1972, *27,* 672–674.

Payne, D. A. *The Specification and Measurement of Learning Outcomes.* Waltham, Mass.: Blaisdell, 1968.

Popham, W. J. *Educational Evaluation.* Englewood Cliffs, N.J.: Prentice-Hall, 1975.

Thorndike, R. L., and Hagen, E. *Measurement and Evaluation in Psychology and Education.* New York: Wiley, 1969.

Torrance, E. P. *Education and the Creative Potential.* Minneapolis: University of Minnesota Press, 1963.

Tyler, L. E. *Tests and Measurements,* 2d ed. Englewood Cliffs, N.J.: Prentice-Hall, 1971.

Wood, D. A. *Test Construction; Development and Interpretation of Achievement Tests.* Columbus, Ohio: Merrill, 1960.

PART FOUR

DELIVERY SYSTEMS FOR INSTRUCTION

This part of the book deals with the final stages of instructional system design, from Formative Evaluation (Stage 11) through Installation and Diffusion (Stage 14). While the chapters of this part are not given titles corresponding to these stages, it will be apparent that the installation of a designed program involves the choice of a system of delivery. Once such a choice is made, it is possible to proceed with tryouts of the instructional system in single classrooms or schools, and in more comprehensive field tests, in order to evaluate the system in both a formative and summative sense. The installation and subsequent diffusion of the new system can then be undertaken, with further evaluation of its total effects.

Systems of delivery are designed to provide one or more modes of instruction chosen as appropriate for instructional goals. Delivery systems must also come within the limits of resources available to designers, as well as to the managers of instruction.

Two of the major categories of delivery systems—group and individual—are described in this section. Chapter 13 considers various forms of group instruction, ranging from the tutoring mode in the two-person group to the instruction of large groups. High precision of instructional delivery in the tutoring situation provides a contrast with the necessarily lower precision of the larger group. The second category, individualized instruction, is exemplified by several systems described in Chapter 14. These systems can be designed to provide highly precise delivery even when the teacher is managing the learning of a large group of students.

Instruction is usually tried out, tested, and revised to improve its effectiveness. This process, described in Chapter 15, is generally called formative evaluation, and its purpose is to improve the instruction which has been designed. A second kind of tryout and test is called summative evaluation, which is intended to summarize the value of the instruction as compared with alternative forms that may be available, or that may have previously been used. The evaluation of instruction brings the instructional design process to a conclusion —which may, however, turn out to be just another starting point.

chapter 13

Group
Instruction

A great deal of instruction is done with learners assembled in a group. When instruction is delivered in this way, one has to bear in mind constantly that learning still occurs within individuals. Older learners, to be sure, may attain a high degree of control over the management of instructional events, to the extent that their learning depends on self-instruction. For learners of whatever sort, the attempt is usually made in group instruction to insure that each instructional event is as effective as possible in supporting learning by all members of the group.

Groups assembled for instruction are of various sizes. The group sizes which seem of particular significance for instructional design include, first, the *two-person group,* which makes possible the *tutoring* mode of instruction. A second commonly distinguished kind of group is simply the *small group,* containing roughly three to eight members, a size which favors *discussion,* as well as what may be called *interactive recitation.* In this latter mode, the performances of individuals are affirmed or corrected by other members of the group. The third kind of group is a *large group,* with fifteen or more members. The most commonly used mode of instruction in such a group is the *lecture,* which may of course incorporate such other presentations as projected or televised pictures and demonstrations. Another mode of instruction with large groups is *individual recitation,* commonly used with such subjects as language, both native and foreign, and sometimes with other subjects as well.

While these three group sizes clearly appear to have different implications for instructional delivery, the distinctions among them are not hard and fast. What can be said, for example, of the group containing between eight and fifteen members? Sometimes instruction proceeds as with a small group (by discussion, for example), but at other times a large group mode (a lecture) might be employed. Division into small groups is also possible. Considering the other end of the scale of group size, one can distinguish a *very large group* (a hundred or more students). In such cases, however, instructional factors differing from those of the large group are likely to be logistic in character, pertaining to seating arrangements, acoustics, and others of this general nature. While these factors have their own peculiar importance, we do not attempt to discuss them here. Otherwise, large group modes of instruction are assumed to be relevant, and applicable to groups which are very large.

CHARACTERISTICS OF GROUP INSTRUCTION

How shall the instructional features of different kinds of instructional groups be characterized? One way would be to describe in detail the various *modes* of instruction, such as the *lecture,* the *discussion class,* the *recitation class.* These various modes do indeed have different characteristics, and vary in their feasibility of use with different sizes of groups. There are, however, variations in what is done by the lecturer, in what happens during a discussion, and in what occurs in a recitation class that appear to be of particular significance for an understanding of the effects of instruction on learning. Systematic knowledge of several of these instructional modes is summarized in a volume edited by Gage (1976).

Rather than describing features of the different modes of instruction, our approach in this chapter is to consider how such varieties of instruction can be planned for delivery to different sizes of instructional group—the two-person group, the small group, and the large group. Our discussion is concerned with questions of what instructional arrangements (including instructional modes) are *possible,* and are likely to be *most effective,* with each of these types of group.

Patterns of interaction in instructional groups

The size of an instructional group is an important determiner of the environment in which learning occurs. Some patterns of interaction among teachers and students are more readily attained with small groups, some with large. Owing to differences in the way they are perceived by students, these patterns may influence the outcomes of learning. Some classroom interaction patterns, similar to those described by Walberg (1976), are depicted in Figure 13–1.

As the figure shows, communication between teacher and student flows in both directions during instruction in a two-person group. When recitation is the adopted mode, with either a small or a large group, mutual interaction occurs between the teacher and one student at a time, while the other students are recipients of a teacher communication. Interactive recitation and also discussion occur in a small group when there is interaction among students as well as between teacher and student. In the lecture mode of instruction, used typically with a large group, the communication flow is from teacher to students.

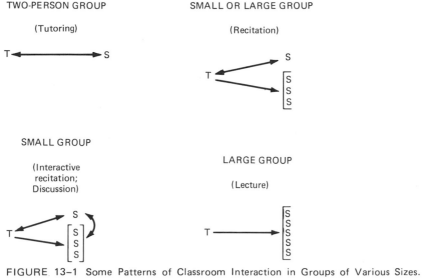

FIGURE 13-1 Some Patterns of Classroom Interaction in Groups of Various Sizes. Arrows Indicate the Direction of Interactions.

Variations in instructional events

Any or all of the *events of instruction* (Chapters 9 and 10) may be expected to vary with group size, both in their form and in their feasibility of use. For example, the event of gaining attention can obviously be rather precisely managed in a two-person group, whereas it can only be loosely controlled for the individual learners in a large group. Learning guidance, in a two-person group, is typically under the control of the instructor (tutor), whereas the semantic encoding suggested by a lecturer is likely to be modified in a number of individual ways by the strategies available to individual learners. In contrast, the feedback provided to a large group can often be controlled with about as much precision as that provided to a small group or to the student of a tutor. This is true of the instructional event (feedback), even though the reinforcing effects of such feedback will vary with the individual student.

The primary factors which appear subject to variation in different types of instructional groups, then, are those pertaining to the events of instruction. The size of group not only determines some of the necessary characteristics of these events, but also sets limits upon their effectiveness in supporting the processes of learning. It is these features of group instruction which we shall be considering in the following sections.

Diagnosing entry capabilities of students

Another factor of some importance in its influence on instructional effectiveness is the assessment of "entry capabilities" of students (cf. Bloom, 1976). Procedures for accomplishing such diagnosis are not instructional events themselves, but they do make possible the design of certain of these events. The ways of conducting diagnostic procedures are likely to vary with the size of the instructional group.

Entry capabilities of students may be assessed at the beginning of a course of study, or at the start of a semester or school year. Student capabilities may be assessed in a finer sense, and "weaknesses" or "gaps" diagnosed, just prior to the beginning of each new topic of a course. Diagnosis of this latter sort is commonly done, for example, in the period devoted to teaching pre-reading skills to children, or at various stages of beginning reading. Other examples of the application of fine-grained diagnostic procedures are sometimes seen in mathematics and in foreign language study. Such diagnoses are likely to be most successful if based upon learning hierarchies. Simple "tests" or "probes" can be administered to students to reveal specific gaps in enabling skills. Diagnosis in this form is not severely affected by group size, since testing for gaps in enabling skills can usually be done as effectively with large groups as with small.

Designing and executing the instruction implied by diagnosis of entry capabilities is, however, greatly affected by the size of the instructional group. This fact provides the basic rationale for instruction which is "individually prescribed." The effects of group size on instruction are particularly critical when the concern is with diagnosis relevant to each *lesson,* or in other words, with the *diagnosis of immediate prerequisites.* Depending on what has happened previously to prepare students for a particular lesson, a different individual pattern of prerequisite capabilities may conceivably appear for each student in a group. Thus, one might discover twenty different patterns of capability in enabling skills within a group of twenty students. Such patterns of instructional needs may readily be managed in a tutorial situation; in fact, this feature is often considered the most prominent advantage of the tutoring mode. The same finding about individual patterns of immediate prerequisites, however, presents a considerable challenge to the teacher of a twenty-person group, for example. Some further implications of this circumstance will be discussed in a later section.

INSTRUCTION IN THE TWO-PERSON GROUP

Instructional groups of two persons consist of one student and one instructor or tutor. Groups of this sort may, however, be composed only of students, one of whom assumes the tutoring role. In schools, the tutoring of younger students by older ones is not an uncommon practice. However, "peer-tutoring" has also been successfully done, even in early grades (Gartner, Kohler, and Riessman, 1971). The alternation of student-tutor roles by pairs of older students or of adults is sometimes chosen as a mode of instruction. Regarding any of these possible arrangements, it is worthy to note that learning gains are about as frequently reported for tutors as they are for students (Ellson, 1976).

As noted in the previous chapter, systems of individualized instruction are usually designed so that diagnostic tests of student weaknesses (or "gaps") will be followed by prescriptions of specific instruction designed to fill these gaps. In such systems, teachers are essentially behaving as tutors when they follow up the prescription with oral instruction. Individualized instruction, then, although it frequently calls upon the learner for self-instruction, often also involves tutoring in a two-person group.

Events of instruction in tutoring

The group composed of a single student and a single tutor has long been considered a kind of ideal situation for teaching and learning. The primary reason for this preference would appear to be the opportunities the two-person group provides for the *flexible adjustment of instructional events.* Thus, the tutor can employ just enough stimulation to gain the attention of the student; or can increase the amount if a first attempt fails. The tutor can suggest a number of alternative schemes for the encoding of information to be learned; if one doesn't work well, another can be employed. The student's comprehension of a new idea, and his storing of it, can be assessed immediately, and again after a lapse of time, in order to affirm its learning and to reinforce it.

Some of the main features which exemplify flexible adjustment of instructional events for a two-person group may be described as follows:

1. *Gaining attention.* Assuming that the student participates willingly in the tutorial situation, the gaining of attention (in the sense of "alertness") may readily be accomplished. The tutor may demand attention by giving a verbal direction, and watch for the overt signs that are typical of an attentive state. Obviously, immediate adjustments of the stimulation necessary to bring about attention can be made if the student's attention wanders.

2. *Informing the learner of the objective.* In the case of this event, flexibility may typically be achieved by repeating the objective in different terms, or by demonstrating an instance of the performance expected when the learning is completed. Of course, if the objective is already known by student, an event such as this may be entirely omitted.

3. *Stimulating recall of prerequisite learnings.* The possibility of flexible determination of this event gives the tutoring mode a definite advantage in the support of learning. Assuming that diagnosis of the prior-learned prerequisites has been made, the tutor can proceed to fill in the gaps of missing student capabilities, should that be necessary. Being assured that prerequisites have been acquired, the tutor can then proceed to require recall by the student. These acts of the tutor in making prerequisite skills accessible in the working memory will do much to insure that learning proceeds smoothly.

4. *Presenting the stimulus material.* Here, too, there is a great flexibility of choice available to the tutor. Selective perception may readily be aided: the tutor can give emphasis to lesson components by changes in oral delivery, by pointing, by drawing a picture, and in many other ways. If a foreign language is being learned, for example, the tutor can choose just the right oral expression to illustrate the grammatical rule to be taught. If varied instances are required, as

in the teaching of a new concept, the number and varied features of these instances can be carefully chosen to meet the student's need, as indicated by an immediately preceding performance.

5. *Providing learning guidance.* This event is also one in which the flexibility of the two-person situation results in an important advantage. In fact, it is in this connection that the phrase "adapting instruction to the needs of the learner" has its clearest meaning. The tutor can employ a variety of means to encourage *semantic encoding* on the part of the learner. Furthermore, the tutor can try such means one after another, if necessary, until one is found which works best. Rule applications can be demonstrated; pictures can be used to suggest visual imagery; organized information can be provided as a meaningful context for the learning of new knowledge. The tutoring mode offers many opportunities for the selection of effective communications by the tutor, all aimed at supporting the learning processes of the student.

6. *Eliciting the performance.* In the two-person group, learner performance can be elicited with a degree of precision not possible in larger groups. On a moment-to-moment basis, the tutor is usually able to judge by the learner's behavior that the necessary internal processing has occurred, and that the learner is "ready" to show what he has learned.

7. *Providing feedback.* The provision of feedback is also capable of greater precision in a two-person group than in other groups. Precision in this case pertains not primarily to the timing of feedback, but to the nature of the information given to the learner. The learner can be told, with a high degree of accuracy, what is right or wrong with his performance.

8. *Assessing the performance.* Flexibility in assessment is available to the tutor, in the sense that the performance may be "tested" at various intervals following the learning. The testing of learner performance may also be repeated as many times as deemed necessary for a reliable decision to be made.

9. *Enhancing retention and transfer.* The management of this kind of event may be done with considerable flexibility in a two-person group, and therefore with a good deal of precision. The tutor can select cues which, according to past experience, work effectively to facilitate retrieval in a particular learner. Just enough varied examples can be chosen to aid the transfer of learning. Spaced reviews can be conducted to the extent needed to insure long-term retention for the particular student, based upon previous experience with that student in the tutoring situation.

The flow of instruction in tutoring

It is evident that the two-person instructional group permits maximal control of instructional events by the tutor. As the manager of instruction, the tutor can decide which events to employ, which to emphasize, and which to assign to the learner's own control. The determination of timing for these events can operate to make each act of learning optimally efficient. In addition, the flexibility of choice of exactly how to select and arrange each event makes it possible for a tutor to provide instruction meeting the needs of the individual student. In the tutoring mode, instruction can most readily be *adapted* to the instructional needs of each student.

In practice, tutoring has taken a variety of forms (Gartner, Kohler, and Riessman, 1971). The advantages it appears to offer have often been shown to yield favorable results in student achievement, although not always (Cloward, 1967; Ellson, 1976). The evidence appears to show that the advantages of tutoring do not result from the individual attention provided to the student in the two-person situation. Rather, tutoring works best when the instruction it makes possible is highly *systematic* (Ellson, 1976). In other words, tutoring can be a highly effective mode when advantage is taken of the flexibility it provides in achieving *precision* in the arrangement of instructional events. The freedom made possible by the two-person instructional group does not produce good results if it leads to sloppiness in instruction; on the contrary, favorable outcomes appear to depend upon careful control of the events of instruction.

Typically, an episode in tutoring runs somewhat as follows. We assume a task in beginning reading, having the objective, "Given an unfamiliar printed two-syllable word of regular spelling, demonstrates phonics rules by sounding the word." The printed word is PLUNDER. The tutor is a volunteer, mother of one of the children in a first grade, tutoring a six-year old girl pupil.

First, the tutor gains the child's attention, and tells her of the objective by saying, "Here is a word you probably haven't seen before in your reading (PLUNDER). I want you to show me how you can sound it out." Should the pupil sound out the word immediately, either by correctly using rules or by recognizing the printed word, the tutor says "Good!" and goes on to another printed word. Otherwise, the tutor encourages the child to sound out the first syllable (PLUN), then the second one, and then both together.

Actually, the procedure is one of combining reminders of what the child already knows (recall of prerequisites), such as the sounds of *pl* and *un,* and learning guidance which suggests the strategy called "blending." Thus, the tutor may tell the child to place her finger over the last part of the word, leaving PL exposed, and then ask "What sound does *pl* make?" If the pupil answers correctly, positive feedback is given. If she gives an incorrect response, the child is told what the correct response is, and asked to repeat it. Then the procedure is followed again for each sound, and for successive combinations of sounds, until the entire word can be sounded correctly. At that point, the child is asked to repeat the word, and some acknowledgement is made of her accomplishment. (In fulfilling a secondary objective, the meaning of the word would probably also be explained to the child).

The systematic steps in this tutoring situation can be seen to be those of repeating, as necessary, the events of instruction calling for the stimulation of recall of prerequisites, presenting the stimulus material, providing learning guidance, eliciting and assessing the performance, and providing feedback. Essentially the same steps would be followed in the tutoring of older students or adults in the learning of an intellectual skill, except that somewhat greater dependence might be placed on encouraging the student to institute these events himself. Tutoring at the university level, of course, usually consists almost entirely of self-instruction—the tutor's activities being largely confined to assessing performance and to suggestions of means the student may employ to enhance retention and transfer of learning.

INSTRUCTION IN THE SMALL GROUP

Instructional groups of up to eight students are sometimes found in formally planned education. The university teacher, or the teacher of adult classes, meets with a small group of students on some occasions. More frequently, such groups may be formed by deliberate division of larger ones. In the elementary and middle grades, the schoolteacher may find it desirable to form small groups from an entire class of students, in order to instruct students who have progressed to approximately the same point in their learning of a particular subject.

The employment of small groups for instruction is a common practice in such subjects of the elementary school as reading and mathematics. In the first grade, for example, a teacher may find that some pupils have not yet mastered the oral language skills of reading readiness; others may be just beginning to learn to sound the letters and syllables of printed words; still others may be reading entire printed sentences without hesitation. Obviously, these different sets of students need to be taught different sets of enabling skills. It would accomplish no favorable instructional purpose to present pages of print to pupils who are still struggling with oral language. Nor is it likely to be of advantage to those pupils who already read pages of print to have to suffer through lessons which require them to make oral descriptions of objects shown in pictures. The practical solution which makes appropriate instruction possible is to divide the class into a number of small groups.

Classes of older students or adults are sometimes divided into several sets constituting small groups. The groups thus formed may meet on separate occasions, as in "quiz sections," or they may meet in separate small groups for a portion of the time of a scheduled class. In either case, the aim is to attain some of the advantages of small-group instruction, and also to provide some added variation in the forms of instruction possible with large groups.

Events of instruction in small groups

The control of instructional events in the small group (three to eight students) can best be compared to what is possible in the tutorial situation. This kind of arrangement of teacher and students might be described as "multi-student tutoring." The characteristics of the instructional situation resemble those of the two-person group, and are rather unlike those of the large group. In the small group, the teacher typically attempts to use tutorial methods, sometimes with single students, sometimes with more than one, and most often by "taking turns."

The general result is the management of instructional events in a way that applies to each individual student in the group, but with some evident loss of flexibility and precision.

Procedures of diagnosis may have been used to select the members of a group for small-group instruction. As previously noted, this is typical practice for small groups in elementary reading, language, and mathematics. During an instructional session with a small group, it is also possible for the teacher to diagnose each student's attainment of *immediate prerequisites*. In fact, this may be seen as one of the important features of small-group, as contrasted with large-group, instruction. By suitable questioning of each student in turn, the teacher is able to judge with a fair degree of accuracy that the necessary enabling skills are present in all students. In this way the estimate of students' "readiness" for taking the next step in learning can be made to approximate the degree of precision available in the two-person instructional group.

The possibilities of control of the events of instruction in the small group are discussed in the following paragraphs:

1. *Gaining attention.* In a small group, arranged so that the teacher can maintain frequent eye contact with each member, gaining and maintaining student attention poses no major difficulties.

2. *Informing the learner of the objective.* This event can also readily be managed in a small group. The teacher can, as necessary, express the objective of the lesson and assure that it is understood by each member of the group. Of course, it may take a bit more time to insure understanding of objectives for eight students than it does for only one (as in the two-person group).

3. *Stimulating recall of prerequisite learnings.* By questioning several students in turn, the teacher is able to be fairly sure that necessary enabling skills, and relevant items of supportive information, are accessible in the working memories of *all* students. Using best judgment, the teacher may direct questions that require selected students to recall relevant items, while the same questions have the effect of reminding other students of material that is already available to them.

4. *Presenting the stimulus material.* The materials for learning may be presented in ways appropriate to the objective, but without necessarily being "tailored" to individual student characteristics. For example, features of the oral presentation may be given emphasis by voice changes. In pictures or diagrams, particular features of objects and events may be appropriately made prominent. For this particular event, the degree of lessened flexibility compared with that of the two-person group appears to be minimal.

5. *Providing learning guidance.* Here the choice is either to present a communication which is the same for all members of the group, or to present individually "tailored" communications, one for each member of the group in turn. With the first of these alternatives, the teacher is behaving as though in a "large-group" setting; with the second, the event is managed as in the tutoring mode, involving a teacher interaction with one student, then with another, and so on. Obviously, the more students there are in the group the more time the latter procedure takes.

It is not uncommon for the teacher of a small group to alternate between these two approaches, judging one to be more appropriate at one time, one at another. In any case, the function of the event remains the same—providing cues and suggesting strategies which will aid the semantic encoding of material to be learned.

Quite a different kind of learning guidance is provided by the small group which is engaged in *discussion*. In such groups, the discussion may be managed and "led" by the teacher. In other instances, the small groups formed out of large classes may have designated students as discussion leaders. The learning guidance provided by discussion is of various sorts, and its function in support of learning depends on the nature of the objective. More generally, it would appear that discussions place a fairly high degree of dependence on the self-instructional strategies of the individual students. In adult discussion groups, the members are, to a large extent, using the strategies of deciding what they want to learn, and selecting these elements from what they hear or say as part of the discussion.

6. *Eliciting the performance*. It is clear in the case of this event that the only way of eliciting *each* student's performance in a small group is to do it one by one. Since this uses up a good deal of time, it is not always done. Instead, the teacher usually "calls on" one or two students to show what they have learned, and assumes that the learning has been equally effective for those not called upon. As the lesson proceeds, other students take their turns being called upon. Obviously this procedure aims at approximating that of the two-person group, but the precision of the event is considerably reduced. The teacher comes to depend upon a probabilistic estimate of learning outcomes, rather than a precise determination of them.

7. *Providing feedback*. Since this event is tied to the occurrence of student performance, it is subject to the same kinds of limitations in the small group. For the student who is "called upon," feedback may be precisely provided. For the other students, it is only probable, because it depends on which of them has made the same response (perhaps covertly).

8. *Assessing the performance*. Performance assessment may also lose some precision of control, since only one student's performance can be assessed at one time, by oral questioning. The other students must wait their turns; this means that a sample of performances will be assessed for each student, but not the entire repertoire he is supposed to have learned. Of course, a test covering an entire lesson or topic may later be given to the entire group of students (a technique equally applicable to large groups).

9. *Enhancing retention and transfer*. For instructional groups in the elementary grades, the teacher is able to estimate the desirability of varied examples and additional spaced reviews, in providing favorable conditions for retention and learning transfer. Such estimates are made by a kind of "averaging" of the group's performance, and thus do not have the precision afforded in the tutoring situation of the two-person group. In the case of older students and adults, the conduct of discussions has as one of its major purposes the enhancement of retention and transfer.

Instruction in the small group—recitation

We suppose that a teacher has assembled a small group of pupils who are to learn the skill of adding fractions with dissimilar denominators. Since one of the steps in this procedure is "finding the least common multiple of the denominators," it may be assumed that diagnostic tests have indicated that students already possess such prerequisite concepts as "numerator," "denominator," "factor," and "multiple," as well as rules for multiplying and dividing small whole numbers, and the rule for adding fractions with identical denominators.

Once the attention of all members of the group is gained (in a "highly probable" sense), the teacher tells the students the objective of the lesson, using an illustration such as $2/5 + 4/15$. Calling upon one or two members of the group in turn, the teacher stimulates recall of prerequisite concepts and rules. For example, students may be asked to add $2/13 + 5/13$, to obtain $7/13$. Having assurance that prerequisite skills are readily accessible, the teacher presents a single example such as $2/5 + 3/7$ as stimulus material. The next step is to provide suitable learning guidance for the learning of the rule having to do with the finding of a least common multiple. This may be done by demonstrating the multiplication of denominators ($5 \times 7 = 35$); alternatively, a discovery method may be employed, initiated by such a question as, "How might we make it possible to change these into fractions that could be added?" In this case, one student of the group is called upon for an answer while others await a later turn. A different student may then be called upon for performance, that is, in arriving at the changed expression $14/35 + 15/35$, and in supplying the sum $29/35$. Feedback, in the form of affirming the correct response or correcting a wrong one, is then provided.

The subsequent instructional events are conducted in such a group by calling on different students, using different examples. Thus, performance is followed by appropriate feedback for the students in the group by "taking turns." The immediate performance of each student is assessed in this manner. The varied examples used serve the function of enhancing retention and transfer, assuming that students other than the one called upon are responding in a covert manner while learning.

Instruction in discussion groups

Instruction which takes the form of discussion is said to be characterized as "interactive communication" (Gall and Gall, 1976). One student speaks at a time, and is listened to by the entire group. The order in which students initiate or respond to speech is not predetermined. Often, one student is responding to the remarks or questions introduced by another student. The teacher may interpose remarks or questions, and sometimes may call upon individual students to speak. Of course, small groups of this sort may be organized with students as discussion leaders.

Three kinds of objectives are often considered appropriate for instruction via group discussion: subject-matter mastery, attitude formation, and problem solving (Gall and Gall, 1976). It is not unusual for a class discussion to have more than one of these types of objectives.

The formation and modification of attitudes is usually the major aim of *issue-oriented discussion,* examples of which are to be found in the "jurisprudential model" and the "social inquiry model," as described by Joyce and Weil (1972). The discussion may be initiated by the account of an incident illustrating a social issue (such as freedom of speech, job discrimination). The teacher or group leader may then ask for one or more opinions about the issue. Comments are made about these opinions, either by the discussion leader or by other students. As the discussion proceeds, the leader attempts to achieve progressive sharpening and clarification of the issue by introducing different examples, and by encouraging statements by various group members. Often, what is aimed for is a group consensus, as represented by a set of statements to which no major disagreements remain. This attitude-forming situation may be conceived as a particular kind of learning guidance, namely, one involving communications from a number of "human models," the latter being members of the group and its leader. This kind of learning guidance, particularly effective in attitude formation, is followed by performance (choice of action) by the individual students, and by feedback in the form of group consensus.

Problem solving is also a commonly adopted goal for discussion groups (Maier, 1963). It appears that the kinds of problems which provide the most effective instruction in discussion groups are those with multiple solutions, as well as those which include attitudinal components. Maier (1971) points out that small group divisions of large college classes can increase the opportunities for student participation, and can be used to form discussion groups for problem-solving and other related purposes. Maier suggests the presentation of problems or issues that capture student interest and emotional involvement, as a means of enlisting motivation. With this kind of objective, small groups have the chance to practice both communication skills and problem-solving strategies. Obviously, this type of instructional group is one which depends very largely upon the students to manage instructional events for themselves. The students must provide themselves with the stimulation to recall relevant knowledge, and must employ their own cognitive strategies of encoding and problem solving. Attitude change objectives are a secondary, although not necessarily less important, outcome of this type of discussion session.

LARGE GROUP INSTRUCTION

In instructing large groups, the teacher employs communications which do not differ in function from those employed with two-person groups or with small groups. For a large group, the teacher initiates and manages the events of instruction which are specifically relevant to the primary objective of the lesson. Because the teacher's cues for timing and emphasis come from several (or many) sources rather than from a single student, there is a marked *reduction in precision* in the management of instructional events. Teachers of large groups cannot be sure they have gained the attention of *all* students; they cannot always be sure that *all* students have recalled prerequisites, or that the semantic encoding they suggest will work well with *all* students. The strategy of instruction in a large group is therefore a *probabilistic strategy*. Instruction so designed will be effective "on the average," but cannot by itself be insured as effective for each individual learner (cf. Gagné, 1974, pp. 124–131).

It may be argued that this pattern of large group instruction is the way instruction should be designed, in general. The instruction itself (that is, the communications of the teacher) is "good," and it is up to the student to profit from it. Students, in this view, must do a great deal of organizing of the events of instruction themselves—it is up to them to infer the objective of instruction, to remind themselves to recall prerequisite skills, to choose a method of encoding, and so on. Such a view appears to be widely held, and widely employed in college and university teaching. It may be noted, also, that this conception of instruction runs contrary to the notion of *mastery learning* proposed by Bloom (1974, 1976). The latter conception relates the quality of instruction to the occurrence of events described as providing *cues, participation, reinforcement,* and *feedback/correctives*. This set of instructional features closely resembles the instructional events we have described. It is evident that mastery learning requires the management of events that go beyond the "giving of information" by the teacher.

Instructional events in the large group

In contrast to the case of the two-person or small group, the *effects* of instruction on members of a large group are only *probable*. Since the degree of instructional readiness, the intensity of motivation and alertness, the appropriateness of the semantic encoding suggested, and the accessibility of relevant cognitive strategies are all factors likely to vary with the individuals who make up the group, instruction, as delivered, is relatively imprecise. Any lack of effectiveness instruction may have for one individual may, of course, be overcome by the student's own efforts at self-instruction. For example, what some students fail to learn from a lecture they may learn later by employing their own encoding strategies on notes of the lecture. Other students may find this kind of encoding ineffective, and may prefer to process the information in its oral form as originally given.

1. *Gaining attention.* This event, as all teachers know, is highly important for the effectiveness of instruction delivered to a group. It is surely no more than a probable occurrence in a class of young people, and often little more likely in a class of older students. The occasional use of demonstrations and audio-visual media can aid the gaining of attention at times when other critical instructional events are to follow.

2. *Informing the learner of the objective.* The objective can readily be stated and demonstrated to a large group. It will probably be comprehended by all students, when suitably presented.

3. *Stimulating recall of prerequisite learnings.* As indicated previously, this event may be of critical importance for learning. It is also, perhaps, one of the most difficult events to accomplish with reasonable probability in a large group.

Typically, the teacher calls upon one or two students to recall relevant concepts, rules, or information. Obviously, though, the necessary retrieval may not be achieved by other students, many of whom are hoping to avoid being called upon. As a result, the management of this event may often be inadequately accomplished. Those students who have not recalled prerequisite skills will probably not learn the relevant objective. The cumulative effects of this inadequacy are therefore quite serious. Various means (such as "spot quizzes" for the entire group) are employed to improve the operation of this event. It appears to deserve a great deal of attention by instructional designers.

4. *Presenting the stimulus material.* The content to be learned can be presented in a way that emphasizes distinctive features. This means that the presentation can be made optimally effective "on the average."

5. *Providing learning guidance.* In a large group, learning guidance can be provided in a way which works, in a probabilistic sense, for most members of the group. For example, the encoding of a historical event can be suggested by a picture or dramatic episode, which may be generally effective in the group as a whole. The particular encoding suggested, however, cannot be adapted to the individual members of the group, as it can in smaller groups.

6. *Eliciting the performance.* Control in obtaining the learner's performance is much weakened in the large group. Whereas a tutor can expect several occasions during which the student exhibits what he learns in a single lesson, the teacher of a group cannot manage this for each student in the group. Instead, in a typical class, the teacher "calls on" one or two students at a time. Other students in the group may occasionally be responding covertly, but this is not a highly likely possibility. Accordingly, it may be seen that student response has a low degree of precision as an instructional event in the large group.

Quizzes and tests are often given in an attempt to overcome the difficulty of eliciting student performance. To be most effective as instructional events, quizzes should be frequent. Even daily quizzes, however, cannot approximate the frequency with which the tutor is able to ask for student performances that reflect capabilities learned in a just-prior moment.

7. *Providing feedback.* Since this event is inevitably tied to the occurrence of performances by the students, it is subject to the same limitations as those occurrences. Feedback to students in a large group occurs with low frequency, and is likely to be confined to results of tests covering a number of different learning objectives.

8. *Assessing the performance.* Similar comments may be made concerning this event in the instruction of large groups. The more frequent and regular assessment (followed by corrective feedback) can be, the better will be the outcome of learning. For example, regularly scheduled quizzes following segments of study material are considered to be the most valuable feature of some computer-managed courses in college subjects (Anderson, Anderson, Dalgaard, Wietecha, Biddle, Paden, Smock, Alessi, Surber, and Klemt, 1974). When the computer is

used for assessment, this event can be managed with a degree of precision that is impossible for the teacher of a large group.

9. *Enhancing retention and transfer.* Events of this nature can be accomplished by the teacher of a large group, again in a probabilistic sense. That is, the teacher can use the varied examples and spaced reviews which have been found to work best "on the average," but is unable to adapt these techniques to differences in individual learners.

The lecture

Surely the most common mode of instruction for the large group is the lecture. The teacher communicates orally with students assembled in a group. The oral communication may be accompanied by occasional demonstrations, pictures, or diagrams; and these may be presented in various media, including the chalkboard. The students listen, and some take notes, which they may use later for recall or as a means of generating their own semantic encodings.

As pointed out by McLeish (1976), the lecture can accomplish some positive instructional purposes. In particular, the lecturer can: (1) inspire an audience with his own enthusiasm; (2) relate his field of study to human purposes (and thus to student interests); and (3) relate theory and research to practical problems. The lecture attains these goals with the utmost economy, which doubtless accounts for its preservation as an instructional mode over two thousand years of higher education.

McLeish's interpretation implies that the "good" lecture can attain certain instructional objectives very well, because it is able to implement certain instructional events effectively. For example, "inspiring students with his enthusiasm" implies that the lecturer often functions as a human model in establishing positive attitudes toward the subject of study. The motivational effects of lecturing are also incorporated in the idea of relating a specialized field of study to the more general concerns of human living. As for the concept of relating research findings to practical problems, this purpose of the lecture functions to provide a context of cues which will aid retention and learning transfer.

As pointed out in the previous section, the communications delivered to groups of learners via the lecture can be aimed at optimizing the effectiveness of many of the events of instruction in a probabilistic sense. For example, attention can be gained by dramatic episodes; instructional objectives can be simply and clearly stated; suggested encoding of material to be learned can be provided by summary statements, visually presented tabular arrays or diagrams; and so on. It is clear that many of the events of instruction can be appropriately presented within a lecture, although they cannot be managed with precision. Their momentary effects cannot be insured for all students; neither can their specific forms be adapted to individual differences in students.

Viewed from the standpoint of instructional events, perhaps the weakest features of the lecture reside in its lack of control over (a) the recalling of prerequisites, and (b) the eliciting of student performance, with its succeeding provision of corrective feedback. The lecturer can "remind" students of what they need to recall as prerequisite knowledge, but he cannot take the steps necessary to insure such recall. Again, the lecturer can "encourage" students to practice the capabilities they are learning, but he cannot require them to exhibit the performances which reflect what they have learned. Thus, when the lecture is used as the sole mode of instruction, there is heavy dependence upon the student to institute these events for himself. This degree of self-instruction is a common expectation in college and university instruction, as well as in adult education. It is worth noting that quizzes and tests are able to overcome this limitation of the lecture only to a small degree, since they are typically both infrequent and "coarse-grained" in their assessment of specific learning objectives.

The recitation class

Another form of large group instruction, more frequently used with some subjects than with others, is the recitation class. This mode of instruction partially overcomes some of the limitations of the lecture, at least in a probabilistic sense. In a recitation class, the teacher calls on one student after another to respond to questions. In a class in foreign language, for example, one student at a time may be answering questions posed in that language, or otherwise continuing a conversation in the foreign tongue.

The teacher's *questions* in a recitation class may represent several different instructional events at different times during a single lesson. A question may be designed to stimulate recall of a prerequisite capability, bringing it to the forefront of the student's memory. Or, a question may be one which asks the student to perform—to show what he has learned. A different kind of question may be used to suggest a direction of thought to the student (in the manner of "guided discovery"), and thus to guide his learning in the sense of semantic encoding. Still another kind of question may require the student to think of examples of application of a newly learned skill or body of knowledge—a process which will contribute cues useful for recall and learning transfer. For instance, having learned the concept of "homeostatic control," questions might direct students to describe several examples of practical devices of this category.

In recitation classes, some instructional events are often left for the student to manage. This is typically the case when recitation follows a homework assignment. In such instances, it is usually expected that events such as control of attention, gaining information about the objective, semantic encoding, and the provision of corrective feedback will be managed by the student himself as he does his homework. These events are obviously relevant to the student's study activities in reading his textbook, practicing his newly learned skills in examples, or rehearsing the statement of organized information. Good "study habits" are, in these circumstances, the determiners of effective learning.

The control of instructional events in the large recitation class is decidedly imprecise, so far as their effects on individual students is concerned. When questions are asked, for whatever purpose, there is time for only a few students to respond. Should the teacher call upon students who are typically "well-pre-pared," and thus engage in relative neglect of students who may be less able to guide their own learning? Or should the teacher call upon the less able students, and through the necessity of supplying corrective feedback, bore those who have already learned correctly? It is clear that what usually happens in the use of recitation with a large class is that the necessary events of instruction affect only a few students on any one occasion. Time does not permit the teacher to allow everyone to "take a turn." All too frequently, students learn to resort to the game of avoiding being called upon to recite. This, of course, is the wrong game so far as the learning of lesson objectives is concerned.

Overcoming the imperfections of large-group instruction

In general, in large groups, instructional events which should be affecting all students end up exerting their effects on only a few. When self-instructional strategies can be brought into play by the remainder of the students, large group instruction may work well enough to be considered adequate. Such is usually the case, for example, with classes of college students and adults, in which there is heavy dependence upon individual initiative for learning. In contrast, the imperfections of the lecture method are likely to be highly apparent even to an occasional observer of a class of seventh-grade students.

Methods of large-group instruction, including lecture and recitation, may be combined in various ways with small group, two-person group, or individualized instruction in order to overcome some of the inadequacies which have been described. Perhaps the simplest scheme is to divide the large group into small groups for part of its meeting time, or into classes of smaller groups for meetings subsequent to a large-group lecture or recitation. Either of these arrangements is intended to make possible a degree of precision in the control of instructional events which surpasses that of the large group.

Other systems of teaching make fairly direct attempts to introduce precision by individualizing the management of instructional events. Particularly, methods have been proposed, and extensively tried out, which supplement large-group modes of teaching with *diagnostic progress testing* and *feedback with correction procedures.* Outstanding among these is the system called *Mastery Learning* (Bloom, 1974; Block and Anderson, 1975).

Mastery Learning   In using this system, the teacher divides a course of study into units of approximately two weeks' length, each unit having clearly defined objectives. Following the teaching of the unit (by large-group methods), students take a test to determine who has mastered the objectives. The test is "diagnostic" of which objectives have or have not been acquired. Those students who exhibit mastery are permitted to engage in self-instructional "enrichment" activities. For those who have not yet shown mastery, additional sessions of instruction are provided, such as small group study, individual tutoring, or additional self-study materials. These students are again tested when they believe themselves prepared, with the intention that all will eventually show mastery of the objectives.

The addition of progress and feedback diagnostic procedures with correction in large group instruction makes a distinct change in instructional precision. As can readily be seen, the procedure gives emphasis to individual assessment and feedback in ways which are not otherwise practical in large-group instruction. Evidence of the system's effectiveness has been reviewed by Block and Burns (1976).

SUMMARY

The nature of instruction delivered to groups is determined in many important respects by the size of the group. For purposes of distinguishing the characteristics of instruction, it is useful to consider three different group sizes: (a) two-person groups; (b) small groups containing approximately three to eight students, and (c) large groups of fifteen or more members.

The characteristics of instruction applicable to groups of these three different sizes can be understood in terms of the *degree of precision* with which instructional events can be managed by the teacher. Generally speaking, the two-person situation, consisting of a tutor and a student, affords the greatest degree of precision for instructional events. As the size of the group increases, control over the management of instructional events grows progressively weaker. That is to say, the effects of necessary instructional events on *individual learners* decreases from near certainty to lesser degrees of probability as the group size grows larger. Learning outcomes, accordingly, come to depend increasingly upon the self-instructional strategies available to the individual learner.

A particular feature of the instructional situation which is typically more difficult to manage as group size increases is the diagnosis of entering capabilities. Means of assessing what the individual students know or do not know at the beginning of each lesson are readily available to the tutor, but become more difficult to accomplish with larger groups. This factor is of particular importance for the execution of the instructional event *stimulating recall of prerequisites,* since students will obviously be unable to recall that which they have not previously learned. The control of this event is thus likely to grow weaker with larger groups, and the result may be a cumulative deficit in student learning.

The two-person group, using tutoring as a mode, makes possible relatively precise management of instructional events, from early ones such as gaining attention to the late ones providing for retention and learning transfer. In the small group, precision of control of instructional events is attained largely by "multi-person tutoring," that is, by initiating each instructional event for the different members of the group in turn. In such circumstances, some events become only probable (rather than certain) for some students on some occasions. With the aid of self-instructional strategies of individual students, small group instruction can attain considerable effectiveness. Small groups are frequently formed by dividing larger groups. Examples of small groups formed in this manner are those for instruction in basic skills in the elementary grades, and student-led discussion groups in college classes.

Large group instruction is characterized by weak control of the effects of instructional events by the teacher. The gaining of attention, the cueing of semantic encoding, the eliciting of student performance, and the provision of corrective feedback can all be instituted as events, but their effects upon the learning processes of students are only probable. Sometimes, indeed, the effects of these events on the individual learner have quite low probabilities. Learning from large group instruction therefore depends to a considerable degree on the learner's own strategies of self-instruction. This circumstance is more or less expected in college students and adult groups.

Typical modes of instruction in large groups are the lecture and the recitation class. A number of techniques have been suggested for overcoming the weaknesses of these large-group instructional methods. Frequently, large groups are divided into smaller groups, and sometimes into two-person groups, in order to bring about some of the advantages of increased precision of control over instructional events. One system for the improvement of large-group instruction is Mastery Learning, in which units of instruction are managed so that diagnosis and corrective feedback follow the learning of each unit until mastery is achieved. Thus, this system supplements large-group instruction with certain instructional events normally available in the tutoring situation, or in individualized instruction.

References

Anderson, T. H., Anderson, R. C., Dalgaard, B. R., Wietecha, E. J., Biddle, W. B., Paden, D. W., Smock, H. R., Alessi, S. M., Surber, J. R., and Klemt, L. L. A computer based study management system. *Educational Psychologist,* 1974, *11,* 36–45.

Block, J. H., and Anderson, L. W. *Mastery Learning in Classroom Instruction.* New York: Macmillan, 1975.

Block, J. H., and Burns, R. B. Mastery learning. In L. S. Shulman (ed.), *Review of Research in Education: 4.* Itasca, Ill.: Peacock, 1976.

Bloom, B. S. An introduction to mastery learning theory. In J. H. Block (ed.), *Schools, Society and Mastery Learning.* New York: Holt, Rinehart and Winston, 1974.

Bloom, B. S. *Human Characteristics and School Learning.* New York: McGraw-Hill, 1976.

Cloward, R. D. Studies in tutoring. *Journal of Experimental Education,* 1967, *36,* 14–25.

Ellson, D. G. Tutoring. In N. L. Gage (ed.), *The Psychology of Teaching Methods.* Seventy-fifth Yearbook of the National Society for the Study of Education. Chicago: University of Chicago Press, 1976.

Gage, N. L. (ed.). *The Psychology of Teaching Methods.* Seventy-fifth Yearbook of the National Society for the Study of Education. Chicago: University of Chicago Press, 1976.

Gagné, R. M. *Essentials of Learning for Instruction.* New York: Dryden Press-Holt, Rinehart and Winston, 1974.

Gall, M. D., and Gall, J. P. The discussion method. In N. L. Gage (ed.), *The Psychology of Teaching Methods.* Seventy-fifth Yearbook of the National Society for the Study of Education. Chicago: University of Chicago Press, 1976.

Gartner, A., Kohler, M., and Riessman, F. *Children Teach Children.* New York: Harper & Row, 1971.

Joyce, B., and Weil, M. *Models of Teaching.* Englewood Cliffs, N. J.: Prentice-Hall, 1972.

Maier, N. R. F. *Problem Solving Discussions and Conferences.* New York: McGraw-Hill, 1963.

Maier, N. R. F. Innovation in education. *American Psychologist,* 1971, *26,* 722–725.

McLeish, J. The lecture method. In N. L. Gage (ed.), *The Psychology of Teaching Methods.* Seventy-fifth Yearbook of the National Society for the Study of Education. Chicago: University of Chicago Press, 1976.

Walberg, H. J. Psychology of learning environments: Behavioral, structural, or perceptual? In L. S. Shulman (ed.), *Review of Research in Education, 4.* Itasca, Ill.: Peacock, 1976.

chapter 14

Individualized Instruction

Teachers long have sought ways to make teaching more precise while also adjusting both the objectives and the methods of learning to the needs and characteristics of individual learners. These efforts have largely been frustrated because teachers have had no *delivery systems* designed to adjust instruction to the individuals in a group of twenty-five or more learners. Although teachers have traditionally divided their time between working with individuals and with groups of varying sizes, this arrangement often leaves some pupils unoccupied and unable to progress for some periods of time. Little is accomplished by teachers merely asserting a determination to adjust their teaching to the individual needs of pupils. They need a delivery system designed to achieve such a purpose.

Early efforts to design delivery systems to assist teachers to "individualize" instruction were made before the event of more recent technology such as the current models for the design of instructional systems, represented, for example, by this book. Also, the early efforts were largely local ones, because there was no marketing agency concentrating on development and diffusion of special materials and media to support the plan for individualization. Many early experiments in schools thus left too great a burden on the teacher. In short, a total support system for individualized instruction was lacking.

In recent years, universities and private research and development agencies have developed comprehensive delivery systems for individualized instruction. The design and development phases for the delivery system were often supported in part by federal or state funds, while private funding made possible the diffusion of the developed system. The purposes of these delivery systems, broadly defined, were:

1. to provide a means for assessing the entry skills of pupils;
2. to assist in finding the starting point for each pupil in a carefully sequenced series of objectives;
3. to provide alternate materials and media for adjustment to varying learning styles of pupils, including choices between print and non-print materials;
4. to enable pupils to learn at their own rates, not at a fixed pace for the entire group; and
5. to provide frequent and convenient progress checks so that pupils did not become "bogged down" with cumulative failures.

In total, the above measures were to enable all pupils to work each day on objectives within their individual needs, capacities, prerequisite skills, and rates of learning. This was accomplished, in part, by designing the learning materials and media which could carry more of the support for more of the instructional events. Team efforts were often employed to design, develop, evaluate, and diffuse the learning materials as a component of the entire delivery system. In short, a systems design model was employed to provide teachers with a total delivery system to support the classroom activities.

NATIONALLY DIFFUSED SYSTEMS

Three individualized-instruction delivery systems have been used widely in the elementary and middle schools throughout the nation. The three systems vary somewhat in subject areas covered and in age range of pupils. Generally speaking, all were eventually intended to include the areas of reading, mathematics, science, and social studies from kindergarten through the upper elementary and sometimes to the secondary levels. The three programs referred to have been described by their designers in books edited by Weisgerber (1971) and by Talmage (1975). The names of the programs are: Program for Learning in Accordance with Needs (Project PLAN); Individually Prescribed Instruction (IPI); and Individually Guided Instruction (IGE). Other widely diffused systems for individualizing instruction are also described in the book edited by Weisgerber (1971).

The three nationally diffused systems are the subjects of an evaluation report (EPIE, 1974). Other reports describe the operations of the programs in the schools, and provide guidance for school administrators and teachers concerning their potential selection, adoption, or adaptation to meet local needs (Edling, 1970; Briggs and Aronson, 1975).

LOCALLY DEVELOPED SYSTEMS

Some schools or school districts have undertaken either to make adaptive changes in one of the widely marketed systems of individualized instruction, or to develop entirely new systems locally. Thus some schools have adopted an available system with few modifications; some have made major modifications of available systems; and some start at the beginning to develop their own systems. When the objectives of a school coincide closely with those of an available system, it seems wasteful to repeat the entire instruction design when it has already been carefully designed by the originators of available systems. Of course, schools sometimes purchase certain materials or components of a system, and locally develop others.

In visits to two non-overlapping samples of schools employing one or another system of individualized instruction, great variations in specific classroom applications were found, although all were directed generally toward the five purposes previously described. Edling (1970), who visited 46 schools, highlighted both the common and the unique features of operation. Briggs and Aronson (1975), who visited 42 schools, described typical operations in selected schools, and summarized the various factors to be considered by schools when plans are made to initiate a new program. These factors pertain to information needed by school boards, parents, administrators, teachers, and pupils.

VARIETIES OF ACTIVITIES

Once a system of individualized instruction is in operation in a school, what typical activities might be observed? The following description (adapted from Briggs and Aronson, 1975) represents a typical hour in an individualized reading program in a classroom with one teacher, one teacher aide (who might be a paid para-professional or a volunteer parent), and 25 third-grade pupils.

Several children are still learning to visually discriminate the letters of the alphabet. They are working individually with programmed instruction booklets. Each page shows a letter at the top; the child is to underline which of two letters placed lower on the page matches the letter; feedback is provided when the page is turned. These children learn slowly, but they *are* learning, and so will experience success rather than failure during this hour. These children were in a "regular" classroom last year.

Two other children can discriminate the letters, and now they are learning to pronounce the names of the letters. They are taking turns running cards through a machine; each card has a letter printed on it, and a sound recording pronounces the name. The children imitate the pronounciation.

Five children are sitting in a corner of the room with the teacher. These children can read, pronounce, and give their own definitions of many words, and they can read some sentences. However, they need help on word attack skills for unfamiliar printed words. After some instruction in this small group, the teacher will assign various lessons to be completed at another corner of the room. There each child will work with a booklet accompanied by a sound tape describing the exercises and providing feedback. The tape is paced to give instruction, to pause for pupil responses, and to give correct-answer feedback.

Three pairs of children are reading aloud to each other, taking turns. They pause frequently to explain the meaning of the story to each other, or to question each other about the meaning.

Four children are listening to "read along tapes," while silently reading from a printed text.

One child is taking an oral test administered by the teacher aide. Another child has in his hand a completed written test over an objective; he is waiting for it to be checked by the aide. One child is "checking off" an objective for himself on a record sheet on the wall; he has passed a "self-graded" test, using an answer key. Another child is at the materials file, looking up the material indicated by a sheet giving him a new objective for study.

The noise level in the room is higher than in a conventional classroom, but it is mainly "productive" noise, and the children are no longer distracted by it. The teacher pauses from her small-group work to reprimand one boy who is annoying a classmate who is trying to read.

Over in the far corner of the room, one boy is lying on the floor reading a sixth-grade level book.

How can a teacher arrange for all these activities, and also conduct some direct instruction with individuals and small groups? The diagnostic and placement tests are "keyed" to objectives in a sequence, which in turn are "keyed" to varieties of materials available for the objectives. The materials are arranged in files which the students have learned to use to gain access to materials. They also have learned to return non-expendable materials to their proper places in the file.

Still the children do not spend a major portion of their time working alone. In the next hour "show and tell" is scheduled for everyone, since they can all communicate at a common level of oral speech although they vary widely in reading ability. Also, in this particular school, only reading and mathematics instructions are "individualized." Other subjects are taught by conventional methods. The children are able to operate the variety of equipment available. The equipment is simple to operate, and instruction on its operation was given at the beginning of the year.

IMPLEMENTING INSTRUCTIONAL EVENTS

As may be inferred from such a sketch of a typical hour of activity, media are often employed for some of the events of instruction. Careful attention is also given to the sequencing of objectives, and to each child's progress in the sequence.

Taking account of prior learning

Diagnostic and placement tests are given at the beginning of the school year to determine just which skills, in a carefully ordered sequence of objectives, each pupil already has mastered and can recall at the time of testing. The results of such tests determine which objective represents the starting point for an individual child. Frequent subsequent testing helps to keep up to date individual records of mastery of prerequisites for later objectives in the series. In the case of reading and mathematics, a single sequence of objectives is often adopted for all learners, but the materials used and the pace of learning vary among learners. In science and social studies, there are often core objectives assigned to all learners, with enrichment or "excursion" objectives selected by the pupil according to personal interest.

Gaining attention

This event usually presents fewer problems in an individualized program than in large group instruction. Each child is usually eager to begin a new objective, having achieved success on the previous objective. As soon as pupils obtain the materials (and in some cases, the equipment) for a new objective, they usually turn at once to the learning task. It is rare that more than one student at a time is not actually working on the assigned objective.

Maintaining attention also is seldom a problem. The systematic cycles of presenting a problem, requiring a response, and providing feedback, which are built into the material, tend to maintain attention. Children are often encouraged to "turn off the machine" or to "read for fun" or to turn to something like clay modeling when they tire of a task. They then will usually return to the task without prompting.

Informing the student about objectives

Owing to the highly structured nature of much of the learning materials, the objective is often evident to the learners. However, each objective in the sequence usually carries both a number and a name—the number to facilitate the filing of material, and the name as a shortened form of the objective. The children thus become aware of the various objectives in the series. In small-group sessions, when the teacher undertakes to initiate a new skill or to verify completion of objectives, the objective is made evident if it is not already known to the members of the group. It may be noted that under individually-paced programs, the composition of small groups shifts constantly. A group of five who are all at the same point of progress on one day may not be at the same common point on another day.

While in general there is no reason why objectives should not be given to learners in terms that they can understand, this event does not appear to have as much importance for highly structured material as it does for loosely structured material. In the latter type of material, the student needs the objectives to determine which portions of the material are most relevant, so that selective reading and review may be undertaken.

Stimulating recall of prerequisites

Recall of prerequisite learning also may be easy to achieve in a carefully sequenced, highly structured program. The careful sequencing makes recall of immediately prior learning highly probable, and the structure of materials makes more probable the initial mastery of prerequisites. Also, the frequent progress checks (usually after study of each objective) prevent accumulative forgetting that could slow further learning.

Presenting the stimulus materials; eliciting the response; providing feedback

Since individualized programs for elementary schools make much use of self-instructional materials, it follows that there are built-in cycles of presenting the stimulus information, requiring a response, and providing feedback. This feature is commonly found in the various print and non-print media used for individualized instruction. It may be the appropriate and precise management of these events of instruction that represents one of the strongest features of individualized programs. This strength, it may be noted, is primarily a feature of the *materials.* The primary strengths of the *teacher* in such programs lie in managing and monitoring the entire system in the classroom, and insuring that personal guidance is available when provided materials and tests fail to function adequately for an individual learner.

Providing learning guidance

Much of this event is also designed into instructional materials in the form of prompts, cues, and suggestions to the learner. This function may be blended in with the event of *providing the stimulus material* in a somewhat more precise manner than can be provided by a teacher, except when using the tutorial mode of instruction.

Teachers, however, are often able to give a more general form of guidance than the provided encoding cues. Teachers discuss with pupils which alternate materials may be best for them, and which enrichment or excursion objectives they might wish to choose. One of the advantages of individualized delivery systems is to give the teacher time to spend with individual pupils. Once the pupils learn the basic procedures of pre-testing, learning, and post-testing, and how to locate materials and equipment, the basic system "runs itself." This does not mean that the teacher is not busy. Often there are times when pupils are "stacked up" to see the teacher for guidance or testing. But gradually pupils learn to signal the teacher of their needs, and to turn in the meantime to enrichment activities.

Individualized systems can be a great boon to slow learners, protecting them from inappropriate tasks and inappropriate instruction, and hence helping them to avoid failure. These systems can also free fast learners from the boredom of unnecessary instruction, allowing more time for more challenging activities. It is the teacher, of course, who must see that learning arrangements are suitable for each learner.

Assessing the performance

For some objectives, learners may test themselves by use of an answer key. But at least periodically, and more often than in large-group instruction, the teacher makes the assessment, with or without the use of written tests. Again, time freed from other instructional events is available for this assessment by the teacher.

Enhancing retention and transfer

Once the teacher has assessed a performance, and found it to be satisfactory in terms of mastery, or adequate according to acceptable standards, attention may be turned to enhancing retention and transfer of learning. As shown in Chapter 13, group instruction is often suitable for this purpose. When several learners have been assessed and found to be at the same point of progress in mastery of given objectives, discussion led by the teacher can be lively, interesting, and effective. Pupils can hear each other's applications of skills or information, and at the same time steps may be made toward terminal objectives pertaining to attitudes or cognitive strategies. Other techniques for enhancing retention and transfer may be designed as part of the materials, or may take the form of projects selected to match student interests.

Because the events of instruction can be arranged in the ways described, learning in an individualized program is often perceived to be less difficult (and perhaps more enjoyable) than in a large-group situation. While it is frequently mentioned that an individualized program requires self-management and self-instruction, it may also be the case that given adequate motivation, such a program is more precisely helpful to the learner than instruction in a large group. Therefore, it need not be concluded that individualized instruction is effective only for mature learners. Owing to the insured appropriateness of each lesson in the series, and to the precision of the instruction, it might be said that this form of instruction is needed more by less mature learners. Adults and college students, on the other hand, are expected to be able to sort out appropriate from inappropriate materials and to provide many of the instructional events for themselves. This is not to say that individualized programs are not appropriate for mature learners; but the form and structure of such programs may be expected to differ from those designed for children.

SYSTEMS FOR OLDER STUDENTS

In college-level instruction, several individualized methods have been developed and fairly widely adopted. Some of the best-known include the Keller Plan (Keller, 1966; Ryan, 1974) and the Audio-Tutorial Approach (Postlethwait, Novak, and Murray, 1969).

As might be expected considering the maturity of the learners, the individualized methods employed at the college level are not as fine-grained and precisely controlled as those of the systems for elementary schools. Generally, the procedures are designed to utilize an economical combination of large-group lecture sessions, smaller "quiz sessions," and independent study. Tests are employed to enable students to participate in the most appropriate activities. Insofar as possible, the mastery learning concept is adopted, within the limits of administrative policies concerning the pursuit of courses beyond scheduled academic terms.

In college programs of this sort, students concentrate their study in the areas needing the most work, as indicated by progress checks. Less use is made of the small-step variety of learning materials. Instead, laboratory assistants are available to provide some individual tutoring when other methods fail. The typical combination of conventional and special procedures results in a degree of instructional precision which is perhaps intermediate between that obtained in large groups and that described previously for elementary programs. This may represent a reasonable degree of control in trying to enhance learning for adult learners without undue costs.

An earlier strategy for individualizing learning at the college level was developed by Pressey in the 1920's. He later termed the procedure "adjunct autoinstruction" (Pressey, 1950). The strategy was quite straightforward; a regular college textbook was employed, along with sets of "practice-test" questions over each chapter. Mechanical devices were used to provide "right-wrong" feedback after each response to a practice-test question. This procedure was employed in regular classrooms, in independent study programs, and in special classes for superior students (Pressey, 1950; Briggs 1947, 1948). Adjunct autoinstruction was not widely adopted as a regular classroom procedure. Interestingly enough, after a considerable period of time, research studies exploring the effects of various ways of placing the adjunct questions in an overall study procedure have become prominent in recent years (Frase, 1970; Hiller, 1974; Rothkopf and Bisbicos, 1967).

VARIETIES OF INDIVIDUALIZED INSTRUCTION

Apart from the types of delivery systems described earlier for elementary and secondary schools and for college instruction, the term "individualized instruction" has been used in reference to a diverse array of educational methods. Some of these may be described as follows:

1. *Independent study plans,* in which there is agreement between a student and a teacher on only the most general level of stated objectives to indicate the purpose of studying. Students work on their own to prepare for some form of final examination. No restrictions are placed upon students as to how they may prepare for the examination. A course outline may or may not be provided. The task may be described at the course level in such terms as "preparing for an examination in differential calculus," or at the degree level as in "honors programs" in English universities. A similar procedure is used in the United States in preparing for the doctoral comprehensive examination in many fields.

2. *Self-directed study,* which may involve agreement on specific objectives, but with no restrictions upon how the student learns. Here the teacher may supply a list of objectives which define the test performances required to receive credit for the course; the teacher may also supply a list of readings or other resources available, but the student is not required to use them. If a student passes the test, he or she receives credit for the course.

3. *Learner-centered programs,* in which students decide a great deal for themselves, within broadly defined areas, what the objectives will be and when to terminate one task and go to another. This degree of "openness" is sometimes

found in public schools, and has been the customary style of operation for a few private, special schools. Usually in public schools, learner choice is permitted only for "excursions" or "enrichment" exercises, and then only after certain required or "core" skills have been mastered. Often such excursions are offered as an incentive to the student to learn the core skills.

4. *Self-pacing,* in which learners work at their own rates, but upon objectives set by the teacher and required of all students. In this case all students may use the same materials to reach the same objectives—only the rate of progress is individualized.

5. *Student-determined instruction,* providing for student judgment in any or all of the following aspects of the learning: (a) selection of objectives; (b) selection of the particular materials, resources, or exercises to be used; (c) selection of a schedule within which work on different academic subjects will be allocated; (d) self-pacing in reaching each objective; (e) self-evaluation as to whether the objective has been met; and (f) freedom to abandon one objective in favor of another one.

This description in itself implies the possibility of more than twenty different ways in which instruction may be said to be "individualized" or "learner-determined," if various permutations and combinations of elements controlled by the learner are considered.

Clearly, most of the varieties of individualized instruction just named tend to place greater responsibility upon students for providing the events of instruction than is the case for the delivery systems discussed in previous sections. For the most part, these varieties also permit greater freedom of choice as to what the objectives will be, and how the objectives may be attained. For these reasons, such methods have most often been employed only for selected groups of students.

THE MANAGEMENT OF INDIVIDUALIZED INSTRUCTION

Systems of individualized instruction may provide a large number of materials, each separate item of which is keyed to an objective. Alternatively, use may be made of existing materials to form a "module" of instruction by giving printed directions on how to use the materials to achieve one or more objectives. For younger children, often an objective will be so limited in scope that it can be mastered in an hour or less. For older students, a "module" may require a week or two of study, and evaluation may be made for a cluster of objectives rather than for a single objective.

The management of the day-to-day progress of pupils is related closely to the frequent progress checks which are "keyed" either to single objectives or to groups of objectives representing modules. Thus the frequency of formal checks upon pupil progress tends to decrease with the age of the learners. In a similar vein, the frequency of responding (followed by feedback) may often also be decreased for older learners; this feature is adjusted either by the way self-instructional materials are designed or by the way a module is assembled. The management of learning, then, is usually centered around single objectives for young children, and around modules for older children.

Sometimes the module will contain all the instructional materials needed to pass a test over the objective. It usually also contains "practice tests" which the students can use to judge their readiness for taking the actual test. In the event that materials and resources physically independent of the module itself are to be used, directions for how to locate and use them are included. Thus the module itself, and its directions for using related materials, allow the learner to go about the learning task without directions from another person, except when difficulties are encountered.

We now give further consideration to the nature of materials for individualized procedures that are applicable to young learners, and to those applicable to adults.

Components for young learners

A typical individualized program of instruction for children may be expected to have somewhat different components than a program for adults. The procedures for using the materials will also be different. The following are brief descriptions of typical components of modules designed for children of about the sixth grade level, who are assumed to have some reading ability.

A List of Enabling Objectives   Often the learner may benefit from seeing both the target objective for the module and the prerequisite capabilities to be acquired. These may be shown simply as a list, or they may be in the form of a learning hierarchy (described in Chapter 6).

A Suggested Sequence of Activities   In part, the sequence of activities may be derived from the sequence of enabling objectives, and in some instances alternative sequences may be chosen. The sequence as a whole needs to make suitable provision for the enhancement of retention and transfer. Sometimes alternative materials, resources, or exercise may be offered as options. Students may be encouraged to find out for themselves which materials seem suitable. One student may prefer or profit most from a programmed text; another may find a slide-tape presentation more effective.

A Menu of Modules   Some programs contain only required modules. The total menu, however, should be designed to meet the needs of fast learners, not solely those of slow learners. Alternatively programs may offer both "core" (required) and "excursion" (enrichment) modules, while still others may consist entirely of student-chosen modules. The student-selected modules may be designed to provide only self-evaluations of student performance, since the objectives represent what the student wants to learn.

Programs may be designed to make use of the principles of contingency management—using a preferred (high reward) activity as an inducement to undertake a study activity. Often such programs include procedures which give the student opportunities to make "contracts," with some required minimum number of modules to be completed by each student. The student may receive a number of "points" at the outset, which he can "spend" to negotiate time to complete a module; and he may, in turn, earn points for successful completion within the contract period. The earned points, within limits, may then be spent to earn free time for preferred new learning, or for other kinds of preferred activity.

A more extreme curriculum philosophy holds that there should be no "modules" and no objectives. According to this view, the learner would simply be put into a learning environment which includes learning resources, laboratory materials, supplies, etc., perhaps attractively arranged to induce interest, but with no requirements, "points," or other rewards, other than the intrinsic reward of enjoyment of learning.

Opinions differ greatly on whether the student should be required to learn or even to try to learn anything he does not voluntarily undertake. Opinions also differ on how specific objectives for individual learning should be. Those who dislike specific objectives usually shun the use of modules, preferring an "open environment" which permits the student to choose what is to be learned. It would seem, however, that society must take responsibility for teaching children how to live in our culture as productive, happy, responsible, adult citizens. Since it is difficult to determine the exact nature of human capabilities a given child will need to achieve his goals and to solve problems not yet foreseen by today's adults, emphasis needs to be placed on intellectual skills and problem-solving strategies, rather than simply upon presently known "facts" (cf. Rohwer, 1971). Programs in science and social studies are often designed to emphasize the attainment of "process" objectives.

Alternate Materials for Single Objectives   It is evident to most teachers that some children master a given learning objective better by using one book, medium, or exercise, than by using another which may have equally good content. In some cases the reason may be obvious; a poor reader will understand a tape-slide series better than a book. In less obvious cases, "individual learning styles" are cited, although the specific meaning of this phrase is not entirely clear. Research studies, however, have identified few intellectual and personality characteristics which can be related to success with specific forms or media of instruction (Briggs, 1968). This finding may result either from the existence of differing entering capabilities which match the specific content of various materials, or from the fact that instructional events more appropriate to some individuals occur to a greater extent in certain materials. It may be that features of the "style" of the instructional materials—small versus large steps; inductive versus deductive; concrete versus abstract; or other characteristics of this sort can be shown to be differentially effective for different learners. At any rate, providing several versions of a module is often worthwhile. One version might have a simpler vocabulary; one might employ a shorter sentence length; and another might combine an outline or "advance organizer" (Ausubel, 1968) with a terse presentation.

The alternate module concept clearly raises an economic question. Research is needed to assess the extent of advantages of alternate materials so that these can be considered in light of costs. Similar data are need relevant to the instance in which one form of materials is superior to other, less costly materials for most learners.

A Feedback Mechanism   For young learners and lengthy modules, it may not be wise to wait until a test is given to provide feedback. Feedback after small increments of study is usually desirable. Feedback at frequent intervals is a built-in feature of programmed instruction, and can also be designed for media that normally present uninterrupted messages, such as television or films. The effectiveness of many media can be improved by building in explicit provisions for learner responding and feedback. In addition to enhancing learning, such responding and feedback may suggest the need for diagnostic testing and remedial instruction, or for restudy of the module when performance is poor.

Mechanical devices and chemically-treated answer sheets can be used to provide feedback after each response to practice questions. Television teachers can pose questions after a brief lecture segment, pausing for the viewer to write his answer or just to think of the answer; after the pause, feedback can be given. Questions used with live lectures have also been found to benefit learning and usually, retention, also. Classroom devices can be employed to provide immediate automatic recording of students' answers (to multiple-choice questions), for viewing by the teacher who can "reprogram" the lecture on the spot.

When a module is brief, or when the learner typically succeeds readily, a parallel form of the formal test on the objective can be used to give feedback after learning is completed. Some form of self-testing or responding-with-feedback can usually be devised as part of each module. This enhances learning and saves time for the teacher, who can then do individual remedial teaching when all other means fail—a valuable activity for which teachers have too little time when employing conventional group instruction. Such a procedure provides an added bonus—the teacher has time to guide thinking and give added feedback on an individual basis when most needed.

Components for adult learners
The nature of both the materials and the procedures may properly be less highly structured for college students or other experienced adult learners.

Objectives   Course objectives for adults may sometimes be quite precise and specific. However, it may still be assumed that evaluation of learner performance can be made at less frequent intervals than would be the case for children. Whether one broad objective or many more specific ones are employed in modules, checks on the performance of the adult learner are typically not made until after a rather long period of study.

Directions Directions for pursuing study may also be greatly abbreviated for adult learners. The learners may be provided with a list of resources, or simply be told to "use the library and the laboratory." The objective itself may be the main source of directions.

Learning Materials Materials for learning may be highly structured, as in a programmed text; semistructured, as in an outline or laboratory guide; or unstructured, as would be the case when the student does library research on a topic.

Evaluation of Performance Adult students may have a few weeks or an entire semester to complete an instructional unit. While working on the unit, the student usually receives feedback from a teacher or advisor, and from conferences providing reactions to draft plans and preliminary reports. Students may also receive direct instruction on a variety of subordinate capabilities, such as writing skills, techniques for finding sources, and others. Usually the evaluation is based on the appropriateness of procedures employed, competence in reporting and interpreting data, and ability to defend a rationale for the product or study which has been completed.

Functions of modules

Modules may specify activities for groups, small or large. In such instances, a class chart shows the progress of each pupil, and is used to form groups which are at the same point of progress.

Modules can also be designed as directions for laboratory or field exercises, or for independent learning not based on instructional materials. In one industrial course for adults, the learners were given the entire set of course objectives, and shown where they could go to take tests. They were then free to visit employees in appropriate departments to observe, ask questions, or seek other ways to learn.

It should be noted that modules need not be restricted to cognitive objectives. Objectives in the affective or motor domain can be devised equally well. In shop courses, where machine time must be carefully planned, all needed cognitive learning can be made to take place before a skill is practiced with the equipment. This not only saves money for duplicate machines, but also avoids injury to persons and damage to equipment by insuring that the trainee knows safety precautions and correct procedures before he has access to the machine. In many cases, a simulator of the actual machine also brings benefits in cost, safety, and efficiency. Simple simulators can be used for parts of the total task, reserving the more expensive complex simulator for consolidation of skills and practice of emergency procedures in a safe environment.

USE OF MATERIALS IN INDIVIDUALIZED INSTRUCTION

A particular set of instructional materials has been developed for use with the individualized system called PLAN (described in Weisgerber, 1971). This particular system will be described in order to provide a concrete illustration of how such materials are employed in individualizing instruction. PLAN is used by a number of schools throughout the United States.

The instructional objectives of PLAN form the basis of a curriculum in language arts, social studies, science, and mathematics for grades 1–12. Within each grade and subject, these objectives are organized into modules of study for use by students. Usually, five or six objectives constitute a module. A program of studies is developed by the student and teacher, and this program guides the student in selecting modules appropriate to his needs and interests.

A central feature of the PLAN system involves the use of a computer, a terminal for which is usually located in each school. PLAN is a "computer-supported" system. The computer receives and stores records about each student's previous study, his progress, and his performance record. On a daily basis, information is printed out for the teacher indicating (1) which lesson objectives have been completed by which students, and (2) what activities have been begun or completed by each student. In addition, the computer furnishes periodic reports of progress on each student. In general, the information stored in the computer constitutes a base of essential information for planning individual student programs and guiding student learning activities.

Modules and TLU's

The module is a unit of study lasting approximately two weeks, on the average. Sometimes modules deal with single topics, sometimes not. They may be collections of activities representing closely related objectives, such as those in writing, speaking, and spelling. In any case, modules are composed of several *teaching-learning units* (TLU's), each of which has a single objective.

The TLU begins with the learning objective which tells the student what he is going to learn. Following this is a list of a number of learning activities. A typical TLU pertaining to a social studies module for the seventh grade is shown in Figure 14–1.

As will be seen, the TLU describes the learning activities to be undertaken by the student, and the references to be studied. Self-test questions and discussion questions are also included. In the early grades, pictorial techniques are used to communicate the objective and the learning activities to pupils. An accompanying sheet, called the Activity Sheet, describes additional activities for the student to do in learning about the topic of the TLU. Once the student has completed the activities given in the TLU and the Activity Sheet, he should be able to do what is called for in the objective. Then he is ready to take a performance test. If his performance is satisfactory, he is ready to move forward to a new TLU; if not, he undertakes additional work as suggested by the teacher.

Teacher Directions   The Teacher Directions which accompany each TLU are designed to communicate the objective, the plan for student activities, materials needed, and test directions. Using this sheet, the teacher is able to see at a glance what kinds of activities must be planned—whether discussions, game-playing, field trips, or self-study by the student. The Teacher Directions make evident what modes of instruction may be needed, such as small-group work, partners working together, tutoring, or other modes. Thus it is possible for the teacher to advise the student about options for learning activities.

Instructional Guides   Other materials which sometime accompany TLU's are Instructional Guides. Such guides may provide direct instruction to the student when it is unavailable in published sources. They often make it possible for the student to develop an intellectual skill necessary for his further progress in a TLU. Figure 14–2 is an example of an Instructional Guide in fourth-grade language arts, related to the objective, "given a root word, change its form-class by adding suffixes."

Performance Measures   When the student has completed a TLU, he takes a test, designed to assess his performance on the stated objectives. In some instances, the test has a multiple-choice format which can be scored by the computer. In others, his performance is observed and evaluated by the teacher in accordance with definite standards. The teacher then transmits this evaluation to the computer for record-keeping purposes. Computer printouts of performance records for all students are ready for the teacher's use on the next day.

Materials handling

One distinctive feature of materials in modular form is that they tend to be arranged in smaller "chunks" than is the case with traditional instruction. The materials for a single objective must be either physically separate from the materials for other objectives, or they must be clearly identified and indexed to match the objective and the test for the module.

Whether the materials for a module represent one chapter in a book, several chapters from different books, or a specially designed programmed instruction sequence, there must be a system by which the student, the teacher, and any teaching aides can locate the materials quickly. This requires either an indexing system or the separate physical packaging of all materials for each module. The materials may be collected into a folder which is properly stored for easy retrieval. Some kind of numbering system is convenient to use, both for planning and record keeping for each pupil, and for locating and storing materials. It is handy, for example, to have "Module No. 1, converting fractions to decimals," listed on planning sheets, record sheets, and on the materials themselves, when filed on shelves or in cabinets.

A planning sheet of some kind is needed for each student, particularly where some freedom in choosing objectives is given to the student. In this case, the

Patriots and Politicians

OBJECTIVE

Identify reasons for the development of political parties in the United States.

1   When the founders of our country were writing the Constitution, there were many different opinions about what should be done. Read *The Promise of America*, pp. 140-143, and *Promise of America: The Starting Line*, pp. 129-134. Make a list of at least four issues on which the authors of the Constitution disagreed. Were these the first differences of opinion among Americans?

2   When George Washington became President, there were no political parties. Read *The Promise of America*, pp. 153-155. With a partner, look at the filmstrip, **The Beginning of Political Parties.** If you were in George Washington's place, what problems would you have had to deal with? Discuss this question with your partner.

3   Raising money was a big problem for President Washington and his Secretary of the Treasury, Alexander Hamilton. Read *The Promise of America*, pp. 157-162. Which groups in the colonies supported Hamilton's policies? Why? Which groups opposed them? Why?

4   Americans also differed on how to treat foreign countries. Read about these differences in *The Promise of America*, pp. 164-167, and *History of Our United States*, pp. 206-208. Why did some Americans favor France and some favor England?

5   Not long after Washington became President it became apparent that there were two major groups with different solutions to our problems. One of these groups was called the Federalists; the other was called the Anti-Federalists, or the Republicans. These two groups became the first two political parties. Political parties are organizations of men with similar views who work together for the same goals. Read about the beginnings of political parties in *History of Our United States*, pp. 205-206, and *The Promise of America*, pp. 162-164. Now do the Activity Sheet.

6   Have a debate with a partner. Pretend that you are a farmer and a supporter of Jefferson. Your partner is a merchant and a supporter of Hamilton. Try to convince your partner that your party's programs are best for the United States.

7   George Washington was very disappointed by the development of political parties. He believed that everyone should be able to agree on policies that were good for everyone in the country. Discuss the following questions with a partner.

        a. Were Hamilton's programs "better" for everyone in the country than Jefferson's programs?

        b. Can we say that there really is one program that is best for the *whole* country?

        c. Why do some people favor one program rather than another?

        d. Today's political leaders also say their programs will be good for everyone in the country. Is it possible that these programs might be good for some people and bad for others?

Look through the newspaper. Can you find examples of politicians who disagree about what is good for the whole country?

8   In the filmstrip there is a statement that "the formation of our first political parties was an important development in the democratic process of government." Would Washington have agreed with this statement? Do you agree? Do you think that it is possible to have a democratic government without competing parties? Can you think of any alternatives to the two party system?

OBJECTIVE

Identify reasons for the development of political parties in the United States.

FIGURE 14-1   An Example of a TLU from PLAN, with an Objective in Seventh-Grade Social Studies

(By permission of the copyright owner, Westinghouse Learning Corporation.)

Food for Thought

INSTRUCTIONAL GUIDE

Every pet needs pet food, **EVEN** pet words like the little feller you see here.

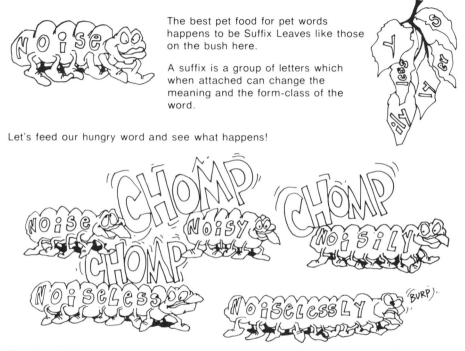

The best pet food for pet words happens to be Suffix Leaves like those on the bush here.

A suffix is a group of letters which when attached can change the meaning and the form-class of the word.

Let's feed our hungry word and see what happens!

Now let's find out if our pet word has changed form-class. Remember the test sentences:

Noun:	I have one **noise.** I have many **noises.**
	noiseless noiseless.
Adjective:	The **noisy** boy seemed very **noisy.**
	noisily. **Noisily**
Adverb:	The boy ate the cake **noiselessly.** **Noiselessly** he ate the cake.

Can the pet word **noise** change form-class to become a verb? Try the verb test to find out! Write your answer below. Discuss your answer with a partner.

FIGURE 14–2 An Example of an Instructional Guide from PLAN

(By permission of the copyright owner, Westinghouse Learning Corporation.)

student may confer with the teacher at intervals to plan in advance for taking one or more modules. If, on the other hand, all students begin with Module No. 1, and complete as many modules as time permits, a single sheet for the entire class may be used for planning, monitoring, and record keeping.

It is no small task, even after the modules themselves have been designed and developed, to be sure there is a sufficient supply of each module, and that the supply is stored for ready access, selection of material, and return of material. If some of the materials are expendable, someone (perhaps an aide) must be sure that after each use, the expendable portion is restocked and made ready for use again.

TEACHER TRAINING FOR INDIVIDUALIZED INSTRUCTION

At first glance, the task of storing, arranging, and using modules for instruction may lead one to believe it is all more trouble than it is worth. Indeed, teachers need training in how to manage individualized instruction. At first, such training may lead the teacher to feel that his most cherished functions are being usurped by the system, and that the teacher is being asked to perform only the tasks of a librarian or clerk. This is because some of the teacher's tasks *are* new and strange as compared to those required under a conventional method of teaching. All teachers need special training for conducting and managing individualized instruction, and they cannot be expected to function adequately, let along enthusiastically, without such training. In the future as such training is more frequently included as a regular part of preservice teacher training programs, the problem will likely be handled at that point in the teacher's education rather than later on.

Even with appropriate training, not all teachers will like the individualized approach. Some experienced teachers will not wish to relinquish their familiar role. Others, who are tired of saying approximately the same thing year after year in class, will welcome the change in role. Once teachers are trained and experienced in the new role, most come to prefer it, usually after one year (Briggs and Aronson, 1975).

Monitoring student progress

Monitoring the progress made by students consists of two related functions—knowing what each student is undertaking to learn, and knowing how fast and how well each is progressing. A glance at the class chart can show which modules a student has finished, and which one he or she is currently attempting. For a module to be recorded as "finished," the student must have met some minimum standard of performance on a test or other evaluation of his or her achievement of the objective. Sometimes this standard is stated in the objective, as "by solving correctly 8 of 10 linear equations." At other times a product is to be evaluated: a laboratory report, a work of art, or an analysis of an editorial with respect to evidence of bias. To make such evaluations as objective and reliable as possible, a "grading sheet" or "criterion sheet" may be used; this sheet lists the features to be looked for in the student product, and some system for deciding whether it meets the standard. For example, points may be assigned on each separate feature to be evaluated; or the number of features present and satisfactory may be counted. Either of these techniques is preferable to making a single overall judgment, not only because it improves the evaluation, but also because it can serve a diagnostic function—it can show the student where he or she needs to improve. This same criterion sheet can be given to the student at the outset of instruction, and thereby functions to inform him or her what is expected, suggesting how it may be done and stating how the product will be evaluated.

Some evaluations can be done orally. By discussing the module and the work done on it by the learner, the teacher can often test in a more probing fashion than can be done in written form, and the assessment can also involve the planning of the next work to be undertaken or the remedial work needed. While oral tests may be less standardized than written ones, they are often convenient and effective when conducted with an individual student.

Regardless of how progress is monitored, the teacher usually knows more about the progress of each student in a well-designed individual plan than when group instruction is used. One reason is that in individualized instruction every student responds to every question. Even if all students work on the same objectives, this is a desirable feature. Of course, when students work on unique objectives or unique clusters of them, evaluation must be done individually.

Assessment of student performance

The performance of students is assessed throughout the conduct of an individualized instruction program to achieve a number of purposes: (1) initial placement of students in an approximate "level" with respect to first assignments in each subject; (2) assessment of mastery of each module, and of the completion of instructional objectives on enrichment tasks; (3) diagnosing learning difficulties in order to identify needed assignments; and (4) measuring student progress in areas of the curriculum over a yearly period.

Placement Testing At the beginning of each school year, pupils may be given placement tests in various areas. Testing is done on an individual basis when necessary (as, for example, in oral reading for young children). On the basis of performance in these areas, a general plan is made for each student covering a six-week period, and initial assignments are made accordingly. In the case of subjects where the objectives are to be chosen by students, performance scores and records of activities performed in the previous year are used to complete the six-week plan, forecasting desirable activities in these subjects from which choices can be made.

Assessment of Mastery   The assessment of student performance is of particular importance to an individualized system, particularly in the area of intellectual skills where new assignments are made on the basis of mastery of prerequisite skills. Such day-to-day assessment should not be considered a matter of formal "testing," but instead likened to the informal "probing" typically done by every teacher in the classroom. It differs from the latter, not in its formality of administration, but in its provision of pre-established standards ("criteria") used by the teacher or by the student, to judge when mastery has been achieved. Criteria for mastery are specified in programs designed for individualized instruction, along with procedures and items used for the observation of individual student performance.

Diagnostic Testing   When a student encounters a difficulty with an assignment, a brief diagnostic test is administered by the teacher or aide. Diagnostic procedures provide an indication of prerequisite skills and information which have been inadequately learned or forgotten by the student. They therefore provide an indication to the teacher of a desirable next assignment or review assignment which will re-establish the necessary competence in the individual student.

Attitude Assessment   The assessment of student attitudes in areas such as cooperation, helping, control of aggressive acts, displaying kindness, and others, will be done by the teacher by means of checklists completed on each child at periodic intervals. Other socially desirable attitudes, such as those attitudes of citizenship which may be prominent objectives in social studies instruction, can be assessed in other ways, as by means of questionnaires. Records of student attitudes often form the basis for reports by teachers to parents, or serve as items to be discussed in parent-teacher conferences.

Yearly Testing   Tests of student achievement are also administered to students near the end of each school year, or more frequently. Scores from these tests are used to compare the performance of pupils with the performance of other groups, as provided by age-level norms. Norm-referenced tests (see Chapter 12) are often employed for this purpose.

Typical daily activities

The various activities of managing an individualized system suggest typical daily activities of students, teachers, teacher aides, and (when applicable) student tutors. As all these participants gain experience with individualized methods, things go more smoothly. At first there may be quite a bit of "slack time" while a pupil is waiting for help or to be told what to do next, and while the teacher attempts to keep everything going. Gradually the pupil becomes more skilled as an independent learner, and he "finds his way about" within the system and with the resources. Progressing from a rather harrassed feeling at first, to a calm, easy pacing, the teacher also becomes both more skilled and more at ease. Initially it may seem that there are too many things to keep track of, but this changes with time.

Student activities are often quite varied over a relatively short time period. Especially when an entire school, rather than just one course or one classroom, is engaged in an individualized system, the concept of "flexible scheduling" is combined with individualized instruction. Then a student may spend most of one day on one subject, but the next day he may be engaged in brief activities ranging over many subjects. This freedom to concentrate heavily at one point but to diversify at other points relieves schooling of much of the boredom resulting from the same schedule every day. If school architecture has been designed to enhance such a flexible mode of scheduling of pupil activities, often more teachers and other resources are literally in sight of the pupil at any given moment. Team teaching arrangements are also compatible with these concepts of space usage and flexible scheduling.

A student may thus move from a study carrel, to a slide-tape area, to a small-group activity, to a conference with one or more teachers, to a test station, and on to band practice or basketball, all in less than one complete school day. At other times, a three-hour laboratory and writing session may complete the work in chemistry for a week.

Teachers usually spend some time each day for advance planning sessions with one to six students; they may review progress and test results and give next assignments to other students. On still other occasions, the teacher may do individual diagnosis and remedial instruction, or confer about a change in a planned schedule. Usually the teacher arranges and conducts small group sessions for groups of students who are at approximately the same point in their learning progress.

To a great extent, students and aides keep the materials files straight, once they are taught the filing system. Teacher aides often administer and score tests, help keep records, and help students find materials they need. They may also serve as tutors, and generally provide back-up assistance when the teacher is especially busy. In general, their role is to help implement the plans agreed upon between teacher and student.

Classroom control

While in general the principles of classroom control and discipline are the same for individualized as for group instruction, several factors usually tend to minimize discipline problems in the individualized method. First, the personal attention and consideration given to the student and to his wishes, plans, ambitions, and interests, all tend to motivate him positively toward achievement of success. Second, the method itself is designed to promote success in learning, and this becomes rewarding in itself and motivating for continued effort. Third, the teacher spends less time "teaching" the class by a group procedure; this leaves fewer opportunities for a student to engage the attention of the entire class with his attention-seeking behavior. The teacher's dealing with a disturbance or a lack of attention to work on the part of a student is less likely to be noticed by the entire group, thus removing some of the fun of "baiting" the teacher. All these factors help lessen the traditional adversary relationship that tends to grow between teachers and students.

Since a system of individualized instruction is clearly designed to help each pupil succeed, fair-minded youngsters usually respond favorably. Just as the system discourages "baiting" of the teacher, it also discourages public confrontations in which neither side wishes to "back down." Finally, it removes temptation for a teacher to employ sarcasm or ridicule of poor work. It quietly reminds the teacher that the goal is learning, not platform performance or crowd psychology. Most important of all, an individualized system emphasizes learning and achievement, privately attained and privately evaluated, by a student who has accepted major responsibility for his learning.

Contingency Management   Techniques of contingency management are of enormous usefulness in the administration of a system of individualized instruction. In simply stated form, these are techniques the teacher uses to arrange successions of student activities in such a way that an initially non-preferred activity will be followed by a preferred activity, thus providing reinforcement for the former. The concept of reinforcement contingencies has been developed and elaborated by Skinner (1968). Application of the techniques of contingency management to school situations has been described by a number of writers (Homme, Czanyi, Gonzales, and Rechs, 1969; Buckley and Walker, 1970; Madsen and Madsen, 1970).

When used properly, contingency management aids in the accomplishment of three objectives which form a part of successful instruction:

1. Establishing and maintaining orderly student behavior, freeing the classroom from disruption and distraction, and aiming students toward productive learning activities.
2. Managing learning so as to instill in students a positive liking for learning and for the accomplishments to which it leads.
3. Capturing the interest of students in desirable problem-solving activities as sources of satisfaction for mastery of the intellectual skills involved in them.

In general, the teacher needs to learn to identify differences in the interests, likes, and dislikes of individual students, and to employ these in selecting specific contingencies to achieve a task-oriented learning environment.

SUMMARY

Individualized instruction is designed by the same processes of planning that apply to design of individual lessons for conventional group instruction. Our previous descriptions of performance objectives, learning hierarchies, sequencing, and employment of appropriate instructional events and conditions of learning, apply to the design of "modules" for individualized instruction.

It is the "delivery system" that primarily distinguishes the design of modules from the design of lessons. The characteristics of materials for individualized instruction include the following:

1. Modules are usually more distinctly self-instructional than are conventional lessons. More of the needed instructional events and conditions of learning are designed into the materials making up the module than is the case for conventional materials.

2. The materials incorporated into modules do more of the direct teaching, while in conventional methods the teacher presents more of the necessary information. Thus the role of the teacher changes somewhat. Individualized instruction depends to a lesser degree on the teacher's function as provider of information; more stress is placed on counseling, evaluating, monitoring, and diagnosing.

3. Some systems provide alternate materials and media for each objective, thus letting the selection vary according to the learner's preferences as to style of learning.

Modules for individualized instruction sometimes contain all the materials, exercises, and tests needed. In other instances, they refer the learner to external materials and activities at appropriate times. A single module usually includes as a minimum:

1. A performance objective
2. A set of materials and learning activities either self-contained in the module, or external to the module itself
3. A method for self-evaluation of mastery of the objective
4. A provision for verification of the learning outcome by the teacher.

As a consequence of its nature, individualized instruction typically provides more frequent feedback and more frequent progress checks than is the case for conventional instruction. It may permit more freedom of choice on the part of the learner, depending on the extent to which objectives are "optional" or "required." Usually, as a minimum, the learner sets his own pace in learning activities.

Management of individualized instruction requires a way to index and store modules, a way to schedule modules to be used by each learner, a way to monitor pupil progress, and a way to assess performance. Sometimes "contracts" are arranged to provide for required work, for enrichment work, and for earned free time for activities the learner prefers.

Classroom control problems are usually less in individualized instruction than in conventional instruction. Teachers usually need special training in the management of such systems. Once they master the necessary routines, they often prefer individualized to conventional methods.

References

Ausubel, D. P., Novak, J. D., and Hanesian, H. *Educational Psychology: A Cognitive View.* 2d. Ed. New York: Holt, Rinehart and Winston, 1978.

Briggs, L. J. Intensive classes for superior students. *Journal of Educational Psychology,* April 1947, 207–215.

Briggs, L. J. The Development and Appraisal of Special Procedures for Superior Students, and an Analysis of the Effects of Knowing of Results. Columbus, Ohio: Ohio State University, unpublished doctoral dissertation, 1948.

Briggs, L. J. Learner variables and educational media. *Review of Educational Research,* 1968, *38,* 160–176.

Briggs, L. J., and Aronson, D. *An Interpretive Study of Individualized Instruction in the Schools: Procedures, Problems, and Prospects.* (Final Report, National Institute of Education, Grant No. NIE-G-740065). Tallahassee: Florida State University, 1975.

Buckley, N. K., and Walker, H. M. *Modifying Classroom Behavior: A Manual of Procedures for Classroom Teachers.* Champaign, Ill.: Research Press, 1970.

Edling, J. V. *Individualized Instruction: A Manual for Administrators.* Covallis, Ore.: DCE Publications, 1970.

EPIE. *Educational Product Report: An In Depth Report.* No. 58, Evaluating Instructional Systems, January 1974.

Frase, L. T. Boundary conditions for mathemagenic behavior. *Review of Educational Research,* 1970, *40,* 337–348.

Hiller, J. H. Learning from prose text: Effects of readability level, inserted questions difficulty, and individual differences. *Journal of Educational Psychology,* 1974, *66,* 202–211.

Homme, L., Czanyi, A. P., Gonzales, M. A., and Rechs, J. R. *How To Use Contingency Contracting in the Classroom.* Champaign, Ill.: Research Press, 1969.

Keller, F. S. A personal course in psychology. In R. Ulrich, R. Stochnik, and J. Mabry (ed.) *The Control of Behavior.* Glenview, Ill.: Scott, Foresman, 1966.

Madsen, C. H., Jr., and Madsen, C. K. *Teaching/Discipline: Behavioral Principles Toward a Positive Approach.* Boston: Allyn & Bacon, 1970.

Postlethwait, S. N., Novak, J., and Murray, H. T., Jr. *The Audio Tutorial Approach to Learning,* 2d ed. Minneapolis: Burgess, 1969.

Pressey, S. L. Development and appraisal of devices providing immediate automatic scoring of objective tests and concomitant self-instruction. *Journal of Psychology,* 1950, *29,* 417–447.

Rohwer, W. D., Jr. Prime time for education: early childhood or adolescence? *Harvard Educational Review,* 1971, *41,* 316–341.

Rothkopf, E. Z., and Bisbicos, E. E. Selective facilitative effects of interspersed questions in learning from written materials. *Journal of Educational Psychology,* 1967, *58,* 56–61.

Ryan, B. A. *PSI: Keller's Personalized System of Instruction. An Appraisal.* Washington, D.C.: American Psychological Association, 1974.

Skinner, B. G. *The Technology of Teaching.* New York: Appleton, 1968.

Talmage, H. (ed.). *Systems of Individualized Education.* Berkeley, Ca.: McCutchan, 1975.

Weisgerber, R. A. *Developmental Efforts in Individualized Instruction.* Itasca, Ill.: Peacock, 1971.

chapter 15

Evaluating Instruction

Every designer of instruction wants to have assurance that his topic, or course, or total system of instruction is valuable for learning in the schools. This means that he wishes to at least know whether his newly designed course or system "works" in the sense of achieving its objectives. More importantly, perhaps, he is interested in finding out whether his product "works better" than some other system it is designed to supplant.

Indications of how well an instructional product or system performs are best obtained from systematically gathered evidence. The means of gathering, analyzing, and interpreting such evidence are collectively called methods of *evaluation,* which is the subject of this final chapter. The placement of this chapter, by the way, should not be taken to indicate that the planning of evaluation for instruction should be undertaken as a final step. Quite the opposite is true; as will be shown, the design of evaluation requires principles of instructional planning that have been described in every chapter of this book.

Evidence sought in an enterprise whose purpose is the evaluation of instruction should be designed to answer at least the following specific questions concerning a lesson, topic, course, or instructional system:

1. To what extent have the stated objectives of instruction been met?
2. In what ways, and to what degree, is it better than the unit it will supplant?
3. What additional, possibly unanticipated, effects has it had, and to what extent are these better or worse than the supplanted unit?

As will be seen in this chapter, these questions in turn give rise to others which must be answered in a prior sense. It is also true that these are but a small subset of the questions that are posed in the field of educational evaluation in general (cf. Popham, 1974). These three questions may best be considered critical ones for the evaluation of an instructional *product* or *procedure*. Before discussing them further, we attempt in the next section to provide a brief review of the larger context to which they belong.

EDUCATIONAL EVALUATION

In its most general sense, evaluation in education is to *assess the worth* of a variety of states or events, from small to large, from the specific to the very general. One can speak legitimately of the evaluation of students, of teachers, of administrators. Evaluation can be undertaken of educational *products,* the producers of such projects, or even of evaluation *proposals* (Scriven, 1974). Methods of evaluation applicable to many different aspects of educational systems and institutions have developed rapidly over the past several years. The subject of educational evaluation requires a book of its own. Here, we shall be able to indicate only the main ideas of some prominent methods.

Scriven's evaluation procedures

Scriven has proposed and tried out evaluation procedures which he considers applicable to educational products, courses, curricula, and projects which propose educational change (Scriven, 1967, 1974). One of the outstanding conceptions proposed by Scriven is called *goal-free evaluation.* In essence, this means that an evaluation undertakes to examine the effects of an educational innovation and to assess the worth of these effects, whatever they are. The evaluator does not confine himself to the stated objectives of a new product or procedure, but rather seeks to assess and evaluate outcomes of any sort. Thus, changes in teacher attitude might occur with the introduction of a scheme for using parent volunteers to tutor children in arithmetic. Such a change in attitude would be assessed in a goal-free evaluation, not simply as an "unanticipated outcome," but as one of a number of effects that a new procedure might produce.

The total scope of educational evaluation, as Scriven sees it, extends from the establishment of a need through the assessment of effects to a determination of cost-effectiveness and the likelihood of continued support. The following are his suggestions of the assessments of worth that need to be made in evaluation of a new educational program or product (Scriven, 1974):

1. *Need:* establishing that the proposed product will contribute to the health or survival of a system.
2. *Market:* determining the existence of a plan for getting the product used.
3. *Performance in field trials:* evidence of performance of the product or program under typical conditions of use.
4. *Consumer performance:* the appropriateness with which the product is addressed to, and likely to be used by, true consumers (teachers, principals, students).

5. *Performance: Comparison:* performance of the product compared with critically competitive products.
6. *Performance: Long-Term:* data indicating performance over a period extending beyond initial field trials.
7. *Performance: Side Effects:* outcomes other than the primary objective, revealed by goal-free assessment.
8. *Performance: Process:* indication that the processes of instruction are as proposed in the product.
9. *Performance: Causation:* demonstration that the effects observed are caused by the product or program.
10. *Performance: Statistical significance:* a quantitative indicator of effect.
11. *Performance: Educational significance:* in view of the achievement of the product or program as indicated by items 3 through 10, evaluating the importance of the gains thus identified for the educational institutions concerned.
12. *Costs and cost-effectiveness:* estimation of inclusive costs of a new program, and comparison with competitors.
13. *Extended Support:* continued monitoring and updating of the product.

According to this system, judging the worth of a new educational product or procedure is a complex matter, based upon various kinds of information. The judgments made about each single factor may be recorded on a profile graph, which can then be used to make a systematic judgment of appropriateness and general worth of the product.

Stufflebeam's evaluation methods

The model of evaluation developed by Stufflebeam and his associates (1971) was originally designed to apply to any of a variety of educational improvements which might be considered for adoption, or actually adopted, by a school or school system. The model is called CIPP, in which the letters stand for Context, Input, Process, and Product.

The CIPP model considers evaluation as a continuing process. The information to be dealt with in evaluation of an education program must first be *delineated,* then *obtained,* and finally *provided.* The information produced by evaluation has the primary purpose of guiding decision making. Typically, Stufflebeam's procedures for evaluation can be thought of as having the purpose of guiding the decisions of a school superintendent who is faced with a proposal to institute a new curriculum program.

The kinds of decisions toward which evaluation may be oriented are four: planning, structuring, implementing, and recycling. Planning decisions are guided by *context* evaluation, which involves the determination of problems and unmet needs. Evaluation of the *input* includes consideration of alternative solutions (programs, products), their relative strengths and weaknesses, and their respective feasibilities (structuring decision). *Process* evaluation deals with information about the educational processes set in motion by the new program. These are implementing decisions an example of which would be a decision about the appropriate use of tutoring as specified by a new mathematics program. Finally, there is *product* evaluation, which serves to guide decisions about recycling. An example of this type of evaluation would be identifying and assessing how well a new course of study is working, leading to a decision to continue the program, to drop it, or to modify it.

Stufflebeam (1974) accepts Scriven's suggestion of goal-free evaluation, not as a substitute for, but as a valuable supplement to, goal-based evaluation. The distinction between formative and summative evaluation is also maintained in the CIPP model. Formative evaluation is seen as serving the needs of decision making about program development, whereas summative evaluation provides a basis for accountability.

It is apparent that there are few, if any, points of actual conflict in ideas between the evaluation models of Scriven and Stufflebeam. We note that "continuous planning" is a major emphasis in the Stufflebeam model, whereas "verified performance" is the emphasized concern of the Scriven system. Both models appear to view evaluation in a highly comprehensive manner, and both are most obviously relevant to the "large" decisions about educational procedures which must be made by the people responsible for the management of total school systems, on the one hand, or for the support of programs of widespread educational innovation on the other.

EVALUATION OF INSTRUCTION: TWO MAJOR ROLES

The view of evaluation assumed in the remainder of this chapter is more circumscribed than those of the general models already mentioned, but is otherwise not in conflict with them. Here we shall examine the logic and the procedures of evaluation as they apply to a single course of instruction. Such a course, we assume, would have been designed in accordance with the principles described in previous chapters of this volume. The questions to be addressed are: How does one tell whether the design process is working so as to achieve a worthwhile result?; and How does one tell whether the product designed has made a desirable difference in educational outcome?

The account of instructional evaluation to be given here is based upon the premise that a course (or smaller unit) of instruction is being designed, or has been designed, to meet certain specified objectives. Thus, the evaluation procedures to be described are concerned primarily with the *performance* aspects of Scriven's model, and with *process* and *product* evaluation, as these terms are used by Stufflebeam. At the same time, we employ the customary distinction between *formative* evaluation and *summative* evaluation, as defined in an article by Scriven (1967). These two roles of evaluation lead to decisions about program revision, in the former case, and about program adoption and continuation, in the latter.

Formative evaluation

Evidence of an instructional program's worth is sought for use in making decisions about how to revise the program while it is being developed. In other words, the evidence collected and interpreted during the phase of development is used to *form* the instructional program itself. If one discovers, by means of an evaluation effort, that a lesson is not feasible, or that the newly designed topic falls short of meeting its objectives, this information is used to revise the lesson, or to replace portions of the topic, in the attempt to overcome the defects which have been revealed.

The decisions made possible by formative evaluation may be illustrated in a number of ways. For example, suppose that a lesson in elementary science has called for the employment of a particular organism found in fresh-water ponds. But when the lesson is tried in a school, it is found that without taking some elaborate precautions this particular organism cannot be kept alive for more than two hours when transplanted to a jar of ordinary water. Such an instance calls into question the practical *feasibility* of the lesson as designed. Since evaluation has in this instance revealed the specific difficulty, it may be possible to revise the lesson by simply substituting another organism and changing the instructions for student activities appropriately. Alternatively, the lesson may have to be rewritten completely, or even abandoned.

Another type of example, illustrating *effectiveness,* may be provided by an instance in which a topic such as "use of the definite article with German nouns" fails to meet its objective. Evidence from a formative evaluation study indicates that students use the definite article correctly in a large proportion of instances, but not in all. Further examination of the evidence reveals that the mistakes students are making center about the identification of gender of the nouns. The designer of instruction for the topic is consequently led to consider how the lesson, or lessons, on the gender of nouns can be improved. He finds, perhaps, that some necessary concept has been omitted, or inadequately presented. This discovery in turn leads him to revise the lesson, or possibly to introduce an additional lesson, designed to insure the attainment of this subordinate objective. A detailed description of such procedures is given by Dick (1977a).

Conducting Formative Evaluation   The manner of conducting formative evaluations varies widely. Obviously, some observations, such as those pertaining to feasibility, may be made with only a few students or none at all. In contrast, the evaluation of an entire course is likely to require at the least a reasonably large number of students in several classrooms. Thus, no simple rule can be given for the extensiveness of student, teacher, or classroom involvement in a formative evaluation effort. It is always a matter of seeking evidence that is *convincing.* When a lesson's objective is successfully met by a single bright student, this is hardly convincing evidence that the lesson would work with students possessing the entire range of abilities typical of a total class. However, if the same lesson's objective is achieved by virtually all the students in a class which is representative of the population for whom the lesson is intended, this *is* a reasonably convincing piece of evidence.

Formative evaluations often are characterized by informality. The instructional entity—the lesson, topic, course, or system—is being tried out, and many kinds of observations are being made at the same time. Lessons and topics are carried through to their conclusions, and the collection of data is not permitted to interfere to any great extent with the progress of instruction. Observations of the students may be made while they are at work on the lesson (by the teacher or other observer), and still other observations are left until the lesson has been completed. Some of the teacher's observations may be recorded from memory following the conduct of the lesson, rather than during it.

The informality of data collection procedures, however, need not be permitted to affect the precision of the data themselves. Quantitative data are definitely necessary for formative evaluation. The teacher's opinion, for example, that "students did well in this lesson" fails to meet the standard of convincing evidence. If one seeks evidence that the lesson's objectives have been met, no evidence is as convincing as an assessment of the performance of students on a properly designed test of these objectives.

Evidence Sought   In order to make good decisions about the further development of an instructional entity, various kinds of evidence are needed. As an initial step (one which is repeated or later occasions when other evidence becomes available), the essential accuracy of the content must be reviewed by a "subject-matter expert," usually a person who has much knowledge of the field in which the instruction lies. Knowledge of the field of genetics, for example, may be used to detect inconsistencies in a lesson on hybrid animals; similarly, a historian's knowledge may be brought to bear on the accuracy of events reported in a lesson on United States tariff policy.

Having satisfied himself that accurate communications will be made, the designer is interested in evaluating both the feasibility and the effectiveness of instruction. Usually, this means that data must be sought from both teachers and students, and preferably also from an "observer" who may be a member of the design team (or the designer). Typically, each formative evaluation study uses its own particular methods for collecting data, designed in part to meet local conditions; there are, therefore, no thoroughly standardized methods. The kinds of data sought may be listed as follows:

From the *observer:*
1. In what respects are (are not) the materials and media employed in the manner intended by the designer?
2. In what respects does (does not) the teacher carry out the procedures and make the decisions intended?
3. In what respects do (do not) the students follow the general procedures specified?

From the *teacher:*
1. What practical difficulties are encountered in conducting the lesson? (Examples: running overtime, setting up equipment, etc.)
2. Estimate the degree of interest or absorption of the students in the lesson.
3. What difficulties were encountered in carrying out the intended teacher procedures?

From the *student:*
1. How likely are you to choose to do the things you learned in this lesson?
2. How likely are you to recommend this lesson to your friends?
3. Results of a test of performance of the lesson's objectives.

It needs to be emphasized again that this list is intended to identify the *kinds of evidence* sought, and that it does not represent the content of the instruments used to collect this evidence. The student question, "How likely are you to choose to do the things you learned in this lesson?" for example, does not represent an actual question to be asked of students. Finding the answer to this question is likely to require a number of specific questions designed to reveal the students' attitudes. As given here, the question simply reflects what the evaluator wants to be able to conclude from the data collected.

For formative evaluation purposes, evidence relevant to these questions is normally collected on each lesson. The evidence may then be collated in some appropriate manner as it applies to topics or to an entire course. Needs for revision or expansion of these larger units of instruction is usually revealed by data on the lessons which comprise them.

Interpretation of the Evidence   These various kinds of evidence, collected by means of observational records, questionnaires, and tests, are now employed to draw conclusions as to whether a lesson needs to be kept as is, revised, reformulated, or discarded.

The question of *feasibility* may be decided, for example, by considering reports of the difficulties experienced by teachers or students in the conduct of the lesson. The question of *effectiveness* is a somewhat more complex judgment. It may depend, in part, on the reports of the observer to the effect that the materials could not be used in the manner intended, or that the teacher did not carry out the intended procedures. It may also depend, in part, on the attitudes of students that are incidentally established by the lesson, as revealed by answers to questions to both teachers and students. And, of course, it may depend to the most important degree upon the extent to which the performance of students, as revealed by tests, is successful.

It will be evident that formative evaluation, in contrast to summative, is most cogently concerned with Question 1, to what extent have the stated objectives of instruction been met? This is one of the principal kinds of evidence which may be brought to bear on the revision and improvement of the designed instruction. On occasion, evidence may also become available which permits comparison with an alternative or supplanted instructional entity (Question 2), and such evidence may also be utilized for formative purposes. Similarly, observations which reveal unanticipated effects (Question 3), good or bad, may surely have an effect on decisions about revision or refinement of instruction. However useful these additional pieces of evidence may be, it remains true that Question 1 defines an essential kind of evidence leading to decisions about revising and improving the instructional unit which is being developed.

Summative evaluation

Summative evaluation is usually undertaken when development of an instructional entity is in some sense completed, rather than on-going. Its purpose is to permit conclusions to be drawn about how well the instruction has worked. Such findings permit schools to make decisions about adopting and using the instructional entity (cf. Dick, 1977b).

In general, summative evaluation concerns itself with the effectiveness of an instructional system, course, or topic. Individual lessons may of course be evaluated as components of these larger units, but rarely as separate entities. The evaluation is called summative because it is intended to obtain evidence about the *summed* effects of a set of lessons making up a larger unit of instruction. Naturally, though, such evidence may include information pointing to defects or positive accomplishments of particular lessons, and this can be used in a formative sense for the *next* development or the *next* revision.

The main kind of decision for which the evidence of a summative evaluation is useful is whether a new course (or other unit) is better than one it has replaced, and therefore should be adopted for continued use. Conceivably, it may be no better, in which case considerations other than effectiveness *per se* (such as cost) will come to determine the choice. Also conceivably, it might be worse than what it has replaced, in which case the decision would likely be an easy one to reach.

Suppose that a newly designed course in American government has replaced one of the same title, and has been adopted by a school for the purpose of trying out the new course. A summative evaluation finds that student enthusiasm for the new course is little changed compared with that for the old; that 137 of the 150 defined objectives of the new course are adequately met by students (the previous course did not have defined objectives, nor means of assessing them); and that a test on American government given at the end of the semester yields an average score of 87 as opposed to 62 on the same test in the previous year. The new course is liked by teachers, for the specific reason that it permits them to take more time for individual student conferences. Now, provided that the new course does not cost more than the old, this set of evidences would very likely lead to a decision to adopt and continue the new course, and to abandon the old.

In contrast to formative evaluation, summative evaluation usually has many formal features, some of which are indicated by this example. Measures of student attitudes, for example, are likely to be based upon carefully constructed questionnaires, so that they can be directly and validly compared with those of last year's students. The assessment of mastery of each objective is also systematically done, in order that there will be a quantitative indication of the accomplishments of the entire course. In addition, measures of achievement are taken from a test serving as a "semester examination." As is true of formative evaluation, each of these summative measures needs to be obtained with the use of methods that make possible the collection of convincing evidence of effectiveness.

Evidence Sought   Summative evaluation of a topic, course, or instructional system is primarily concerned with evidence of learning outcomes. As will be discussed in the next section of this chapter, obtaining such evidence requires the collection of data on "input measures" and "process measures," as well as on those measures which directly assess outcomes. Learning outcomes are assessed by means of observations or tests of human capabilities, as reflected in the objectives specified for the instruction. Accordingly, the measures of outcomes might consist of any or all of the following types:

1. Measures indicating the mastery of *intellectual skills,* assessing whether or not particular skills have been acquired. Example: A test requiring solutions for designated variables in linear algebraic equations.
2. Measures of *problem-solving ability,* assessing the quality or efficiency of the student's thinking. Example: Exercises requiring the design of a scientific experiment to test the effect of a particular factor on some natural phenomenon, in a situation novel to the student.
3. Tests of *information,* assessing whether or not a specified set of facts or generalizations has been learned. Example: A test requiring the student to state the names and roles of the principal characters in a work of literature. Alternatively, tests assessing the breadth of knowledge attained by the student. Example: A test which asks the student to describe the major antecedents of a historical event.
4. Observations or other measures of the adequacy of *motor skills,* usually with reference to a specified "standard" of performance. Example: An exercise in which the child is asked to print the alphabet in capital letters.
5. Self-report questionnaires assessing *attitude.* Example: A questionnaire asking the student to indicate "probability of choice" for actions concerned with the disposal of personal trash.

Interpretation of Summative Evidence   The various measures appropriate for the outcomes of learning are interpreted mainly in comparison to similar measures obtained on an instructional entity representing an alternative method of instruction. Thus, the primary emphasis of evidence obtained for summative purposes is on the answer to Question 2, (In what ways, and to what degree, is this entity better than some other?) Usually, the comparison to be made is with a topic or course which the newly designed unit is intended to replace. Sometimes, two different newly designed instructional entities may be compared with one another. In either case, such comparisons require methods of data collection that can demonstrate that "all other things are equal," which is by no means an easy thing to do.

Answers to Question 1 and 3 are also desirable outcomes of a summative evaluation. One wants to determine, as a minimal condition, whether the objectives of the new instructional unit have been met (Question 1). Should it turn out that they have not, this result will obviously affect the possible conclusions to be drawn from comparison with an alternative unit. In addition, it is always of some importance to explore whether the newly designed instruction has had some unanticipated effects (Question 3). A topic designed to teach basic musical concepts, for example, might turn out to have some unexpected effects on attitudes toward listening to classical music.

CONDUCTING AN EVALUATION

The various measures of outcomes of instruction that have been mentioned obviously require a good deal of careful thought and effort. In some instances, the required measures, tests, observation schedules, or questionnaires can be purchased or adapted from instruments already available. In most cases, however, they must be *separately developed* to meet the needs of the instructional design effort. Methods for the development of outcome measures have been described in Chapter 12.

Besides the development of tests or other types of measures, the enterprise of evaluation, both formative and summative, requires careful scientifically based methods which serve to insure that the evidence obtained is truly convincing. To describe these methods in full detail would require at least a separate volume; in fact, a number of books are available that deal with the design of evaluation studies (for example, DuBois and Mayo, 1970; Isaac and Michael, 1971; Popham, 1975). In this chapter, we can deal only with the *logic* of evaluation studies, beginning with the logic of data collection and interpretation already introduced. Beyond this, however, is the rationale for identifying and controlling variables in evaluation efforts, in order that valid conclusions can be drawn about instructional outcomes.

The variables of evaluation studies

The intention of studies to evaluate an instructional entity is to draw conclusions about the effects of the instruction on learning outcomes—on the human capabilities the instruction has been designed to establish or improve. But these capabilities are affected by other factors in the educational setting, not only by the instruction itself. It is therefore necessary to *control or otherwise account for these other variables,* in order to draw valid conclusions about instructional effectiveness. Considered as a whole, the educational situation into which instruction is introduced contains the classes of variables described in the following paragraphs.

Outcome Variables   We begin to list the variables of the educational situation with outcome variables, the dependent or measured variables which are the primary focus of interest. These have already been described as measures of the human capabilities intended to be affected by instruction. The classes of variables that influence educational outcomes, and their various sources, are shown in Figure 15–1.

Process Variables.   What factors in the school situation might influence the outcomes, given the existence of an instructional program? Obviously, there may be some effects on how the instructional entity (topic, course, system) is conducted. Outcomes may be influenced, in other words, by the *operations* carried out to put the instruction into effect, typically by the teacher (cf. Astin and Panos, 1971). For example, the instruction as designed may call for a particular type and frequency of teacher questioning. To what extent has this been done? Or, the designed course may call for a particular sequence of intellectual skills, some to be mastered before others are undertaken. To what extent has this operation been carried out? As still another example, the designed instruction may specify that a particular sort of feedback is to be incorporated in each lesson (see Chapter 9). Has this been systematically and consistently done?

One cannot simply assume that process variables of the sort specified by the designed instruction, or intended by the designer, will inevitably occur in the way they are expected to. Of course, well-designed instruction provides for whatever action may be required to insure that the program operates as planned; for example, provisions are often made to train teachers in these operations. Nevertheless, such efforts are not always fully successful—teachers are no more free of human inadequacies than are the members of any other professional group. Designers of new programs of individualized instruction, for example, have rather frequently found that the operations specified for these programs are not being

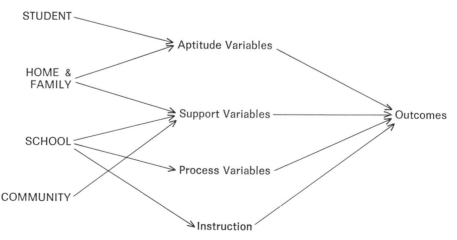

FIGURE 15–1   Variables Influencing the Outcomes of an Instructional Program

executed in the manner originally intended. As a consequence, it is essential that assessments of process variables be made and this is particularly so when the newly designed instructional entity is being tried out for the first time.

Process variables comprise many factors in the instructional situation which may directly affect student learning. Such factors, then, may concern matters of *sequence,* or matters of institution and arrangement of the *events of instruction,* both of which are described in Chapter 9. Another factor is the *amount of time* devoted by students to particular lessons or portions of a course. Naturally, one of the major variations to be found in topics or courses of instruction is the degree to which these classes of process variables are specified. A textbook, for example, may imply a sequence for instruction in its organization of chapters, but may leave the arrangement of events of instruction entirely to the teacher, or to the learner himself (as does this book). In contrast, a topic designed for instruction in language skills for the sixth grade may not only specify a sequence of subordinate skills, but also particular events such as informing the learner of objectives, stimulating recall of prerequisite learnings, providing learning guidance, and providing feedback to the learner, among others. Regardless of the extent to which process variables are prescribed by the designed entity, it is necessary to take them into account in a well-planned evaluation study. After all, the outcomes observed may be being substantially affected by the ways a new instructional program is *operated,* whatever its designed intentions.

Typically, process variables are assessed by means of systematic observations in the classroom (or another educational setting). This is the function of the observer, not the teacher, in the conduct of the evaluation. The observer may employ a checklist or observation schedule as an aid in recording his observations. Such instruments normally have to be specially designed to meet the purposes of each particular evaluation study.

Support Variables   Still another class of variables, occurring partly in the student's home and community, has to be considered as potentially influential upon the outcomes of an instructional program. These include such factors as the presence of adequate materials (in the classroom and the school library), the availability of a quiet place for study, the "climate" of the classroom with reference to its encouragement of good achievement, the actions of parents in reinforcing favorable attitudes towards homework and other learning activities, and many others. The number of different variables in this class is quite large, and not enough is known about them to make possible a confident differentiation among them with regard to their relative importance.

The general nature of this class of variables is to be seen in their effects on the *opportunities for learning.* Materials in the classroom, for example, may present greater or fewer opportunities for learning, depending on their availability; parents may make opportunities for adequate attention to homework more or less available; and so on. In contrast to process variables, *support variables* do not directly influence the process of learning as the former set of factors is expected to do. Instead, they tend to determine the more general environmental conditions of those periods of time during which process variables may exert their effects. For example, the designed instruction may call for a period of independent study on the part of the student. In operation, the teacher may make suitable time provisions for this independent study, thus insuring that the process variable has been accounted for. But what will be the difference in the outcome, for (1) a student who has a relatively quiet place in which to pursue his learning uninterrupted, and for (2) a student who must perform his independent study in an open corner of a noisy classroom? This contrast describes a difference in a *support* variable. The opportunities for learning are presumably less in the second case, although the actual effects of this variable on the outcome cannot be stated for this hypothetical example.

Support variables require various means of assessment. What parents do in encouraging homework may be assessed by means of a questionnaire. The availability of materials relevant to a topic or course may be assessed by counting books, pamphlets, and other reference sources. The "climate" of a classroom may be found by the use of a systematic schedule of observations. Other measures of this class, such as number of students or the pupil-teacher ratio, may be readily available at the outset of the study. For any of a number of support variables, it is likely to be necessary to select or develop the technique of assessment best suited to the particular situation.

Aptitude Variables   It is of great importance to note that, of all the variables likely to determine the outcomes of learning, the most influential is probably the student's *aptitude for learning*. Whatever may be accomplished by improved methods of instruction, by arrangements of process variables, and by insuring the best possible support for learning, it is important to keep in mind that this entire set of favorable circumstances cannot influence learning outcomes as much as can student aptitude.

The aptitude for learning that a student possesses at any given point in time is undoubtedly determined in part by his genetic inheritance. It is also determined in part by environmental influences, some of which (like nutrition) may exert their effects even before birth. An individual's aptitude is partly determined also by the kinds of prior learning he has done and by the opportunities he has had to learn. It should be clear, then, that aptitude is a variable that has its own multiple determinants. As it enters an evaluation study, however, aptitude is usually an *input* variable (Astin & Panos, 1971). As such, it is not subject to alteration by the evaluation; it can only be measured, not manipulated.

Traditionally, aptitude for learning is measured by instruments called *intelligence tests*. Many well-designed and carefully validated tests of this sort are available. Criticisms of "unfairness" are sometimes raised concerning intelligence tests, based in part upon the demonstrable fact that they contain items sampling information and skills that may be more readily available to one ethnic group than they are to another. We cannot devote space to a consideration of this criticism in these pages. For the purposes of conducting evaluation studies, however, it may be noted that the important characteristic sought in a test of learning aptitude is not "fairness," but *predictive power*. This phrase means the power of an aptitude test score to predict variations in the achievements of different students, considered as learning outcomes. That intelligence tests do accomplish such prediction is a fact that has been shown in studies too numerous to cite. On the whole, these studies have shown that intelligence (aptitude for learning) may account for as much as 50 percent of the variations in learning outcome, measured as student achievement in capabilities falling in the categories of information, intellectual skills, and cognitive strategies.

Obviously, then, the aptitude for learning which a student brings to the instructional situation is likely to have a very great effect on his learning, when the latter is assessed in terms of its outcomes. This is true, so far as is known, quite independently of the student's ethnic or racial background. Thus, if effectiveness of an instructional program is to be assessed, the effect of the instruction itself must be demonstrated by instituting controls which make possible the separation of the influence of the student's "entering" aptitude for learning.

While measures of learning aptitude are often most conveniently identified by scores on intelligence tests, other measures are sometimes employed. A *combination* of several aptitude tests may be used to yield a combined score to assess learning aptitude. (Actually, most intelligence tests are themselves collections of subtests sampling several different aptitudes.) Another procedure involves the use of measures which are known to *correlate* with intelligence scores to a fairly high degree. Previous school grades exhibit such high correlations, particularly in subjects such as reading comprehension and mathematics. Still another correlated measure is family income, or family socioeconomic status (SES). It seems reasonable, though, that while correlated measures are sometimes useful, they are not to be preferred in evaluation studies over measures which attempt to assess learning aptitude in the most direct manner possible.

INTERPRETING EVALUATIVE EVIDENCE

We have pointed out that measures of the outcomes of an instructional program—that is, measures of learned intellectual skills, cognitive strategies, information, attitudes, motor skills—are influenced by a number of variables in the educational situation, besides the program itself. Process variables in the operation of the instructional program may directly affect learning, and thus also affect its outcomes. Support variables in the school or in the home determine the opportunities for learning and thus influence the outcomes of learning that are observed. And most prominently of all, the learning aptitude of students strongly influences the outcomes measured in an evaluation study.

If the effectiveness of the designed instruction is to be evaluated, certain *controls* must be instituted over process, support, and aptitude variables, in order to insure that the "net effect" of the instruction itself is revealed. Procedures for accomplishing this control are described in this section. Again it may be necessary to point out that only the basic logic of these procedures can be accounted for here. However, such logic is of critical importance in the design of evaluation studies.

Controlling for aptitude effects

The assessment of outcomes of instruction in terms of Question 1 (To what extent have objectives been met?) needs to take account of the effects of aptitude variables. In the context of this question, it is mainly desirable to state what *is* the level of intelligence of the students being instructed. This may be done most simply by giving the average score and some measure of dispersion of the distribution of scores (such as the standard deviation) on a standard test of intelligence. However, correlated measures such as SES are frequently used for this purpose. Supposing that 117 out of 130 objectives of a designed course are found to have been met; it is of some importance to know whether the average IQ of the students is 115 (as might be true in a suburban school) or 102 (as might occur in some sections of a city, or in a rural area). It is possible that, in the former setting, the number of objectives achieved might be 117 out of 130, whereas in the latter, this might drop to 98 out of 130. The aims of evaluation may best be accomplished by trying out the instructional entity in several different schools, each having a somewhat different range of student learning aptitude.

When the purposes of Question 2 (To what degree is it better?) are being served in evaluation, one must go beyond simply reporting the nature and amount of the aptitude variable. In this case, the concern is to show whether any difference exists between the new instructional program and some other—in other words, to make a *comparison*. Simply stated, making a comparison requires the demonstration that the two groups of students were *equivalent* to begin with. Equivalence of students in aptitude is most likely to occur when successive classes of students in the same school, coming from the same neighborhood, are employed as comparison groups. This is the case when a newly designed course is introduced in a classroom or school, and is to be compared with a different course given the previous year.

Other methods of establishing equivalence of initial aptitudes are often employed. Sometimes, it is possible to assign students *randomly* to different classrooms within a single school, half of which receive the newly designed instruction and half of which do not. When such a design is used, definite administrative arrangements must be made to insure randomness—it cannot be assumed. Another procedure is to select a set of schools which are "matched" insofar as possible in the aptitudes of their students, and to try out the new instruction in half of these, making a comparison with the outcomes obtained in those schools not receiving the new instruction. All of these methods contain certain complexities of design which necessitate careful management if valid comparisons are to be made.

There are also statistical methods of control for aptitude variables—methods which "partial out" the effects of aptitude variables and thus reveal the net effect of the instruction itself. In general, these methods follow logic such as this: If the measureed outcome is produced by A and I, where A is aptitude and I is instruction, what would be the effect of I alone, if A were assumed to have a constant value, rather than a variable one? Such methods are of considerable value in revealing instructional effectiveness, bearing in mind particularly the prominent influence the A variable is likely to have.

Whatever particular procedure is employed, it should be clear that any valid comparison of the effectiveness of instruction in two or more groups of students requires that equivalence of initial aptitudes to be established. Measures of intelligence, or other correlated measures, may be employed in the comparison. Students may be randomly assigned to the different groups, or their aptitudes may be compared when assignment has been made on other grounds (such as school location). Statistical means may be employed to make possible the assumption of equivalence. Any or all of these means are aimed at making a convincing case for equivalence of learning aptitudes among groups of students whose capabilities following instruction are being compared. No study evaluating learning outcomes can provide valid evidence of instructional effectiveness without having a way of "controlling" this important variable.

Controlling for the effects of support variables

For many purposes of evaluation, support variables may be treated as "input" variables, and thus controlled in ways similar to those used for learning aptitude. Thus, when interest is centered upon the attainment of objectives (Question 1), the measures made of support variables can be reported along with outcome measures in order that they can be considered in interpreting the outcomes. Here again, a useful procedure is to try out the instruction in a variety of schools displaying different characteristics (or different amounts) of "support."

Similarly, the comparisons implied by Question 2 and part of Question 3 require the demonstration of *equivalence* among the classes or schools whose learning outcomes are being compared. Suppose that outcome measures are obtained from two different aptitude-equivalent groups of students in a school, one of which has been trying out a newly designed course in English composition, while the other continues with a different course. Assume that, despite differences in the instruction, the objectives of the two courses are largely the same, and that assessment of outcomes is based on these common objectives. Class M is found to show significantly better performance, on the average, than does Class N. Before the evidence that the new instruction is "better" can be truly convincing, it must be shown that no differences exist in support variables. Since the school is the same, many variables of this sort can be shown to be equivalent, such as the library, the kinds of materials available, and others of this nature. Where might differences in support variables be found? One possibility is the "climate" of the two classrooms—one may be more encouraging to achievement than is the other. Two different teachers are involved—one may be disliked, the other liked. Student attitudes may be different—more students in one class may seek new opportunities for learning than do students in the other. Variables of this sort which affect opportunities for learning may accordingly affect outcomes. Therefore, it is quite essential that equivalence of groups with respect to these variables be demonstrated, or taken into account by statistical means.

Controlling for the effects of process variables

The assessment and control process variables is of particular concern in seeking evidence bearing on the attainment of stated objectives (Question 1). Quite evidently, an instructional entity may "work" either better or worse depending upon how the operations it specifies are carried out. Suppose, for example, that a new course in elementary science presumes that teachers will treat the directing of students' activities as something left almost entirely to the students themselves (guided by an exercise booklet). Teachers find that under these circumstances, the students tend to get into situations raising questions to which they (the teachers) don't always "know the answers." One teacher may deal with this circumstance by encouraging students to see if they can invent a way of finding the answer. Another teacher may require that students do only what their exercise book describes. Thus the same instructional program may lead to quite different operations. The process variable differs markedly in these two instances, and equally marked effects may show up in measures of outcome. If the evaluation is of the formative type, the designer may interpret such evidence as showing the need for additional teacher instructions or training. If summative evaluation is being conducted, results from the two groups of students must be treated separately to disclose the effects of the process variable.

In comparison studies (Question 2), process variables are equally important. As in the case of aptitude or support variables, they must be "controlled" in one way or another in order for valid evidence of the effectiveness of instruction to be obtained. Equivalence of groups in terms of process variables must be shown, either by exercising direct control over them, by a randomizing approach, or by statistical means. It may be noted that process variables are more amenable to direct control than are either support or aptitude variables. If a school or class is conducted in a noisy environment (a support variable), the means of changing the noise level may not be readily at hand. If, however, a formative evaluation study shows that some teachers have failed to use the operations specified by the new instructional program (a process variable), instruction of these teachers can be undertaken, so that the next trial starts off with a desirable set of process variables.

Unanticipated outcomes (Question 3) are equally likely to be influenced by process variables, and accordingly require similar control procedures. A set of positive attitudes on the part of students of a newly designed program *could* result from the human modeling of a particular teacher, and thus contrast with less favorable attitudes in another group of students who have otherwise had the same instruction. It is necessary in this case also, to demonstrate equivalence of process variables before drawing conclusions about effects of the instructional entity itself.

Controlling variables by randomization

It is generally agreed that the best possible way to control variables in an evaluation study is to insure that their effects occur in a random fashion. This is the case when students can be assigned to "control" and "experimental" groups in a truly random manner, or when an entire set of classes or schools can be divided into such groups randomly. In the simplest case, if the outcomes of Group A (the new instructional entity) are compared with those of Group B (the previously employed instruction), and students drawn from a given population have been assigned to these groups in equal numbers at random, the comparison of the outcomes may be assumed to be equally influenced by aptitude variables. Similar reasoning applies to the effects of randomizing the assignment of classrooms, teachers, and schools to experimental and control groups, in order to equalize process and support variables.

Randomization has the effect of controlling not only the specific variables which have been identified, but also other variables which may not have been singled out for measurement because their potential influence is unknown. Although ideal for purposes of control, in practice randomizing procedures are usually difficult to arrange. Schools do not customarily draw their students randomly from a community, nor assign them randomly to classes or teachers. Accordingly, the identification and measurement of aptitude, support, and process variables must usually be undertaken as described in the preceding sections. When random assignment of students, teachers, or classes is possible, evaluation studies achieve a degree of elegance which they do not otherwise possess.

EXAMPLES OF EVALUATION STUDIES

The four kinds of variables in evaluation studies—aptitude, support, process, and outcome—are typically given careful consideration and measurement in any evaluation study, whether formative or summative. Interpretation of these measures differs for the two evaluation roles, as will be seen in the following examples.

Evaluation of a program in reading for beginners

A varied set of lessons in reading readiness and beginning reading was developed and evaluated over a two-year period by the Educational Development Laboratories of McGraw-Hill, Inc., and by the L. W. Singer Company, of Random House, Inc. This system of instruction is called *Listen Look Learn.* In brief, the instructional materials include: (1) a set of filmstrips accompanied by sound, designed to develop listening comprehension and oral recounting; (2) an eye-hand coordination workbook dealing with the identification and printing of letters and numerals; (3) a set of filmstrips providing letter-writing tasks, accompanying the workbook; (4) letter charts for kinesthetic letter-identification; (5) picture sequence cards, and other cards for "hear and read" practice; (6) a set of colored filmstrips for the analysis of word sounds and the presentation of words in story contexts.

As reported by Heflin and Scheier (1968), a systematic formative evaluation of this instructional system was undertaken, which at the same time obtained some initial data for summative purposes. Table 15–1 summarizes some of the main points of the study, abstracted from this report. The purpose of the table is to illustrate how the major classes of variables were treated and interpreted; naturally, many details of the study covered in the report cannot be reported in the brief space of such a table.

Classes of first-grade pupils from schools located in eleven states were included in the evaluation study. A group of forty classes comprising 917 pupils were given instruction provided by the *Listen Look Learn* system, and a group of 1000 pupils in forty-two classes was constituted as a control group. Control group classes used the "basal reading" instructional system. Each school district was asked to provide classes for the experimental and control groups which were as equivalent as possible in terms of characteristics of teachers and pupils.

Aptitude Variables   Owing to differences in the availability of aptitude scores in the various schools, no initial measures of aptitude were employed. Instead, information was obtained concerning the socioeconomic status of the pupils' families, as indicated in Table 15–1. When aptitude measures were administered during the second year of the study (Metropolitan Readiness, Pintner Primary IQ), verification was obtained of a broad range of aptitude, as well as of equivalence of the experimental and control groups.

For purposes of formative evaluation, one wishes to know that the classes selected for instruction have included a range of student aptitudes that is representative of schools in the country as a whole, since that is the intended usage for the system being evaluated. From the report (Heflin and Scheier, 1968), it would appear that the schools taking part in the study represented a great majority of United States elementary schools, although by no means all of them. For example, inner-city schools were apparently not included. Nevertheless, the study offers reasonably good evidence that a broad range of pupil aptitudes was represented. In addition, it is clear from the reported data that the two groups of pupils were reasonably equivalent in aptitude.

Support Variables   The range of SES of pupils' families provides the additional indication that support for learning, insofar as it may be assumed to originate in the home environment, exhibited a suitable range of variation for the study. Other evidences of learning support are inferred from measures of the characteristics of teachers, as indicated in Table 15–1. The inference is that teachers having a typical range of educational backgrounds will conduct themselves in ways that provide a range of differential opportunities for learning. A reasonable degree of equivalence is also demonstrated on these variables between experimental and control groups.

Other measures of support for learning, not systematically obtained in this study, are perhaps of greater relevance to summative evaluation. Such variables

TABLE 15-1   Variables Measured and Their Interpretation for Formative and Summative
Evaluation in a Study of a System of Instruction for Beginning Reading
(*Listen Look Learn*)*

Type of Variable	How Measured	Interpretation
Aptitude	Initially, by means of socioeconomic status (SES), a correlated measure. During second year, standardized test scores for IQ and Reading Readiness	*Formative:* A variety of classes providing a range of SES from high to low. *Summative:* Equivalence of SES, and later of aptitude, shown for experimental and control groups
Support	(1) Level of formal education of teachers (2) Amount of teacher education in reading methods (3) Years of teaching experience	*Formative:* Range of these variables typical of most elementary schools. *Summative:* Reasonable equivalence of experimental and control groups on these variables
Process	(1) Appropriateness of lessons as judged by teachers (2) Success of program components as judged by teachers (3) Strength and weaknesses of individual lessons judged by teachers	*Formative:* Judgments of appropriateness used to test feasibility. Indirect indications of effectiveness of pupil learning, based on teachers' estimates
Outcome	Metropolitan Primary I Achievement Word Knowledge Means: LLL Group–25.5 Control Group–24.1 Word Discrimination Means: LLL Group–25.9 Control Group–24.7 Reading Means: LLL Group–27.3 Control Group–25.2	*Summative:* Achievement scores on standardized test indicate scores on component reading skills significantly higher than those of an equivalent control group

Information and results abstracted from Heflin and Scheier, The Formative Period of Listen Look Learn, a Multi-Media Communication Skills System. *Huntington, N.Y.: Educational Development Laboratories, Inc., 1968.*

as "availability of reading materials," "encouragement of independent reading," and others of this general nature would be examples. In the *Listen Look Learn* study, incomplete evidence was obtained of the number of books read by individual children, and this number was found to vary from zero to 132 (Heflin and Scheier, 1968, p. 45).

Process Variables   As Table 15–1 indicates, a measure of the feasibility of the various parts of the program was obtained by asking teachers to judge the appropriateness of the materials for groups of fast, medium, and slow learners. Various features of the individual lessons might have contributed to appropriateness, such as the familiarity of the subject of a story or the difficulty of words employed. Teacher's judgments led to conclusions about feasibility which resulted in elimination or revision of a number of elements of the program.

Teachers' estimates also formed the bases for evidence of the "success" of the various activities comprising the *Listen Look Learn* program. Such measures are of course indirect evidence bearing on process variables, as contrasted with such indicators as how many exercises were attempted by each student, how long a time was spent on each, what feedback was provided for correct or incorrect responses, and other factors of this nature. The materials of this program do not make immediately evident what the desired process variables may have been. Consequently, teachers' reports about "how effective the lesson was" were probably as good indicators of these variables as could be obtained in this instance.

Outcome Variables   Learning outcomes for this program were assessed by means of standardized tests of word knowledge, word discrimination, and reading (portions of the Metropolitan Primary I Achievement Test). As can be seen from Table 15–1, mean scores on these three kinds of activities were higher for the experimental group than for the control group, which had been shown to be reasonably equivalent so far as the operation of aptitude and support variables were concerned. Statistical tests of the difference between the various pairs of means indicated that these differences were significant at an acceptable level of probability.

It should be pointed out that the evidences of learning outcome obtained in this study were considered by its authors as no more than initial indications of the success of the *Listen Look Learn* program. Further studies were subsequently conducted to evaluate learning outcomes in a summative sense (Brickner and Scheier, 1968, 1970; Kennard and Scheier, 1971). In general, these studies have yielded data and conclusions which show improvements in early reading achievement considerably greater than are produced by other instructional programs they are designed to supplant (usually basal reading approaches).

Evaluation of an individualized arithmetic program

A second example of an evaluation study, summative in character, is provided by an investigation of an individualized instruction system developed by the Learning Research and Development Center, University of Pittsburgh (Cooley, 1971). In this study, a program of individualized instruction in arithmetic for the second grade of the Frick School was compared with the previously used program. The new program had undergone several years of formative evaluation and development. It provided for individual progress of pupils in attaining arithmetic skills, based upon mastery of prerequisite skills.

Table 15–2 summarizes the treatment of variables in this evaluation study, and presents the major outcome findings.

Aptitude Variables   First, it will be seen from the table that aptitude variables were measured from year to year at the time the children first entered the school. Over a period of several years, the aptitude of entering classes was found to be essentially the same. In addition, the correlated variable of socioeconomic status

TABLE 15-2   Variables and Their Interpretation in an Evaluation of an Individualized Program in Arithmetic for the Second Grade, Frick School*

Variable	How Controlled or Measured	Interpretation
Aptitude	Classes of pupils used in Control and Experimental Groups equivalent in aptitude when they entered school SES of pupils in both groups shown to be equivalent	Aptitude of classes of pupils remains unchanged in this school from year to year
Support	Same school facilities present for both groups, and same teachers involved. SES of pupils equivalent	Specific support variables of the school and the home are equivalent
Process	Contrasting process in individualized and regular instruction Same teachers involved in both groups	Effects of process variables in individualized instruction to be examined; other specific process variables equivalent in both groups
Outcome	Wide Range Achievement Test—Arithmetic Mean Scores in Second Grade: Experimental Group (1971)-25.22 Control Group (1970)-23.40	Significant differences obtained in outcome scores for equivalent groups

*Information and results abstracted from Cooley, W. W. Methods of Evaluating School Innovations. Pittsburgh, Pa.: Learning Research and Development Center, University of Pittsburgh, 1971 (26).

(SES) was found to remain stable. Accordingly, it was considered a reasonable assumption in this study that successive classes of pupils would have the same initial aptitudes. An experimental group (individualized instruction) in the second grade in 1971 could be compared with a control group (regular instruction) who were in the second grade in 1970.

Support Variables   So far as support variables were concerned, these were not specifically singled out and measured individually. Instead, there was a demonstrated equivalence of classrooms and teachers. Under these circumstances, particular support variables were assumed to be equivalent for both groups. Similarly, those support variables originating in the home could be assumed equivalent, in view of the demonstrated absence of differences in SES variables for the two classes.

Process Variables   The most important process variables, those associated with the specific technique of individualized instruction, were deliberately contrasted in the two groups, and this variation was verified by classroom observations. Other process variables (such as the encouragement provided by teachers to pupils) could be assumed to be equivalent because the same teachers were involved for both experimental and control groups.

Outcome As a consequence of this study design, certain influencing variables in the categories of aptitude, support, and process are either shown to be, or reasonably assumed to be, equivalent in their effects on both groups of pupils. Outcome variables are therefore expected to reflect the effects of the changes in instruction in an unbiased manner. Measures of arithmetic achievement, as shown in the final row of the table, indicate a significant improvement when the new (individualized) instruction is compared with the previously used instruction.

A generalized example

Every evaluation study presents the evaluator with a different set of circumstances to which he must apply the logic we have described. In practice, compromise must sometimes be made, because of the existence of inadequate measures of learning outcomes, the difficulties of achieving equivalence in groups to be compared, the occurrence of particular events affecting one school or class without affecting others, and many other possibilities too numerous to mention. Part of the evaluator's job, of course, is to judge the severity of these occurrences, and the ways in which they must be taken into account to arrive at convincing evidence.

A reference set of representative evaluation situations is shown in Table 15–3, together with their most likely interpretations. These situations serve as one kind of summary of our previous discussion of the types of variables affecting learning outcomes.

The hypothetical comparisons of Table 15–3 suppose that School A has been trying out a newly developed course (also labeled "A"), and that its outcomes are being compared with those from School B, which has been using a different course ("B"). In all cases, it is further supposed, the measures of outcome have been found superior in School A to what they are in School B.

TABLE 15–3 Comparisons of Learning Outcomes in School A (Using Course A) and School B (Using Course B), and Their Interpretation

Situation		Outcome Comparison	Most Likely Interpretation
1. Aptitude variable:	A > B	A > B	Most of the outcome difference, if not all, attributable to aptitude differences
Support variables:	A = B		
Process variables:	A = B		
2. Aptitude variable:	A = B	A > B	Differences may be caused by instruction, by support, or both
Support variables:	A > B		
Process variables:	A = B		
3. Aptitude variable:	A = B	A > B	Differences may be caused by instruction, by process differences, or both
Support variables:	A = B		
Process variables:	A > B		
4. Aptitude variable:	A = B	A > B	Difference is attributable to effects of instruction
Support variables:	A = B		
Process variables:	A = B		

Situation 1 is that in which support variables and process variables have been controlled, that is, shown to be equivalent. Aptitude variables indicate higher intelligence, on the average, in School A than in School B. Since this variable is such a powerful one, the effects of instruction cannot be expected to show up, and the likely interpretation is as shown in the final column. Situation 2 is one in which all influencing variables have been shown equivalent except for the support variables. Differences in outcomes may be caused by these variables, by the instruction, or by both in some unknown proportion. Similarly, Situation 3, in which process variables differ, can lead only to the conclusion that either process or instruction, or both, have produced the observed differences in outcome.

Situation 4 is what is aimed for in studies of summative evaluation. Here all the influencing variables have been shown to be equivalent, by one method or another. This situation is one that makes possible the interpretation that outcome differences are attributable to the instruction itself.

SUMMARY

Evaluation of courses, programs, and instructional programs usually has at least the following questions in view: (1) have the objectives of instruction been met; (2) is the new program better than one it is expected to supplant; and (3) what additional effects does the new program produce?

Formative evaluation is undertaken while the new unit is being developed. Its purpose is to provide evidence on feasibility and effectiveness, so that revisions and improvements can be made. It seeks evidence from observers, teachers, and students.

Summative evaluation is concerned with the effectiveness of the course or program, once it has been developed. Mainly, the evidence sought is in terms of student performance. Measures are taken of the kinds of student capabilities the program is intended to establish.

When summative evaluations are undertaken to compare a new instructional unit with an "old" one, other variables besides the unit itself must be taken into account. The outcomes of instruction are influenced by variables whose effects must be "controlled," in order to test the effects of instruction. These variables include the following:

1. Aptitude variables, reflecting the students' aptitude for learning
2. Process variables, arising from the manner of operation of instruction in the school
3. Support variables—conditions in the home, school, and community which affect opportunities for learning.

Evaluation studies use various means to control these influencing variables, in order to demonstrate the effects of the newly designed instruction. Sometimes, the operation of these variables can be made equivalent by assigning students, schools, or communities in a "randomized" way to different groups to be instructed. More frequently, statistical means must be employed to establish the equivalence of groups to be compared. If two courses or systems of instruction are to be evaluated to determine which is better, evaluation logic requires that control be exercised over these other variables. Ideally, everything should be equivalent except the two instructional programs themselves.

References

Astin, A. W., and Panos, R. J. The evaluation of educational programs. In R. L. Thorndike (ed.), *Educational Measurement,* 2d Ed. Washington, D.C.: American Council on Education, 1971.

Brickner, A., and Scheier, E. *Summative Evaluation of Listen Look Learn Cycles R–40, 1967–68.* Huntington, N.Y.: Educational Development Laboratories, Inc., 1968.

Brickner, A., and Scheier, E. *Summative Evaluation of Listen Look Learn 2nd Year Students, Cycles R–70, 1968–69.* Huntington, N.Y.: Educational Development Laboratories, Inc., 1970.

Cooley, W. W. *Methods of Evaluating School Innovations.* Pittsburgh, Pa.: Learning Research and Development Center, University of Pittsburgh, 1971 (26).

Dick, W. Formative evaluation. In L. J. Briggs (ed.), *Instructional Design: Principles and Applications.* Englewood Cliffs, N.J.: Educational Technology Publications, 1977a.

Dick, W. Summative evaluation. In L. J. Briggs (ed.), *Instructional Design: Principles and Applications.* Englewood Cliffs, N.J.: Educational Technology Publications, 1977b.

DuBois, P. H., and Mayo, G. D. (ed.). *Research Strategies for Evaluating Training.* AERA Monograph Series on Curriculum Education, No. 4. Chicago: Rand McNally, 1970.

Heflin, V. B., and Scheier, E. *The Formative Period of Listen Look Learn, and Multi-Media Communication Skills System.* Huntington, N.Y.: Educational Development Laboratories, 1968.

Isaac, S., and Michael, W. B. *Handbook in Research and Evaluation.* San Diego, Ca.: Knapp, 1971.

Kennard, A. D., and Scheier, E. *An Investigation to Compare the Effect of Three Different Reading Programs on First-Grade Students in Elk Grove Village, Illinois, 1969–1970.* Huntington, N.Y.: Educational Development Laboratories, 1971.

Popham, W. J. (ed.). *Evaluation in Education.* Berkeley, Ca.: McCutchan, 1974.

Popham, W. J. *Educational Evaluation.* Englewood Cliffs, N.J.: Prentice-Hall, 1975.

Scriven, M. The methodology of evaluation. In R. Tyler, R. M. Gagné, and M. Scriven, *Perspectives of Curriculum Evaluation.* AERA Monograph Series on Curriculum Evaluation, No. 1. Chicago: Rand McNally, 1967.

Scriven, M. Evaluation perspectives and procedures. In W. J. Popham (ed.), *Evaluation in Education.* Berkeley, Ca.: McCutchan, 1974.

Stufflebeam, D. L. Alternative approaches to educational evaluation: A self-study guide for educators. In W. J. Popham (ed.), *Evaluation in Education.* Berkeley, Ca.: McCutchan, 1974.

Stufflebeam, D. L., Foley, W. J., Gephart, W. R., Guba, E. G., Hammond, R. L., Merriman, H. O., and Provus, M. M. *Educational Evaluation and Decision Making.* Itasca, Ill.: Peacock, 1971.

Indexes

Name Index

Subject Index